1986

CATHEDRALS AND ABBEYS
OF ENGLAND AND WALES

THE BELL HARRY TOWER, CANTERBURY.

CATHEDRALS AND ABBEYS
of England & Wales

EDITED BY PROFESSOR T. G. BONNEY,
D.SC., LL.D., F.R.S.

Bracken Books

LONDON

First published 1891
in two volumes by Cassell & Company Limited as
Cathedrals, Abbeys and Churches of England and Wales

This edition published 1985
by Bracken Books, a division of Bestseller Publications Limited,
Brent House, 24 Friern Park, London N12 9DA, England

and copyright © Bracken Books 1985.
ISBN 0 946495 54 8

Printed and bound by R. J. Acford, Chichester, England

CONTENTS

CONTENTS

LIST OF PLATES

LIST OF ILLUSTRATIONS

14 CATHEDRALS AND ABBEYS

INTRODUCTION.

HE cathedrals of England, in design and plan, are more nearly related to those of North-Western France than of any other part of Europe. This is of course only what might be expected, seeing that the connection between the two countries was, for so many years, so close, and, for a time at least, the centre of civilisation of the united kingdom of England and Duchy of Normandy was on the other side of the Channel. There were men of mark among the clergy, and buildings of some fame among the churches of England, long before the battle of Senlac; but there can be no doubt that, whatever ill may have been done by the invader, he brought with him a more learned clergy, and a higher standard in the arts of civilisation, especially ecclesiastical. One of his first steps was to replace, as quickly as possible, the English bishops by Norman prelates; and these, almost without exception, busied themselves in rebuilding the cathedrals of their dioceses. Of the chief churches anterior to the Norman invasion only a few fragments now remain, incorporated (generally beneath the surface of the ground) into the buildings by which they were replaced, but of their architecture we can form some slight idea from the more considerable portions of parochial churches which are still scattered up and down the country. From Earls Barton and Barnack, from St. Michael's at Oxford and St. Benet's at Cambridge, from Holy Trinity at Colchester, and several others which it is needless to name, we see that, except as a matter of antiquarian interest, there is little to regret in the fact that the Norman prelates adopted a policy so "thorough" in their dealings with the architectural past. The cathedrals erected by them were at first closely related to the churches of the land in which they had been reared. In what remains of the work of Lanfranc at Canterbury, of Gundulf at Rochester, and of Walkelyn at Winchester, we see buildings which might almost be called copies of the churches which they had left behind in their own Normandy. The workmanship was at first inferior—the cathedrals of England must have appeared to the French visitor as "provincial" or "colonial" in design and execution—full of good intentions unskilfully fulfilled, or of great designs imperfectly executed. But in no long

c

time the plant from a sunnier soil took root, and became acclimatised. It was modified by the influences of its environment, and obeyed the laws of growth and development. English church architecture assumed its own characteristics, and became a specific variety, distinguishable from and fully comparable with the indigenous descendants of the French stock from which it had sprung. The distinction, of course, becomes more marked as time proceeds; the divergence becomes readily perceptible in the later period of the Romanesque or round-arched style, to which the name Norman is commonly given; the influence is only occasionally seen, and that chiefly in the south-east of England, in the first period of the use of the pointed arch, that commonly called the Early English; and after this the differences between the churches of England and of North-Western France become so marked as to be perceptible on the most cursory glance. There is, however, not much in common between the English cathedrals and those of Northern Germany, even at the earliest period; while the difference is no less marked from those of the more southern parts of France, and still greater from those of Northern Italy.

The chief architectural distinctions will be presently noticed. There is, however, another which should not be entirely forgotten—the distinction of site. The French cathedrals, as a rule, stand in the heart of the towns; they are hemmed in with houses, which in many cases actually rested against, and were encrusted upon their walls, an encroachment which seems to have been permitted from a very early period. Thus, as it has been often remarked, notwithstanding all that has been done of late years to clear away these encumbrances, it is extremely difficult to obtain any good general view of the exterior, and it is only when at a distance from the town we see the huge mass of sculptured stone rising high above the subordinated roofs that we can fully appreciate its grand proportions and its vast dimensions. English cathedrals, on the contrary, are generally surrounded by ample open spaces; this may be in part due to the fact that they were almost invariably connected with some great monastery, that they were not only the mother churches of a diocese, but also what we might call "college chapels," as is still the case with the Cathedral of Christ Church at Oxford. This connection appears much more rare in France; except it be for an episcopal "palace," one treads, on quitting the door of a French cathedral, upon the pavements of the streets, and passes abruptly from the peace within to the turmoil of the city. In this there may be a gain as well as a loss; perhaps we may have in it some ground for the mutual insulation, once very marked, of the cathedral and the townsfolk. But whether or not because they so commonly were incorporated into the spacious precincts of an important monastic foundation, the fact remains that the English cathedrals stand in spaces far more open than is usual in France, and frequently occupy sites remarkably beautiful.

The differences also in plan are considerable; these are less conspicuous in the older cathedrals, though even there a distinction may often be noticed. In those of Norman date in England the dominant ground-plan is almost always a Latin cross with well-developed arms. There is no trace whatever of the basilica type, though possibly this may once have been visible in the churches of earlier date in this country, as it is certainly more permanently impressed on those of France. But when we come to the cathedrals built in the Pointed styles, the difference is even more persistently marked. Contrast, for example, the ground-plans of the Cathedrals of Paris, Amiens, Rheims, or Chartres with English buildings. All of these, even the last, cover spaces of ground large in proportion to their length; their area being in the case of Notre Dame (the smallest), 64,108 feet, and of Amiens (the largest), 71,208 feet. Salisbury, which is rather longer than Notre Dame, covers less ground by full 9,000 feet; and York, which is quite fifty feet longer than Amiens, and is one of the most spacious of our cathedrals, occupies an area but slightly greater.

The French cathedrals are generally more lofty* than the English; this produces a result which, however impressive at first sight, is sometimes open to criticism. Mr. Fergusson says, not without justice: "A great charm of English cathedrals is their repose of outline; a French cathedral is surrounded by a multitude of pinnacles, flying buttresses, and other expedients, to keep the building from falling. It is true that these objects were made ornamental, but though it is vicious to conceal construction, it is bad architecture to let the devices of construction predominate over the actual outline of the main building itself. Not only does it suggest weakness, but it produces a flutter and a perplexity that can never be satisfactory. . . . All this exemplifies the observation made above, that the French were always working up to the limits of their strength, always trying to make their piers as light, their windows as large, and their vaults as high as possible; doing all they could, and striving to do more, while the soberer English architect, on the contrary, attempted nothing over which he had not full command." French cathedrals not seldom have double side aisles. Chichester alone among English cathedrals lays claim to these, and the peculiarity is confined to the nave. Another distinctive feature of our cathedrals is the extreme rarity of a chevet at the east end. Apsidal terminations were not rare in those of Norman date, but they appear to have been more pleasing to French and Teutonic than to English-born architects, and could not maintain their footing in this country. The original Norman chevet remains with modifications at Norwich and Peterborough, and to some extent at Gloucester. It was retained

---

* The average in English cathedrals of height to breadth in the centre aisle is 2·36 to 1, and is often as low as 2 to 1. In French cathedrals it is commonly 3 to 1 (as at Westminster Abbey).—Fergusson, "Handbook of Architecture," book viii., chap. i.

in the reconstruction of Canterbury, and in a modified form is a feature at the eastern extremity of Lichfield and Wells, but the majority of the English cathedrals are square-ended, so that to obtain a really characteristic example in the Pointed style, we must turn from our cathedrals to the Abbey Church at Westminster. The change, in the writer's opinion, is to be regretted. Contrast, for example, the choir of Laon with that of the neighbouring Cathedrals of Soissons or of Rheims: how poor and flat the termination of the first appears. Hence we find that the east ends of our English cathedrals are the least satisfactory parts. The bold attempt at Durham to solve the difficulty by a perfectly original treatment cannot be called a success; the east ends of Lincoln and of York are comparatively poverty-stricken. From the interior, no doubt, the effect of a double row of lancets or of a fine Decorated window is sometimes very striking, but it may be questioned if this atones for losing the rich effect of the converging ribs of the roof, and the apparent increase of dimensions which is given by the sweep of the chevet, while externally everything seems sacrificed to the window, and the architect always appears to have been in a difficulty as to how to complete his design. Eastern transepts are a much commoner feature in England than in France, and these generally are a great enrichment both within and without. Continental architects also, as a rule, appear to have succeeded better with their west fronts than the English. Wells and Lichfield are undoubtedly beautiful, Peterborough and Lincoln are unique, but both are incomplete, and the latter is certainly open to criticism; York, indeed, is very good, but several, including even Salisbury, are almost failures. It is difficult to find one to compare with the harmonious beauty of Notre Dame at Paris, or with the magnificence of Amiens or Rheims. In one respect, however, the English architects generally bear away the palm—in their towers and steeples. This is, perhaps, in great part due to the use made of a central tower—a feature comparatively rare in France. Laon (which, had all its towers been built, would have been a marvel) and St. Ouen at Rouen show what several of the French cathedrals have lost. We may challenge our kinsmen across the Channel to match the central towers of Canterbury and of Gloucester, or the groups of York, Wells, Durham, and Lincoln, the steeples of Chichester or of Salisbury, or the triple spires of Lichfield, and thus we may venture to assert that there are charms in the architecture of ecclesiastical buildings in England hardly less great than in France.

Our cathedrals have been passing during the last forty or fifty years through a period of restoration in a double sense of the word—a restoration to something of their pristine beauty, and a restoration to use. As for the former it cannot be said that the efforts have been invariably successful—the ravages of time or neglect cannot wholly be obliterated in the beauty of a building, any more than on the face of a woman.   Let the mouldering stone be replaced by new, the crumbling carving exactly copied, yet the building has lost its interest; it has become a mere model, and is no longer a record of the works and thought of men who lived and played a part in this world.   A much "restored" building is hardly better than a copied picture, a manuscript reproduced in photozincography, a scarce old book reprinted in exact fac-simile —it may be instructive, but it loses almost all its interest.   Over-restoration has been the fate of not a few cathedrals.   Not only has the progress of decay been arrested, not only has the new work been done which was needful for the stability and permanence of the building, not only (a task involving actual reconstruction, sometimes of a very conjectural kind) have the deformities been excised and the excrescences swept away which an age of architectural barbarism had introduced, but also, not seldom, the architect has been turned loose on the building to work his will almost unchecked, to impress his own individuality on the cathedral, to run up a big bill, to advertise his name, and advance a stage towards knighthood.   Whether from interested motives or from sheer ignorance, our English cathedrals, like so many of our churches, have, in many cases, suffered almost as much as they have benefited by the epidemic of restoration through which the land has been passing.   No doubt the mischief has not seldom been the result of well-meaning ignorance.   The architect found, or thought he found, a part of the building in a critical condition, and did not possess enough either of knowledge or of genius to reproduce the thoughts of his predecessor and give the world a second, and almost as excellent an embodiment of the same idea.   The later restoration is, in this respect, generally much better than the earlier.   Scott, for instance, was far more conservative and more capable than Cottingham; but still, even in his case, it may sometimes be doubted whether he has not been over-bold, and has tampered with that which had been better left alone.   It must, however, be remembered, as an excuse for the architects and those (supposed to be) in authority over them, that it was often absolutely necessary to do something.   Our cathedrals, some half a century since, were in many cases in a state of dis-repair that threatened to become dilapidation, and their beauties were marred by whitewash, by huge wooden boxes, and by all kinds of eighteenth-century abominations.   I can remember more than one in its unrestored days, and it was not possible to let things remain as they were.   Still zeal, as it so often does in everything connected with religion, has sometimes outrun discretion, and though our cathedrals have rarely suffered from the restorer as those of France did during the Second Empire, though he has rarely worked his will with so little control as he has done at the Fondaco dei Turchi at Venice, and is attempting to do at St. Mark's, yet there has been much mischief perpetrated, together with a very considerable amount of good.

At any rate we may hope that the majority of our cathedrals are now structurally secure. The catastrophe of Chichester, and that which has only been averted by taking down the central tower of Peterborough, would, in all probability, but for the "Gothic revival" of the nineteenth century, have been a common fate.

Structurally, it is probable that, on the whole, our cathedrals suffered more from the neglect of the last century than from any mischief wrought by the iconoclastic zeal of the Puritans. Their injuries rarely went further than the destruction of details, and, in the worst cases, the fifteen years of desecration was not a long enough time to allow the fabric to suffer any serious damage from neglect; but the long period of utter carelessness, from which the present is a reaction, was most detrimental. In one respect, however, our cathedrals have been more fortunate than those of the Continent. The middle part of the seventeenth century marks an epoch, after which for a very long time all structural changes cease in our cathedrals. The opposite influences both of the Puritans and of the courtiers of the restored Stuart diverted men from attempting to enlarge or beautify structures with whose architecture the age was entirely out of sympathy. This was fortunate. Had not the "church revival" of Laud and the earlier Stuarts been so rudely suppressed, seventeenth-century architects might have been let loose upon our cathedrals to deal with them as did Inigo Jones with old St. Paul's, and as Christopher Wren with the façade of Westminster Abbey. But from that, in most cases, Hanoverian apathy has saved us. It is difficult for the present generation to understand the mental condition of its ancestors during the eighteenth century in relation to the architectural remains of the Middle Ages. There has been during the last thirty years a reaction against the architecture of the Renaissance (though the latest craze, dressing as a Florentine of the Medicean epoch, and dwelling in a mansion supposed of the reign of Queen Anne, has produced some turn of the weather-cock). Still, notwithstanding this reaction, and notwithstanding a deliberate preference for "Gothic" instead of Renaissance, on ethical grounds as well as for reasons of taste, few Englishmen would allow the best work of Inigo Jones or of Christopher Wren to fall to ruin, or would attempt to gothicise the present Cathedral of St. Paul. Inconceivable as it may seem, our great-grandfathers appear to have thought that they were actually improving a cathedral when they blocked the vistas of its aisles by screens of plaster and of glass, when they hid the fret-work of a vaulted roof by a flat plaster ceiling, and replaced its carved stall-work by big boxes lined with green baize. All poetic feeling in art appears to have been utterly extinct in England during the later half of the last century. While ready to bestow ponderous epithets of admiration on the results of a "classic taste," their architects were rarely able to produce a work which is even tolerable in its kind; all sense of poetry seems to have been smothered under beef and pudding, or drowned in beer and port wine. However, except in those cases where, as at Lichfield, Hereford, Salisbury, and Durham, Wyatt (whose name it is difficult to write without prefixing an opprobrious epithet) was let loose on a cathedral, the policy of "let alone" was in most cases followed, and the worst sin of commission, except whitewash, wood and plaster work, and hacking at details, was the intrusion of a greater or less quantity of monuments, always conspicuous and often hideous. The feeling of Englishmen, from clownish Squire Western to the more cultured Matthew Bramble, towards the great works of the Middle Ages, can be best summed up in these excerpts from a well-known work of Smollett: "The cathedral (of Durham) is a huge gloomy pile. . . . . As for (York) minster, I know not how to distinguish it, except by its great size and the height of its spire, from those other ancient churches in different parts of the kingdom which used to be called monuments of Gothick architecture, but it is now agreed that this style is Saracen rather than Gothick, and I suppose it was first imported into England from Spain, great part of which was under the dominion of the Moors."

It must not, however, be forgotten that the existence of anything like a conservative spirit in architecture is a thing of extremely modern growth. Mediæval builders effaced without a moment's hesitation the work of their predecessors. At first there was gain as well as loss in this; many of our most noblest works in the Early English and Decorated styles—veritable poems in stone—have replaced simpler and in some cases much less beautiful "Norman" buildings; but as time went on the changes became more wanton, the improvement much less marked. Very much of what was done by the architects of the century preceding the Reformation we could wish undone; their alterations, with the exception of a few fine towers, have been almost invariably for the worse, and it was generally the oldest work, and historically the most interesting work, that suffered most at their hands. The proportions of a Norman nave would be destroyed by raising the roof to enlarge the clerestory windows; the design of a façade would be irretrievably spoiled by the insertion of a huge window of the most commonplace character—a mere frame for stained glass. Taste was decaying and, as is usual, was giving place to sumptuousness; the old faith was dying, and its custodians were trying to galvanise it to life by appealing to superstition —the results are a matter of history. Had the clergy of England headed the reforming movement, the plunder and the wasteful perversion of the property of ecclesiastic corporations in the sixteenth century, the iconoclastic fury of the seventeenth, and the apathy of the eighteenth century, might perhaps have been averted; but the history of the Church, not of England only, is too often the history of lost opportunities, and "too late" is the verdict which posterity is compelled to pronounce upon its efforts.

Half a century since our cathedrals were too often falling into decay—gloomy, deserted piles, in which a few clergy droned through the prescribed duties, and the people of the city felt little interest. All this is changed; the old exclusive policy of the "cathedral close" is a thing of the past; deans and canons admit themselves to be but ordinary mortals, and work as hard as their brother-men; the cathedrals are decently, in many cases sumptuously, restored, services are numerous and attractive. The cathedral has become, as it should be, a centre of religious life and instruction, the great common church of the several parishes of the town. At all reasonable times it is open, and in most cases the visitor can move unrestricted through all parts where a more special custody is not needed. Not seldom also the cathedral has become a centre of intellectual activity for the town, and the mainspring of every good work. It would be invidious to particularise, for the writer naturally would speak of those which he knows best (though these are not few), but it may be asserted in general terms that life in a cathedral city to one outside the charmed circle of the "close" is now a very different thing to what it was forty or fifty years ago. The English cathedrals are becoming in the land a great power for good (we do not restrict the term to the English Church), and they will, we trust, be yet more so in the future. The chief danger to the Church of England at the present day—at any rate from within—is zeal without discretion. If the patronage of our cathedrals is wisely bestowed, they will be —like our universities—in the non-political sense of the word, great conservative institutions; places where men will be found who will not be blown about by every wind of doctrine, or be swayed by every whim of the day, whether the fashion set towards superstition or towards infidelity.

T. G. Bonney.

The Cathedral Churches
OF
England and Wales.

CANTERBURY CATHEDRAL, FROM THE SOUTH-WEST.

CANTERBURY.

AMONG our cathedrals, Canterbury, as is befitting a metropolitan, has a rightful pre-eminence. Few surpass it in picturesqueness of outline, in beauty, or in interest of architecture. No mistaken zeal of a comparatively late age as at St. Peter's in Rome, no overpowering necessity as at St. Paul's in London, has broken its historical continuity and obliterated all traces of the work of earlier generations. Centuries of history do not, indeed, look down from its towers in so full a sense as from the Egyptian pyramids, for above ground there is no remnant of any structure

B

earlier than the Norman Conquest; but since this epoch in our annals, generation after generation has left its mark upon the building, and Canterbury Cathedral is a history writ in stone of every age up to and even beyond the English Reformation.

We have spoken of St. Peter's at Rome: the Cathedral of Christ Church at Canterbury, the metropolitan church of the *alterius orbis papa*, while more venerable as a building, occupies a site not less august. Its title by possession, as a place of worship, may be carried back to the earliest days of Christendom in Britain. We cannot, indeed, fix the precise date when the first church was reared on the little plain in the valley of the Stour, but when the Roman missionaries in the days of Gregory came to win back England to the Church of Christ, Ethelbald gave to Augustine, adjacent to the palace which he transferred to the new-comers, an ancient building which had formerly been a church of the British Christians, and had been erected, so ran tradition, by King Lucius. This Augustine restored—perhaps enlarged and in part rebuilt—and so as the centre of his monastery of Christ Church it became the first cathedral of Canterbury, the mother church of English Christianity.

For almost a century and a half the restored church remained nearly as Augustine had left it. In conformity with the Roman custom, neither he nor his immediate successors were buried within its walls, but in the extra-mural cemetery of the church of Peter and Paul. But in the year 740, Cuthbert, the tenth successor of Augustine, obtained permission from the Pope to depart from this Latin custom and to bury the Archbishops of Canterbury in their own church, "to the intent that they might have their resting-place where they had ruled in honour." Accordingly on his return he erected, "to the east of the 'great church' and almost touching it," a second church, which was dedicated in honour of St. John the Baptist. Within its walls, in due season, his body was laid, and thus began the long series of archbishops, who, when their work was ended, rested in their own cathedral. Of Cuthbert's church also every trace has disappeared, but some have thought that the singular circular termination of the present cathedral, which now bears the name of "Becket's Crown," may be a souvenir of the tomb-house of Cuthbert. In the days of Odo, the latter half of the tenth century, a new roof was needed, and at that time the walls were raised, probably by adding a clerestory. But an evil time was coming in the days of Alphege. The monastery and city were stormed and sacked, the church was plundered and set on fire, the monks were slaughtered, the archbishop was dragged away a prisoner to be insulted and at last murdered by the conqueror. Twelve years later, with a Dane upon the throne, quieter times returned, and the remains of the archbishop were translated with great pomp to a resting-place among his predecessors, Canute himself giving his crown of gold as an atonement, to be hung up "at the head of the great cross in the nave."

A worse calamity, however, occurred. In one of England's darkest years, that which followed the death of Harold at Senlac, a fire broke out in Canterbury city, and the flames laid hold on the monastery; almost all its buildings, the mother church itself, and the tomb-house of the archbishops, with all their store of relics, perished in the flames. Stigand the Englishman was still archbishop, but three years afterwards he was deposed, and Lanfranc the Norman was appointed to the vacant see. Monastery and church alike lay in ruins, but the new prelate quickly addressed himself to the task of reconstruction. One hundred and fifty Benedictine monks were established in the former, and in seven years the church was rebuilt.

In this work, as we are in effect told, all traces of the Saxon church were swept away—he carried out in stone and wood a policy thoroughly Norman. Thus with the first archbishop of that race the chronicle of the present fabric begins. The nave and western towers rest probably on the foundations of Lanfranc's building; portions of his walls yet remain in the lower parts of the two western transepts. The great central tower is raised on piers, which have as their core those which supported the humbler central tower of Lanfranc's church. East of this all is of later date, and in most respects of newer design. As there had been in the Saxon church, and as there is in the present building, so was there a crypt beneath Lanfranc's choir, but this, it is almost certain, consisted only of two bays. Lanfranc's choir had not a long existence. It seemed inadequate to the enlarged ideas of the next generation, and in the days of Anselm, Lanfranc's successor, was pulled down and rebuilt on a far grander scale, by Ernulph, prior of the monastery. The work, however, was not completed by him, but by his successor Conrad, whose name was generally attached to the building, which was dedicated with great pomp in the presence of Henry, King of England, David of Scotland, and all the English bishops, in the year 1130. It was in this church—begun by Lanfranc and completed by Conrad—that the murder of Becket and the humiliation of the king took place, shortly after which events (1174) the glorious choir of Conrad became a heap of ruins. A fire broke out in some cottages on the south side of the church, just beyond the monastic precincts; a strong gale was blowing from that quarter; the glowing embers were carried up, hurled against the roof of the church, and dropping through some interstices ignited the woodwork within. The fire smouldered for a while unperceived, and was not discovered until it had got firm hold upon the roof. The people flocked to save the pride of their city, working, praying, even raving and blaspheming in the excess of their grief; but all efforts were in vain, and the choir was utterly destroyed, the stones in many parts being so calcined by the heat of the conflagration that rebuilding became a necessity. This task was entrusted to one William of Sens, a man " of lively genius and good reputation," under whose charge the work went on from the autumn of 1174 to the year 1178, when " through the vengeance of God or spite of the devil " he fell from a scaffolding and received such serious injuries that he was obliged to give up the charge of the work. He was succeeded by an Englishman, also William by name, by whom the work was completed in the course of six years. The architects followed the lines of Conrad's choir as far as its eastern extremity, where it ended in a chevet, flanked by two towers, and terminated by an oblong chapel dedicated to the Holy Trinity.   These towers were retained, but the Trinity Chapel was rebuilt on a grander scale and practically incorporated with the building,

the floor being raised yet higher to make a more stately resting-place for the relics of the new saint —Thomas of Canterbury —and beyond this, and so considerably to the east of the outermost wall of Conrad's building, was raised the singular structure called " Becket's Crown," which unfortunately was left incomplete in the upper part. All this part still remains almost unaltered; but the architects had not yet done with Canterbury. Nave and transepts were rebuilt in the days of Prior Chillenden, between the years 1378 and 1410, and the great central tower was not carried up to its present height till the end of the latter century, when Prior Goldstone ruled the monastery.

This   tower — " Bell Harry Tower " as it was

BELL HARRY TOWER.

called, from a small bell hung at the top—replaced the "Angel Steeple," from whose summit a gilded angel, glittering from afar in the sun, first attracted the eyes of pilgrims as they approached the sacred shrine at Canterbury. This was the last great work executed in the cathedral, if we except the rebuilding of the north-west tower in the present century, and it was the crowning glory. It would be impossible to find its equal in England, difficult in the world. Whatever might be the faults of the later fifteenth-century architects, and they were not few, they could build towers. The predominance of vertical lines in their designs—often unpleasing, even defeating itself, and causing a feeling of flatness in buildings of less elevation—produces its full effect in one of these lofty structures. We may admire the more ideal perfection of the spires of Salisbury or Chichester or Norwich, and the triple group of Lichfield, but the towers of Gloucester and of Canterbury—of which in our judgment the latter is much the finer—are a marvellous combination of grandeur and of grace.

BECKET'S CROWN.

THE CRYPT.

There is, perhaps, no cathedral in England of which the distant view is more impressive than that of Canterbury. It has not the advantages of situation possessed by Durham or Lincoln or Ely. Standing in the open valley of the Stour, it is surrounded—though fortunately at a distance — by higher ground, but it rises above the clustering houses of the city, above the surrounding meadows and undulating fields, like a three-peaked mountain of stone.

The western towers are comparatively low, though lofty enough to break the monotony of the long line of the nave roof, and to lead the eye duly upwards towards the central peak.   Of these, the southern was completed by Goldstone, having been begun by Archbishop Chichele, while the northern was rebuilt in the present century, being completed in the year 1834.   This replaced one of the old Norman towers which had survived the reconstruction of the nave, and bore the name of the " Arundel Steeple," from a peal of bells placed in it during the primacy of that archbishop.

The principal entrance to the cathedral, approached from the town through the great gateway, another work of Prior Goldstone, is by the south porch, as it was even in the time of the Saxon structure. This occupies a rather unusual position, as it opens into one of the western towers. It corresponds in style with the nave, and formerly—as we learn from Erasmus—bore on a panel above the doorway sculptured representations of Becket's murderers.

THE CHOIR SCREEN.

Through this we enter the nave—a very characteristic work in the Perpendicular style. At the first glance, one of the most distinctive features of Canterbury Cathedral attracts the eye. It is the commencement of the great ascent by which the pilgrims went up to the house of their Lord—the first of the flights of steps which led to the elevated platform in the retro-choir which supported the shrine of Thomas à Becket. Commencing beneath the central tower, the floor rises in a gradual ascent of three stages to the foot of the massive screen of stonework, which almost shuts off the choir from the nave, while shorter but steeper staircases lead from the floors of the transepts to the choir aisles.

Thus the nave produces on the spectator the effect of a great hall, and this is increased by the elevation of the aisles and the comparative thinness of the piers which support the main walls. Instead of a triforium there is a panelled wall of stone, forming a part of the design of the clerestory, as though the lower half of a large Perpendicular window had been blocked up. The result of this is comparatively poor, and the nave of Canterbury, notwithstanding the greatness of its scale, is an example of the decadence of ecclesiastical architecture, when true poetic feeling was fading away and was being inadequately replaced by an ostentatious effort at magnificence. The nave of Canterbury is nearly of the same age as, and closely resembles, that of Winchester, but in the latter the original Norman piers were transformed, not rebuilt; thus Winchester exhibits a strength of design which is painfully wanting in Canterbury, while a rich balcony to some extent atones for the absence of a triforium. Doubtless the painted panes, which in ancient days filled all the windows, as at King's College Chapel, in Cambridge, added greatly to the splendour. These iconoclastic zeal destroyed, and all that remains has been pieced together to fill the western window.

Since the Puritans completed what a Tudor king began, the nave has been but little altered, except that a considerable amount of new stained glass has been introduced. Flags have been hung up on its walls, memorials of warfare by Kentish men in many lands, and monuments, not a few, give some slight relief to the general bareness, though they are but seldom of any particular interest, either architecturally or historically.

The southern transept has a fine stained-glass window, and in the eastern chapel, dedicated to St. Michael, called also the " Warrior's Chapel," is a good piece of Perpendicular work dating from about the year 1400. The centre is occupied by the great altar-tomb erected by Margaret Holland to the memory of her two husbands—John Beaufort, Earl of Somerset, half-brother of Henry IV., and Thomas of Clarence, second son of that monarch, killed by a lance-thrust on the field of Baugé, 1421. But at the east end is a tomb of yet greater interest—a stone coffin, over-arched, so that the head alone projects into the building—wherein rests the dust of Stephen Langton, who has left his mark upon the Bible by the division into chapters, and a yet more important mark upon the history of England, as the contriver of the Great Charter. It was a position which " Old Gandolf " might have envied, for there as he lay beneath the altar stone he could have heard " the blessed mutter of the mass," and tasted " good strong thick stupefying incense smoke ! "

But even now the north transept generally obtains the first notice, as it did from the Canterbury pilgrims, for here Becket received the martyr's crown. We must not, however, suppose that there is much left to recall the scene. Since that dark December evening when the deed of blood was done, all the architectural features

of the building have been changed, but some of the ashlar-work in the lower part
of the wall is a remnant of that which echoed to the stroke of sword and the
groans of the murdered man; some of the slabs in the irregular stone pavement
are those which were sprinkled with his blood.

In order to obtain a mental picture of the place where Becket died, we must
sweep away the noble tomb of Archbishop Peckham and all the later monuments.

PLACE OF THE MARTYRDOM.

We must take away the present staircases and arrange them like those which still
remain in the southern transept. We must replace the sumptuous eastern chapel,
with its elaborate vaulting, by a simpler apsidal structure, and the lofty open transept
of Chillenden by the massive Norman work of Lanfranc, yet more obstructed by
a solid stone gallery, as at St. Stephen's at Caen, and at Winchester, which was
supported by a great central column. Through the doorway in the western wall
Becket and his terrified attendants entered, followed in brief time—for he would
not have it barred—by the four knights. From the stairs he descended out of the
gloom to confront his foes. By that column the final struggle took place: between

it and the entrance to the Benedict Chapel the archbishop fell, and on the stone pavement the sword of Richard the Breton snapped in twain as he dealt that last fatal stroke which smote off the crown of the skull.

From the "transept of the martyrdom" flights of steps lead downwards into the crypt, and upwards into the northern choir aisle, or up to the plat-

form already named as be-
neath the arches of the central
tower. Mounting this last, we
pass beneath the fine stone
screen, a work by an unknown
architect in the fifteenth century, and enter the choir. This,
it will be remembered, is the
work of the two Williams—
architects respectively representing France and England—
replacing the "glorious choir"
of Conrad. The style is Early
English, or First Pointed, as
some people prefer to call it,
but it retains, especially in the
earlier part, distinct traces of
the preceding style, semicircular arches being freely used.
The great length of the building is the first characteristic to
impress the mind. We seem
to have entered a second church,
style and arrangement are so
different from that which we
have left. Even the choir of
Conrad, without the Trinity
Chapel, fully equalled the nave

THE CHOIR.

in length, but the design of William, in which that building was not only in-corporated into the choir, but was considerably lengthened, gives us the longest choir in England. The next feature to attract notice is the singular contraction of the walls beyond the eastern transept. This marks the position of the chevet of Conrad's choir, and is caused by the desire of the architect to retain two flanking towers, which appear to have escaped the conflagration, while he carried the building on considerably to the east of the ancient Trinity Chapel. In fact,

c

the more we examine the plan of the choir, the more we are struck with its singularity. To begin with, its total breadth is somewhat greater than Conrad's choir, and the outer walls in consequence at first expand a little, and the walls of the Lady Chapel and of St. Michael's Chapel make an oblique angle with those of the transept. They then approach together beyond the eastern transept, where the greater of the two ascents to the platform of the high altar is constructed, and lastly attached to the chevet we have the structure known as Becket's Crown. Though the unusual elevation of the floor at the eastern part of the building causes the whole to appear rather low for its length, and the above-named contraction of the walls produces an effect more singular than beautiful, yet it is impossible to look at the choir of Canterbury, with its well-balanced members, piers, arches, triforium, clerestory, its felicitous combination of Romanesque dignity with the grace of the First Pointed style, and its many exquisite details, without a fervent tribute of admiration to the architect who conceived the design. In the western part he was doubtless strongly influenced by the preceding Norman building, a few fragments of which he had incorporated into his own. His English successor, who took up the work when it had advanced to about the level of the eastern transept, appears for a time to have continued on nearly the same lines, so that the work of the two is not easily separable, but on approaching the Trinity Chapel the later architect seems to have emancipated himself from all traditional influences, and terminated the building with a structure which is characteristically Early English in design.

The stalls and seats in the choir are quite new, the work of a restoration which was concluded only a very few years since. An effort is now being made to obtain a new organ; the present instrument, which stands above the choir screen, was built by Green in the last century, and was enlarged by Hill in 1842. A defect, which is more patent to the eye—we may say the only thing that still cries for improvement—is the reredos. This is an erection of about the middle of the present century, when it replaced an elaborate Corinthian screen, being an imitation " of the screen-work of the Lady Chapel in the crypt." Imitation may be the sincerest flattery, but in stone it is often unsuccessful, as it is here. The predecessor of the Corinthian screen, a fine piece of fourteenth-century work, fell a victim to Puritan zeal. Very different from the present simple aspect of the communion table and its surroundings was the high altar in the days before the Reformation. Richly adorned itself, in a grated vault beneath was a treasury of gold and silver vessels, in presence of which, says Erasmus, Midas and Crœsus would have seemed but beggars. As artists we may regret the change, as members of the Church of England we cannot even sigh for the " most idolatrous costly glory cloth " which Laud gave and the Puritans destroyed. Right and left of the altar, and enhancing the glories of the choir, stood formerly the shrines of Alphege and of Dunstan. The one has utterly disappeared; of the other, the position of its altar is indicated by some diaper work in the wall. By it are the monuments of Archbishop Stratford, Chancellor of Edward III., with whom he had no small strife, and of Archbishop Simon of Sudbury, victim to the rage of a London mob; and the screen-work round the choir is the work of Prior Henry d'Estria, in the first decade of the fourteenth century. One other relic of ancient days must be noticed: this is the marble pavement of a part of the choir between the two eastern transepts. When this is disturbed " it is usual to find lead which has run between the joints of the slabs, and spread on each side below," supposed to be the result of the great fire of 1174, when the molten lead streamed down from the roof.

In the windows of the north aisle, along which the pilgrims passed on their way to the shrine of the martyred Thomas, is some excellent thirteenth-century stained glass. Here, too, is the fine monument of Archbishop Chichele. Yet further is the stately tomb of Cardinal Bourchier, bishop or archbishop for fifty-one years, who died in the year 1486; and near it a cenotaph to Archbishop Howley, who was buried at Addington. In the basement storey of St. Andrew's Tower was once the sacristy, where was kept a marvellous store of vessels of gold and of silver, with relics yet more precious, such as Becket's pastoral staff, his handkerchief, stained with his blood, and even rags which had served him for the homeliest purpose. These were preserved in a black leather chest, and when it was exhibited the faithful knelt in reverence. The pilgrims retired after their visit to the shrine by the south aisle, where are the tombs of Walter, the archbishop elected during Richard's crusade, and Reynolds, once tutor of Edward II., but in the end faithless to him; and a mark on the wall denotes the place of the monument of Winchelsea, who opposed Edward I. on the question of clerical subsidies, but was open-handed to the poor of his diocese. Anselm, the learned philosopher and the champion of his church in the "War of the Investitures," rests in the chapel of the tower which bears his name, and from the chamber above watch was kept by night over the treasures of his successor's shrine.

This stood, as we have said, in the centre of the retro-choir; an arched structure of marble supporting on high the sacred chest wherein the saint's relics were laid. Hither they were brought from their tomb in the crypt below on a memorable day—Tuesday, July 7, 1220—followed by a crowd of prelates and nobles from either side of the Channel, with the young King Henry III. at the head of the procession. The shrine itself was a wonder of art, " blazing with gold and jewels; the wooden sides were plated with gold, and damasked with gold wire, and embossed with innumerable pearls and jewels and rings, cramped together on this gold ground." All these treasures, when times had changed, were swept off to the royal treasury; the bones of Becket were buried in an unknown and unhonoured grave, the shrine was utterly destroyed, and now only a roughly-paved space enclosed between two mosaics—one composed of rare stones, brought doubtless from the classic ruins of Rome, and one of figures inlaid with white marble on black—marks the site. A crescent attached to the roof high above, surrounded by staples which may once have supported flags, is probably the last remnant of the varied offerings which were formerly gathered about the shrine of Becket.

THE CHOIR STALLS.

In such a holy place no ordinary man might be laid to rest, so for many years the martyr's remains occupied this Trinity Chapel in solitary state. At last, at a time of national mourning, Edward the Black Prince was entombed, not as he had directed in the crypt below, but here on the floor above, " on what was then thought to be the most sacred spot in England." The tomb has fortunately escaped well from the chances of some five centuries. The brass effigy reposes on an altar-tomb beneath a canopy; the features, still uninjured, showing the type of the Plantagenet face, "the flat cheeks and the well-chiselled nose, as in the effigy of his father at Westminster and of his grandfather at Gloucester." The canopy above yet retains the painting, a quaint representation of the Trinity, with which it once was decorated. From it hang the prince's gauntlets and helm, his surcoat and shield, and the scabbard which once held his sword; this, men say, was taken away by the hand of Cromwell.

Opposite, on the north side of the chapel, is the tomb of Henry IV. and his second wife, Joan of Navarre, who survived him twenty-four years, dying in 1437. The Yorkist stories asserted that this, so far as the king's body went, was but a cenotaph, the body having been cast into the sea during a storm as a Jonah offering;

but an examination in the year 1832 showed the tale to be no more true than those of politicians generally are. East of this king's monument is one to Wotton, first Dean of Canterbury after the Reformation, placed here, it may be, in order to show that the reverence for the great Thomas was indeed a thing of the past. At the feet of the Black Prince is the tomb of Archbishop Courtenay, his executor, but whether he is buried here is uncertain; and, yet further east, lies Odo Coligny, Cardinal Chatillon, who died at Canterbury as a refugee in the days of Elizabeth.

At the extreme eastern end of the chancel stands Becket's Crown, which is an octagon in plan, terminating the cathedral like an apsidal tower, if the phrase may be allowed. In this remarkable structure some have seen a memorial of the tomb-house of the Saxon archbishops, others a remembrance of the seat assigned by Pope Pascal II. to the *alterius orbis papa*, in the " corona " in the Lateran; but whatever may have been its motive, the building is the work of English William, and one of the most graceful parts of his design. Here, when the shrine was standing in the adjoining part of the cathedral, were the shrines of Archbishop Odo, and of Wilfred of York, with " a golden reliquary in the form of a head, containing some relic of Becket, perhaps the severed scalp." Here also

THE BAPTISTERY.

is the tomb of Cardinal Pole, kinsman of Queen Mary of ill memory, the last archbishop entombed in the cathedral. Of late years the patriarchal chair has been brought back to the Corona. Tradition states that it was the throne of the heathen kings of Kent, given by Ethelbert to Augustine, and has ever since been the *cathedra* of the Archbishops of Canterbury. It is fashioned of three pieces of Purbeck marble, and is probably of later date than tradition assigns to it. By the latest authority (Canon Robertson) it is assigned to the year 1220.

One other marked feature of Canterbury Cathedral yet calls for notice—the spacious crypt which supports all the eastern part of the building, and causes the long ascent which has been already mentioned. There are four others in England, which like it are anterior to the year 1085. These are Winchester, Gloucester, Rochester, and Worcester, and no cathedral of later date has included a crypt in its design, though one which had previously existed may have been rebuilt. The western or lower part of Canterbury crypt is the older. A little of Lanfranc's work remains, but in the main it is a relic of the cathedral of Ernulph. The eastern part, beneath the Trinity Chapel and the Corona, was the work of English William. This not only supported the sacred shrine, but also over-arched the spot where for a time Becket's body was laid between his death and its translation. Thus the actual building, beneath whose massive arches in the gloom of a December day the last rites were paid to the blood-stained corpse, that, too, in which a King of England was forced to humble himself before a crowd of monks, remains no longer, but all the western part—that along which the body was brought to burial—is still unaltered. Towards the eastern end of the crypt, enclosed by open stonework of Perpendicular age, is the chapel of our Lady Undercroft, once the richest treasure-house of the cathedral, surrounded in the days of Erasmus by a double rail of iron, and displayed only to a chosen few among the thousands of pilgrims. Here was laid the body of Cardinal Morton, who united the houses of Lancaster and York in the persons of Henry VII. and Elizabeth. In the crypt also is a memorial of the Black Prince, the chantry founded to commemorate his marriage.

In the days of Elizabeth a number of French and Flemish refugees, mostly clothiers and silk-weavers, settled at Canterbury; and the crypt was granted to them by the queen. They set up their looms in the main part, and worshipped in the south side-aisle. The looms have fortunately vanished with the trade, but the descendants of the refugees still meet in the aisle for worship, after their fathers' ways and in the French tongue.

We pass now to the exterior of the cathedral, into the precincts of the great Benedictine monastery of Christ Church. The conventual buildings at Canterbury were situated on the northern side of the cathedral; that edifice standing near to the boundary of the enclosure, both on the west and on the south. A massive wall surrounds the whole, so that it was like the temple of old, at once a fortress and the house of God. This wall, though of earlier date than the Norman Conquest, was greatly strengthened by Lanfranc. Much is of later date, but probably some parts which still remain are his work. The main approach to the cathedral from the town is by Christ Church Gate, at the end of Mercery Lane—a grand structure in the Later Perpendicular style, built by Prior Goldstone in the year 1517. As we enter this the cathedral, vast in height as in length, at once confronts us. The intervening strip of ground was once the cemetery, and that south and east of the choir was the monastery garden. Somewhere here was the school founded by Archbishop Theodore, when he introduced the study of Greek, so long as twelve centuries ago. The comparative narrowness of the open space makes it impossible to obtain a very complete general view of this southern or of the western face. The part of the cathedral which is more immediately opposite to the visitor is the nave of Chillenden, with the southern porch and the comparatively low western tower, whose date has been already given, while from the other end rises on high the magnificent Bell Harry Tower. But to appreciate the building as a whole, its grand sky-line and majestic proportions, we must seek some spot at a little distance from the town, where we can see it rising high above the roofs, like a great mountain of hewn and sculptured stone.

Near the eastern end of the church, on the northern side, are the ruins of the infirmary, now to a considerable extent freed from the houses into which they had been incorporated, and not far off an ancient house which once formed a part of some guest chambers belonging to the prior. We must not forget to notice a beautiful little Norman structure, with an upper storey, attached to the north-eastern transept, called the " Baptistery." The name is incorrect, but the lower part was connected with the water supply of the monastery. The passage leading to the cloisters, called the " Dark Entry," recalls a tale in the " Ingoldsby Legends," and retains a remnant of good Norman work in its arches. The cloisters are Late Perpendicular, though some fragments of the Norman structure, through which Becket passed to his death, still remain incorporated into their walls, and there is a door on the site of that which communicated with his palace. The refectory was on the north, the chapter-house is on the east. The latter is a grand hall, built by Archbishop Arundel about the year 1400, with a handsome roof of Irish oak. There is a fine view of the Bell Harry Tower, with the transept and chapter-house, from near the north-west angle of the cloisters.

The palace of the archbishop has been swept away, but round the green court on the northern side of the cloisters no inconsiderable portion of the monastic buildings still remain, though often masked by more modern dwelling-houses. The deanery includes a portion of the prior's lodgings. It also contains an interesting series of portraits of the Deans of Canterbury from the time of Wotton to the present. The Grammar School occupies the ancient almonry. This, with some adjoining buildings, was appropriated by Henry VIII., who set up a mint in one part and founded a school in the other. Since then the buildings of the latter have been augmented, as its number and its fame have increased. Its hall is a modern structure, built on the site of one which belonged, it is supposed, to the steward of the monastery courts, but its external staircase is a fine specimen of Norman work, and is the only one of its kind that remains in England. But all around this court there is much to delight the antiquary, which space forbids us to describe minutely. We must merely, in conclusion, indicate the porter's gate, also in the main a late Norman structure, in

CHRIST CHURCH GATE.

former times the chief entrance from the town to the monastery. An arched doorway in the adjoining street—Palace Street—is almost all that remains of the home of the Archbishops of Canterbury from days long anterior to the Norman Conquest.

Of the lives of its occupants, and of those who in later days have been Primates of All England, we have but spoken incidentally, as space is wanting for a subject so great.   For many centuries the history of the see of Canterbury is to no small extent the history of England, and though of later years, since the days of the Reformation and of the great Civil War, the annals have been less eventful and the Archbishop of Canterbury has been less of a prince among the nobles, yet he may have been a power for good certainly not less potent.   When we note that the seed once planted here by a band of missionaries has spread unto the ends of the earth, and the daughter churches of the Church of England may be found in all lands, we see in the fabric of Canterbury Cathedral a visible token of how " a small beginning could lead to a great and lasting good," for there is no place in Britain " which carries us more vividly back into the past or more hopefully forward to the future."

T. G. BONNEY.

RUINS OF THE INFIRMARY.

D

GENERAL VIEW OF YORK.

YORK MINSTER.

Sir Walter Scott calls this cathedral "the most august of temples, the noble Minster of York," and its most devoted lover can never complain that it has not in every age received its due share of veneration. From the time that Alcuin spread its fame in the country of his adoption, telling with a son's pride of the beauty of its decorations, the learning of its priests, and the treasures of its library, in the court of France, this "glorious temple in the north" has never been without its historians, or its prelates without their biographers. From this overwhelming mass of information it is no easy task to extract and condense a few pages that shall be generally interesting, yet sufficiently explicit.

Let us look first at the west front, that exquisite specimen of Gothic art, which "has been compared with the celebrated façade at Rheims Cathedral for richness, sublimity, and beauty of architectural design; it is certainly not surpassed by that of any church in England in its fine proportions, chaste enrichments, or scientific arrangements." An eight-pinnacled tower rises at each side, and between is a gable with perforated battlement, surmounted by a crocketed pinnacle. The whole front is divided into three parts by massive buttresses, enriched with tabernacle work on every face, and in each of these divisions is an entrance to the church. In the two side ones are three windows, one above the other, the two lower ones Decorated, those in the towers Perpendicular, the upper and lower having enriched pediments. The central doorway is divided into two by a slender shaft, as is not unusual, but the space beneath the deep vaulting of the arch is filled with a circular six-light window, which is an uncommon, if not unique, arrangement. Over this is a crocketed gable, in the centre of which is a niche containing the statue of Archbishop Melton, who finished the building of the western part of the nave. " He sits, graven in stone, in his archiepiscopal attire, with his hand still raised, in the attitude of benediction. Over his head is the finest Gothic window in the world, built in all probability by himself, and still beaming with the glowing colours with which he adorned it nearly five hundred and fifty years ago. On either hand is an effigy of a benefactor of the church, the heads of the noble houses of Vavasour and Percy, bearing in their arms the wood and stone which they once gave."

The nave was begun by Archbishop Romaine in 1291, and finished by Archbishop Melton in 1330. The aisle windows are Decorated, and so is the clerestory, though rather later in style. It is divided into a centre and two side aisles by seven clustered columns, which support acutely-pointed arches, rising to the height of about forty feet. Above these is the triforium, which forms, so to speak, the lower part of the clerestory windows, as the same mullions continued upwards separate the arcades of the one and the lights of the other. One slender outside column of each cluster, with one still more slender on each side of it, rises straight from the ground to the spring of the clerestory arch, where it branches off into three ribs, which meet those from the opposite side in the groining of the roof. The roof is of wood painted like stone, covered with lead—new since the fire of 1840; the aisles retain their original stone vaulting. In the archives of York Minster are two agreements entered into by plumbers, dated 1367 and 1370, for repairing and covering with lead, where required, that cathedral, the belfry, and the chapter-house. The first time we hear of lead being used was when St. Wilfrid (archbishop 669—709), fresh from the glories of the Eternal City, and reinstated in the see of York, grieved to find the church there built by Edwin and Oswald so fallen into decay, set to work on a thorough restoration. He put on a new roof of lead, placed for the first time glass in the windows, so that the birds could no longer fly in and out and defile the sanctuary within, covered the walls with plaster, and decorated the altar. This same Wilfrid was one of the five saints of whom

York can boast; the others are Paulinus, St. Chad, St. John, generally called "of Beverley," and St. William. His life teems with interest. He was a great and good man, though fiery and imperious, and always in hot water. One feels

YORK MINSTER, WEST FRONT.

glad to read that though "his life was like an April day, often interchangeably fair and foul, after many alterations he set fair in full lustre at last."

The nave is paved in a geometrical pattern, designed by Kent under the supervision of the Earl of Burlington, about 1736; the materials used, partly Huddleston stone, given by Sir Edward Gascoign, of Parlington, partly—alas, that it must be owned!—old gravestones cut into shape! The former pavement must have been interesting and peculiar. It had a row of circular stones about two feet in diameter and two feet apart up each side, and one row of fewer and larger down the middle, supposed to be to show where, on grand occasions, the different church dignitaries should stand. The intervening space was filled with graves, all trace of which is, of course, now lost. The only monument of any interest left in the nave is that commonly ascribed to Archbishop Roger (though dates are irreconcilable), which being absolutely in the wall could not be easily removed, though Drake does tell us that in his time any curious osteologist might have the pleasure of poking his walking-stick through the open work in front, and even touching the coffin!

This Archbishop Roger (1154—1181) rebuilt the choir with its crypts, with the archiepiscopal palace to the north of the cathedral, and the Chapel of the Holy Sepulchre between the two buildings. He gave one of St. Peter's bones and part of his sandals to the church. These were put into a crucifix of gold, and were among the things sent for the ransom of Cœur-de-Lion, but were afterwards

THE NAVE, LOOKING EAST.

redeemed. He waged long and actively the war with Canterbury about the question of supremacy and "bearing the cross," the right to carry that symbol erect belonging exclusively to the Primate. At the Council of Westminster, September, 1102, Gerard of York kicked over the chair prepared for him, because it was on a lower level than that put for Anselm of Canterbury. Roger vindicated his claim in an even more amusing and undignified way, and this also at a Council at Westminster. Huguccio, the Pope's legate, of course sat in the middle, and the Archbishops of Canterbury and York were to be one on each side. When Roger arrived he found that Richard had got there before him and taken the place of honour on the right. What was to be done? He pushed in between the legate and his rival, and ended by sitting on his knee! This the Canterbury people could not quite suffer. They pulled him off, threw him on the ground, and beat and trampled him unmercifully, and when at last they allowed him to rise, it was in sorry plight, with a torn cope and "covered with dust and shame!" and, sad to relate, when he complained to the king (Henry II.) he was only laughed at. Pope Alexander, however, put an end for a time to such brawls by settling the question according to the decree of Gregory the Great, which gave precedence to the senior; but on the 20th of April, 1353, a composition was made by the king between the archbishops, which practically made Canterbury the head, though on all public occasions they were to be as equal as possible. In addition to this the Pope ordained that York should be called "Primate of England," but Canterbury, "Primate of *all* England." York, however, retains the old privilege of crowning the queens.

This is the largest nave in any English cathedral, and, as in the case of that other St. Peter's, in a sunnier city, the proportions are so exquisite that the eye takes some time to realise the size. All is so simple, so grand, and fault-finders add "so cold." Perhaps there is a little want of colour, but where form is so perfect one could scarcely wish, even for the sake of warmth, to risk the loss of purity. Most of the windows retain their original glass, fairly perfect, and here and there a shimmering bit of colour is cast to the ground, but this is never by the oldest glass, which always transmits pure light. No conclusive explanation has been given of this, and some say it is a "lost art;" is it not more probably the result of the outside surface of the old glass being roughened by the corrosive action of the weather and producing interference?* The glass of many of the windows is very much out of plumb, owing to the melting of the lead which binds it together during the fire of 1840. This catastrophe took place on the night of May 20th, when the whole nave was burnt up to the central tower; this the fire could not pass, as there was nothing in it to burn. It originated in the south-west tower, where some workmen are supposed to have left a light. The metal of the melted bells poured down among the ruins, and was collected, and for years snuff-boxes, &c., made of "bell-metal," were a staple commodity among the curiosity vendors of the city. The new bells rang for the first time on July 4th, 1844. "Great Peter," who occupies the other tower, does not "utter forth his glorious voice" quite as often as some of us could wish. He has to be struck by a hammer, because, owing to his enormous weight, the machinery has never been arranged for ringing him.

Let us pass up the nave, now noticing a stone dragon which projects from the triforium, and from which at one time hung the canopy of the font, and

* Investigations made after these words were written have shown this to be the correct explanation.

now wondering if Charles I. were not right after all when he ordered the organ to be removed because it spoilt the view of the east window. We pause at the south-east corner of the nave. It was upon this spot that Archbishop John Romanus stood on April 6th, 1291, to lay the foundation stone of this his great work, and to call down the blessing of the Holy Ghost upon it. What would he look round and see? To the right Roger's Norman choir, almost above his head the great tower, and beyond it the north transept, both of which his father had built—noble example to any son. The "Five Sisters" would look down on him much as they do now on us; behind him would be the transept and tomb of Walter Gray, and before him the ruins of the Norman nave, built by Thomas, burnt in 1137, and which he was preparing to make even as we see it now.

The central tower, the largest in England, was built about 1260 by John Romanus the elder, treasurer of the cathedral, who enclosed the Norman piers in the present many-shafted pillars. It was "clothed upon" by Archbishop Thoresby, with help from his friend and private chaplain, Walter Skirlaw, afterwards Bishop of Durham, and as William of Wykeham was at that time a good deal in York, and also a friend of the archbishop's, probably so energetic a builder would have a hand in it too. The bells were removed from it to their present abode about 1409, when the lantern tower was made open to the top as at present. The tower is Perpendicular, with a groined roof and two fine windows on each face. A rich arcade runs round it between the arches and the windows, and in each of the eight spaces below this is the coat of arms of some donor to the fabric. This is the same in the nave.

Across the two eastern pillars of the tower is the magnificent screen so justly celebrated. The carved work of the canopies is very rich. There are seven niches on one side of the central doorway, and eight on the other, containing statues of the Kings of England from the Conqueror to Henry VI. The iron gate was given in the early part of last century by a Mrs. Mary Wandesford, a maiden lady, who took "brevet rank." She also endowed an "old maids' hospital" for her poorer sisters. York has always been a great place for single ladies, and the memory of five of the number is exquisitely perpetuated in the next lovely object which meets our gaze—the celebrated window of the "Five Sisters." It consists of five equal-sized lancets of the most perfect Early English. The sisters are each said to have done one panel in needle-work, and then had it copied in glass by foreign artists, but the exact when and where are not known. It is a most beautiful specimen of late thirteenth-century painted glass, and the peculiar blending of the grisaille tints is quite unrivalled. This window fills the whole of the end of the central aisle of the north transept, which was built by John Romanus the elder, in the reign of Henry III.

The south transept was built by Archbishop Walter Gray at a rather earlier
date than the north, and both are good specimens of Early English, and very
much alike. It is interesting to notice in the triforium that the large arches,

THE CHOIR.

which each enclose four small pointed ones, are sometimes round and sometimes
slightly pointed, marking one step in the transition.   In both the transepts the
clerestory and triforium are distinct architectural compositions.   Each transept
has two aisles, and is divided into three bays.   There is a strange monument behind one of the pillars in the north transept, of a man worn to skin
and bone.   It is in memory of John Haxby, treasurer, died 1424, of whom

is told the usual legend, that he tried to fast for the forty days of Lent, and so died. Also near here is the very fine tomb of Archbishop Greenfield, behind which the maniac, Jonathan Martin, hid himself. He watched every one out of the minster after evening service, and then piled benches and straw hassocks in a heap under the organ, and put a light to them, causing

THE MINSTER, FROM THE EAST.

the fire of 1829, when the organ and all the choir were burnt. The coloured glass of the bottom part has never been refilled, and it remains clear, as a remembrance. The front of the south transept has a pretty rose window, with lancets underneath, the lower ones spoilt by bad modern glass. This part was restored by Street, under the late dean, and is generally thought to be architecturally the most perfect of any. The painted grey roof has been removed, and a wood one with emblazoned bosses substituted. In the central bay of the east

E

aisle is the tomb of the founder, Walter Gray—a noble monument to a noble man. He died May 1st, 1255, having been archbishop thirty-nine years. He is represented in his mitre and robes, his head resting on a cushion, his right hand raised to bless, his left hand holding the pastoral staff, and thrusting it into the mouth of a dragon under his feet. Over his head is a massive canopy supported by nine slender pillars, and it was a well-believed tradition that he was buried in this canopy and not in the earth, because as he died under excommunication he might not be buried in consecrated ground! But unfortunately for this tale he was never excommunicated, and when the canopy was examined by Drake, the historian, he found nothing more interesting than rubble. Side by side with Walter Gray's is another beautiful monument, a modern one, but in wonderful harmony with the surroundings. It is in memory of the late dean, Dr. Duncombe, the restorer of the transept, and a great benefactor to the church and city. The slender columns of dark grey Purbeck marble, interspersed in the grey stone clusters, form a striking feature in this part of the building; until a few years ago they were whitewashed, to preserve them from iconoclastic hands.

Entering the choir by the door in the screen, the magnificent east window bursts into view. It is the largest in England which retains its original glazing. The number of subjects represented in glass is about one hundred and fifteen, from the Old Testament and the Revelation. The figures are generally about two feet high, the drawing is good, and the faces are exquisitely finished, resembling in style the work of the early Italian painters. It was begun by John Thornton, of Coventry, in 1405. He was to have four shillings a week, and five pounds a year in addition, and to finish it in three years, and, if the work were really well done, ten pounds at the end of that time.

The architecture of the choir is much the same as that of the nave, though rather later; the clerestory is Perpendicular instead of Decorated, and the roof more complicated, which is a doubtful improvement. It is made of teak, painted stone-colour. The Norman choir of Roger was in existence till the time of Thoresby (1352—1373), and was only removed bit by bit as the workmen came to each part. They began from the east end, and a slight difference in style is discernible in the three eastern bays. One noticeable architectural peculiarity in the choir is the introduction of small transepts midway between the great transepts and the east end. Some think they owe their origin to Roger, and that he meant them for the bases of towers like those of Canterbury —he was Archdeacon of Canterbury before he came to York. Another idea is that the long window which extends the whole height of them was designed to throw additional light on the altar, which at one time stood between them. It was put backwards into its present position about 1730, thus adding to the body of the church the space between it and the altar-screen, which was once a sort of vestry for the archbishops to robe in before consecration, and above which, in front, was a gallery for music. The altar-screen is an exquisite specimen of Perpendicular work, in perfect harmony with its surroundings, and it is unfortunate that the same cannot be said for the reredos, which is not what one might wish either in form or colour. The moulding of Tinworth's terra-cotta "Crucifixion" and the wood-carving are both good, but cannot atone for covering so much of the east window. Just below the little transepts stand the pulpit on one side, and the archbishop's throne on the other. The carving of their canopies and those of the stalls is very good, copied from those which were there before the fire; the pinnacles are sometimes thought too slender. Thoresby pulled down the old Manor House at Sherburn, and used the materials for building this choir as far as they would go. In 1385 a contract was entered into for Huddlestone stone, of which the western part is mostly built.

Descending a few steps into the south aisle we cross to the vestry, where a great many interesting relics are preserved. First and foremost of these is the horn of Ulphus, a Saxon prince, who, hearing his sons quarrelling about the division of his property, punished them by giving it to the minster (about 1036), and laid his drinking-horn on the altar, as the tenure by which it was to be held. It is an elephant's tusk, beautifully carved with winged quadrupeds, thought to be of Oriental workmanship. The lands lie to the east of York, and are still in the possession of the dean and chapter. There are some silver chalices and rings taken from the tombs of the archbishops; a silver pastoral staff given by Catherine of Braganza to her confessor, James Smith, when James II. made him a bishop; an ancient chair, rather like the throne of Dagobert, in which several kings are said to have been crowned; a magnificent oak chest of the time of Henry V.; a "Mazer" bowl, promising an indulgence to all who drank from it, given by Archbishop Scrope to the Cordwainers' Company; two velvet-bound books, given to the church by Charles I.; and last but not least, a wooden head of Archbishop Rotherham, found in his coffin where his own ought to have been. Why it was put there no one can make out; he died of the plague in 1500.

Adjoining the vestry is the beautiful Early English room called Archbishop La Zouche's Chapel. He began building it in 1350, intending to be buried there, but was called away in 1352, before it was ready for him, so he was laid in the nave. This archbishop beat the Scots and took their king prisoner in a battle at Bewre Park, near Durham, while Queen Philippa remained in York to pray for his success. The chapel is now used for the meeting of Convocation. It contains St. Peter's well, in a very picturesque recess.

Leaving the vestry, we turn to the right along the south aisle of the choir towards the Lady Chapel. The principal monuments are in this part of the cathedral, and it must be owned there are very few of any great interest or beauty. To the left, by the choir-screen, is that of Archbishop Dolben, in his youth a Royalist soldier. To the right that of the Hon. Thomas Wentworth, nephew of the Earl of Strafford. Near this is an amusing inscription to a certain Lady Downe, which after twenty-seven lines enumerating her perfections, refers the enquiring reader to the *Gentleman's Magazine* of May, 1812, for further particulars! The window next the east end of the south aisle—the meeting of Mary and Elizabeth—originally adorned the east window of St. Nicholas', Rouen, and was given to the dean and chapter by the Earl of Carlisle in 1804. The design is supposed to be by Sebastiano del Piombo, a pupil of Giorgione. The splendid tomb of Archbishop Bowet, who died in 1423, was injured in the last fire and has not been restored, but in spite of its ruinous condition, from either side it is a lovely study of light and shade, a temptation to any artist. It is in the best style of Henry VI.'s time, and similar to that of Cardinal Kemp at Canterbury. It fills the

THE FIVE SISTERS.

space between the two pillars of the easternmost end of the south aisle. In the corresponding position on the north side rests Archbishop Scrope, beheaded for high treason after a mock trial, June 8th, 1405, in a field between Bishopthorpe and York—the first prelate who suffered death in England by any form of law.

Between these two monuments—for there is no altar here now—are, in various states of repair, memorials to Archbishops Rotherham, Frewen, Matthew, Sewell, and Sharp. We are now immediately beneath the east window, but cannot see it so well as in the choir, where it has been described, but the stone arcading which doubles each mullion can be well seen, and the gallery which crosses the window half-way up, the effect of which is beautiful and peculiar. At the back of where the present altar stands was the gorgeous shrine of St. William, to which his bones were removed from the nave, January 8th and 9th, 1284, in the presence of Edward I., Queen Eleanor, eleven bishops, and the whole court. Thirty-six miracles are recorded of him, and oil is said to have flowed from his tomb, so no wonder pilgrims flocked to it. The shrine was entirely swept away at the Reformation. Just in front of this is the place where Thoresby laid six of his predecessors, leaving room for himself to rest in their midst. The monument of Archbishop Sterne, which faces down the north aisle, is amusingly realistic. He was a staunch Royalist, and died of the gout, and his statue is half recumbent, with one leg thicker than the other. He was grandfather of Laurence Sterne. Passing the tombs of Charles Howard, Earl of Carlisle, Chancellor Swinburne, and Sir Henry Bellasis, and the St. William window in the little transept on the right, we come to the only link with royalty the minster possesses, the tomb of William of Hatfield, second son of Edward III. and Philippa, who died at the age of eight. The face is injured, but the figure is in good preservation. The feet rest on a lion. A series of canopies reach to the roof. In this aisle are two large triangular boxes, ornamented with beautiful iron-work, in which copes were kept.

TOMB OF ARCHBISHOP WALTER DE GRAY.

The first crypt is nearly square. It has a groined roof supported by six short pillars, some of which have Norman capitals, all different, and some very beautiful. One has figures dancing round. The whole effect is interesting, and, with the dashes of sunlight that find their way in, quite charming, but it is perplexing to find stones of many different styles in this part of the building, so that no date can be assigned to it, and records are not explicit.

We descend a few more steps and are in the crypt proper—Roger's glorious work—begun in 1171. Four of the original magnificent pillars remain with their zigzag and diaper pattern, and the remains of four slender pillars round each. Between them are the bases of small columns. Outside these are some walls of the older Norman church, which in some places encase the herring-bone stonework of the Saxon. But the interest of this most interesting place centres in an earthy mound just under the site of the Norman high altar. And here let us pause.   This is the spot hallowed for centuries as that upon which King Edwin was baptised, and where his head was brought home to be buried. Long before that—looming out from the mists of antiquity—we see, if uncritical, King Ebrauc and his chiefs celebrating their pagan rites, and then the Romans with their stately worship, for here stood a temple to Diana, or as some say, Bellona.   Then came the dawning of Christianity, and the mission of St. Sampson and others, for the light of the Gospel had penetrated these northern glooms before the little Yorkshire boys had charmed St. Gregory in the Roman slave market, and he had sent Augustine to convert us to be " not Angles but Angels."   Then, after St. Sampson had been driven away by pagan invaders, came King Arthur to restore the desolated churches; he left his chaplain, Pyramus, as bishop.   Much of this is legend.   The first date that stands out clear and certain is April 12th, Easter Day, 627, when Paulinus baptised King Edwin, two of his children, and " many other persons of distinction and royal birth."   A little wooden hut was the beginning of York Minster, but over it rose a larger church of stone, which Edwin did not live to finish.   That task was accomplished about 642 by Oswald, his successor.   It was repaired by St. Wilfrid about 720, and destroyed by fire in 741, rebuilt by Egbert (732—766), first archbishop since Paulinus, and demolished by the Danes.   Thomas of Bayeux—chaplain to King William, and first archbishop after the Conquest— rebuilt the church, but it was again burnt in 1137—this time only partially— along with St. Mary's Abbey and thirty-nine parish churches!   This was in the episcopacy of Thurston, and perhaps his time was too much occupied with military matters, and rousing up the monks of St. Mary's, for him to begin any restoration.   This work was taken in hand by Roger, his successor, who lived to finish the Norman choir, and the crypt of which we now speak.

St. Olaf, King of Norway, who died in 1030, is said to have sent over to the King of England for the plans of York Minster, to be used in the building of Trondheim Cathedral.   The two churches have something in common, but the points of resemblance belong mostly to a later date.

The only part of the interior of the building remaining undescribed is the chapter-house, by some considered the gem of all.   It is entered from the north transept through a very beautiful doorway, divided into two by a slender shaft, which leads into an L-shaped vestibule.   This doorway, with the vestibule beyond, forms an exquisite study of light and shade.   There have been great disputes about the date of the chapter-house, and perhaps the most received opinion is that it was built by Walter Gray about the same time as the south transept, because a figure of him in one of the windows is like that on his tomb, and the arms of several of his contemporaries are in some of the other windows, and still more because the style resembles that of his age rather than that both before and after. On the other hand the windows and buttresses and the grotesque carvings resemble those of the west end of the nave. It is octagonal in shape with no central pillar, a window on each side with six arches below each, and a seat under each arch separated by pillars of Purbeck marble. All sorts of quaint little carvings are in the canopies of these stalls. One is a devil taking the crown from a king's head; another a monk and a nun kissing. The original glass, mostly heraldic, of Early Decorated date, remains in all except the east window, which is modern and very humiliating. The ceiling was covered with frescoes coeval with the building; remnants of this may be seen in the vestibule. On a pillar by the door is the celebrated inscription, " Ut rosa flos florum, sic est domus ista domorum." The chapter-house was restored in 1844. It must originally have stood alone, for the vestibule is built both on to it and to the transept. This latter also contains some good carving, and the window arches are peculiar, not having their points in the middle.

Northwards from the north transept, and adjoining the deanery, is a stone building with an Early English five-light window very like the " Five Sisters." It is now the minster library, but anciently it was the private chapel of the arch- bishops and adjoined their palace. Of the palace itself nothing remains except a few arches. To his everlasting disgrace, Archbishop Young (1560—1568) sold the lead off the roof and pocketed the proceeds, and Roger's palace fell into decay. Young was, notwithstanding, deemed worthy of sepulture in the north aisle of the choir, but the exact place is not known.

Looking back along the vale of years, how many memories come thronging up as we gaze upon York Cathedral or linger beneath its over-arching roof ! Kings and saints have knelt where we kneel, have prayed where we pray. Here from age to age have come the warrior in his strength, the old man with his hoary "crown of glory," the sinner with his burden, the maiden with her joy. Here (in 1221) the Princess Joan, daughter of King John, though only eleven years old, was married to Alexander II. of Scotland, and here thirty-one years later came her little niece, Margaret of England, to be united to Alexander III. That was indeed a gay Christmas. Henry III. and his queen and court were there, and the royal family of Scotland, to witness the union of the two children. Neither the bride nor the bridegroom was yet eleven ! A thousand knights in robes of silk attended the bride, while the King of Scotland was surrounded by the most distinguished vassals of his crown, and by the highest dignitaries of the Scottish Church. Tournaments and balls and processions suc- ceeded each other for many days; and such was the number of the guests and the profuse hospitality of the hosts, that six hundred oxen were killed for one feast. In the midst of the festivities an attempt was made to get the King of Scotland to do homage for his kingdom to the King of England ; but the boy, with a spirit and discretion above his years, refused to take a step of such importance without the consent of the estates of his realm. It will be remembered that King William had been entrapped into that very act of homage at York by Henry I. (1175), and placed his spear and shield on the altar. At that altar (January, 1328) another and even more distinguished young couple began their long and happy married life, Edward III. and Philippa of Hainault. He was not yet seventeen, and she was only fourteen years of age. Yet another princess bride came to York, Margaret Tudor, sister of Henry VIII., when on her way to be married to James IV. of Scotland (July, 1503). She lodged in the palace of the archbishop, and went more than once to the minster, and St. William's head was brought for her to kiss. She wore a gorgeous dress of cloth of gold. In after-years she would perhaps look back at the days in York as among the palmiest of her life, for her husband hated his father-in-law, and visited his repugnance upon his wife.

From wedding to funeral—so is the way of the world. Here was buried the head of King Edwin, founder of the church, and Eadbert, one of his successors on the throne of Northumbria. Here the remains of Tosti, Tiger of the North, brother of Harold, were brought after the battle of Stamford Bridge, to rest quietly at last. Here, when pious hands brought Archbishop Gerard home to his grave (1108), the crowd pelted his coffin with stones, because he had died with his head on an astronomical book! Here is the last home of two of our noblest archbishops, Scrope and Nevill, the first put to death by the fourth Henry, the second "done" to death by the fourth Edward, in revenge for the deeds of his brother, the king-maker; and here was laid in the cold earth the fiery Harry Hotspur. These are the towers which Cardinal Wolsey, Archbishop of York, saw from Cawood; he was summoned south before he had taken a nearer view.

In conclusion, let me quote from old Drake's time-honoured volume: "Let it be then the prayer of all good men that this glorious building, the great monument of our forefathers' piety, may never want a governour less devoted to its preservation than the two last actually were or the present seems to be. That this fabrick may stand firm, and transmit to late posterity the virtues of its founders, and continue, what it has long been, not only a singular ornament to the city and these northern parts, but to the whole kingdom."

CONSTANCE ANDERSON.

DURHAM, FROM THE RAILWAY STATION.

DURHAM.

THE central shrine of Northumbrian Christianity, in its situation,
its character, and its history, Durham stands unique among the
cathedrals of England. The Wear, winding deep in its rocky bed,
by a sudden turn forms a peninsula of horseshoe shape; a mass
of cliff, precipitous and woody, rising perpendicularly above the river.
From west to east across its centre this islet is spanned by the massive cathedral—the old Benedictine abbey. To the south the crest
is occupied by the old monastic buildings, the deanery, and the houses and
gardens of the canons. To the north, stretching as far as the isthmus, as if to
shield from attack the sacred fane, rises the massive pile of the old castle, with
its clustered buttresses, and crowned by its grand feudal keep; for centuries
the fortress of the Prince-Bishops of Durham, and now the home of the
University of the North.

The view of this stately mass, "half church of God, half castle 'gainst the
Scots," from the viaduct and railway station high on the opposite western slope
of the river, is one of surpassing grandeur; the most magnificent embodiment
in stone and mortar of the old English idea of Church and State which our
island affords. The contrast between this marvellous position and that of most
other monasteries is indeed great. Instead of some retired spot by a river's

F

bank, speaking of peace and contemplation, and shadowing a yearning for calm and repose to come, here the church boldly faced the world, in strong antagonism to the ignorance, oppression, and cruelty which raged in this border-land.

One peculiarity meets us at once. From its position on the edge of a precipitous cliff, there is no accessible western front or entrance. The western façade approaches to within a few feet of the extremity, and the steep slope is built up with massive masonry to form a platform on to which the Norman west door once opened, but which is now wholly covered by the Galilee or Lady Chapel, transferred, contrary to the almost invariable practice, from the east to the west end.

The only entrances to the cathedral are, therefore, on the north and south sides, the latter through the cloisters and monastic buildings. We approach it from the north, on which side we have an unbroken view of its whole length, from the wide cathedral graveyard and the great open space called the Palace Green. With the exception of the eastern end and its transepts, the Galilee Chapel, and the upper part of the central and western towers, we see the abbey almost as Flambard in 1128 completed the work left by Carilef in 1096.

An older and humbler fane, the church of Aldhune (first Bishop of Durham, 990), had occupied the site on which, on the 12th of August, 1093, Bishop Carilef, in the presence of Malcolm, King of Scotland, laid the foundation stone of the existing church. The old northern porch of the sanctuary, with its chambers above, was destroyed and barbarised by Wyatt at the end of the last century; fourteenth-century windows have been inserted in the transepts; while the upper part of the central tower, including the galleries of the lantern, was gradually rebuilt from 1406 to 1474. Much more interesting and beautiful are the imposing western towers, built, no doubt, before the central tower, although we have no record of their exact date. The series of arcades from the Norman below to the fully-developed Early English clustered shafts of the upper stages, point to their completion at a period not later than the beginning of the thirteenth century. The arcades are formed of round-headed and pointed arches alternately, and the only modern portion are the parapets and turrets, added a century ago, in lieu of the wooden spires covered with lead, which surmounted them till the year 1670. Grand, however, as is the general effect of the north front, the details have been somewhat blurred by the fatal paring of four inches from the whole surface, perpetrated by Wyatt, who irretrievably destroyed the depth and boldness of the mouldings and the pilasters.

Let us now enter the sacred building. On the door is still fixed the grotesque bronze sanctuary knocker, many and many a time clasped, and not in vain, by some unfortunate offender, to whom the shrine of St. Cuthbert held for centuries a protecting hand, and interposed to save him from the avenger. Watchers remained night and day in the chamber above to receive the suppliant, who was maintained by the convent for thirty-seven days. We possess the register of the sanctuary for sixty years, from 1464 to 1524, with the particulars of 330 fugitives, of whom no less than 283 were for murder or homicide. No doubt the privilege was often abused, " yet in the rapine and tumult of the Middle Ages, the right might as often be a shield to innocence, as an impunity to crime."

ANCIENT KNOCKER.

When we have entered the church, and look down the nave, we must admit that no grander Norman building exists. It is homogeneously majestic in its wondrous solemnity. " Look at the perfect symmetry of the great arcades, of choir and nave: the pillars are neither too short and broad, nor are they again too lofty and slender, but are admirably adapted to carry out the proportions of the whole. Look how the triforium and clerestory, neither dwarfed into insignificance nor made too asserting by their importance, unite with the arcade which support them, and form together a design of perfect and consistent excellence." There is massiveness, without the heaviness which marks the Norman portions of Norwich and Winchester.

We said that Durham is the central shrine of Northumbrian Christianity. It shelters the hallowed dust of its two great apostles, Cuthbert and Bede. As the former is the *raison d'être* of the existence of Durham, we will pass at once to his shrine at the east end of the choir, now a simple massive platform of masonry, projecting into the "Nine Altars," as the east end and transepts are called; with a slab in the centre, under which lie the coffin and bones of the saint. Very different was its appearance before the visit of the commissioners of Henry VIII. We can yet see in the flooring the sockets that once held the supports of the rich canopy, under which lay the relics of St. Cuthbert, laden with costly gems and gifts, which are said to have surpassed in value those of the shrine of St. Thomas of Canterbury, "and accounted to be the most sumptuous and richest jewels in all this land." Very shortly must we give the story of our patron saint. A shepherd boy in Scotland, trained in the Abbey of Melrose, a wandering preacher of mighty power from the Tweed to the Forth, he was selected to be Prior of Lindisfarne, and in 685 its bishop, the sixth successor of Aidan. In the Church of Holy Island he was buried. Fragments of his wooden coffin—the oldest, out of Egypt, in the world—are still, with Saxon

THE WEST FRONT, FROM THE RIVER.

carving and letters, in the chapter library. In 875, driven by the Danes from
Lindisfarne, the monks wandered over moor and fell in Southern Scotland and
Northern England, always bearing with them the body of the saint. They
halted at Craike, in Yorkshire, at Chester-le-Street and Ripon, and finally settled,
in 995, on this lordly seat, then a primæval forest. Here, under a chapel of

boughs, they laid the coffin, while Aldhune, the first Bishop of Durham, erected the first cathedral, of which not a trace remains. Carilef's cathedral originally terminated in an apse, in the centre of which was Cuthbert's shrine. This having become ruinous, the present "Nine Altars Chapel" was commenced in 1242, so named from the nine bays of its eastern façade, each of which contained an altar. This singularly beautiful structure is the only post-Norman portion of the cathedral, and is a specimen of the highest perfection of the Early English style. The arcade, with its graceful trefoiled arches supported by slender marble shafts, the lofty clustered columns which divide the bays, with shafts of

THE CHOIR, LOOKING WEST.

IN THE NAVE.

Stanhope black marble and sandstone alternating, the sumptuously decorated vaulting of the roof, crowded with various and graceful sculptures both of foliage and figure subjects, fitly complete the building, in harmony, not in contrast, with the Norman simplicity of the rest of the structure, the east bay of the choir having been beautifully enriched, both in the capitals and the vaulting, with sculpture, so as to blend harmoniously with the later style. As Dr. Greenwell has asserted, "Truly, no more majestic vaulting crowns any church in our country."

Next in importance, as in date, after Cuthbert, of the holy men of Durham, comes the Venerable Bede. To visit his tomb we retrace our steps to the west end of the building and enter the Galilee Chapel. Before reaching it, between the piers just west of the north and south doors, we cross a line of blue marble, eastward of which no woman was allowed to pass, such was the reputed distaste of St. Cuthbert for the sex. This, however, was by no means in accordance with the character of the friend and guide of St. Hilda during his life, and is a monkish invention which cannot be traced further back than four hundred years after his death. We descend by several steps into the Galilee. This chapel was erected about 1175, and is a unique specimen of late twelfth-century work. It consists of five aisles of four arcades each; the semicircular arches, richly decorated with zigzag, are each supported by two slender shafts of Purbeck marble, to which were afterwards applied two others of sandstone, so that each column is now a cluster of four shafts, the added ones giving no support to the arch, but having been built merely for appearance sake. The rich simplicity of this chapel renders it one of the most interesting portions of the fane. Its walls were once decorated with fresco, of which a portion remains tolerably perfect, in the north-east recess, with figures of St. Oswald and St. Cuthbert. But the interest of the Galilee centres in the tomb of Bede, covered with a plain slab, and the inscription "Hac sunt in fossâ Bedæ venerabilis ossa." Bede, though peculiarly Durham's saint, for in this county he was born, lived, and died, yet is the common possession of the English Church. He was not a man of action, but a saint, a student, an expounder of Holy Writ, a man of science. Born at Fulwell, close to Wearmouth, about 674, he spent his whole life in the monastery of Jarrow, a voluminous author on arithmetic, geography, history, astronomy, and theology. At Jarrow, in 735, he died, but his bones were carried to Durham by a monk, who thought he ought to be near his beloved Cuthbert, and not till 1370 was he removed from St. Cuthbert's coffin and placed in a magnificent shrine of gold and silver, on the spot where his bones still remain. Several MSS., claiming to be in Bede's own handwriting, and one at least unquestioned, are to be seen to this day in the chapter library.

The dust of many great men lies by the side of Bede in the Galilee Chapel. Bishop Neville desired to be buried there, and in front of the central altar of Our Lady, which occupied the original western doorway of the abbey, is the massive tomb of Cardinal Langley (1406), the only Bishop of Durham before Bainbridge and Wolsey who attained to that dignity, and who made great repairs in the Galilee, which he found in a ruinous condition. The Galilee was in olden times, and is to the present day, the bishop's consistory court.

Returning to the choir we may examine the insertions or fixed furniture. One of the most beautiful features of the interior of Durham is the reredos, or Neville screen, which separated St. Cuthbert's shrine from the high altar west of it. It was built, chiefly at the cost of Lord Neville, in 1380, as a thank-offering for the victory of Neville's Cross over the Scotch, and is of graceful pointed architecture, of Dorsetshire stone, though commonly said to be Caen, and till the Reformation had a hundred and seven figures in its niches, the removal of which, though lamented by some, adds to the graceful lightness of the structure.

In the next bay, on the south of the choir, is the bishop's throne, an integral part of the tomb of Bishop Hatfield, who lies below, with his recumbent figure in alabaster, in pontifical robes, under a beautifully sculptured canopy. The throne above it has once been richly gilded and coloured, and is the loftiest episcopal seat in England. The whole was erected by Bishop Hatfield in his lifetime (1345—1381). Of the brass of Bishop Beaumont (1333) only the matrix remains.

In the north aisle of the choir is a stone bench with the arms of Bishop Skirlaw (1388—1405), who is buried close by; and the letters W. D., on the pavement of the sacrarium, mark the resting-place of William Van Mildert (1836), the last Prince Palatine of Durham. The only remaining monuments to be noticed are the altar-tombs of Ralph, Lord Neville, who led the English army at the battle of Neville's Cross, 1346, and died in 1367; and of his son, John, Lord Neville, and Matilda Percy, his wife, both piteously defaced, and removed to their present position from what was once the Neville chantry in the south aisle. It is true that most of the great early prelates of Durham were buried in the chapter-house, but the tombs of several bishops and of many priors have utterly disappeared in the troublous scenes enacted here. The interior of the cathedral was literally gutted by the unfortunate Scotch prisoners, whom, to the number of 3,000, Oliver Cromwell, after the battle of Dunbar, shut up in winter in the cathedral. It is not to be wondered at that they destroyed the wood-work for fuel, and that scarce a fragment of the old stained glass, one of the glories of Durham, remains. The liberality of many friends has, however, within the last few years supplied the place of much that has been destroyed, and few finer specimens of modern stained glass can be found than the compositions which mellow the light in many of these windows. While deploring the devastation which left the interior of the cathedral a desolate waste, at the epoch of the Restoration, it is impossible to read the description of the fane, before the Reformation, as given in "The Rites of Durham," without arriving at the conclusion that the general effect of the whole must have been much inferior to what it is at present. A solid stone screen behind the "Jesus altar," at the east end of the nave, entirely cut off the choir; the south aisle was completely blocked by the solid stone wall of the Neville chantry, which occupied its two eastern bays; while thirty altars, with all their elaborate and inharmonious furnishing, besides nearly as many tombs, must have marred the simplicity of the Norman architecture. Nothing, however, can ever have interposed to affect the majestic beauty of the long line of the triforium, clerestory, and vaulted roof.   It is to Bishop Cosin that we owe the thorough restoration

THE EASTERN TRANSEPT.

of the interior after 1662.   He erected the stalls with the canopy work over them; a magnificent close screen of elaborately and richly carved oak, surmounted by an organ of Father Schmidt, now all swept away; and the canopy over the font.   This woodwork, though characteristic of the time when it was executed, harmonised well, by its bold and vigorous carving, with the building in which it was placed.   He also paved the choir with white marble, effectively

THE GALILEE.

relieved by chequers of black, which has recently been replaced by a costly and elaborate, though feeble and ineffective tesselated mosaic of Byzantine design.   Three most interesting specimens of woodwork of different epochs escaped destruction by the Scotch, only to be reserved for unprovoked demolition in the present generation. These were the fine clock-case, under the windows of the south transept, originally erected by Prior Castell (1404), with later additions by Dean Hunt (1620); an oak screen, which surmounted the platform of St. Cuthbert's shrine, one of the few remains, and a very fine one, of the decorative art of the time of Philip and Mary; and lastly, the splendid ancient reredos of the altar over Cardinal

Langley's tomb, containing paintings of the early part of the fifteenth century. Of this not a vestige now remains. These acts of vandalism were perpetrated in the years 1844–45. Thus in the course of its history the cathedral has experienced the effects of revolving cycles of epochs of destruction and of intrusion. A few years ago most important but questionable changes were made in its interior furniture. The present sumptuous Byzantine pulpit was erected under the lantern; and opposite to it the massive metal lectern, scarcely to be

THE CHOIR.

admired either for its material, design, or execution; while the choir, which since the destruction of Bishop Cosin's woodwork had been open to the nave, was barred by the introduction of the heavy though richly-carved Decorated screen of alabaster, which is not only utterly incongruous in its florid ornamentation with the rest of the church, but entirely cuts the perspective of the reredos and grand east end, when viewed from the nave.

It is under the flooring of the chapter-house that most of the illustrious bishops of olden time are laid. This once noble building, adjoining the south transept on the south, but separated by the monk's parlour, is entered from the cloister, and *was* the finest Norman chapter-house in England. Within it were buried the first three bishops — Aldhune, Eadmund, and Eadred, Carilef and his eleven immediate successors, and Bishop Kellow. The bones of Aidan, first

G

Bishop of Lindisfarne, were brought here from Holy Island. It is remarkable that since Neville in 1457, only three of its bishops have been buried in Durham. The treatment of the tombs of those buried in the chapter-house ought not to be forgotten. By an act of barbarism, scarcely credible, in 1796 this splendid hall, 77 feet long, and paved with the slabs and brasses of sixteen bishops of Durham and many priors, was destroyed in order to make a comfortable room for the chapter. The keystones of the groining were knocked out, when the whole vaulting fell in and crushed the pavement below, not a single inscription of bishop or prior having been preserved or even copied. Of the stone throne at the east end, in which every bishop, from Pudsey to Barrington, had been enthroned, not a relic remains. Upon the ruins of the western portion of the chapter-house a flooring was laid, and the present room erected, part of the old walls being utilised, but the arcading plastered over. The greater portion was levelled and thrown into the deanery garden. In this part have recently been exposed the slabs of Bishops Flambard, Geoffrey Rufus, and William de St. Barbara, when, as well as their bones, their pastoral staves, and their episcopal rings set with sapphires (the latter now in the chapter library), were found in the stone coffins.

Several of these bishops claim especial mention. First of them is Ralph Flambard, Chancellor of William Rufus, and completer of Carilef's work. He was the friend of Robert of Normandy, a politician perhaps unscrupulous, but a man of great energy, and of equal liberality, except towards the monks. Not only the cathedral, but the castle and the city owe him much, for he built the existing bridge over the Wear, known as Framwellgate Bridge, probably the earliest example of the elliptic arch in England. His successor, Geoffrey Rufus, was also Chancellor of England under Henry I. Hugh Pudsey, King Stephen's nephew, and eleventh Bishop of Durham, was one of the most prominent statesmen of his day. He has left his mark on Durham, by the building of Elvet Bridge, the founding of Sherburn Hospital, and especially by the erection of the Galilee Chapel. His illuminated Bible, in four huge folios, is one of the most precious gems in the unique MS. library of the chapter. A great warrior-bishop was Anthony Bek (1283), a man of noble birth, large private fortune, and more at home in court or camp than church. He led 140 knights to the Scottish wars, and received the submission of the king, Baliol, on behalf of Edward I. He was made by the Pope, Patriarch of Jerusalem, by Edward II. King of the Isle of Man, and died king, patriarch, palatine, and bishop. He sold Alnwick Castle to the Percys, founded the collegiate churches of Chester-le-Street and Lanchester, with deans and prebendaries. The ruins of his house at Eltham, in Kent, still exist. Very different in character was Richard de Bury (1333), tutor of Edward III. and Chancellor of England; but especially distinguished as a scholar and a great book collector. Among his successors are Fox, afterwards Bishop of Winchester, founder of Corpus Christi College, Oxford; Cardinal Wolsey, who, for the six years he held the see, never visited it, and then, on the death of his predecessor Fox, resigned it for Winchester. He was succeeded by Tunstall, translated from London, the bitter opponent to Tyndal's New Testament, who remained bishop till deposed by Elizabeth, although imprisoned on a political charge of treason during the latter part of King Edward's reign. Of later prelates, Cosin, as already mentioned, left his mark on Durham, as did his contemporary, Dean Sudbury, to whom the chapter owes its library. Lord Crewe was his successor, whose political course may be criticised, but who was a noble benefactor to the diocese. The learned Butler, one of the most illustrious, or rather the greatest of the prelates who have occupied the throne of Durham, only lived for two years after his translation, too short a time for him to leave any trace of his episcopate, save a single charge; nor is he buried here. Of his successors, Bishops Barrington and Baring, not to mention others, have left behind them the proofs of a truly princely liberality.

The cloisters, which existed from the earliest times of the monastery, were rebuilt by Bishops Skirlaw and Langley, but have been much altered. They are enclosed on the south and west by the ancient refectory and dormitory, both now occupied as the chapter library, the latter a magnificent chamber, 194 feet long and 41 wide, still covered with its original solid and massive roof of oak trunks, scarcely touched by the axe. It was divided into forty little wooden cells, one for each monk, and is over a fine crypt, the common house of the fraternity. Besides the book-cases, it contains an interesting local archæological collection, from Roman and Saxon times, of altars, crosses, Anglo-Saxon inscriptions, and much Runic sculpture. In the refectory, now called the old library, re-roofed by Dean Sudbury, are many priceless treasures. Besides the MSS. of Bede and the episcopal rings already mentioned, are the pectoral cross, the gold embroidered stole and maniple, and the Gospels of St. Cuthbert, though the celebrated MS. which once graced the high altar has unaccountably become the property of the British Museum; while the manuscript chamber contains one of the most valuable collections of MSS. to be found beyond the precincts of the universities.

Finally, we claim for Durham, in spite of all that she has suffered from the hand of the spoiler, that she still sits on her rocky height peerless in majesty among the historic fanes of this ancient land.

H. B. TRISTRAM.

OLD ST. PAUL'S, FROM THE SOUTH.

(After Hollar.)

ST. PAUL'S.

 THE site now occupied by the Cathedral of St. Paul, by far the most important ecclesiastical building in the style of the Renaissance which exists in England, has for long been the position of the mother church of London. Two cathedrals had already been built, had received for generations their crowds of worshippers, and had been swept away, before Sir Christopher Wren laid the foundations of the great structure which now rises from the summit of Ludgate Hill. The site, indeed, was holy ground at a still earlier time. Here the Romans had built a temple, and had dedicated it, so antiquaries say, to Diana. Brito-Roman graves, as well as those of Saxon date, were found by Sir Christopher Wren in digging the foundations for a part of the cathedral. The temple fell into ruins, like so many other Roman buildings, after their troops had abandoned the island, and in the seventh century Ethelbert of Kent founded a monastery, which he endowed with the manor of Tillingham, in Essex, and dedicated to St. Paul.

At that time Mellitus, a companion of Augustine, was Bishop of London, and the first of the long series of occupants of this post of labour and honour. Of the details of this, the first church of St. Paul, we are ignorant. Doubtless it was comparatively small in size and rude in style; but it was destroyed after the Norman Conquest in a fire which devastated London. According to Dean Milman, this happened in the year 1087 or 1088, but there are difficulties in

CHAPTER-HOUSE AND CLOISTER, OLD ST. PAUL'S.
(*After Hollar.*)

fixing precisely the date. The rebuilding was begun at once by Maurice, then Bishop of London, and some of the materials were taken from the ruins of a strong castle near the Fleet, then called the Palatine Tower, which was William the Conqueror's subscription to the work; other stone was obtained from Caen, in Normandy. This cathedral, with various modifications, existed till the great fire in the year 1666. Of its appearance old engravings and descriptions enable us to form a fair idea, and in Mr. Longman's "History of the Three Cathedrals Dedicated to St. Paul" plates are given embodying the results of a careful study of the existing materials by Mr. E. B. Ferrey. At first the new building progressed but slowly; forty years had passed and it was still unfinished. Then another great fire—in the year 1136—broke out and raged all the way from London Bridge to the Church of the Danes, greatly injuring—some historians even go so far as to say destroying—the still incomplete cathedral. At last, however, the work was ended; and then, in no long time, men began to desire a more sumptuous structure, so in the early part of the thirteenth century the central tower was rebuilt, and afterwards the whole of the choir, the work being completed in 1240. Other alterations and important repairs were made towards the end of the same century, but then the building remained almost unaltered until after the Reformation.

The Cathedral of St. Paul, as thus completed, was one of the finest in all England. In plan it was cruciform, both choir and nave consisting of twelve bays. The transepts projected for four bays beyond the outer wall of the nave and choir, and from the intersection of these rose a lofty stone tower, crowned by a spire covered with lead, its summit attaining an elevation of about 460 feet, or even more, according to some authorities. In length the cathedral exceeded Winchester, being at least 596 feet. The ridge of the roof of the choir was 142 feet from the ground; that of the nave slightly less; and the wooden spire covered with lead, which rose above the central tower, was probably rather more than 200 feet. The nave, a fine Norman building, internally not unlike that of Gloucester, with a rather plain west front, remained unchanged, at any rate externally, except that the clerestory had been altered and a vaulted roof had been added. The transepts and choir were rich examples of the Decorated style, and, unlike almost any other English cathedral, a grand rose window was the chief feature of the eastern end. In the south-west angle, between the nave and transept, was a small cloister, in the centre of which stood the chapter-house; and at the south side, abutting on the western end of the nave, and probably like it, Norman in style, was a small parish church, dedicated to St. Gregory. The choir, as at Canterbury, was elevated on a crypt, the vaulting of which was above the ground-level. Part of this, after the year 1256, was dedicated to St. Faith and used as a parish church, the old church of that name having been destroyed for the enlargement of the cathedral. A wall and gates surrounded the building, and in the churchyard, at the north-east angle, stood the famous Paul's Cross, where our forefathers assembled in fine weather to hear sermons from the most eloquent and learned preachers of the day. East of the cathedral was a school, and a belfry tower, in which hung a noted peal of bells, and to the north was the College of Minor Canons, of which the name is still preserved in Canon Alley. West of this was the bishop's palace; the deanery was on its present site, and gardens and the early monastic buildings lay to the south.

Thus the cathedral remained till the middle of the fifteenth century. Then it was again endangered by its old enemy, fire, for in the year 1444 the steeple was struck by lightning, and was so seriously injured that it was eighteen years before its restoration was completed. Yet worse befell it in 1561, after the Reformation, when the steeple was again struck during a storm, set on fire, and utterly destroyed; and not only this, but the flames caught the roofs on each side, and they also were burnt. The decline of the ancient reverence had now rendered the building, especially the nave, liable to all kinds of desecration; "Paul's Walk" was a general rendezvous and a covered place of exercise, combining the varied attractions of Burlington Arcade and the old Quadrant of Regent Street; a place where all inventions were emptied and not a few pockets; the "land's epitome," where men transacted business, gallants swaggered, and strumpets flaunted. A partial repair was indeed effected, but the whole building bore a ruinous appearance in the days of Elizabeth's successor, who took an active part in its restoration. This was entrusted to Inigo Jones, who built a classic west front, and with the best intentions generally maltreated the church. The work of restoration was continued till the crash came which shook down king and bishop, and was carried far enough to diminish our regret at the destruction of the cathedral after the Stuarts came back to the throne.

At that time still greater changes were under consideration, including the substitution of a grand dome for the central tower, for neglect and wanton injury combined had wrought great damage during the period of Puritan ascendency; but on September 2nd, 1666, the "great fire" broke out, and before long the flames reached the cathedral. Once more its ancient enemy raged within its walls, and this time more uncontrollably than ever, and "that most venerable church" was reduced to a heap of ruins.

These, however, were not long suffered to remain untouched. Dr. Christopher Wren was appointed one of the "Commissioners for the reparation of St. Paul's," as well as principal architect for rebuilding the whole city. He at once fitted up a portion of the ruins for temporary use in public worship, and the commissioners proceeded to deliberate upon the next step to be taken, for at present they hesitated between restoration and rebuilding. At first, contrary to the advice of Wren, attempts were made in the former direction, but as time went on the difficulty—one might say the hopelessness—of producing any satisfactory result became more evident, and in 1670 it was determined to clear away the foundations of the old cathedral and prepare to build a new one. Wren had already made a design, prior to the fire, for a new cathedral, but at the request of Dean Sancroft he now produced a fresh design, which he described as "something coloss and beautiful, conformable to the best style of Greek and Roman architecture." Of this a model was made, which may still be seen at the South Kensington Museum. The plan is a Greek cross, with the angles filled in by quadrants of a circle.   The arms are short; a large dome rises from the centre, and a smaller dome rises from behind the west façade.   The novelty of the design, as imperfectly cruciform, displeased the clergy, and it was accordingly rejected.   Then Wren prepared various designs, one of which was approved by King Charles, licence, however, being given to make alterations.   Of this clause Wren fortunately availed himself, construing the permission in the widest sense, so that the present

THE CHURCH OF ST. FAITH, THE CRYPT OF OLD ST. PAUL'S.

(From a View by Hollar.)

cathedral has but little resemblance to the design which was approved by his Majesty.   In this case second thoughts proved far the best, for the design as originally prepared was distinctly inferior both to the present building and to that which had been rejected.   As to the comparative merits of these two, opinions differ; but there is a general tendency among the best qualified judges of the classic style to prefer the present one, although it is in some points admittedly inferior to the older design, as indicated by the Kensington model.   All, however, must agree that the design which was honoured by royal approval, and from which evidently London had a narrow escape, was in some respects absolutely hideous.

On the 1st of May, 1674, Wren began to clear away the ruins for the new foundations—a work of no little difficulty. To lay these took some time, for Wren was too great a man to run any risk that his building should fall into ruins. He,

THE CHOIR, BEFORE THE REMOVAL OF THE SCREEN.
(*From a Print published* 1754.)

like the Romans, built for eternity rather than for time; and it was not until June 21st, 1675, that the first stone was laid. The old and the new cathedrals, roughly speaking, occupy the same site, but as the latter is considerably shorter than the former, and as the end of its eastern apse is not far away from the east wall of the earlier building, the present west front is some distance within the boundary of the former one. The work went on, and by April, 1684, more than

H

a hundred thousand pounds had been expended, the stone being brought from the quarries in the Isle of Portland. The choir was opened for divine service on the thanksgiving day for the Peace of Ryswick, December 2nd, 1697, and the dome was completed in 1710. It is painful to relate that the closing years of Wren's work at the cathedral were darkened by wrongful and insulting treatment. There had been a commission appointed to superintend the progress of the works, the majority of whom were no more fitted for the duty than have been some modern ediles. An idea took possession of their minds that Wren wanted the work prolonged as much as possible in order that he might continue to enjoy his sumptuous salary (£200 a year!) as architect. Accordingly, three years before the close of the seventeenth century, a clause had been inserted in an Act of Parliament which had authorised them to suspend the payment of one-half his salary till the work was finished. When the building was substantially complete Wren was still only able to obtain this by petitioning the Crown. But disputes about this comparatively paltry sum were not all; the commissioners continued to meddle with the work and to thwart the architect. Contrary to his strongly-expressed wishes they cooped up the cathedral within an enclosure consisting of a stone wall surmounted by a heavy cast-iron railing, which since, and with such good effect, has been removed from the west front. The iron-work of this was cast from ore smelted in the furnaces of the Sussex Weald, and has thus the one solitary interest of being a monument of a vanished industry. The commissioners insisted upon crowning the side walls of the cathedral with a balustrade, since this, to quote Wren's words, "was expected by persons of little skill in architecture," and by ladies, who "think nothing well without an edging." At last they brought their disputes to a close by a crowning act of insult and ingratitude. As the result of a miserable court intrigue they obtained from George I. the dismissal of the illustrious architect from his office of Surveyor of Public Works. Wren, then in his eighty-sixth year, but in full possession of his faculties, bore this ill-treatment with equanimity, retired to his house at Hampton Court, and resumed his studies in philosophy and theology, until, four years later, he passed quietly away from this world. His successor, a court favourite, named Benson, has received as his reward a place in the "Dunciad," without which his name would already have been forgotten.

The principal dimensions of Wren's building are as follows:—The length, including the portico, is 500 feet; the greatest breadth, across the transept, but without reckoning the porches, is 250 feet; the general width of the nave is 115 feet; but this at the western end is augmented by the projection of the towers. The monuments of old St. Paul's had, of course, been destroyed by the fire, the effigy of Dean Donne in his shroud alone escaping comparatively unhurt; of the rest only fragments were left. But the loss was less severe than would have been the case in some of our cathedrals. The monuments were hardly so numerous, so magnificent, or so interesting historically as one might have expected.

Two early Saxon kings rested here—Sebba, the East-Saxon, and Ethelred the Unready. Of royal lineage, after the Norman Conquest, there was only the grand tomb of "Old John of Gaunt, time-honoured Lancáster." There was also a handsome monument to John de Beauchamp, to which Duke Humphrey's name was perversely affixed, though he rests, as is well known, at St. Albans. Here, in the days of Paul's Walk, the men of empty pockets lingered, to while away the hour of dinner, and so gave rise to the familiar saying. Some workers of the Elizabethan days had been laid to rest beneath the arches of St. Paul's, among them Nicholas Bacon, father of a yet greater son; Sidney, brought from the field of Zutphen; Francis Walsingham, shrewd adviser of Elizabeth, and others less illustrious. These monuments, with the exception of a few fragments, one being a portion of the effigy of Nicholas Bacon, all perished in the flames. For many years after the new cathedral was completed, not, in fact, till 1796, was any monument allowed to be erected within its walls, but since then they have become numerous. Of these the more important will be mentioned later.

It has been already mentioned that the ground-plan of the exterior is a Latin cross, at the centre of which is placed the dome, the distinctive feature of the building, rising to a height of about 365 feet. St. Peter's at Rome, with which it is natural to make a comparison, has the following dimensions:—"Length, 630 feet; breadth, 440; width of nave, 220; and height of dome, $437\frac{1}{2}$." The exterior of St. Paul's consists throughout of two orders, the lower being Corinthian, the upper composite; its two most distinctive features are the west front and the dome. The former has a noble portico, divided like the rest of the building into two storeys, the lower consisting of twelve coupled columns, the upper only of eight, above which is an entablature and a pediment decorated with sculpture of moderate merit depicting the conversion of St. Paul. This portico is flanked by the lower storeys of the western towers; each of them, where it rises above the mass of the building, consists of a square base supporting a circular turret flanked with columns and crowned by a cupola. The effect of the whole is remarkably harmonious. Difference of opinion will naturally exist as to the results of Classic and of "Gothic" architecture, a preference for the one or the other being the result of natural feeling as well as of education. At the present day the majority prefer the poetic beauty of many English and foreign cathedrals in the "Gothic" style to the balanced regularity and ordered magnificence of such buildings as St. Paul's and St. Peter's, just as they would prefer a curve of natural growth to the more elaborate and intricate design that a machine can draw; but, accepting the fact that the natural bent of Wren's mind and all the influences of his age led him to prefer to build after classic models, we must admit, whether we sympathise in our inmost heart with the Roman adoptions of Greek designs or even with the originals themselves, that it would be difficult to imagine anything more successful, as a classic work, than the Cathedral of St. Paul. To the writer—one of those who can admire but cannot love the works of the Renaissance—its western front appears far superior to the corresponding façade of St. Peter's, which, notwith-standing its larger dimensions, has always seemed in this respect poor in conception

THE CHOIR.

and almost insignificant in effect. The dome, indeed, is more doubtfully superior to that of St. Peter's; in fact, we ventured to prefer that which Wren originally designed, and which may now be studied in the South Kensington model. The chief external feature of St. Paul's dome is a circular colonnade around the drum, consisting of thirty-two columns, the base of which is some twenty feet above the roof ridge of the church. Every fourth intercolumniation is filled with masonry, which masks the projecting buttresses of the inner shell or true wall of the dome—a most ingenious device. It may, however, be doubted whether the abrupt break produced by the balustrade which crowns this colonnade has not the effect of diminishing the height of the dome and somewhat interfering

with its harmony of composition.   The dome is surmounted by a stone lantern,
which is covered by a cupola supporting a ball surmounted by a cross.   The
device adopted by Wren for insuring the stability of his dome is unusual, and

ST. PAUL'S, FROM THE SURREY SIDE.

in a certain sense is an unfair one, because the dome visible from the exterior
is to a great extent a mere ornamental shell, and does not support the weight
of the lantern.   From the upper part of the lower storey of the drum he built
up a strong cone of masonry, on the top of which the lantern is carried.   Outside or
this the roof of the outer dome is constructed, and within it another dome —
the one visible from the interior—is built.   By this device strength and stability

are amply secured; but obviously the dome of Sir Christopher Wren is a much less daring effort of the architect than that of Michael Angelo or of Brunelleschi, and is liable to the objection of not being what it seems. This, however, opens a question on the ethics of architecture into which we do not propose to enter.

The interior of St. Paul's is hardly less impressive than the exterior. Its smaller scale does not, indeed, produce the overpowering sense of vastness which gradually creeps over us in St. Peter's when we begin to realise the scale of every part, and the want of marble and mosaic produces a chilling and an almost poverty-stricken effect. But we cannot remain long in St. Paul's, especially beneath the dome, without being impressed with the grandeur as well as the harmony of the design, and the defect of colour is due to the building having been left without the finishing touches of the master-hand. St. Paul's Cathedral is even now incomplete, though efforts have been of late years, and are being still made, to bring it nearer to perfection. Certainly there is no cause to regret that the enemies of Wren were obliged, by want of funds, to withhold their hands; in every possible respect they were acting, as it would seem in mere malice, in the direct opposite to his wishes. They had prisoned his building within a massive and ugly fence; they had erected a heavy organ-screen, cutting off the choir from the dome—this also has disappeared during the recent alterations; and they had bedaubed the interior of the dome with the unsightly paintings of Sir John Thornhill, in this respect also acting contrary to the wish of the architect, who had intended to employ mosaics largely in the decoration of the interior of the building. Some have recently been placed in the spandrels of the arches supporting the dome, and it is to be hoped that the liberality of the citizens of London will speedily continue this series.

The general symmetry of the style employed in St. Paul's Cathedral renders a lengthy description of the interior needless. It is divided by two massive arcades, supported by pilasters, into a body and two aisles, the latter being low compared with the former. The roofs are vaulted; there is a clerestory but no triforium, the windows being introduced into the curved space formed by the intersection of the vaulting with the outer walls; this does much to avert monotony from the design. Below the drum of the dome is the well-known Whispering Gallery, a rather conspicuous feature in the interior view, so called from its remarkable acoustic properties, and the piercing of the centre of the cupola allows the eye to travel as far as the summit of the cone which supports the lantern. The view of the dome from the interior, its great expanse and elevation, is undoubtedly far the most impressive part of the cathedral, which sometimes certainly does give an opportunity to the lover of Gothic to emphasise the merits of his favourite style; but could the dome be completed—as doubtless it existed in the mental conception of the architect—with marble and mosaics, glowing with rich colour, instead of disfigured with the daubs of Thornhill, even the most unfriendly critic of classic art would have to admit that Christopher Wren had produced a work which few could rival.

In the fittings of the choir is some fine carving by Grinling Gibbons, the most cunning workman in wood that this country has ever seen. Wren had contemplated the erection of a grand baldachino over the altar. This is now supplied by a marble reredos, which some think more fitted for St. Peter's than St. Paul's. Be this as it may, it is, in our opinion, too large for the building, and thus injures the effect of the apse, while the columns supporting only an entablature—forming a gigantic " post and rail " arrangement—on either side of the centre-piece seem as ugly as meaningless.

It will be remembered that the ancient cathedral was supported by a crypt —in which was the Church of St. Faith—and perhaps readers of " Old St. Paul's " may remember the tragedy of which its vaults were the imaginary scene. This feature was retained by Wren, and there is a crypt beneath the whole of the present church; its vaulting is supported by piers answering to each of the piers above, but of far more massive structure. Those corresponding with the eight great piers which support the dome are of surprising strength and solidity. Again, of these eight dwarf piers, the two to the east are of much larger proportions than the rest, so as " to give to the central chamber enclosed between them . . . the appearance of a rock-hewn cave." In the crypt are interred the many illustrious men who have been honoured with a resting-place in St. Paul's Cathedral, and whose monuments decorate or disfigure the church above. Here have been laid many of the greatest artists of England, among them Reynolds, Lawrence, and J. M. W. Turner. Wren himself is buried at the eastern end of the south aisle, and other architects of less note are gathered in the same halls of the dead. Soldiers and sailors, too, are there whose lives have been spent in the service of their country; and St. Paul's crypt claims for itself the honour of being the resting-place of the greatest admiral and the greatest general in the last long struggle of this nation with France. Beneath the very centre of the dome the body of Admiral Nelson was deposited in a black marble sarcophagus, which is elevated above the pavement of the chapel. The history of this receptacle is a curious one: it was designed originally for Cardinal Wolsey, and intended to be placed in his memorial chapel at the eastern end of St. George's, at Windsor, now the royal vault. But he died in disgrace, and a less honourable place of sepulture was deemed good enough for his corpse, so the black marble sarcophagus remained without a tenant, until it was at last removed from Windsor to serve as the tomb of Nelson. Near to him rests Collingwood, his brother-in-arms, and the Earl of Northesk. To the east in another chamber is laid the body of Wellington. Him a yet grander tomb has received.   A massive granite pedestal supports a huge sarcophagus of simple form, sculptured from a great block of one of our rarest British rocks. It is that called luxulyanite, consisting chiefly of quartz and black tourmaline, in which minerals, as a ground mass, are scattered large crystals of red felspar.

THE WELLINGTON MONUMENT.

The dominant tint of purple-black is in harmony with the purpose, while the spots of red relieve the stone from the rather monotonous effect of basalt.   No tomb of porphyry for emperor of Rome, nor of greenstone or granite for Egyptian king, surpasses this sarcophagus of the Iron Duke in sombre   magnificence. The funeral car on which the duke's coffin was borne through the streets of London is placed in an adjoining chamber.

The body of the church is well filled with monuments, although it was not till very late in the last century that a beginning was made.   The first erected was to the honour of John Howard, the philan-
thropist. Samuel Johnson, though buried in the abbey at Westminster, was the next, followed by Sir Joshua Reynolds, and by Sir William Jones, the Oriental scholar.   These are placed each against one of the four great piers of the dome. Then "Parliament, . . . perhaps with ill-judging but honourably prodigal liberality, voted large sums for monuments, which could only be expended on vast masses of marble, more to the advantage of the artists than of their sublime art. Fames and victories, and all kinds of unmeaning allegories, gallant

men fighting and dying in every conceivable or hardly conceivable attitude, rose on every side, on every wall, under every arch." In short the monuments in St. Paul's, interesting as they may be historically, are, as works of art, for the most part worthy of an age which, though fruitful in great men and great deeds, seems to have reached the very nadir of taste in everything connected with architecture. Among the more modern monuments some improvement is visible, although perhaps the worst in the whole cathedral is that to the memory of the late Viscount Melbourne. Chief among them in splendour, and usually one of the first to attract notice, as it is placed in the chapel on the southern side of the western end of the cathedral, is that erected to the memory of Arthur, Duke of Wellington. It is very sumptuous, very magnificent, and we believe is generally admired. The materials are white marble and bronze, in themselves perhaps not the happiest possible combination. The details are well executed, but the design does not strike us as in any way remarkable; and the figure of the duke appears too large for the sarcophagus on which it rests. On the whole it may be said of the Wellington monument, as of many others, that the result produced is not adequate to the money spent.

Among the other soldiers commemorated are Ponsonby and Picton of the French war, and Charles James Napier of Scinde, Heathfield of Gibraltar, and Cornwallis, greater in the state than on the battle-field; Sir John Moore of Corunna, Sir Ralph Abercromby of Egypt, with a host of others of worthy but less splendid fame. Among illustrious sailors we find the monuments of Riou and Charles Napier, of Rodney, of Howe, of Collingwood, and of Nelson. Among authors there are Hallam and Dean Milman, Samuel Johnson and William Napier. There are Edmund Lord Lyons, Mountstuart Elphinstone, and Henry Lawrence; Bishop Heber of Calcutta, and Bishop Blomfield of London, are commemorated. As for Wren, we see a memorial inscription on the entablature of a portico in the north transept (removed hither from the more conspicuous position of the organ screen), "Si monumentum requiris, circumspice."

The opening out of the choir to the dome by the removal of the screen and organ has been among the more important of the late series of changes. A pulpit also has been erected at the south-east side of the dome, so that its vast area is utilised for services. The work of improvement progresses, and among the additions has been a bell of exceptional size.

The cathedral library is in a room over the chapel containing the monument of Wellington; the ancient collection was almost wholly destroyed in the great fire, but the present library contains many valuable books. It owes its beginning to the munificence of Bishop Compton, and has been augmented by many other donors. The proper approach to it is by the "geometrical staircase," one of the sights of the cathedral, a spiral staircase attached only to the outer wall—seemingly almost hanging in the air.

But on a clear day no one should omit another of the "sights"—the ascent to the gallery above the dome. By this means the great size and the constructive massiveness of the cathedral can be better appreciated, and the panorama of London is something marvellous: below are roofs and churches and public buildings; miles of streets, with their endless throngs of foot-passengers and vehicles; the river, with its bridges, its fleet of boats and ships and steamers.

It is impossible, within these brief limits, to sketch even in outline the careers of the distinguished men who have occupied the see of London. Among them were many who in the Middle Ages were prominent among the statesmen and the churchmen of England, but the list of those connected with the present building begins with Compton, who had taken an active part in inviting over the Prince of Orange. Robert Lowth the Hebraist, Charles James Blomfield, and the late primate, Archibald Campbell Tait, are among the more conspicuous of his successors. But among the Deans of St. Paul's have been men of hardly less eminence than among the bishops. Indeed, the deanery has not seldom been either the stepping-stone to a higher rank, or has been held by a bishop. Among the deans of the old cathedral we find the name of Colet, founder of the great school which for so many years had its home in the precincts of the cathedral, but which has now been transplanted to a more ample space in the suburb of Kensington.

Alexander Nowell, author of the catechism used in the Church of England, must not be forgotten, nor Overall, author of the Convocation book, nor Donne, eminent as a preacher hardly less than Colet. At the time of the fire Sancroft was dean. Among his successors at the deanery were Stillingfleet and Tillotson. Later on came the profound thinker, Joseph Butler, who died Bishop of Durham. Dean Secker afterwards became Archbishop of Canterbury. Dean Newton was noted in his day for his "Dissertations of the Prophecies." In the present reign there has been Henry Hart Milman, poet and historian, who began both the restoration and the good work of opening the church as a place of worship for the people of London. His annals of St. Paul's must not be forgotten in this place. Henry Longueville Mansel, his successor, was distinguished as a metaphysician, but had only a brief tenure of office, when he died suddenly, and was succeeded by the present dean, Richard Church, also honourably known in the world of letters.

T. G. BONNEY.

THE CHOIR, LOOKING EAST.

WINCHESTER.

 IN the fair valley of the Itchen, where the downs on either hand draw near together, has stood from prehistoric days a little town which grew to be Winchester, one of the most important capital cities of England. The first authentic records of it are those which have been dug out of the soil, not written in books.

During the Roman occupation there was, in all probability, a Christian church on or close by the site of the present cathedral; in the close stood at least one Roman villa; relics of the ancient Church of St. Amphibalus may perhaps still be embedded in the walls of the cathedral crypt. This earlier Christianity was, however, swept away by the Saxon invaders; not till after the year 635, when King Cynegils was baptised, did the first English church rise from its foundations. It was finished by his son Cenwalh, who endowed it with all the lands round about the city. This first church, rude, no doubt, and small, and in large part built of wood, was dedicated to St. Birinus, to the Holy Trinity, and to the honour of St. Peter and St. Paul.

Round this primitive house of God grew by degrees a great religious community, though the Benedictines were not finally established here till, at the bidding of St. Dunstan, the secular clergy were turned out in 964, and monks from the great Abbey of Abingdon set in their room by Bishop Æthelwold. He

THE NAVE.

also rebuilt the church, and in 971 translated into it the relics of the patron saint, Swithun. The new church was completed by 980, and hallowed to St. Swithun as well as to St. Peter and St. Paul.

There is a doubt whether this Saxon cathedral was on the site of the present building, or a little to the northward of it; at any rate, whatever Saxon work there may be in it has been completely incorporated, and we shall not go wrong if we consider that the existing church was begun by Bishop Walkelyn in 1079. Though to the east it was considerably shorter than it is now, ending, as the crypt below shows, with a noble apse, after the Norman fashion, still the total length was little less than at present; for it extended some forty feet farther to the westward, as the bases of two grand western towers still testify. The magnificence of this effort of Norman skill and piety may still be understood by any one who will make careful study of the two transepts, which remain almost as Walkelyn left them in 1093. From them we may picture the glory of the long and lofty nave, its massive piers, broad deep triforium, and dignified clerestory. The whole

CHANTRIES OF FOX AND BEAUFORT.

FOX'S TOMB.

church was of the same height as now; and the tower was open, as a lantern, from floor to topmost roof. The original tower, however, was not destined to stand long. Soon after William Rufus was buried under it in 1100, whether from faulty construction, or uncertain foundations in the wet ground, or from being weakened by excavating too near the piers; or whether, as the resentfully pious held, from the cankering wickedness of the Red King's bones—from whatever cause, in 1107 the tower fell in with a mighty crash over the monarch's tomb. In a few years a new tower was built at the junction of the cross, though the masons feared to raise it to a sufficient height; it was called "Walkelyn's Tower," although erected some time after his death. It is in itself a noble specimen of Norman work, though ill-proportioned to the height and length of the church, so that it gives it a heavy and dull effect. The monotony of the long nave and the low elevation of the tower make the outside of the cathedral far less imposing than the inside.

This grand Norman structure did not long remain unchanged. About seventy years after the finishing of the tower, Bishop Godfrey de Lucy swept away the whole of the Norman Lady Chapel, except the crypt, and broadened the entire church to the width of the nave. He built on wooden piles, which soon gave way; so that his south wall is far out of the perpendicular, and has for centuries worn a look of painful insecurity. Bishop Lucy's work, and especially his arcading, inside and out, forms a charming example of Early English style.

There is but little in the church of Decorated or Middle-Pointed style; four bays of the choir, unrivalled in grace and richness of mouldings, and the tracery of one or two windows, are all that Winchester can show of the most beautiful and exuberant period of English architecture.

Satiated with the rich ornamentation and variety of the period, men, in the latter half of the fourteenth century, turned towards a harder and a simpler manner of building, a severe architectural Puritanism. They trusted for effect to height and repetition, even to monotony, and to the upward pointing of reiterated vertical lines. And Winchester Cathedral early felt the influence of this change of taste. First, Bishop William of Edington, then the more famous William of Wykeham, attacked and "reformed" the massive and noble Norman work. Edington began at the west end, altering the façade completely, and converting to modern style two bays on the north and one on the south. His work, carried on from 1360 to 1366, is one of the earliest examples of strictly Perpendicular architecture. The huge west window, which forms the main feature of the façade, has been mercilessly criticised and condemned by Mr. Ruskin in his "Stones of Venice" (vol. i., chap. xvii.), who first draws a caricature of the window, and then condemns his own creation.

The work thus set in hand by Edington was carried through by William of Wykeham, who, through his colleges, imposed the unimaginative Perpendicular style on England. He did not pull down the ancient Norman nave, but encased the columns with the poor mouldings of this later Gothic, clearing away the circular arches which supported the broad triforium, and carrying the work up to a quasi-triforium, with a monotonous though effective clerestory above; the whole crowned by a masterpiece of stone groining, which gives to the nave of this cathedral its special character and magnificence. For though somewhat hard in character, and deficient in fancy, the roof is singularly effective, and gives a marked impression of power and dignity to the whole building. Any one who penetrates into the dark recesses above the vaulting of the aisles will find in many places heads of Norman columns, and sometimes portions of Norman arches and other early work, which show themselves above the veneering of Perpendicular stonework with which they have been encased below. At the very end of the fifteenth century, Bishop Langton transformed the Early English chapel on the south side of the Lady Chapel into a Perpendicular chantry, destined to be his own burial-place. He gave it a new groined roof, covered with bosses carved with the canting heraldry of the time; he fitted the chapel also with exquisite woodwork, now much defaced and damaged, and placed in the centre a fine tomb, with a brass, since lost. Bishop Fox, his successor, carried on Langton's work, and brought to bear on the choir of the church the changed tastes of the new age: in his work we find both specimens of Perpendicular style and also Renaissance ornamentation. He rebuilt the clerestory of the choir, walls, and roof, above the Middle-Pointed chancel arches. In so doing he gave to the eastern part of the church a dignity and interest which it lacked before; for to him are due the bold flying-buttresses, the most characteristic feature of the building, which support the thrust of the roof, and combine most graceful lightness with a feeling of perfect strength and security. He also built up the east end of the choir, placing in the central pinnacle a life-like statue of himself. To him also is probably due, in its striking height and exquisite elaboration of detailed canopy work, the finishing of the great reredos, which is repeated, with less happy effect of proportion, at St. Albans.

Fox roofed in the choir with wooden vaulting, crowded with ornament, on which the incoming of the " new monarchy" is very distinctly marked. Blazoned shields and coats of arms and royal symbols tell us plainly that England had passed out of the impotence of the Civil Wars into the strong hands of the Tudor kings. The decoration all indicates a warmer though undoubtedly more debased taste, as may perhaps be also seen in the fine east window which we owe to him. Around the presbytery, Fox, in the year 1525, built up a stone screen in the Late Perpendicular style, with a cinque-cento frieze above, marking thereby the tardy invasion into English architecture of the fine Italian taste of the Renaissance. Over the frieze, again, he placed six beautiful wooden coffers, to contain the bones of English bishops, saints, and kings.

Just before and in his day, Priors Hunton and Silkstede pushed out the Lady Chapel some twenty-six feet in the later Perpendicular manner. This additional bay of the Lady Chapel, with its stiff ornament and half-obliterated frescoes, made this church the longest cathedral in England.

With the death of Bishop Fox in 1528, the structural changes in the fabric come almost to an end. Later additions or alterations were but small; such as the closing of the fine Norman lantern of the tower by a wooden groining, erected under the eyes of Charles I., as we see by the bosses and ornaments; there is the royal monogram in many forms, and royal badges, and the initials of the king and queen, C.M.R. (Carolus Maria R.), and a large circular medallion displaying in profile the royal pair themselves; in the centre is an inscription giving us the date of this work, 1634. The library, a lean-to along the end of the south transept, was built to hold Bishop Morley's books after his death in 1684; and the porch at the west end was restored in the present century.

THE EXTERIOR, FROM THE NORTH-WEST.

Within the walls the most striking object of interest is the famous Norman font of black stone, which was probably placed in the church by Bishop Henry of Blois, brother of King Stephen; it portrays in bold if rude relief the life and miracles of St. Nicolas of Myra. Next after the font may perhaps be noted the fine carved spandrels, fourteenth-century work, of the choir-stalls, with the quaint misereres of the seats; then Prior Silkstede's richly-carved pulpit of the fifteenth century, and the very interesting and valuable Renaissance panels of the pews, put in by William Kingsmill, last prior and first dean, in 1540.

The chantries and tombs in this church are of unusual beauty and interest. Three founders of colleges at Oxford lie buried here: Wykeham, of New College and St. Mary's Winton; Wayneflete, of Magdalen College; and Fox, of Corpus Christi College. William of Wykeham lies buried in the nave, between two of the great piers; the altar in his chantry has been removed, as have also the statues, otherwise his alabaster effigy and the stonework of the canopies remain un-injured; and the great bishop's serene countenance, with the three characteristic little Benedictines at his feet, has been handed down to later generations in life-like truthfulness. In the retro-choir, on the north side, is William of Wayneflete's splendid chantry; and just at the rear of the great screen is the tomb of Bishop Fox, a strikingly elaborate example of Late Perpendicular work. No effigy of the bishop is here; he built the tomb himself, and perhaps thought it enough to be seen on the pinnacle outside or in the great east window; there is a richly-ornamented altar and reredos, and behind it a little chamber, still called his study, because in his old age, when blind, the good bishop was daily led thither to sit and rest and pray. On the outside of this chantry, and of that of Bishop Gardiner over against it, are placed two ghastly *memento mori* figures, such as are not unusual on the monuments of foreign prelates, evidences of that morbid feeling about death which pervaded the period just before the Reformation, and made men depict on so many walls these emblems of corruption or the corresponding and still more ghastly-humorous dances of Death.

In no English church, except Westminster Abbey and St. Paul's, lie so many men of name. For just as the features of the cathedral represent all the succes-sive phases and changes of the art of building, until it has been styled a "School of English Architecture," so it is the home and centre of our early history. Long is the roll of kings and statesmen who dwelt in its shadow, and whose bones here lie at rest. Cynegils and Cenwalh, West-Saxon kings, founders of the church, are here; Egbert was buried here in 838; Ethelwulf also, and Edward the Elder, and Edred. The body of Alfred the Great lay awhile in the church, then was transferred to the new minster he had built, and finally rested at Hyde Abbey. And most splendid name of all, the great Cnut was buried here; as was also his son Harthacnut, as bad and mean as his father was great. The roll of kings was closed when Red William's blood-dripping corpse came jolting hither in the country cart from the New Forest. Here also lie Emma, lady of the English, whom her mean son, Edward the Confessor, treated so ill; and Richard, the Conqueror's second son, and one of the greatest of Englishmen, Earl Godwin, and his nephew, the Earl Beorn. Of churchmen there is also good store. Besides the prelates mentioned above, St. Birinus and St. Swithun, and Archbishop Stigand, and Æthelwold, parent of the Benedictine priory, Walkelyn, the master-builder, and the saintly Giffard, lie here; so, too, do Henry of Blois, the first founder of the Hospital of St. Cross; Peter des Roches

J

also, guardian of the realm in the youth of Henry III.; and Edinot, builder of the western front, and in later days Peter Mews, and Morley, and Hoadley, with many another of lesser fame. There are but few men of letters here: in a chapel in the south transept Izaak Walton is buried; and in the north aisle of the nave lies the well-known novelist, Miss Austen. Near the west end of the church is Flaxman's monument to Joseph Wharton, the critic, and head master of Winchester College. There is hard by another specimen of Flaxman's work in a graceful group on the monument to Mrs. North, the bishop's wife. Bishop North himself kneels in effigy (one of Chantrey's masterpieces) at the other end of the church, against the east wall of the Lady Chapel. And finally, in the south transept stands Scott's elaborate memorial to the late Bishop Wilberforce, ill-placed among the surroundings of the massive Norman work.

In this great church many stirring scenes of English history have been enacted. The early kings made Winchester their home and the cathedral their chapel. Here it was that Egbert, after being crowned *in regem totius Britanniæ*, with assent of all parties, issued an edict in 828 ordering that the island should here-after be always styled England, and its people Englishmen. Here King Alfred was crowned and lived and died. Here in 1035 Cnut's body lay in state before the high altar, over which was hung thenceforth for many a year, most precious of relics, the great Norseman's crown. Here William the Conqueror often came, and wore his crown at the Easter Gemôt; here, too, clustered many of the national legends: St. Swithun here did his mighty works, and here were the forty dismal days of rain; hard by is the scene of the great fight between Colbrand the Dane and Guy of Warwick; in the nave of the church Queen Emma trod triumphant on the red-hot ploughshares as on a bed of roses; hither came Earl Godwin's body after his marvellous and terrible death, one of the well-known group of malignant Norman tales. It was in the Cathedral of Winchester that Henry Beauclerk took to wife Matilda, to the great joy of all English-speaking folk. Here Stephen of Blois was crowned king; and here, on the other hand, the Empress Maud was welcomed by city and people with high rejoicings; here, too, was drawn up and issued the final compact, in 1153, which closed the civil war of that weary reign, and secured the crown to the young Prince Henry. He in his turn often sojourned here, and befriended the growing city. In the dark days of John the king was here reconciled to the English Church in the person of Stephen Langton; Henry III. and his queen Eleanor were here in 1242; and on May-day of that year "came the queen into the chapter-house to be received into the Society" as a kind of honorary member of the convent. In 1275 Edward I. and his queen were welcomed with great honour by the prior and brethren of St. Swithun, and attended service in the church. The christening of Arthur, Prince of Wales, elder brother of Henry VIII., was here; and here Henry VIII. met his astute rival, the Emperor Charles V. It was in Winchester Cathedral that the marriage of Philip and Mary took place, and the chair in which she sat is still to be seen in the church. The Stuart kings loved the place; here in the great rebellion was enacted that strange scene when, after the capture of the city, the mob rushed into the cathedral, wild for booty and mischief, and finding in the chests nothing but bones, are said to have amused themselves by throwing them at the stained windows. It was at this time that Colonel Nathaniel Fiennes, a Parliamentary officer and an old Wykehamist, stood with drawn sword at the door of Wykeham's chantry, to protect it from violence. Since the days of the Merry Monarch, who was often at Winchester, and loved it so well that he built his palace here, no striking historical events have been enacted within its walls. The church quickly recovered from the ruin of the Commonwealth time, and has had a quiet, happy life from that time onward, a tranquil grey building sleeping amidst its trees, in the heart of the most charming of all South English cities.

G. W. KITCHIN.

THE SOUTH-EAST CORNER.

GENERAL VIEW OF NORWICH.

NORWICH.

The ancient bishopric of East Anglia extended over all that large district which now includes the counties of Norfolk and Suffolk and the larger portion of the Isle of Ely. The bishop's chair was first fixed at Dunwich in Suffolk, but the diocese was subsequently divided, the Bishops of Dunwich presiding over Suffolk, the Bishops of Elmham having the oversight of Norfolk only. So things continued for more than three hundred years; but during the tenth century the two counties were once more united under one diocesan, the Bishops of Elmham being Bishops of East Anglia as before, until in 1078 another change took place—the see was transferred to Thetford, then an important and flourishing town, and occupying a convenient and central position, from which the diocese might be worked.

At no one of these earlier episcopal residences does it appear that there was ever any great church of commanding appearance or magnificent proportions, and until the close of the eleventh century it may be said that East Anglia had never had what we now understand by a cathedral. It was not till it had been determined to make Norwich the seat of the East Anglian bishopric, and not till Herbert Losinga, then Bishop of Thetford, became first Bishop of Norwich, that any serious attempt was made to erect a cathedral church worthy of a great diocese. Bishop Herbert was one of the foremost men of his time and one of the richest, and Norfolk and Suffolk, especially the former, were then the most thriving counties in England. Norwich was the second city in the kingdom; and the ports on the eastern coast were full of vessels, which carried on a large trade with the continent of Europe, and brought wealth to the merchants, who were not wanting in open-handed liberality. When Bishop Herbert signified his intention to build a great mother church in Norwich, he was supported with munificence by all classes. The first stone was laid in 1096, and the choir is said to have been opened for divine service in five years from its commencement.

To understand the real greatness of Bishop Herbert's design, the visitor must, before entering the church, take his stand opposite the western door, a few yards from the Erpingham Gate of the close, facing eastward. Before him rises the mighty church. To the left—*i.e.*, on the north of that church— stands the bishop's palace, which, till twenty-five years ago, actually communicated with the cathedral, and which, in fact, is a survival of the original residence provided by the founder for the bishops of the see. The old Norman cellars and storehouses constructed for this ancient building are still used, and may be seen by the curious who can gain admission to them.

Why was this palace built to the north, under the huge shadow of the cathedral, where no sunbeam could get at it from morn to dewy eve, and where it must needs have lain in perpetual gloom? Because Norwich Cathedral was the church of a great monastery, and the abbot's house of a great monastery was almost invariably placed on the north of the monastic buildings. The founder of Norwich Cathedral was a monk before he was a bishop, and in setting himself to carry out his ambitious design he resolved to found a vast monastery, of which the church was only a portion, though it might be the most important portion, of his audacious undertaking. In theory the first Bishop of Norwich was first abbot of the great Benedictine house of Norwich—though there never was any actual abbot—and as such he lived, though bishop of the see, on the north side of the church of the monastery. The prior and his sixty monks lived on the south, and were the officiating clergy of the sacred edifice.

Retaining our position still facing the great western door, and now turning our eyes to the right or southern side of the cathedral, we see before us the wall of the cloister in which the monks for the most part spent their day. Just in the angle between the western wall of this cloister and the cathedral doors stands a building which now serves as the choristers' school, and which a few years ago formed a part of one of the canons' houses and was then used as a kitchen. This was the porter's hall of the monastery, and is well worth a visit. If we enter it we shall see the handsome Norman hall through which any one who sought admission to the monastery in the old days had to pass, and through which, for centuries, the monks did pass in and out when business or inclination led them away from their seclusion to mix with the busy outer world. To the right of this porter's hall—*i.e.*, further to the south—the visitor will notice another and a very beautiful fragment of the monastic buildings of which it is difficult to give a satisfactory account. It was evidently a covered portico, open to the air on all sides, and dates from some time in the thirteenth century. As yet no explanation wholly free from objections has been given of the purpose which this construction was meant to serve; and as we have no space for discussing conjectures, we will leave the ruin to be admired, and pass on. Before entering the cathedral, however, it will be well to notice that the two lesser doors—one on the north and the other on the south—of the main entrance have been left as they were,* their plain semicircular arches with the simple mouldings indicating that they date from the twelfth century, and early in that century, before the pointed arch appeared in our architecture. During some excavations made in 1881 the *débris* which had accumulated in front of the great doors was removed, and the old stone steps, much worn by the feet of generations of worshippers, were exposed. The visitor may see one of these steps trodden into a deep depression—the stone being almost worn through—in the southernmost of the three entrances. The whole work of the *central* portion of the west front has been altered from its original appearance by taking out the narrow and barbaric doorway of the earlier architect, by removing bodily the whole mass of masonry pierced with small and mean windows which surmounted this doorway, and by substituting for it the enormous west window, which now seems to occupy the whole west front, and which is filled with staring gaudy pictures in stained glass, inserted as a memorial to Bishop Stanley—the father of the late, better known, Dean of Westminster. This immense window was inserted by the executors of Bishop Alnwick, who occupied the see of Norwich from 1426 to 1436. In the spandrels of the central doorway are the bishop's own arms and those of the see, with the inscription "Orate pro Anima Domini Willielmi Alnwyck, Epĩ."

And now let us pass through this great central door. Before us stretches the grand length of the vast nave; with the single exception of St. Albans, the longest nave in England, for it extends 250 feet to the intersection of the transepts. The massive nave piers rise up almost without any relief to the eye a sheer 70 feet, and originally supported a flat timber roof, which was replaced by the present magnificent stone roof—technically known as *lierne-vaulting*—in the days of Bishop Lyhart, who died in 1472. The two side aisles of the nave support the mighty triforium, along which from end to end two waggons might easily pass abreast. The triforium was originally lighted by narrow semicircular arched

---

* The pinnacles surmounting the flanking turrets, however, are the productions of a nineteenth-century genius.

THE NAVE, NORWICH.

Norman windows, which let in very little light.   Tradition says they were destroyed in the reign of Queen Elizabeth, who complained of the darkness and gloom; and it is said that Dr. Gardiner, then dean of the cathedral, hacked away the walls and inserted the present hideous windows, which at any rate admit some gleams of sunshine.   Till Bishop Alnwick inserted his huge west window the nave at Norwich must have resembled a long tunnel, and the lighting

1. THE ERPINGHAM GATE.   2. THE ETHELBERT GATE.
3. ENTRANCE TO THE BISHOP'S PALACE.

of so large an area, filled as it often was from end to end with people, must have demanded a consumption of wax tapers on great festival days which only a very heavy charge upon the funds of the monastery could have supplied.

Over the great open arches of the triforium rises the clerestory, in which the original Norman windows may still be seen, just as they were more than seven hundred years ago.   The nave comprises fourteen bays—*i.e.*, spaces arched over and included between the piers.   Three of these bays are, however, included in the choir, which is entered through a heavy stone screen, which supports the organ.   Very soon after the Restoration a movement was set on foot to replace the old organ, and a subscription was begun in the summer of 1663.   The money required was soon raised, and the new organ placed where it now stands in 1664.   The old organ was destroyed by the mob who broke into the cathedral in 1643, and looted the building, smashing the glass, plundering the vestments and ornaments, and robbing all they could lay their hands on.   Bishop Hall has given us a most graphic account of the scene that ensued, in his " History of his Troubles."

THE CHOIR, LOOKING EAST.

On passing through this screen we see before us the magnificent display which the central tower, with the two transepts and the glorious presbytery or chancel, affords.   The clerestory of the presbytery may perhaps be regarded as the most strikingly beautiful feature in Norwich Cathedral.   It was erected in the bishopric of Thomas Percy (1356—1369), and was then covered over with a timber roof, which was replaced by the present stone vaulting in the days of Bishop Goldwell, about a century afterwards.*   And here it may be well to notice that the roof of Norwich Cathedral is unique.   No church in Britain can boast of such a glorious stone covering, stretching over an expanse that occupies more than half an acre of ground.   With the exception of the timber roofs which surmount the triforium, there is not a single foot of Norwich Cathedral that is not protected by a stone vaulting, and hardly a foot of that vaulting which is not in some way adorned by

* In the " Handbook to the Eastern Cathedrals," and elsewhere, the *clerestory* is erroneously attributed to Bishop Goldwell.

sculpture more or less elaborate.   Nor was this all : the stone was not only carved, but richly adorned with colour, and in every bay the artists represented some Scripture scene.   Dean Goulburn some years ago began to remove the white-wash from these sculptures, but was deterred by the great cost of the under-taking, and nothing more has since then been done to them.   The renovation of the roof of the presbytery has, however, been completed.   Here the sculpture consists of little more than the *rebus* of Bishop Goldwell.*   The last

portion of this stone vaulting was, it is said, executed in the days of Bishop Nix, who died in 1536, three months after the first Act for the dissolution of the monasteries had passed.

When the suppression of Norwich Priory took effect, the monastery and its church had been standing for more than four hundred years.   During the first two centuries of this period there can have been very little change in the look of the cathedral inside and out ; during the next two centuries a vast change was effected. On the 17th January, 1362, a terrific hurricane swept over England, and among other in-juries that it wrought was a total destruction of the lofty

THE CATHEDRAL, FROM THE SOUTH-EAST.

belfry surmounting the central tower at Norwich.   This belfry crashed down upon the roof of the presbytery, reducing the upper portion to a mass of ruins. Bishop Percy set himself to the work of restoration ; hence the erection of the clerestory and the spire.   With this began the fashion of " beautifying "—*i.e.*, altering and improving the original design ; and the opening out the great west window, the throwing the stone roof over the nave, then over the presbytery, and finally over the transepts, followed one another probably with hardly an interval.

---

* A *rebus* is a term used in heraldry, whereby a name is represented by a pictorial device upon a shield. In Norwich Cathedral there are at least three good instances.   The name of Bishop Walter Lyhart is represented by a *hart lying in water* ; Bishop Salmon by a shield with three *salmon* ; Bishop Goldwell by a *golden* bucket and *well* on the presbytery roof.

K

Only four of the many chapels which were once to be seen in Norwich Cathedral remain in anything like their former condition. These are the Jesus Chapel on the north, St. Luke's Chapel and the Beauchamp Chapel on the south of the presbytery, and Bishop Nix' Chapel, which occupied the seventh and eighth bays in the south aisle of the nave. St. Luke's and the Jesus Chapels have been very beautifully renovated by Dr. Goulburn. The former serves as the parish church for the inhabitants of the cathedral close. Outside this chapel stands the ancient font of the cathedral, which must have been at one time a marvel of exquisite sculpture, and which now serves as an instructive monument of the frenzy of iconoclastic bigotry which in the reign of Edward VI. enacted that all remnants of idolatry should be destroyed. Immediately behind the high altar stood, we are told, the Lady Chapel, which in Bishop Herbert's original design was meant to harmonise with the St. Luke's and the Jesus Chapels. But did Herbert's Lady Chapel ever exist at all? I am inclined to believe that (although the foundations were certainly prepared) no Lady Chapel existed till Bishop Walter de Suffield erected his Lady Chapel in the middle of the thirteenth century, and that if such a massive appendage as was clearly contemplated by the founder had ever been erected, no sane man would have gone to the vast expense of demolishing it less than one hundred and fifty years after it was first built and raising another. Bishop Suffield did, however, build a Lady Chapel, of which not one stone remains; the entrance to it from the east end of the choir aisle may still be seen, and the beautiful arches which served as a double doorway to this chapel are almost the only specimens of Early English architecture in the cathedral.

The monuments in Norwich Cathedral are few and devoid of interest, the destruction and obliteration by the mob in 1643 of all that was worth preserving having been too complete to leave anything for posterity to admire. Such vestiges of the old grandeur as remain may be easily turned to by the help of the printed cards with which this cathedral is furnished, and which the visitor will find ready for his use hanging up in conspicuous positions on the walls. One beautiful piece of modern sculpture, the last work of Chantrey, and perhaps his masterpiece, is the life-size figure of Bishop Bathurst, in white marble, which is now placed in the south transept.

Before we leave the choir one last peculiarity of this cathedral should be remarked upon. Behind some curtains—in front of which the altar now stands—may still be seen the ancient episcopal throne. It is a stone chair of great weight and very plain in design, and is supported upon a semicircular arch, which may be seen from the aisle behind the throne. Here the bishop sat on state occasions, and from this he gave his blessing upon the congregation assembled. Round him, but on a level several feet below, stood the assistant priests in a semicircle. The pavement is still marked with an indenture to indicate the exact position which the bishop's assessors were expected to occupy. This is the only example in England of a bishop's throne being so situated, and it is said to furnish incontestable evidence that the Bishops of Norwich in the twelfth century consecrated the elements at the Eucharist facing not east but west.

We have hitherto dealt only with the inside of the church, and that, too, but superficially. The external features are almost as full of interest as the interior. The church is best left by the prior's door in the south aisle of the nave; this leads us into the splendid cloisters, which, like the church, are vaulted over with a stone roof, richly sculptured with scenes from the lives of the saints and Scripture subjects. The prior's door should not be passed through without notice. A cast of this door in plaster of Paris was made for the Exhibition of 1851, and is now deposited in the South Kensington Museum. The lavatory of the monastery, in excellent preservation, may be seen at the southern angle of the western walk, close to the door which once served as the entrance to the monks' refectory. A very striking view of the tower and spire, with the intersection of the southern transept and the nave, may be obtained by standing just inside the grass plot—technically called the *garth*—in front of the lavatory. By far the most imposing view of the whole building, however, is afforded from the extreme end of the grammar school cricket-field within the close, not far from the old water-gate to the westward. No one who has the opportunity should miss walking round the east end and observing the glorious aspect of the flying buttresses; they bear almost the whole weight of the wonderful stone roof which spans the presbytery. Obviously the delicate shafts and the slight walls which are seen from the interior could never hold up the enormous weight of the ponderous mass of sculptured stone which they seem—but only seem—to be supporting.

The monastic buildings at Norwich have almost utterly disappeared. The northern wall of the refectory still remains, however; and some traces of the reader's desk or pulpit may still be recognised. In the eastern walk of the cloisters the entrance to the chapter-house was opened out some thirty years ago, after being blocked up for centuries. The Lady Chapel and the chapter-house were in ruins as early as 1569. The old library was taken down in 1574.

But though so few vestiges of the great priory at Norwich survive, it is otherwise with another and smaller conventual establishment which the cathedral close contained. The grammar school, with the head-master's house, represents a college of six priests with their chapel, and under it a charnel-house, or depository for human bones, which was founded and endowed by Bishop Salmon at the beginning of the fourteenth century. The *shell* of the school-house is precisely as it was left nearly six hundred years ago, the massive and tenacious materials of which the walls consist making any removal of the original fabric too expensive to be contemplated. The old charnel-house serves now as a gymnasium. The old chapel is used as the great school. The old endowment supports the more modern institution.

The two gates of the close are interesting relics of mediæval grandeur. That which stands immediately opposite the west front of the cathedral was erected at the cost of Sir Thomas Erpingham, a local worthy, whose name Shakespeare has immortalised. This gate was designed at the beginning of the fifteenth century. It was probably left unfinished for some time, and completed by an

PULL'S FERRY, AT THE BOTTOM OF THE CLOSE.

inferior architect several years after it had been carried up to the present height of the buttresses, and then for a while abandoned. There is an elaborate description of this gate in Harrod's "Gleanings among the Castles and Convents of Norfolk." The other gate of the close to the southward is St. Ethelbert's, and was built but a few years after the Erpingham Gate. It was the gift of Bishop Alnwick. The upper portion of this gate is a good specimen of inter-mixed flint and stone work, and was executed about seventy years ago.

During its eight centuries of existence on the spot where it still stands up so proudly, Norwich Cathedral has had some bad half-hours. In 1272 the citizens, infuriated by the exactions levied upon them by the prior, besieged the close and set the monastery on fire. The flames consumed a large portion of the archives of the monks and of the see, but the cathedral escaped. It was just ninety years after this that the great belfry was blown down, and almost exactly one hundred years after this latter calamity that another fire wrought much mischief. The last conflagration of which any record remains was in 1512, when the vestry was burnt, and all the vestments and "ornaments" were consumed. The marks of this fire may still be seen in the triforium on the south of the presbytery, where the stone has been extensively discoloured by the fierce heat, and the course of the flames may easily be traced to this day by the ineffaceable marks they have left behind them. The central tower has twice been struck by lightning, once in 1271, and again in 1463.

When we come to the *personnel* of the diocese of Norwich, of the great monastery which existed there for so long, and of the chapter which replaced that monastery, and has inherited no mean portion of its original endowments, it is impossible to help being struck by the remarkable absence of any representative names in the long list of those who have been prominent personages here in their day. Herbert Losinga, the founder, stands out almost a solitary figure conspicuous among the foremost men of his time, alike in politics and literature. For more than four centuries after Bishop Herbert's death there is literally not a single Bishop of Norwich or prior of the monastery whose name is known to literature or science, or who has even gained a reputation for pre-eminent sanctity of life. Bishop Parkhurst was the first literary Bishop of Norwich, and appears as a kind of episcopal Sydney Smith of the sixteenth century. Bishop Hall's name will always be honoured, his writings will always be read, and his character always admired; but he was Bishop of Norwich for scarcely more than a few months; he came only to show how a devout and brave man can suffer without losing his self-respect, and live the higher life in poverty and persecution when his face is set heavenwards. Since Bishop Hall's time the Bishops of Norwich have been blameless in character and prudent administrators, as a rule respectable scholars, and sometimes a little more, but representative men they have not been. So it has been with the deans of the cathedral. If we except Dr. Prideaux, author of the "Connection of the Old and New Testament," Dr. Goulburn was absolutely the first Dean of Norwich who ever had the smallest reputation as a man of learning; the rest have been cyphers. Perhaps no former dean, single-handed, effected so much, or made such great sacrifices, to keep up and adorn the fabric of the cathedral; certainly no previous Dean of Norwich enjoyed so high a literary reputation, or deserved it so well.

AUGUSTUS JESSOPP.

LINCOLN.

 " BEAUTIFUL for situation; the joy of the whole earth: upon the north side lieth the city of the great King." These words of the Psalmist rise instinctively to the lips as the traveller approaches Lincoln, and sees the cathedral reposing in serene majesty on the lofty brow of its "sovereign hill." "Beautiful" indeed, pre-eminently beautiful, St. Mary's minster is "for situation." Beautiful beyond all English cathedrals and minsters, with the exception, perhaps, of St. Cuthbert's mighty fane at Durham. There is a brilliant passage in one of Mr. Froude's "Short Studies" which must have been penned with Lincoln vividly present to his mind's eye. Nowhere do you feel more powerfully as you approach that "the cathedral, with its huge towers, majestically beautiful, is the city." Nowhere is the contrast more striking between the vastness of the edifice, standing out clear and sharp with its exquisite beauty of outline and refined harmony of proportions, and "the puny dwelling-places of the citizens," which "creep at its feet" and stream down the hillside in motley confusion. Nowhere do you more vividly realise that "the cathedral is the one object which possesses the imagination and refuses to be eclipsed."

The approach to Lincoln Cathedral from the lower town reveals to the visitor as he slowly climbs the hill the loveliness of the building, with a gradual and ever-varying development which adds no little to its effect. The summit at last reached, we pass under the vaulted archway of the massive Edwardian gate-house which protects the entrance to the close, and stand awe-struck with the marvellous façade that rises before us. We can perhaps hardly call it beautiful; impressive is the more fitting term. A vast wall, unrelieved by buttress or projection, leaps at one bound from base to parapet; the few windows which break its surface are set so deep in the three rude cavernous recesses—a fragment of the earliest cathedral of Remigius—that they hardly affect the general windowless aspect. Plain almost to savageness in the Norman centre, the broad lofty wall is saved from monotony by the decorative arcading which profusely covers the later portion, tier above tier, partly late Norman, partly Early English of more than one date. A sharply-pointed gable finishes the composition in the centre, encrusted with ornamentation of the most exquisite design, the work of the age of Grosseteste. The façade is terminated at each angle by tall octagonal stair-turrets, capped with spirelets.   From the summit of that to the south the mitred effigy of St. Hugh looks down calmly on the building which owes its present form to his personal munificence, and to the veneration for his saintly memory.   On the northern apex is perched "the Swineherd of Stow," blowing his horn to gather his herd, a thirteenth-century "Gurth," who, according to ancient tradition, gave a peck of silver pennies, the savings of his lifetime, to the building on which he is handed down to all time.   Behind this vast broad wall rise the two matchless towers, St. Mary's to the north, St. Hugh's to the south.   The lower storeys belong to the age of Stephen, and were the work of the prince-bishop, far more warrior than prelate, "Alexander the Magnificent," in the first half of the twelfth century.   The lofty belfry stages, with their spire-crowned turrets, may be placed quite at the end of the fourteenth century. As originally built, these towers were terminated by lofty spires of timber covered with lead.   Time and decay wrought their work upon them.   Often threatened, and in 1727 only saved from demolition by a popular tumult, at last, in 1807, they fell a sacrifice to a misjudging economy and a mistaken idea of symmetry.

Marvellous as the façade is, the charge is, not without justice, brought against it of unreality.   Its richly-arcaded walls give no key to the building behind them.   This undoubtedly is a fault.   There can be no question that the effect of the towers would have been far finer if they had stood out from the ground, without any screen before them concealing their connection with the fabric. But it is worse than useless to find fault, and spoil an enjoyment of what we have by speculations as to what might have been.

Let us now pass to the opposite end and examine the east front.   To estimate the effect of this façade, as well as of the exquisite eastern limb of the cathedral of which it is the crowning glory, it should be approached from below.

Entering the close by another Edwardian gate-house, the cathedral is before us, its grey walls rising in quiet dignity from the smooth greensward.   The first portion to come into view is the vast decagonal chapter-house, capped by its tall pyramid of lead, with its widely-spreading flying buttresses, like huge arms propping up the vaulted roof. With the exception of that at Worcester, which is of Norman date, this is the earliest of our polygonal chapter-houses, and though simpler and less ornate than its younger sisters, especially that "rose among flowers," the lovely chapter-house at York, it yields to none in stateliness of outline.   A few steps further the glorious "Angel Choir" comes into view, the first complete specimen of English Gothic art, after it had attained its highest development in the latter half of the thirteenth century.

The great east window of eight lights, with its lofty mullions, simplicity of conception, and pure and bold tracery, is the very noblest specimen of its

THE CATHEDRAL, FROM CANWICK HILL.

date.   The richly-crocketed gable, bearing in its apex the Virgin Mother with
the Infant Saviour in her arms, flanked by tall spire pinnacles of elaborate
luxuriance, with its two equally lovely aisle gables, is one of the most delicious
of architectural works.

Leaving the east end we may pass westwards and watch the gradual
development of the varied architectural features of the building.   First, the
side elevation of the Angel Choir, with its lovely windows, as perfect as the great
east window on a smaller scale, divided by tall gabled buttresses, where pedestals
and canopies await—let us hope not in vain—the army of statues which once
peopled them.   Then follows the deeply-recessed south porch, with its solemn
sculptures of the Doom, the seated Judge, the yawning tombs, the rising dead—

recalling on a smaller scale, more perfectly than any other doorway in England, the vast cavern-like portals of Rheims or Chartres. On either side of this marvellous porch the late but rich monumental chapels of Bishop Russell, the tutor of the boy-king, Edward V., and celebrated by Sir Thomas More, on the right, and of Bishop Longland—"longa terra mensura ejus," as his punning motto has it—

THE CATHEDRAL TOWERS, FROM THE SOUTH-WEST.

the persecutor of sacramentaries and ghostly counsellor to Henry VIII., on the left, are dwarfed into insignificance—"mere trinkets for the watch-chain"—by the vast proportions of the building to which they are attached. The high narrow eastern transept, the work of the sainted Hugh of Avalon, with its tall lancets and apsidal chapels, is succeeded after a short interval by the far more sturdy and less elegant western transept, with its broader windows and ponderous buttresses, at the intersection of which with the body of the church rises the glorious

L

central tower, the "Lady Bell Steeple," as it used to be called before a vulgar desire to make the great bell known as "Great Tom" bigger still consigned to the melting-pot the lovely little peal of mediæval bells which formerly day by day rung out the "Ave Maria." An amusing story, told by Matthew Paris and several of the mediæval chroniclers, enables us to fix the date of the lower portion of this tower with precision. In the early years of the episcopate of Robert Grosseteste, the big-headed, lion-hearted asserter of his rights against all con-traveners of them, whether the chapter of his cathedral or the Pope himself, when his claim to visit his cathedral officially had roused the ire of the dean and canons, one of the latter, while preaching in the nave *ad populum*, appealed to his hearers against the oppressive acts of the bishop; "so intolerable were they," he exclaimed, "that if he and his brethren were to hold their peace the very stones would cry out on their behalf." Scarcely were the words out of his mouth when the central tower, then freshly built in a new-fangled style, came crashing down, burying some of his hearers in its ruins. This was in the year 1237. The new tower was immediately begun. Its magnificent upper storey, the crowning glory of the minster, though shorn of the tall leaden spire—the loftiest save that of old St. Paul's in the kingdom—destroyed by a thunderstorm in 1548, owes its completion to Bishop John of Dalderly, a prelate whose Christian virtues gave him a powerful influence while he lived, and obtained for him a popular canonisation which, however, the Curia of Rome refused to recognise formally, in spite of the repeated petitions of the dean and chapter. It was begun in March, 1307, and was not far from completion in 1311.

At this point the circular window, known as the "Bishop's Eye," challenges our admiration. The corresponding window of the north transept, looking over the deanery, was called the "Dean's Eye," symbolising the watchful care the chief officer of the chapter was bound to exercise against the wiles of "Lucifer," to whom it was inferred, from the words of the prophet Isaiah, "I will sit on the sides of the north" (Isa. xiv. 13), that gloomy sunless quarter was specially subject. The window of the southern transept, looking over the episcopal palace, was similarly known as the "Bishop's Eye," courting the genial influences of the Holy Spirit. There is no record of its erection, but it was probably connected with the "cultus" of Bishop John of Dalderly, who was buried in this transept, where some fragments of his once magnificent shrine are still to be seen.

At the western angle of the transept stands the "Galilee Porch," a very stately vaulted entrance, cruciform in plan, which was probably erected for the reception of the bishop on state occasions. The episcopal palace lies a short distance to the south, and there is an archway in the close wall, originally opened by the second Norman bishop, Robert Bloet, by the express permission of Henry I., exactly in a line with this porch. The porch, which is in the Early

English style, both in position and design is absolutely unique. Above it is a chamber, now used as the muniment room, in which the court of the dean and chapter was formerly held.

At no point are the vast dimensions of the cathedral more impressive than on turning the angle of the Galilee. An entire new church seems to open upon us, with the long buttressed aisle walls of the nave, the large gabled north-west chapel, itself a small church, which flanks it, and the western towers. As we advance the Norman work of the lower part of the towers, and the highly-enriched arcaded gables which project from them, become very striking features. From no point is the picturesque variety of the outline of the cathedral, with its bold defiance of the conventional, more striking.

Before entering the cathedral it will be desirable to give a rapid sketch of its architectural history. The earliest cathedral on this site was erected by the first Norman bishop, Remigius of Fescaup, on the removal of the see from Dorchester-on-Thames, about 1072. From the portions that remain at the west end, both externally and internally, we see that it was a fabric of the sternest Norman character, absolutely devoid of ornament. It ended in a short apsidal eastern limb, the semicircular foundations of which remain beneath the stalls of the choir. After an accidental fire in 1141, by which the roof was burnt off, the whole church was vaulted in stone, by Bishop Alexander, to whom we may also assign the very elaborate western doorways, and the lower storeys of the towers. The cathedral suffered severely from the earthquake of 1185, which we are told by Roger of Hoveden rent it from the top downwards. The year following, 1186, Hugh of Avalon was appointed bishop. He at once made preparations for the rebuilding of his shattered cathedral, of which the first stone was laid in 1192. Hugh died in 1200, by which time he had seen the present ritual choir with the eastern transept completed, and the larger or western transept begun. This portion of the cathedral supplies us with the earliest dated example in England of the pure Lancet Gothic without any trace of Norman influence. Documentary evidence fails us almost entirely for the half-century after the death of Bishop Hugh. During this period the transept was completed, the nave built, and the west front cast into its present shape. The central tower was rebuilt, as has been already stated, after its fall in 1237. The whole of these works are in the same general style, though with many lesser variations, viz., the Lancet Gothic. To the same period belongs the chapter-house, which was in progress during the episcopate of Bishop Hugh of Wells (1209—1235), brother of Bishop Jocelin of Wells, the rebuilder of that loveliest of English cathedrals. The popular veneration for St. Hugh — the earlier bearer of the name — was the cause of the elongation of the eastern limb, by the erection of the Angel Choir, to receive the shrine containing his body, for which work the offerings

of the devotees flocking to the hallowed spot supplied the necessary funds.   It
was begun about 1255, and completed in 1280, in which year the translation
of the saint's body took place, in the presence of Edward I. and his Queen

THE CLOISTERS.

THE ANGEL CHOIR.

Eleanor, his brother Edmund, Earl of
Lancaster, Archbishop Peckham, and an
immense concourse of the leading ecclesiastics and nobles of the day.   The addition of the "Angel Choir" completed the
main fabric of the cathedral.   The cloisters
were added in the geometrical Decorated
style in 1296 and the immediately subsequent years.

On entering Lincoln Cathedral, while
we are struck by the combination of grace
and dignity in the design with richness in
detail, and by the general impression of size
and space, we cannot fail to feel the want
of height.   This defect is not so painfully
apparent in the nave as in the choir and
western transept.   In the latter, which is certainly the clumsiest portion of the
building, the vault is absolutely crushing in its lowness, and cuts off the upper
part of the northern circular window or "Dean's Eye" in a most awkward
fashion.   In the choir the strangely unsymmetrical arrangement of the vaulting

cells, joined to its lowness, gives an unpleasing effect to an otherwise noble design. This is the more provoking as there is no real want of height in the section of the building itself. But a vast space is lost between the groining and the roof, from the want of courage in the architect to lift the stone vault to a more adequate height. In the nave the vault is actually some feet higher, and the point of the springing of the groining and the form of the arch are so arranged as to make it look higher still. The first impression made by the nave is so perfectly satisfactory that it is only slowly and reluctantly that one begins to notice its defects. However, there can be no question that the arches are generally too wide, producing a sprawling effect and a sense of inadequacy of bearing power. The two westernmost bays are narrower, and are so much more pleasing that we can only wish that all had been of the same width, and that the designer had given us eight arches instead of seven. There is some awkwardness also in the way in which the later nave is fitted on to the western towers and the intervening Norman bay. From some unexplained cause—perhaps no more than an error in the original setting out of the new nave—the axis of the two divisions is not the

A CORNER IN THE CLOISTERS.

same, so that the west window, and still more distressingly the western arch, are out of the centre of the vista. This want of symmetry is not improved by the flimsy tracery of the Early Perpendicular window, which has been unhappily substituted for the original Early English triplet of Grosseteste's age.

The impression of space and lightness is much increased by two large chapels, opening into the aisles of the nave by an additional arcade at the western end. That to the north has a tall central column of polished Purbeck marble, of wonderful slenderness, almost as fragile-looking as that of the chapter-house at Salisbury. The corresponding chapel to the south, which serves as the Consistory court, wants the central column.

The ritual choir is divided from the lantern by an elaborately carved screen of Decorated date, of sufficient depth to contain several vaulted chambers. On either side the choir is fenced off from the aisles by arcaded stone screens, introduced after the fall of the tower to strengthen the fabric. In the third arch of the south choir aisle a screen wall, richly panelled in the Decorated style, marks the site of the shrine of Little St. Hugh; a monument of the eagerness to believe the most incredible tales of the vindictive cruelty of the hated Jews, of which so striking an example was presented not long since in Hungary. Beneath the now demolished canopy a tiny stone coffin enshrines the remains of a Christian child, "bonnie Saint Hugh of Lincoln," whose body was found in the cesspool of the house of a Jew, Copin by name, wounded, it was said, in hands, feet, and side in blasphemous mockery of the sufferings of our Lord. The whole story, too long to be narrated here, is to be found in Matthew Paris, who tells how Copin, on the promise of his life, feasted the ears of his judges with the atrocities stated to have been perpetrated on the child, which the leading Jews from all parts of England had flocked to see; how the young King Henry III., happening then to visit Lincoln, annulled the promise as an infringement of his own royal prerogative; how the miserable culprit, tied to the tail of a horse, was dragged through the streets of Lincoln, and hanged on Canwick Hill, "presented both in body and soul to the prince of the power of the air;" and how, finally, near upon a hundred Jews inculpated by him were carted off to the Tower of London and hanged, and their property confiscated. Few subjects have been more popular in ballad literature than this tale of St. Hugh of Lincoln, the Jew's daughter being usually made to play the part of the murderess.

The choir is furnished with three tiers of seats, the upper row of prebendal stalls being surmounted by lofty tabernacle work of the most consummate richness and lightness. They, like the works at the west end, and the vaulted ceilings of the three towers, are due to John of Welbourn, treasurer of the church towards the close of the fourteenth century. The carvings are quaint, and in some cases of a ludicrous character, not very suitable to a religious building. The poppy-head of the precentor's stall exhibits on one side two monkeys churning; on a second side we see a baboon, who has stolen the butter, hiding himself among the trees; on the third side the thief, having been caught, tried, and condemned, is expiating his crime on the gallows, the two churners pulling the rope, while he with clasped hands is praying his last prayer. The miserere of a stall on the tier below shows the body of the butter-stealer borne by his hangmen to burial. This curious series may probably illustrate some once popular but now forgotten poem.

GROTESQUE FIGURE.

No words can do justice to the consummate beauty of the "Angel Choir," which, in the combination of richness and delicacy of ornament and unstinting profuseness of sculpture, leaving scarcely a square foot of plain wall anywhere, knows no rival. The name by which it is popularly known is derived from the sculptures of angels with expanded wings, playing on musical instruments, which fill the spandrels of the exquisitely-designed triforium. In singular contrast to these lovely creations a queer little shaggy Puck or Robin Goodfellow, with horns and huge flapping ears, sits nursing his right leg at the base of the first vaulting shaft on the north side, evidently as fond of mischief for mischief's sake as Shakespeare's "shrewd and knavish sprite."

Lincoln Cathedral is now decidedly poor in monuments. There are but few, and these not as a rule bearing any great historic name. The whole of the sepulchral brasses, many of them of singular beauty, were torn up by the Parliamentary soldiers after the storming of the castle and the close by the Earl of Manchester in 1644, when, as Evelyn says, the military "shut themselves in with axes and hammers till they had rent and torn off some barge-loads of metal, so hellish an avarice possessed them." Besides despoiling the brasses and carrying off an exquisite full-length metal effigy of Queen Eleanor, whose "viscera" were interred here after her death at the neighbouring manor of Harby, the soldiers inflicted so much wanton injury on the other monuments that, under the influence of the prosaic spirit of neatness and uniformity which prevailed during the last century, not a few decayed memorials of historic interest were ruthlessly removed by those who should have been their guardians. Of the monument of Bishop Grosseteste which stood in the south arm of the eastern transept, once the resort of numerous devotees and the scene of many reputed miraculous cures, only a few shattered fragments remain. Not even so much is left of the still more celebrated wonder-working shrine of St. Hugh, the Bishop. This, however, is the less to be regretted, as the whole cathedral may be called his monument. Of Remigius, the dwarfish but energetic founder of the cathedral—"the man of small stature but of lofty soul"—there is a possible but dubious memorial in a sepulchral slab, carved with the tree of Jesse, placed under one of the nave arches. This slab is fractured across the middle, an accident which, we know from Giraldus Cambrensis, happened to Remigius' tombstone from the

LINCOLN CATHEDRAL, FROM WITHAM BANK.

falling of the roof-timbers in the fire of 1142; but the carving is certainly later than Remigius' time.

Of the thirty prelates who filled the episcopal throne of Lincoln up to the period of the Reformation, of whom by far the greater part were interred within the walls of the cathedral, the monuments of only two survive. These are Bishop Henry of Burghersh (1320—1342), the diplomatic agent of Edward III. in French affairs, whose unquiet spirit, so the tale ran, was doomed to walk the earth in huntsman's garb of Lincoln green, with horn and baldrick, until the lands of which he had robbed his poorer neighbours for the enlargement of his own chase had been restored; and Bishop Richard Fleming (1420—1431), by whom the papal decree for exhuming the body of Wycliffe, burning it to ashes, and casting them into running water, was carried out at Lutterworth.

Both of these monuments stand towards the east end of the north aisle of the Angel Choir, that of Bishop Fleming in a chantry chapel erected for its reception. Each consists of an altar-tomb carrying a recumbent effigy of the prelate in full pontificals. According to the taste of the age, a second effigy, towards the aisle where all might see the ghastly *memento mori*, represents the decaying corpse of Bishop Fleming.

On the aisle wall, facing Bishop Burghersh's monument, is the recessed tomb of his elder brother, Bartholomew, Lord Burghersh, who died in 1356, one of the most renowned of the warriors in Edward III.'s French campaigns, fighting at Crecy in the same detachment with the Black Prince, and sent out to reconnoitre before the battle of Poictiers. Of post-Reformation prelates, the only monuments are those of Bishop Fuller (1667—1675), who restored the cathedral after the fanatical outrages of the great Rebellion ; of Bishop Gardiner, whose altar-tomb bears a set of very pleasing sapphics commending the prelate's virtues ; of Bishop Kaye (1827—1853), whose white marble effigy, a graceful and dignified work of Westmacott's, reposes in one of the apsidal chapels of the south arm of the lesser transept ; and of Bishop Wordsworth, presenting a life-size effigy beneath a lofty and elaborate canopy, recently erected in the Angel Choir. The only other ancient monuments are those of Sir Nicholas Cantilupe and Prior Wymbush of Nocton, under tall gabled canopies in the retro-choir ; the much mutilated altar-tomb of Katherine Swynford, the tardily wedded third wife of John of Gaunt, the mother of Cardinal Beaufort, and great-grandmother of Lady Margaret Beaufort, mother of Henry VII. ; and that of her daughter, the Countess of Westmoreland, on the south side of the choir. The Easter sepulchre opposite is an exquisite specimen of Decorated canopy work, the base finely carved with the sleeping guards. The font, of black basalt, which stands beneath the second arch on the south side of the nave, is a gigantic specimen of rude Norman work, with a huge square basin carved with griffin-like figures, supported on four pillars, closely resembling the font of Winchester Cathedral.

The cloisters form an irregular quadrangle to the north of the choir, between the two transepts. They are in the Decorated style, with rich traceried windows and a groined roof of oak. Built like many ancient works, with hardly any foundation, the thrust of the vault has forced the walls out of the perpendicular, and completely thrown down the northern walk.

The chapter-house, which opens out of the eastern wall of the cloister, is one of the grandest works of the thirteenth century. Its stone vaulted roof is supported by a central column of clustered shafts. No part of the cathedral is more full of stirring historical reminiscences. Here in the days when Parliaments were migratory, several Parliaments were held by Edward I. and his two successors.

M

Of these the most remarkable was that of Edward I., in 1301, by which the Great Charter and the other charters on which the liberties of the subjects rested were confirmed, and the claim of the powerful and ambitious Boniface VIII., as supreme Lord of Scotland, to arbitrate between the two countries was firmly resisted, and the political independence of England and England's king of the see of Rome was unhesitatingly asserted. Another Parliament held here by Edward I.'s degenerate son, in 1316, was disgraced by a squabble between Sir John de Ros and the king's unworthy minion, Despenser, who, regardless of the sacredness of the place, struck the former a blow with his fist, drawing blood. Here, too, in 1310, was held the trial of the Knights Templars, before Bishop John of Dalderby, for the crimes of apostasy, idolatry, and gross immorality. The evidence, though utterly worthless, was sufficient to secure a verdict of condemnation, with the complete suppression of that once powerful body. None, however, of the English Templars suffered death, their only punishment being an honourable imprisonment in various monastic houses. Here, also, to pass on a couple of centuries, in October, 1536, in the early days of the popular rising against Henry VIII.'s proposed suppression and confiscation of religious houses, which afterwards came to a head in Yorkshire in the celebrated " Pilgrimage of Grace," the leaders of the Lincolnshire insurgents, 60,000 strong, assembled for consultation on the royal letters just received, recalling the "rude commons" of the " brute and beastly shire" of Lincoln to their allegiance. Treachery on the part of the leaders was suspected. Two hundred, after retiring to the cloisters for conference, returned with the intent of putting the gentry to the sword if they refused to lead them against the royal forces which were approaching. They, however, found the chapter-house empty. A side door in the vestibule, now blocked up, then probably concealed by arras, had afforded an unsuspected exit, and in the twilight of that autumnal evening the intended victims made a hurried escape across the minster green to the house of the chancellor, Christopher Massingberd.

These are only two or three incidents in the varied and stirring annals of the Cathedral Church of St. Mary of Lincoln, which from its first erection has been identified more thoroughly than most others with the national life and the events which have shaped the history of our country.

EDMUND VENABLES.

LICHFIELD.

 ANTIQUARIANS dispute, though legends explain, the origin of the name Lichfield. According to the latter it means "field of the dead," and commemorates the slaughter of a number of Christian converts by the Roman soldiery during the Diocletian persecution. That this derivation is not modern the city arms bear record, as on them we see "an escutcheon of landscape with many martyrs in it in several ways massacred."

More historical, yet not without an admixture of legend, is the connection of Lichfield with St. Chad. A mile or so away from the eastern end of the cathedral, beyond "Stowe Pool," may still be seen a low church tower and a cluster of houses which form the village of Stowe. Here St. Chad took up his abode, near a church, perhaps on the site of that now standing, which had been built by his predecessor Jaruman, and from this centre administered the great bishopric of Mercia. Thus Lichfield, though not without some considerable interruption, has been the seat of a bishopric since the middle of the seventh century. Of Chad's piety and labours, which are doubtless historical, and of the legends which loving memories gathered about the story of his death, there is not here space to tell. The little church and village, the centre of the great Mercian bishopric, began to increase in fame and in size as pilgrims flocked to the grave of St. Chad. In the days of his successor the see of Mercia was divided, and Lichfield became the head of a more manageable diocese. A century later Offa obtained from the Pope for the Bishop of Lichfield the title archbishop, the pall, and jurisdiction over four bishops of Mercia and two of East Anglia. But this glorification of Lichfield was but of short duration, for after the king's death a new Pope annulled the act of his predecessor.

In the eleventh century Lichfield lost for a time the honour of being an episcopal town, for the Norman bishop removed the seat of the see to Chester, the town being considered "inadequate to support the episcopal dignity." Chester, after twenty-eight years, was deserted for Coventry, but in the year 1128, after an interval of rather more than half a century, Lichfield was again, notwithstanding its insignificance as a town, restored to its ancient honour. The date when a church was first built on the present site is a little uncertain; but we learn from Bede that St. Chad was buried near the Church of St. Mary, the first in Lichfield, and that his remains were afterwards translated to the new Church of St. Peter (the present cathedral). Hence this must have been completed some time before 735, the year of Bede's death, though probably it was then a comparatively small and humble structure. After the Conquest this work of English hands was replaced by a Norman church on a grander scale, the exact date of the rebuilding being also uncertain; but this also, with the exception of a few fragments, has been swept away. It was gradually rebuilt, after it had stood for rather more than a century, the western part of the choir, the oldest portion of the present cathedral, having probably been

LICHFIELD, FROM THE SOUTH.

begun about the year 1200. The south transept was next taken in hand, followed some few years later by the north transept; for one at least of these is known, from an old grant giving a right of quarrying stone, to have been in progress about the year 1235. Next the nave was rebuilt, the work being begun about the middle of the same century; and the west front, which does not appear to have been constructed quite continuously with the rest, is dated about 1275. The architects now again took in hand the eastern part of the choir. The work executed at the beginning of the century was destroyed, and the present Lady Chapel and presbytery were erected, the former being the earlier, and the whole work, occupying roughly a quarter of a century, being completed about the year 1325. Since then nothing has been done except by way of improving or restoring the building. Some " Perpendicular" windows were inserted in the fifteenth and sixteenth centuries; the central spire was destroyed during the Civil War of the seventeenth century, and was rebuilt after the Restoration by Sir Christopher Wren; and the minor injuries of the siege, of age, and of perverse architects, have been repaired from time to time, the last work being the restoration of the magnificent west front, which was completed so recently as the year 1884. Wyatt, the destroyer, was let loose on Lichfield in the later part of the last century, and it has cost much to undo

his work, though happily he left his mark less permanently impressed on Lichfield than on some other cathedrals, as he mainly confined himself to blocking up the pier arches of the choir, erecting an elaborate organ screen, and glazing the upper portion of the eastern tower arch in order to protect the canons from the cold; and to removing the communion table to the extreme east of the building, " so as to convert the united choir and Lady Chapel into a long aisleless or apteral chapel." These arches were reopened in the year 1856, and four years later the cathedral was placed under the charge of the late Sir G. G. Scott, with the result, to quote the words of the accomplished

THE WEST FRONT.

author of the "Handbook to the English Cathedrals," "that the cathedral has been enriched with a series of works in wood, metal, and encaustic tiles, unexceeded in beauty or in interest by any which have been produced in England during the present century."

The great event in the history of Lichfield Cathedral (for generally the annals of the town have been as uneventful as those of a small midland town without a river and without manufactures usually are) was the siege, to which allusion has already been made. The town itself was an open one, but the cathedral had been rather strongly fortified by Stephen Langton, its bishop, and a statesman of mark in the reigns of the first two Edwards.   When the strife between king and Parliament resulted in an appeal to arms, it happened that the chief families in the neighbouring districts were strongly Royalist, and so the " close " of Lichfield by their means was occupied by a garrison, and held for the king.   This, in the early part of 1643, was attacked by a Parliamentary army under the command of Robert, Lord Brooke.   He planted one of his batteries in Dam Street, which runs along a kind of causeway at the eastern end of the "Minster Pool," a sheet of water completely protecting the south side of the close. As Lord Brooke was standing in this battery, a shot fired from the battlements of the central tower by a Mr. Dyott, one of the gentry of the neighbourhood, struck him in the forehead and he fell dead.   His fall, however, did not bring a long respite to the cathedral.   The attack was resumed under the command of Sir John Gell. Injured by the cannon shot, the central spire fell and crushed in a part of the roof, and the defenders of the close were soon obliged to capitulate.   The cathedral, battered by the siege, was wrecked by the victors.   They defaced the monuments, hewed down the carved woodwork, and shattered the stained glass, besides destroying many valuable records of the cathedral and of the city, and added to the injury by sundry wanton insults to the religious feelings of the conquered.

After the Restoration Dr. Hacket was appointed to the vacant see and to the charge of a ruined cathedral.   No sooner had he come into residence than he began the work of repair.   The great spire was rebuilt from a design by Sir Christopher Wren, fortunately so as not to differ conspicuously from the others; and by the end of the year 1669 the work was practically finished and the building reconsecrated.   The bishop lived to hear the tenor bell (the first of a peal which he had ordered) rung, and then passed away from this world.

The restoration by Bishop Hacket was by no means complete as to details, and among other things left for future care were the statues adorning the west front, which had been greatly injured.   This work, however, was taken in hand in the middle of the last century, when Roman cement was moulded over the ancient stone cores (for they were sometimes little more), and the west front emerged from the restorer's hands " spick and span," looking almost brand-new.   Of course the details of the restoration were such as might have been expected from the antiquarian science of the time, and the last important work accomplished in the cathedral has been the restoration in stone of the west front and the renewal of the statues.   Its completion was signalised by a great ceremonial, when the west front was "rededicated," in the presence of the Archbishop of Canterbury and others, in the spring of 1884.   The result, of course, has been that much of the detail is now new work, but the rather crumbling nature of the red stone used in the building has unfortunately made this necessary in more than one part, and it is a very careful restoration, founded upon whatever traces could be discovered of the old, so that the cathedral now appears far more like its ancient self than it has done for a couple of centuries.

The three most notable features of the exterior of the cathedral are the west front, the triple group of spires, and the great length of the roof. It may be doubted whether the last is a good feature, the nave and the choir up to the extreme east end being at the same level. But the other two characteristics are of singular beauty. Individually the spires of Norwich or of Salisbury may bear away the palm; indeed, the fact that the central spire of Lichfield is a seventeenth-century rebuilding renders the comparison hardly fair. But such a group does not exist elsewhere in Britain. The charm of the triple grouping is admitted alike in towers and spires, and the superiority of a dominant centre as at Canterbury, Lincoln, or Durham is generally felt; but at Lichfield the substitution of the perfect for the imperfect form, of the steeple for the tower, places the cathedral in this respect before all others. The "Ladies of the Vale," as the spires of Lichfield have been poetically named, are exceptionally beautiful, whether seen from a neighbouring eminence rising above the roofs of the town, or from afar, in pleasant contrast with the woods and meadows of the neighbouring country.

The west front is certainly one of the most beautiful in England. The central doorway and the great west window (the latter a restoration by Scott), both remarkably fine examples of the richest work in the Decorated style, and the intervening arcades with statues, together with the enrichment of every part of the façade, produce a very grand effect, while the composition as a whole is singularly graceful.

It must be remembered that Lichfield is among our smaller cathedrals, the total length being 319 feet; grace, therefore, rather than grandeur is its characteristic, and in this, as we have said, it is seldom equalled. The impression produced by the west front is hardly diminished on entering the nave, in doing which the beautiful old ironwork on the west door should not be left unnoticed. The clustered piers, supporting the nave arches, are good; the triforium, arranged so as to consist of a pair of Decorated arches in each bay, rather like that in Westminster Abbey, is especially fine. The clerestory, however, is peculiar, the windows being curvilateral triangles, enclosing three circles with a trefoil in each. It may be doubted whether the composition is wholly judicious, and the following is the verdict of a very excellent judge: "Nothing can exceed this nave in beauty and gracefulness. But in sublimity it is exceeded by many, . . . and the reason seems to be that a bay of the Lichfield nave is clearly limited in its height. The triforium is made a principal instead of a subordinate feature; you feel that if by the heightening of the pier-arches it were placed at a different level from the eye much of its beauty would be lost." The aisles are exceptionally narrow, but the wall arcades give them a rich appearance. The roof of the nave was grievously injured during the siege, so that only a part is ancient work. Monuments of early date are almost wanting. The blind fury of the Puritans made nearly a clean sweep of those which existed at the surrender of the cathedral, so that only some mutilated fragments remain; but there are several subsequent to that epoch, among them a very ugly one in the south transept to the memory of the officers and men of the 80th (Staffordshire) Regiment who fell in the Sutlej campaign. A marble slab and inlaid brass cross in the opposite wall commemorate Admiral Parker. There are also one or two modern brasses, and among the mural tablets (in itself of no particular beauty) is a small monument with an inscription by Sir Walter Scott to the memory of Miss Seward, a poetess in her day of some note, but now almost forgotten, who lived at Lichfield, and died there in the year 1809. A large Perpendicular window has been inserted in the north end of the north transept, naturally to the injury of the architectural effect. It was filled with stained glass about seventy years since, and consequently can hardly be said to adorn the cathedral. A very beautiful work in metal by Skidmore of Coventry has replaced Wyatt's organ screen. It has the same general character as that at Hereford, and is hardly less elaborate or beautiful. The pulpit, placed against the north-west tower pier, is a modern work in metal by the same artist, and the brass lectern, also modern, is by Hardman of Birmingham, while a handsome new marble font stands in the nave.

THE CENTRAL SPIRE AND CHAPTER-HOUSE.

The choir and presbytery are eight bays long, and at this point the side aisles cease; the Lady Chapel, which is not otherwise marked off from the rest of the building, extends three bays farther to the east, and is terminated by an apse (three sides of a hexagon). The original Norman choir had an apsidal (semicircular) termination, but did not extend beyond a spot between the fourth and fifth piers of the present choir. A square-ended chapel was built east of it about 1180, but was removed at the beginning of the next century, when the choir was taken down and replaced by one in the Early English style which terminated at about the position now occupied by the reredos. Then the Lady Chapel and retro-choir were erected, about a century later, shortly after which the greater portion of the choir was rebuilt. During the recent restorations Wyatt's work has been all undone; his stalls, with their plaster canopies, have been destroyed (the present are without any); the choir has had new seats. The communion table was replaced in the position which

the high altar had occupied from the year 1325 up to the days of Wyatt, namely, at the end of the sixth bay of the choir, where its platform is elevated by three steps above the floor of the presbytery, which itself is one step higher than that of the choir. The pavements are composed of marble slabs and encaustic tiles, the latter the work of Minton, while some of the former are ornamented with incised work. The reredos, designed by Scott, is a graceful structure, and the materials used in it (alabaster, marble, fluor-spar, and malachite) are all found, or might be found, in the limits of the diocese. The windows of the Lady Chapel are filled with stained glass; the two western ones are of the last century, without merit, and may one day be replaced by some more worthy of the position. The remaining seven are filled with glass which once adorned the great Cistercian nunnery of Herckenrode, in the bishopric of

THE CHOIR, LOOKING WEST.

Liége. This, when the French Republicans had overrun the country and propagated their new doctrines of liberty at the point of the bayonet, was suppressed in 1802; the glass which had filled some of its windows was purchased by Sir Brooke Boothby for a sum of £200! and during the Peace of Amiens imported into England. The designs are very good, and so is the colour, though the date is rather late (it ranges from 1530 to 1540). Some portions of glass that remained over after filling these seven windows were inserted in the east window of the south choir aisle, and in one of those in the aisle of the south transept.

It has been already said that the Puritans deprived Lichfield of nearly all its ancient monuments. Still it is exceptionally rich in tombs of later date, and especially of the present century, which rise above the usual dull if not offensive level of modern times. In the north choir aisle at the eastern end is a kneeling figure of Bishop Ryder, by Chantrey, which is one of his last works. The figure is good, but the pedestal is not satisfactory; it was formerly too high, it is now too low. At a similar position in the southern aisle is the first work that brought Chantrey especially into repute, the "Sleeping Children," a marble monument of exquisite grace, too well known to need any description. The children were the daughters of the Rev. W. Robinson, Prebendary of Lichfield, who died in the year 1812. Under the north arcade of the choir, in one of the positions deemed in ancient times most honourable, is a canopied tomb to the memory of John Lonsdale, late Bishop of Lichfield. The design was furnished by Scott, the figure being modelled by G. F. Watts. Another handsome altar-tomb, with a recumbent figure placed in a little chamber on the south side of the Lady Chapel, records the respect felt for his successor, George Augustus Selwyn, the last bishop. In the retro-choir is a handsome monument commemorating Dean Howard, and another to the late Archdeacon Moore; while near the western end of the south aisle are monuments, the one on the southern side to the late Arch-deacon Hodson, who died of cholera while on a tour on the Continent, the other to his distinguished son, Major Hodson, who fell at the taking of Lucknow. Both these were designed by Mr. G. Street. Farther east is the tomb of good Bishop Hacket, to whom the fabric of the cathedral owes so much and his diocese hardly less.

The sacristy and treasury are placed east of the south transept, and approached from the south choir aisle; in their walls are incorporated some slight remnants of the old Norman cathedral, all, in fact, that is left above ground. In a corre-sponding position on the northern side is the vestibule leading to the chapter-house, which is in plan rather exceptional, being an elongated octagon, two of the sides being double the length of the rest; it is of two storeys, having vaulted roofs supported by a central pillar, the lower one being the chapter-house, the upper the library. The date of the building is about the year 1240, or distinctly later than that of the older part of the choir adjoining, but about the same as that of the north transept. The clustered central column and the arcades round the building are worth notice. The Puritans destroyed the books in the old chapter library, so that those in the present one have been collected since the Restoration, though among them are one or two which were saved at the time of the sack of the cathedral. There are several of value, the most remarkable being the "Gospels of St. Chad." It contains at the present time the Gospels of St. Matthew and St. Mark, with a part of that according to St. Luke. Traditionally St. Gildas is asserted to be its scribe, and notes in Welsh on the margin of some of the pages give a certain support to the story. One of these states that it was presented to St. Teilo, the patron saint of Llandaff, by its purchaser, Gelhi. Mr. Westwood inclines to refer it to the latter part of the eighth century, though he thinks it possibly might be as old as the days of St. Chad. At any rate, it appears from another entry to have been at Lichfield as early as the year 1020.

To most of its bishops, if of eminence, Lichfield has been but a temporary resting-place. One, however, noted as a statesman and as a liberal benefactor to his cathedral and diocese, Walter Langton, died Bishop of Lichfield, and was buried in the Lady Chapel of which he was the founder. Of Hacket's good works we have already spoken, and of the last two bishops, John Lonsdale, a man not less revered than loved, an accomplished scholar, a wise ruler, and a good man; and George Augustus Selwyn, translated to Lichfield from the scene of his great mission work in New Zealand, who died at a

THE " SLEEPING CHILDREN."

ripe age, full of zeal and earnest labour to the last. The Deans of Lichfield do not appear to have made any particular mark upon history, though many of them have been useful in their generation.

In the vicinity of the cathedral there is little of interest. The gates of Stephen Langton's fortifications have been swept away, with the exception of a small portion of one near the south-east angle, though the western gate lasted till the beginning of the present century; of his walls also little more than occasional fragments are visible. Perhaps the best indicated continuous portion of the defences, which resisted for a time the attack of the Puritan forces, is at the eastern end of the close, where a parapet rests upon the lower part of the ancient wall, and gives a view into the fosse, now converted into a garden of one of the canon's houses. From this position we look across level meadows to the little church of Stowe, noted, as said above, for its connection with the memory of St. Chad. Langford's palace, with its great hall one hundred feet long, stood at the north-east angle of the close; this, in the year 1687, was replaced by the present structure, a mansion of moderate size and of little architectural interest. For many years previous to the appointment of Bishop Selwyn the usual episcopal residence was at Eccleshall, in a distant part of the county, and the " palace " at Lichfield was let; but the inconvenience caused by the separation of the bishop from the more central part of his diocese and from the cathedral town was so obvious, that after the death of Bishop Lonsdale the palace at Eccleshall was sold and Lichfield became again the dwelling-place of its bishop.   The other houses in the close are of even less architectural interest than that of the bishop, Lichfield having been far less fortunate than many of our English cathedrals in preserving portions of its ancient appanages.

The best general views of the exterior of the cathedral are obtained from the causeways leading over the Minster Pool (on the lines of Bishop Langton's work), from the neighbourhood of Stowe, and from the hilly grounds on the south-eastern part of the town.   Its characteristics may be thus summed up: it is pleasantly situated on the grassy lawn of its close; it has proportionately the longest choir in England (always excepting those which have the nave imperfect); its stained glass (bought plumes, it must be admitted) is, perhaps, the best of its date; it glories in the richest west front and the most beautiful group of spires in this country.

T. G. BONNEY.

HEREFORD.

THE ancient city of Hereford stands on the banks of the river Wye, in the midst of a fertile, well-wooded district. On approaching the town the prospect is not inviting. The houses are mostly built of very red bricks, and no objects are specially visible except the lofty spires of St. Peter's and All Saints' Churches, and the large square tower of the cathedral.

History is altogether silent as to the nature of the fabric which stood here in early Saxon times when Hereford was called Fernleigh. It is recorded that bishops of the early British Church were here in the sixth century. In 676 Putta resigned the see of Rochester and came to reside not far from Hereford. Ethelbert, King of East Anglia, was murdered near Sutton, four miles from Hereford, by Offa, the great Mercian king, with some intention of uniting the kingdoms of East Anglia and Mercia. He was buried at Marden, but his body was soon removed to Hereford by a pious noble named Brithfrid. About 830 the church was rebuilt in stone by Milfrid, a nobleman of Mercia, who, "moved by the renown of miracles wrought at the shrine of St. Ethelbert, sent abundance of money and began from the foundation (*circa* 830) and perfected a superior church built of stone, which he endowed with royal munificence." This Saxon church stood about two centuries.

Bishop Athelstan rebuilt the church in the time of Edward the Confessor.

It was but short-lived, being plundered and burnt in 1056 by a combined force of Welsh and Irish, under Griffith, the Welsh prince. Robert of Lorraine, who was consecrated in 1079, and held the see sixteen years, undertook the reconstruction of the cathedral for the third time. Bishop Reynelm carried on the work (1107—1115), and Bishop Robert de Betun, his third successor (1131—1148), completed it. A Latin cross was the ground-plan of the Norman church, dedicated to St. Mary and St. Ethelbert, with three bays for the choir, an eastern apse, a central tower, and eight bays for the nave. The fabric remained unaltered scarcely fifty years, when Bishop de Vere (1186—1199) commenced the eastern transepts. The erection of the Lady Chapel, now used as the parish Church of St. John Baptist, appears to have been carried on from 1226 to 1246. The clerestory of the choir was built about 1250. The north transept was rebuilt in the time of Bishop Aquablanca, and completed by Bishop Swinfield about 1280 to 1288. The building of the north porch, with a large doorway of remarkable design, was the work of Swinfield (*circa* 1288—1290). He built both the aisles of the nave soon after; also the presbytery aisles and the north-east transept before his death in 1316.

The building of the central tower, which is profusely adorned with the ball-flower ornament, may have commenced soon after 1320, while that formerly at the west end of the nave was erected about the middle of the fourteenth century. The beautiful chapter-house and its vestibule were erected before 1375, and the cloisters in the following century. Bishop Trevenant (1389—1404) rebuilt the south end and groining of the great transept. In the fifteenth century Bishop Stanbury alone made any addition to the fabric by erecting his small chantry (1453—1474). Bishop Audley built his chantry 1492—1502. Bishops Mayo and Booth made the last additions by erecting the outer porch, now forming the principal northern entrance to the cathedral. The building of the present edifice extended therefore over a period of 440 years.

On approaching the cathedral, excellent views of the exterior may be obtained from the well-kept close, especially from the north-east corner. The bishop's palace, the deanery, residences for the canons, and the cathedral school are in close proximity. The college, the residence of the vicars choral, is a picturesque quadrangle attached to the cathedral by its own cloister. The eastern gables of the choir and Lady Chapel were rebuilt from designs by Mr. Cottingham (1841—1850), while the greater part of all other restoration has been carried out by the late Sir G. G. Scott (1856—1877). The ancient spire—wood covered with lead—was taken down in 1797. The western front, with the clerestory of the nave, were constructed in a most debased style by James Wyatt, who also shortened the nave by one entire bay. These works were undertaken in consequence of the disastrous fall, on Easter Monday, 1786, of the west

HEREFORD CATHEDRAL, FROM THE BANK OF THE WYE.

4

end, whereby half the nave and a western tower were destroyed. The Norman west front contained a deeply-recessed doorway, arcaded panels, a few effigies, a large window of six lights, two square turrets, and a central fourteenth-century tower profusely covered with the ball-flower. The substructure being unequal to this great weight, the north-west corner suddenly gave way, when the whole became a hopeless ruin. Two sides of the bishop's cloisters remain, also portions of the ancient chapter-house, where many monuments and ancient stones are preserved. The architectural details of the fabric generally are so excellent that they will be found worthy of careful inspection. The north transept, Lady Chapel, and clerestory of the choir are peculiarly beautiful examples of Early English work in various stages of development.

The roofs of the entire edifice are well covered with lead. Upwards of £50,000 has been expended on the fabric during the last forty years, a large sum being still required to complete the restoration which has thus far been so well carried out. It was the opinion of Welby Pugin fifty years ago that " in this church there is much to admire, a good deal to learn, much to deplore." The points for admiration are now greatly increased, while many unsightly objects have been removed. The cathedral is highly valued by the citizens and all connected with the diocese; the services are conducted most efficiently, and the building is well warmed and lighted, and cleaned with praiseworthy care; the seats are all free, and the edifice is open during the whole day. Entering the cathedral through Bishop Booth's porch and the rich Decorated doorway, a good general view of the interior is at once obtained. The fine massive Norman pillars of the nave, tower, and choir, the superb modern screen, the spacious and lofty central lantern, the reredos with its richly-carved spandrel, the distant view of the Lady Chapel with its rich lancet windows and foliated ornaments, its groined roof and stained-glass windows, the darkness of the choir and the various lights and shades, all combine to impress very deeply the mind of the visitor.

Commencing the survey of the interior in the north transept, the first object of interest that meets us is the tomb or substructure of the shrine of Bishop Thomas de Cantilupe, commonly known as " St. Thomas of Hereford," who died in 1282. It is a rich specimen of Early Decorated work, and has been most carefully restored. The canonisation of this bishop was effected in 1320, many miracles being wrought—as it is said—at this place. The arms of Cantilupe have been adopted for this see ever since, and the registers of the diocese were commenced in his episcopate.

The most ancient and beautiful of the episcopal monuments in this cathedral is that of Peter de Aquablanca (1240—1268). The effigy is a fine and perfect example of a bishop in full vestments. The rich canopy is supported by slender shafts; the carving throughout is so delicate and rich that the tomb is scarcely surpassed by any of its period.   Ten Norman bishops (1079—1216) were buried in this cathedral, effigies being placed over their tombs in the fourteenth century. The beautiful little chantry and the tomb of Bishop Stanbury (*ob.* 1474), who was the first Provost of Eton College, are worthy of careful examination.   The effigy, executed in alabaster, although slightly mutilated, is a valuable example of mediæval vestments.

In the north-east transept a large number of monumental fragments are preserved—forming a rich and varied collection.   There is also a beautiful altar-tomb of alabaster and polished marbles erected as a public memorial to the late dean, Richard Dawes, 1867.   The effigy, by Mr. Noble, is a good likeness of the dean, who was an ardent supporter of the education movement about the middle of this century.   The crypt under the Lady Chapel is small but interesting; it is the solitary example of a crypt in an English cathedral built after Norman times until we come to Truro Cathedral. Dean Merewether, who preceded Dean Dawes, is buried here.   The arduous work of rebuilding the piers of the central tower and other works were accomplished through his zeal.

The south-east transept contains memorials of several Bishops of Hereford.   The remains of Bishop Gilbert Ironside (1701), together with his black marble tombstone, were removed to this place in 1867, when the Church of St. Mary Somerset, London, was taken down.   There are about forty bishops buried in this cathedral, a larger number, perhaps, than in any other church.   Here also may be seen a curious effigy of St. John the Baptist, and a fine marble bust, the supposed work of Roubiliac.   The fine canopied Perpendicular tomb of Bishop Mayo (1516), with effigy fully vested, is on the south side of the **altar.**   In the same place there is a fourteenth-century effigy of King Ethel-

THE TOWER AND NORTH PORCH.

bert, whose murder near this city is depicted in the pavement in the centre of the choir.

On the wall of the south aisle, accessible to the visitor at all times, is preserved the celebrated Hereford "Mappa Mundi" (date *circa* 1282—1300). This is the work of an ecclesiastic, who is supposed to be represented in the right-hand corner on horseback, attended by his page and greyhounds. He has commemorated himself under the name of Richard de Haldingham and Lafford in Lincolnshire. His real name was Richard de la Battayle or de Bello. He held a prebendal stall in Lincoln Cathedral, and was promoted to a stall in this cathedral in 1305, afterwards becoming Archdeacon of Reading. During the troublous times of Cromwell the map was laid beneath the floor of Bishop Audley's Chapel, where it remained secreted for some time. In 1855 it was cleaned and repaired at the British Museum.

This is allowed to be one of the most remarkable monuments of its kind in existence, being the largest and most interesting of all the old maps, drawn on a single sheet of stout vellum. The world is here represented as round, surrounded by the ocean. At the top of the map (the *east*) is represented Paradise, with its river and tree; also the eating of the forbidden fruit, and the expulsion of our first parents. Above is a remarkable representation of the Day of Judgment, with the Virgin Mary interceding for the faithful, who are seen rising from their graves and being led within the walls of heaven. The map is chiefly filled with ideas taken from ancient historians. There are numerous figures of towns, animals, birds, and fish, with grotesque creatures. The four great cities are made very prominent — Jerusalem, Babylon, Rome, and Troy. In Great Britain most of the cathedrals are mentioned.

A number of ancient objects of great local interest are exhibited in a glass case in the vestry.

In the south aisle are two fourteenth-century tombs, with effigies of unknown ecclesiastics. The tomb of Sir Richard Pembridge, Knight of the Garter, in the reign of Edward III., is worthy of special notice as a fine example of the armour of that period. He died in 1375. This is one of the earliest instances of an effigy having the garter on. The Norman font on the south side of the nave is a large circular stone bowl, with figures of the twelve Apostles carved around it, supported by four demi-griffins.

The choir is full of objects of much beauty and interest. The reredos consists of five canopied compartments, with rich sculpture, representing our Lord's Passion, erected in 1851 as a public memorial to Mr. J. Bailey, M.P. for this county. At the back of the reredos is a pier from which spring two pointed arches; the spandrel thus formed is covered with rich modern sculpture, representing Christ in majesty, with angels and symbols of the Evangelists; below

O

is a figure of King Ethelbert. There is also a very curious and early episcopal chair worthy of notice. The bishop's throne and stalls, of good fourteenth-century work, all carefully restored, and the modern book desks and figures of angels on the upper stalls, also deserve attention. The organ is a grand instrument, recently built by Mr. Willis. The screen is a most imposing and magnificent object, designed by Sir G. G. Scott, and constructed in 1862 by Skidmore's Art Company. This and the large central corona were conspicuous objects in the 1862 Exhibition. It consists of an arcade of five main arches on a base of Devonshire marble, with a central gable, terminating in a richly-jewelled cross. A variety of foliage is produced out of thin plates of copper. Mosaic panels and polished stones in great variety form the chief ornaments. It has seven bronze figures and two massive gates. The tower contains a good and melodious peal of ten old bells. There are forty painted glass windows; thirty-six are modern, of varied merit, and four good examples of the fourteenth century.

Hereford Cathedral is one of the old secular foundations. Many eminent men in former times were associated with this place, some having been promoted to bishoprics and other high offices. No attempt is made to enumerate them in the present limited space, but they include Robert of Gloucester, the Chronicler, prebendary in 1291; Nicholas of Hereford, chancellor in 1377—a remarkable man, leader of the Lollards at Oxford; Polidore Vergil, prebendary in 1507—a celebrated literary man, author of a most popular history; Cardinal Wolsey, prebendary in 1510; Miles Smith, prebendary in 1580, promoted to the see of Gloucester—a very learned man, one of the translators of the authorised Bible, 1611; and Dr. R. D. Hampden, who was bishop of the see 1848—68.

The library, it should be added, placed in a room adjoining the north transept, contains many old books in MS. chained to their places. Some of them are fine specimens of ancient handwriting, and contain beautiful illustrations in gold and colour. Among these one of the most valuable is a unique copy of the ancient Hereford antiphonary of the thirteenth century, in good preservation.

FRANCIS T. HAVERGAL.

WORCESTER.

WORCESTER CATHEDRAL, though not in the first rank,* has a beauty of its own. It has not the massive grandeur of Durham or Winchester, but it is, especially in the eastern parts, stately and graceful as Salisbury or Lincoln. The variety of styles is pervaded by a remarkable unity of design: for instance, in the arches of the nave and of the choir, dating, these from the thirteenth, those from the fourteenth century.

It stands in the form of a double or "patriarchal" cross, without transept aisles. The tower, though poor in details, is well proportioned. In position it is awkward, midway between east and west; and the exterior of the cathedral is bare. But, seen from the Shrub Hill, the cathedral rises nobly against the wavy outline of the Malvern Hills; and on a bright evening in spring or autumn the level rays of the setting sun light up the windows across the Severn with a blaze of glory, as if it were illuminated within for some high festival. Inside, the elevation appears at first unsatisfactory, but, as a matter of fact, the width of the nave aisles detracts from the height.

The cathedral is rich in reminiscences. Worcester, on a Roman road and beside a great river, naturally became the bishop's seat in the conversion of the Wiccian province. But there are no traces of the rude structure, St Peter's, the mother church of the province when Mercia was an independent kingdom; nor of the St. Mary's which Oswald raised in the tenth century, a little north-east of the present cathedral—a stately building in those days, with its twenty-seven altars for his monks, who were to supplant their strictly monastic predecessors.

Wulfstan found Oswald's cathedral in ruins, the handiwork of Hardicanute's soldiers, sent to chastise Worcester for rising against the ship-tax. In 1084 he commenced a new cathedral, parts of which stand to this day. In 1089 the eastern portion was ready for the bishop and his fifty monks. But within a quarter of a century the roof was destroyed by fire, and the cathedral was again in flames in 1202. In 1218 the cathedral was reconsecrated with much pomp by Bishop Silvester, in honour of St. Mary, St. Peter, St. Oswald, St. Wulfstan, the young king, Henry III., being present with his court.

The prince-like bishops of the thirteenth century have left their mark on their

---

* Willis places it about fourteenth in length of the cathedrals and conventual churches of England.

cathedral.   William of Blois rebuilt the eastern part; Godfrey Giffard added
the gilt rings, a special feature of the choir and Lady Chapel; of Walter Cantilupe, it is said, a stone effigy remains (see p. 113).   In the next century good
Bishop Cobham revaulted the north aisle of the nave, Bishop Wakefield the two
most western bays of the nave.   Prince Arthur's exquisite little chapel marks
the sixteenth century.   The cathedral suffered little in the Reformation, much in
the Rebellion from Essex's troopers and from Cromwell's.   During the Common-

THE CATHEDRAL, FROM THE SOUTH-WEST.

wealth the usual services here were silenced till April 13th, 1661.   In 1842 the
restoration of the cathedral throughout began under Perkins, and, after his
death, was completed under Scott, in 1870.   A fine peal of bells was provided
through the exertions of Canon Cattley.

The cathedral has passed through many perils from Danish pirates* and
Welsh marauders, as well as from the conflagrations so frequent in the Middle
Ages, and from civil wars.   In 1292—probably not then only—two rival pro-
cessions fought in the cathedral.   In 1641 Essex stabled his troopers, it is
said, in the nave, exasperated by discovering arms hidden in the precincts.
During the siege which took place in 1646 a field-piece was slung up to the

* An old door, now in the crypt, formerly in the porch, is said to be covered with the skin of a Dane,
who lagged behind when his comrades retired to their boats below the west end of the cathedral.

top of the tower; and subsequently the lead off the roof was sold, with much else, by auction.

The cathedral has been distinguished by royal visits and royal gifts, from King Edgar, in the tenth century, downwards. It was a special favourite with the Plantagenets. Henry II. and Henry III. attended mass here soon after

THE CHOIR, WITH KING JOHN'S TOMB.

accession. John, niggardly as he was, could be lavish in his superstitious awe of Oswald and Wulfstan. Edward I. came almost yearly, particularly before his campaigns abroad. Elizabeth visited Worcester in great state, to the cost of Bishop Bullingham. James II. insulted "the faithful city" by preferring a Roman Catholic chapel to the cathedral and a Roman Catholic priest to the bishop. The most solemn pageant of all was the funeral of Prince Arthur, who died at Ludlow, 1502: the tears and sobs of the crowd attested their sorrow for his untimely end. The cathedral was enriched by the offerings of pilgrims flocking to the shrines of Oswald and Wulfstan. The Lady Godiva of Coventry, in the eleventh century, was one of many benefactors.

Traces of old Norman work are fewer and less vivid than they would be, owing to the perishable nature of the stone. Striped layers, white and green, may be discerned, as at Pisa and Sienna. The hand of the Norman builder may be seen in the walls of the transepts, in the juncture of the north wall of the choir with the tower, in the western part of the choir, in the south corner of each western transept (where the circular staircase projects unusually into the cathedral), and elsewhere. The eastern arch of the north transept speaks his skill. A Norman shaft remains in the angle at the west end of the south aisle of the choir. The piers of the tower encase a Norman "core."* On the outside of the western end of the nave are vestiges of two Norman doorways, surmounted by Norman windows, and of a central doorway, decapitated by the great west window inserted in 1380. The crypt is the most perfect relic of Bishop Wulfstan's work. The two most western bays in the nave are semi-Norman, like the arcade in the chapter-house, and are the work of Bishop Simon, in the twelfth century. Wulfstan's central tower fell in 1175 from sheer weight, as Norman towers were apt to fall. His cathedral had no western towers. In 1221 two small towers fell; they had probably flanked the northern transept.

The porch, resembling the porch at Gloucester in the niches and figures, was erected by Bishop Wakefield in 1386, almost the latest pre-Reformation work here. He closed the western entrance overlooking the Severn. In the two western bays of the nave pointed arches are mixed with semicircular. Like the pointed Norman doorway in the cloisters, they retain their Norman character, without the Norman configuration. The naves of Ely and Peterborough terminate similarly in Norman pointed work. The eastern part of the nave is Decorated; the middle part is Decorated on the north, Perpendicular on the south; the foliage of the piers on the north is richer. The Jesus Chapel, with the font, is in the eighth bay from the west end. The pavement of the nave, black and white marble, the munificent gift of the late Earl of Dudley in the recent restoration, is more suitable for Italian architecture. The pulpit, also his gift, is elaborately carved in marble and alabaster. The west end of the south aisle is used for the Consistory Court of the diocese.

The choir, retro-choir, and Lady Chapel are singularly graceful, with slender columns clustering round the piers, and, as it were,

"Alternately
Framed in ebon and ivory,"

or like a sheaf of lances (it has been said) in the hand of a giant. This part of the cathedral was commenced in 1224, under Bishop Blois and, with Lincoln

* Willis.

and Salisbury, is among the oldest specimens in England of the Early English style, which displaced the ponderous architecture of Normandy.* The choir is as high as the nave, but the triforium is shorter. In the retro-choir and Lady Chapel, the floor being lower, the shafts are taller, but the horizontal lines of the tiers of arches remain the same; the narrowness of the arches enhances the height. The eastern transepts, like those of Clugny and of St. Benoit-sur-Loire—Benedictine monasteries both, as was Worcester—are unusually high. The gilt rings round the columns were added by Bishop Giffard in 1269, probably to hide the iron clamps, which here, as at Pershore, welded the stonework together, when the slighter columns began to succumb under the pressure from above. The Norman choir was, as usual, under the tower. The stalls and the misereres, with their quaint carvings, ecclesiastical or social in their meanings, are of the fourteenth century. The canopies are in the style of the Renaissance.

The small oriel window, Perpendicular, in the north aisle of the choir, vulgarly called the "peephole," belonged to the sacristan's "checquer," or counting-house, not his vestry, or robing-room. On the opposite side of the choir is St. John's Chapel, with the floor slightly raised. Here, in the south wall, is the doorway of the stone staircase leading to the treasury, occupied, it is said, by Cromwell after his victory. It was sometimes used for the confinement of refractory monks. There is a modern " Jesse " window in the south-west transept behind the organ. Prince Arthur's Chantry is exquisitely rich and delicate in the fan-tracery of the roof and in the tabernacle-work of the east wall. The tomb is of granite. The adjoining chapel is called the dean's.

In the recent restoration the east front of the cathedral was rebuilt in the Early English style, for the sake of uniformity. The painted glass, by Hardman, in the east window, was given by the citizens. The decoration of the vault, too, is by Hardman. The floor is laid with marble and with ancient encaustic tiles, probably from the monks' kiln at Great Malvern. The sculptures in the spandrels of the arcades resemble those in Wells Cathedral; they were restored by Boulton. The reredos was erected by Dean Peel to his wife's memory, rather more than twenty years ago; the figures are almost life-size. His own memorial, of marble, inlaid with a large cross and with the emblems of the Evangelists, forms the back of the reredos. The old woodwork in the choir was restored under Scott's direction. The bishop gave the throne.

The crypt is specially interesting. The descent into it is from the south-west transept. In 1092, four years after the consecration of it, Wulfstan held a synod of the diocese here. The cross views, through the maze of dwarf Norman pillars, simple and unadorned, reminds one of the mosque at Cordova. The central pillars, said to be distinctive of English architecture, reappear in the

* Willis compares the Lady Chapel with Rochester.

chapter-house. There are only four apsidal crypts in England—at Canterbury, Winchester, Gloucester, and here; and this surpasses the others in the number and comparative lightness of the pillars.* These are placed so as to bear the weight of those above ground.

The recumbent figure of King John, in the choir, is said to be the oldest regal effigy in England. He closed his inglorious reign at Newark in 1216, and, by his express desire, he was interred here before the high altar, between

RUINS OF THE GUESTEN HALL.

the tombs of St. Oswald and St. Wulfstan, to be safe in their companionship. The tomb was moved eastwards with the high altar under Bishop Blois, and was replaced here in the reign of Henry VIII. The bishops are swinging censers. A wild beast at the king's feet gnaws the scabbard—perhaps as a conventional representation of evil trampled under foot ("Thou shalt tread upon the lion and the adder," &c.)—perhaps as denoting the strife between him and his barons. The figures were gilt—a questionable improvement—in the restoration of the cathedral. The tomb, on which traces of colour have been discerned, is by

* Willis.

Alchurch, a sacrist of the fifteenth century.   Horace Walpole pronounced it worthy of Cavallini.

The oldest episcopal effigy here is probably the recumbent figure on the north side of the Lady Chapel, supposed to be of William of Blois, rebuilder of this part.   The other two, to the south, are perhaps Bishops Bryan and Hemendale.   Bishop Giffard intended for himself a magnificent tomb close to the altar, but the archbishop interposed, and Giffard lies where the chantry of Prince Arthur was afterwards erected.   The tombs of Bishops Cantilupe and Carpenter are said to be in the northern transept, those of Cobham and Bransford in the north aisle of the nave.   Philip Ballard, last Abbot of Evesham and first Dean of Worcester, lies just beyond the altar-screen.   Two knights in armour, two mediæval ladies, one apparently of extraordinary stature, are represented by recumbent figures in the Lady Chapel.   Judge Littleton, famous for his book, the basis of Coke's "Commentary," ancestor of the Lytteltons of Hagley, is commemorated in the south aisle of the nave; and Bishop Gauden, reputed author of "Icon Basilike," by a small mural tablet.   A small slab on the north wall of the Lady Chapel is in memory of Izaak Walton's wife, sister of Bishop Ken.   In the north-east transept is a very graceful monument, by Chantrey, to Mrs. Digby.   The monument by Roubiliac, in the north-west transept, to Bishop Hough, who, as President of Magdalen College, Oxford, resisted the arbitrary proceedings of James II., is melodramatic and incongruous.   In the south-west transept is a memorial to Bishop Maddox, who died in 1759, styled by Nash "Institutor of Infirmaries in this county."*   The tomb of the late Lord Lyttelton in this transept, by Forsyth, deserves close inspection.   The tomb is of Derbyshire spar, the figure is of alabaster; the expression and posture are admirable.

The cloisters are entered from the south aisle of the nave, the cathedral forming, as usual in Benedictine monasteries, a screen from the north wind for the other buildings, and the cloisters serving as a sheltered ambulatory for the monks. They were damaged in the Rebellion, but are now in good preservation.   The arcades are of the fourteenth century; the tracery of the panels is better than that of the windows.   The east walk reminded Willis of Gloucester.   The narrow slit or orifice in the stonework of the windows was merely, according to him, to lighten the superstructure; it may have been for the prior or sub-prior to supervise the monks, seated in summer-time, three in each window, at their studies.   The refectory was, as usual, on the south side of the quadrangle; since the dissolution it has been used for the cathedral school.   It is, like the cloisters, in the Decorated style.   The crypt of it is Norman.   The Norman lavatory is seen in the south-west corner of the quadrangle, conveniently near the refectory,

* "History of Worcestershire," ii., App. clv.

P

and the dormitory on the west. Water was conveyed in leaden pipes from Henwick Hill till the Rebellion, when the pipes were used for ammunition.

Passages, or "slypes," lead from the cloisters, one southwards, into the outer court ("curia") of the monastery, one westwards, to the infirmary, one eastwards, bifurcating to the prior's house and to the monks' burying-ground. This last served as the parlour ("locutorium"), where the inmates might speak with pedlars and other visitors. The masonry on the north side is ruder and older than on the other. The library, over the south aisle of the nave, is approached by a winding stair from the north-west angle of the quadrangle. It contains many valuable works, and particularly a digest, in MS., of Roman law, by Vacarius, an Italian canonist, who was brought to England by Archbishop Theobald in Stephen's reign, and who is said to have introduced the study of civil law at Oxford. The well-known slab, bearing only the word "Miserrimus," near the door of this staircase, marks the grave of the Rev. T. Morris, M.A., a nonjuror, who died in 1748, aged eighty-eight, sorrowing to the last for the fallen dynasty. Wordsworth in his pathetic sonnet mistakes the meaning of the inscription.

The chapter-house has been compared to those of Bristol and Rochester.* It is decagonal, with a central pillar, from which the vaulted roof springs. The Norman arcading is transitional, like the western bays of the nave (see p. 110). The rebuilding of the upper walls in the fifteenth century was, it would seem, no caprice of fashion, but necessitated by the pressure of the roof. The chapter-house is frequently used, by the permission of the dean and chapter, for committees, &c., of a religious and charitable kind. But it is not well adapted for acoustic purposes. The monks are said to have ranged themselves in the niches along the walls, and so to have facilitated hearing.

Owing to the friable sandstone and to rough usage in days past, there are but scanty remains of other conventual buildings. These, in plan, resembled those of Durham, a river here, as there, flowing below. The ruins of the Guesten Hall, south-east of the cathedral, close to the site of the prior's house, are very picturesque. It was rebuilt by Prior Bransford, afterwards bishop here, in the fourteenth century. The windows are beautiful specimens of the Decorated style. It was in frequent use for the pilgrims to the shrines of Oswald and Wulfstan. Being too dilapidated to be restored (it had already been refashioned for the deanery), the roof of it was given to Holy Trinity Church, Shrub Hill, when the cathedral was last restored.

The Edgar Tower, east of the cathedral, was the main entrance into the monastic precincts. Perhaps the gateway of the castle was here, while Urso, after the Conquest, encroached on the monastery even up to the southern walls

* Willis.

of the cathedral. The name recalls the son of Ethelred II.; the fabric is of much later date; it is used for the registry.

The charnel-house ("capella carnaria") stood north-west of the porch. Bishop Cantilupe endowed it for four priests, and added a prison. In 1636 it was converted into a school for the city, but through damp and neglect it soon fell into decay. The crypt might perhaps be disinterred.

The deanery, formerly the palace, and probably so to be again, has some very interesting features, particularly the spacious vaulted chamber below. The front was built in the time of Bishop Hough.

The clocherium (or "campanile") rose, with its wooden spire, 150 feet, almost touching the north-east transept. The churchyard cross was on this side, and was used, as at St. Paul's Cathedral, for preaching. Seats for the chief citizens were placed against the north wall of the cathedral. The nave is now employed here, as elsewhere, for this purpose, and listening crowds here, as elsewhere, bear witness to the revival of the spiritual energies of our cathedrals. "Floreat ecclesia cathedralis Vigornensis."

I. GREGORY SMITH.

CHRIST CHURCH, FROM MERTON MEADOWS.

OXFORD.

THOUGH the smallest cathedral church in England, and perhaps in Europe, Christ Church possesses great interest for the architect, both within and without. If there can be a distinctly transitional style, this church is in it, and as the term is used by Sir Gilbert Scott, it is quite admissible here. The use of the word transitional is extremely convenient in discussions on architecture, generally speaking; but in this case it is quite necessary. We presume a mixture of pure elements may be called a pure mixture; and here we have Romanesque, Norman, and Decorated features, all good of their kind. The north-east walls and turrets might remind one of the Cathedral of Mainz or of Trier, while the chapter-house door is noble Norman, and its Early Decorated windows excellent in their way. The architecture, in fact, agrees with the dates now historically assigned to it, that is to say, with the latter part of the twelfth century. Dr. Ingram, in his "Memorials of Oxford," exerts himself with great faith and heartiness (and by no means without support of appearances now better understood) to prove that traces

of the early work of Ethelred II. still remain. It is a devout imagination, and may well be dear to Christ Church men; but there is not a shadow of foundation for it, in the opinion of Sir G. Scott, Mr. J. F. Parker, and the authorities in general.

A short historical sketch is necessary here, beginning, as usual, with credible legend, and excluding the miracles with which the first foundress is credited by Philip, her third Norman prior. The story of St. Frideswide has passed through his hands, through William of Malmesbury's and John of Tynemouth's, and is found in Leland's "Collectanea."

About A.D. 727 an alderman or "subregulus" of the name of Didan is discovered ruling over the populous city of (Mercian)

THE SHRINE OF ST. FRIDESWIDE.

Oxford, in all honour. He and his wife Saffrida have a daughter named Frideswide. She embraces the monastic life with twelve other maidens; her father, at her mother's death, builds a conventual church in honour of St. Mary and All Saints, and thereof makes her prioress. The munificent kings of Mercia also build inns, or halls, in the vicinity; which account seems to anticipate even Alfred's imagined foundation of University College, and therefore (though we fear on no historic ground) is to be faithfully adhered to as dogma by all members of the larger house. St. Frideswide's death took place 735—740, or even later. Her priory became a house of secular canons; and her remains were laid beneath the already-existing tower, until their first translation under Prior Philip

(12th February, 1180), by the Archbishop of Canterbury, to the north choir aisle. She was again translated (10th September, 1289) to a new and more costly shrine in the Lady Chapel, which had been added to that aisle early in the century.

Many casualties passed over the site of St. Frideswide's ancient church before her last translation. It was wholly or partly burnt in 1015, or in 1002, when certain Danes took refuge in its tower from the massacre of that year. It was rebuilt on a somewhat larger scale, and made a "cell" or dependency of the great monastery of Abingdon for some years of the eleventh century. Its canons were, however, reinstated, but soon after the Conquest were dispossessed, probably as violating the law of celibacy. A Norman church must then have been erected in place of the old Saxon one, and it is probable that the doorway of the chapter-house,* which is certainly more ancient than any part of the existing church, may have belonged to this. It is marked by fire, which may, however, be referred to the conflagration of 1190, when a large part of Oxford was destroyed. This was nearly sixty years after the accession of Guimond, the first regular prior, who re-established the foundation as a convent of regular canons of his own Augustinian order; in which state it continued, till Wolsey's reconstruction, in the midst of the European revival of learning, and on the brink of the English Reformation, which he so well foresaw. But both Guimond, and Robert of Cricklade, his successor, seem to have been wise and well-meaning ecclesiastics; and a school was connected with this convent which has really good claim to be considered the original germ of the university, and can be so asserted by archæologists with some historical truth. Robert of Cricklade began the present structure of the church about the middle of the twelfth century. Guimond, who died 1141, had probably been employed in new arrangements of the monastic buildings, which the change from secular to regular canons would certainly involve. And in 1180 the new buildings were far enough advanced for the translation of St. Frideswide from her sepulchre to her shrine.

Their architecture is doubly transitional. They mark a time when builders like Henry de Blois or William of Sens, well versed in theory and skilful in detail, were exerting themselves to perfect the round-arched style, while at the same time the pointed arch was gradually being introduced, and architectural art was undergoing a complete transformation. Everybody knows that Gothic architecture is derived from Roman; but it is not always remembered that, while the use of the arch and so many great principles of stone construction are due to Roman teachers, they still handed over their style to the northern conquerors in a thoroughly impure condition. Their grand vault and arch system had become

---

* The rest of that beautiful building is certainly of much later date, probably towards the middle of the thirteenth century (Scott's Report, p. 7).

encrusted with Greek lintels and pediments. Rome always composed the wrong way, and always would put two beautiful things together with a comparatively bad result, instead of two comparatively ugly things with a good one. Then just at this time of the twelfth century, when the Northern builders were finally eliminating all traces of the Greek or trabeated structure, the new or pointed arch began to present itself, and was used here and there, as it seems unconsciously, for mere pleasure in its form.

This kind of purely transitional architecture may be observed in Christ Church Cathedral, as at Canterbury and Winchester; in St. Joseph's Chapel at Glastonbury, and the chapter-house of St. Mary's Abbey at York. The proportions of the first original may claim to be considered precisely the best possible.* Doubtless it was a beautiful though not a large church, and it is unfortunate that Wolsey's name must be associated with the lamentable shortening of its nave to one half of the original length, as well as with the lowering of all the roofs. The latter operation strikes the eye of the spectator on entering the quadrangle by the great gate, whence the traces of the old and high-pitched roof are painfully visible below the spire; and the former, though partly repaired, distresses his gaze as soon as he enters the restored double porch. Wolsey had designed, and in fact had begun to build, a new and magnificent church on the north side of the quadrangle for his new Cardinal College. He was only allowed to complete three sides, including the hall; and all the works were stopped by his fall in 1529. Henry VIII. refounded the college, to which he gave his own name, in 1532; but suppressed it, and reconstituted the whole foundation, November 4th, 1546. He then removed the new see of Oxford (erected at Oseney in 1542) to St. Frideswide's, and this last, the present foundation, was styled the Cathedral Church of Christ in Oxford; and comprises a dean and canons with other capitular officers, as well as a large body of students, proper to a college. The ancient church has had a twofold character ever since: it is the cathedral of the diocese, but it is also the college chapel; and as the Dean of Christ Church is always there, and the Bishop of Oxford very seldom, the academic uses and appearances prevail over the ecclesiastical, in a manner which has probably been the reverse of satisfactory to more than one occupant of the see of Oxford.

However, the ancient interior, from the twelfth to the sixteenth century, must have been one of considerable beauty, which may be in some degree restored by the late repairs. The side arcades of the nave claim special attention. The pillars in the twelfth-century church were solid enough for any purpose of strength; and the builder therefore ingeniously divided them in their thickness, and left the half, or halves, which faced the aisle, in their natural proportions, while

* The three western bays (out of five) were removed, but one has been recently rebuilt. "A double equilateral triangle, the common base giving the length of the transepts," is the original formula.

he raised those which faced the central nave, so as to embrace the triforium stage. Sir G. Scott is convinced that this was the original design and not the result of alteration, and gives parallel instances at Ramsey, and in the choir of

THE CHOIR.

Jedburgh. These and most of the principal arches in the church are round, though two of those which carry the tower and the clerestory windows of the nave are pointed.

The thirteenth century brought two great additions to the structure, each beautiful and noble in its way: the upper stage of the tower, with its spire; and the chapter-house; not to mention a second northern aisle to contain the new and more precious shrine of 1289. This was built as a Lady Chapel, and has since been called the dormitory, being the burial-place of several deans and canons; which recalls the primitive term of *cœmeterium*, or place of rest. The original shrine was enclosed within the new one, and some fragments of the latter are still preserved. The curious structure at present existing is really the watching-chamber of the shrine erected in the next century. It is raised upon what was in all probability the tomb of the donor of the shrine, and not of St. Frideswide's parents, as is popularly asserted. In the next century a large chapel, now called the Latin and formerly the Divinity Chapel, was added to the north of the northern choir aisle, by appending two bays eastward to the north-east chapel of the thirteenth century just mentioned. Windows were altered from Norman to Decorated, particularly the three windows at the east end, now restored to their original style. Between the two chapels are three interesting monuments, the western most probably that of Sir George Nowers, one of the companions of the Black Prince. The next is a prior's, Robert de Ewelme's, or his successor's, Alexander de Sutton. Between them they completed the translation of St. Frideswide. Further eastward is the tomb of Lady Elizabeth de Montacute, who in 1340 gave the present Christ Church meadow to the convent, in order to maintain a chantry in the Lady Chapel.

There were great alterations late in the fifteenth century. The Perpendicular style was then extending its rigid rule over England, and various parts of the church were conformed to it. The choir clerestory was remodelled, and the rich vaulting added; most of the windows of the aisles were altered, and the present cloisters were built. The great window of the north transept is of the early sixteenth century, with the wooden roof of the transept and tower; that of the nave is later. But in 1524 came Wolsey's great scheme for Cardinal College, to which St. Frideswide's was sacrificed, as we have seen. One may and must admire Wolsey, but the loss of his intended Perpendicular chapel, with all its magnificence, is of much less importance to the architect and historian than that of the west end of the nave, which he destroyed. He was right on the whole; he had a perfect apprehension of the revival of knowledge, and if all English prelates had accepted it

ENTRANCE FROM THE CLOISTERS.

as manfully as he and others of his mind, the worst part of the Reformation might have been saved to England. He anticipated its academic principle, which was to turn monastic seminaries into houses of religious, useful, and real learning. Monasticism had lasted long and done much, but it was clearly coming to an end, and that in the thoughts of very pious and devoted men. Wolsey was in correspondence with Fox of Winchester and Oldham of Exeter. The former had founded Corpus Christi College about ten years before (1515–1517), at first intending to make it a seminary for the Priory of St. Swithin at Winchester, and there is no doubt that he was dissuaded from that purpose by Oldham's terribly accurate vaticination—"What, my Lord, shall we build

Q

houses and provide livelihoods for a company of monks whose end and fall
we ourselves may live to see? No; it is more meet a great deal to have care
for the increase of learning, and for such as shall do good to the Church and
Commonwealth." All three prelates did well and wisely, but contributed to
a result which went far beyond their wishes or anticipations; nor if they
had lived could they have ruled the terrors of the ensuing time. Wolsey
invites his Cambridge students, of unusual promise, but already tainted with
suspicion of heresy. "Some of them," said Dr. London, Warden of New
College, "have already had a shrewd name." Some have, indeed, retained it,
for among them were Frith and Clark, Sumner and Taverner. Just four years
after the date of Cardinal College come Wolsey's directions to Dr. Higdon, the
first dean, for the arrest of Thomas Garret, and his treasures of forbidden
books, New Testaments in particular. His friend Antony Dalaber's narrative
is given us by Mr. Froude; it is one of the most graphic and pathetic
passages in English history, and it gives us a little sketch of the alarm of
heresy, and its intrusion on the Christ Church services. It almost makes one
regret the old order of the choir up to twenty years ago, which must still have
resembled Wolsey's. "Evensong was begun," says Dalaber, "the dean and
canons in their grey amices. They were almost at 'Magnificat' before I came
thither. I stood in the choir door, and heard Master Taverner play, and others
of the chapel there sing, with and among whom I myself was wont to sing also,
but now my singing and music was turned into sighing and musing. As I there
stood, cometh Dr. Collisford, the commissary (Rector of Lincoln), as fast as ever
he could go, bareheaded, as pale as ashes (I knew his grief well enough), and to
the dean he goeth into the choir, where he was sitting in his stall, and talked
with him very sorrowfully." All had reason, and would have more.

Wolsey's destructions in the cathedral may or may not have been partly
balanced by his executing the choir vaulting; that he did this, however, is disputed.
At all events they were not repaired by Dean Duppa's refitting the choir in no
style, or by his munificent and well-meaning present to the church of a quantity
of stained glass by Van Linge, for which all the Perpendicular windows in
the aisles were turned into plain two-light orifices without tracery. So of the
Decorated windows at the end of the choir aisles, &c. But as these and all
the worst mutilations have been happily restored under Sir G. Scott, we will not
waste wrath or lamentation on the doings of the seventeenth or eighteenth
centuries. The last repairs have been happily delayed long enough to fall into
competent hands, and the traces of the original work, and partly those of the
fourteenth-century restorations, have been conscientiously followed.

This paper should not close without some kind of guide or itinerary for the
visitor; and it seems to the writer that he will probably come into Christ Church

under the great gate, and find himself below Wolsey's tower, completed by Wren; with Wolsey's hall on his right, Dr. Fell's northern side of the quadrangle on his left, and only the thirteenth-century spire, right before him, to represent our proper subject. Let him look at that, and note the traces of the old high-pitched roof and the difference of the older Norman masonry of the lower part of the tower from the thirteenth century above. (The spire has been again rebuilt as to its topmost part.) Then let him cross the quadrangle to its south-east or right-hand farther corner, under the hall; let him digress thither, and to the kitchen if he likes—that's not our business—and return to the little cloister quadrangle at the old low level of the buildings. There he will see Guimond's original work, the nave and transept walls; and he can go on to the perfectly restored chapter-house and look at the Norman door, which Dean Liddell considers, with apparent truth, to have been part of an earlier church. The room within is one of the most beautiful of its age and style in existence. Then he had better go back into the great quadrangle, and so in at one of the double western doors. If it is a sunny day, the capital effect of warm white stone and brilliant small windows will strike him; if it is not, the old Norman impression—of low browed arches, as of a rest of warriors—may or may not come to him. Under such vaults the last great race of ravagers, who could build as well as destroy, lay down to rest. Thick walls and narrow lights, and peace, of its kind—

> " No rude sound shall reach thine ear,
>   Armour's clang nor war-steed champing,
> Trump or pibroch summon here
>   Mustering clan, nor squadron tramping."

So the whole frame of the nave, choir, and transepts. The shrine of St. Frides-wide and the best tombs are in the north-east chapel. The new choir furniture is very good; the reredos is unsuccessful, also the choir glass. The great northern transept window will attract attention. Clayton and Bell have done well in the south aisles; but of all window-glass the writer knows, Burne Jones's, by Morris and Faulkner, at the east end of the aisles of the choir, seems most entirely satisfactory.

R. St. John Tyrwhitt.

THE CHOIR.

SALISBURY.

THE last time that Pugin was in Salisbury he stood at the window of a house overlooking the cathedral and exclaimed, "Well, I have travelled all over Europe in search of architecture, but I have seen nothing like this." There is ample justification for such a verdict. The structure itself is vast; the clear space around is probably without a parallel; the spire is exceptional both for its elegance and its height; the colour is determined by the same lichen that has grown through the same generations over the entire mass, and in those grey walls rising out of the greensward, the impression undoubtedly is conveyed that there are points in which Salisbury Cathedral stands without a rival in the world.

There is one characteristic about its architecture which it shares with St. Paul's Cathedral alone amongst English cathedrals—that it was built all at one period. It is therefore no museum of English architecture, as so many similar churches are, in which we can study the movements of the art in their several periods. It is from end to end the monument of one single epoch, the first half of the thirteenth century—it was begun in the year

1220—built, as seems probable, not altogether apart from French influence, yet in its severity, its reserve, its stern disdain of ornament, thoroughly English in its spirit, being indeed the completest survival in this country of what has been often thought the best and purest period of English art.

The lofty spire, upon which the repute of Salisbury Cathedral is popularly rested, seems to have been no part of the original design. The lantern was at first completed a little above the roof of the nave. The piers and foundations below were never intended to carry so vast a weight; and it was not probably till a generation or two had elapsed that some unknown architect, with the daring of a true artist in exhausting the capability of his material, planned the tower and spire, which have since been recognised as amongst the chief glories of the pile. How near he came to overtaxing the capability of the existing building may been seen internally, from the thrust which the added mass of masonry has caused along the arcades in all direc-

THE LADY CHAPEL.

tions. To this extent, therefore, the statement must be modified that the entire cathedral was built at one time. Nor must it be forgotten that so large a building necessarily takes years for its construction, and its own growth witnesses the transition of art from one epoch to another. Remembering, therefore, that the erection of the cathedral began at the east, proceeded towards the west, and concluded with the spire, it is curious to notice how the ornamentation of the several parts marks the progress of English architecture as the years passed on. The ball-flower ornament, for example, does not belong to the period when Salisbury Cathedral was begun. Accordingly it is not to be seen in the eastern parts of the fabric, but it is found in the western façade* and upon the tower, which came so many years later.

This cathedral is peculiarly rich in the survival of consecration crosses, which in mediæval days were carved or painted on the walls of a church. They are to be seen both outside and inside the building. Those on the inside were twelve in number, three on each wall, to the north, south, east, and west. It seems probable, but not perhaps quite certain, that the number of external crosses was the same. The whole ritual of the consecration is extremely curious, and is described by Durandus, a French bishop who was nearly contemporary with the building of Salisbury Cathedral. The deacon was shut up alone in the church, and his business was to light twelve lamps before the twelve crosses painted on the walls. Meantime the bishop, clergy, and people outside thrice made the circuit of the building, the bishop sprinkling the walls with water which he had previously blessed. On their entering the church, a cross in ashes and sand was made upon the pavement, and upon the cross the entire alphabet was written in Greek and Latin characters. The bishop then made the tour of the interior and anointed the twelve painted crosses with the sacred chrism.

The artistic effect of the interior is not at all equal to that of the exterior of the church; and the question arises as to what is the particular respect in which its builders failed? why is it that they who were so great and strong outside have become so feeble and so poor within? It is perhaps open to doubt whether it is the originators who failed at all. Here are at all events many of the same fine qualities within that won our admiration without. Here, as on the exterior, there are size, elegance, symmetry, just proportions, modesty of treatment, and many other such attributes. Yet, judged by its own high standard it fails. The present Poet-Laureate is understood to have framed the criticism that it is deficient in mystery. This result is no doubt in a great measure due to colour, or more strictly speaking to the absence of right colour. Outside the building Nature has done the exquisite colouring with her mantle of lichen; internally the present colour-effect is due to successive generations of men, of whom some have misunderstood and some have even derided the power of colour. As the cathedral has been seen for the last hundred years, and probably for much longer, the whole effect is too light. Until the restoration of the past ten years, when its marble shafts have once again begun to gleam with their dark polish, and the vaulting of the roof has been robed in modern polychrome, the dominant effect was universally, as indeed it still is in part, that produced by a kind of buff wash. But it may be doubted whether we have any idea of the splendour of this interior as its

* The design of the façade, the grouping of the statues, and the stories severally connected with them are given at length in the present writer's work entitled "The Legend of Christian Art."

originators meant it to look. Then, no doubt every pillar in the structure being of marble helped by its dark rich burnish to remove that pale monotony which we have found so painful; then, arch and wall and groining were from end to end aflame with vermilion in arabesque and saint and angel; then, every window—and the wall of this cathedral is nearly all windows—must have flashed its jewels on the floor. It must have been a magnificent interior then. The giant-artists of the exterior were not so feeble directly they got within the porch.

The colour-system of the cathedral which has been so terribly misunderstood—the modern arabesques, for example, are painted upon a white ground; the old ones may still be seen to have been painted upon a deep colouring, making a vast difference in the solemnity of the aggregate effect—but the system, whatever it was, was not confined to the inside, but reaches even to the exterior of the church. On the west portal there is an example of what is very rare in this climate—colour on the exterior of a building. Within living memory that door was known as the " Blue Door." The " restoration " by Wyatt in the last century removed much of the colour, and the recent work has removed still more; but some slight traces of the blue may still be discerned. The same is true of the arcading in the cloisters, where there is still sufficient evidence before the seeing eye for the presumption that their wall-spaces were once covered with cartoons in colour.

One difficulty always strikes the eye of the intelligent spectator about the inside of Salisbury Cathedral. There seems to be no kind of an elevation where the high altar could have been placed. The floor seems perfectly flat. The difficulty is removed by a reference to some of the French churches. The altar probably stood—not as we see it at the end of everything—but on a daïs of its own, covered probably with a gorgeous canopy, rich in sculpture and metal-work, with its superb corona, as we actually know, suspended before it, and girt with every circumstance of splendour. The ritual of Sarum demanded that it should stand free of any wall; and its probable position was at the intersection of the lesser transept with the choir, where the decoration overhead of all three arms of the fabric, in front of it, leads up to the figure of Our Lord in Majesty.

The internal arrangement of Salisbury may serve to correct a popular mistake whereby an expression about " the old monks " is so often hazarded in connection with any and every cathedral. There were no monks at Salisbury; and the choir-stalls all placed east of the transept may serve to remind us of it. The law is correctly laid down by the eminent French writer Viollet-le-Duc, that non-monastic churches had their choir-stalls east of the transept, whilst monastic churches had theirs to the west, in the nave, or across the transept. The arrangement at Westminster compared with that at Salisbury is an example of this.

A very singular feature in the internal structure is the plinth, carried all round the church, upon which the great shafts of the arcade rest. Most probably it was intended for a seat; and in the early days it was perhaps the only sitting accommodation provided in the nave. The sermons of those days, preached in the nave, were certainly not less lengthy than those of our own time; but the bulk of the hearers must either have stood or have rested the arms and chin upon the crutch-shaped leaning-staff (reclinatorium), which was the precursor of the more comfortable arrangements of modern times.

From an artistic point of view there are two or three tombs of exceptional interest at Salisbury. First, there is the thirteenth-century tomb of Bishop Bridport, which has been seriously mutilated by the iconoclastic zeal of the past, but which is still perfect enough to exhibit to us the British architect of that day, in his first efforts to throw off the grim severity of treatment which marks the earliest beginnings of the cathedral. This monument has been copied for the Crystal Palace. The tomb with recumbent effigy of Longspee, Earl of Salisbury, is valuable as a specimen of monumental art partly in wood. Originally it was ablaze with colour, which can still be traced in some profusion. Indeed, the whole series of tombs, which in the last century were arranged down the nave, serves to show that for many generations the old English artists coloured everything. Here it may still be seen that they painted even their alabaster.

Amongst the curiosities of monumental art are two recumbent figures represented as skeletons. Until the recent restoration, only one of these tombs was exposed to view, and it was popularly believed to be the monument of one who had reduced himself to a state of emaciation by excessive fasting. This view received a severe shock when the removal of the old fittings of the choir disclosed a second tomb of a similar character. Such monuments exist, moreover, in other churches; and they belong in fact to a period when it was the fashion to represent the mortality of man in this ghastly form.

Another curiosity is found in the recumbent figure of the so-called " Boy-Bishop." It was the custom of the mediæval Church for a few days after the children's festival of St. Nicholas, in December, to allow a parody of ecclesiastical pomp on the part of the children, one of the number being actually invested with the mock dignity of the bishop. The story went that one such boy died during his term of office, and that this was his tomb. In this case likewise the popular story has been exploded by comparative science. Similar monuments in miniature are found elsewhere; and two explanations of them are possible. Either there was a fashion at one period of constructing monuments of diminutive size, as there was at other periods of aiming at colossal size; or, what is more probable, the small stone was made to cover the relics of some eminent person when only little of them could be recovered. What if, in the present instance, the eminent person was no less a figure than St. Osmund himself— the nephew of William the Conqueror, the founder of the see, and in his use of Sarum, the father of the worship of the whole English Church? His relics—what little had survived of them—were certainly collected at the time of his canonisation in 1457, when there was a great festival at Salisbury, and when no fewer than forty thousand persons came to pass in front of his shrine. There is no trace of any cover for so eminent

THE CATHEDRAL, EXTERIOR.

R

a treasure either recorded or surviving in Salisbury Cathedral unless it be this unexplained stone.

One of the most beautiful monuments of Early English art still surviving in the cathedral is the screen which for nearly a century has stood in the north-east transept. This was long thought to have been the original screen dividing the choir from the nave. Subsequent investigation, however, has shown that this could not have been the case; though from an old print still extant it may be inferred that it was placed in that position as far back as the time of the later Stuarts, when a large organ was erected over it by Renatus Harris, the famous organ-builder of the Restoration period. It is well known that after the fire of London, Renatus Harris supplied organs to many of Sir Christopher Wren's churches; and as Wren was employed upon Salisbury, it is just possible that the transfer of this fine Gothic screen as a facing for the organ loft may have been effected under his influence. In the present generation Sir Gilbert Scott saw at once that the niches in the screen were meant for seats; and it is matter for learned conjecture as to where these seats were originally required.

H. T. ARMFIELD, F.S.A.

RIPON CATHEDRAL.

To those who have never visited this fine old minster we may introduce it in the words of one of the southern prelates, who, on visiting it a few years ago, remarked, "I never thought that you had such a gem in Yorkshire;" and certainly, small though it be in size, its many styles of architecture, telling its varied history so well, lend to it an interest of no ordinary kind. It is a very picturesque object, whether viewed from the country above the river Ure, which adds so much to the beauty of the neighbourhood, or whether approached from Kirkgate, with its fine west front before us. Visitors to Yorkshire will miss a great deal if they fail to see this fine old building, and its neighbour, Fountains Abbey.

Archæologists differ in opinion as to its earliest history; that is, whether the present building occupies the same site as that referred to by the Venerable Bede, or whether the crypt, known as "St. Wilfrid's Needle," does not belong to a second church erected by Wilfrid. We have, however, the authority of the late Sir Gilbert Scott and of Bishop Stubbs for the view that the minster occupies the site of the Abbey Church of St. Wilfrid, and, anyhow, this crypt bears such a resemblance to that beneath the Priory Church of Hexham, also founded by Wilfrid, as to leave little doubt as to its origin.

ST. WILFRID'S NEEDLE.

This is one of the most interesting relics of pre-Norman times. It is entered from the floor of the nave; and after descending several steps, and traversing a dark passage forty-five feet long, the visitor reaches a cylindrically vaulted cell, seven feet nine inches wide by eleven feet three inches long, in which are niches of the rudest description. The "needle" has been formed by perforating the wall on the north side, so as to communicate with a passage behind. Many are the opinions hazarded as to its use in early days: one of them that it was a medium for the confessional.

To "thread the needle" at Ripon is not so difficult as it looks, and not a few are the folk nowadays who are dragged through by the vergers as a species of charm.

A word or two about St. Wilfrid. A great man was he, with all his faults; he may be regarded as the star of the Anglo-Saxon Church. It is not

THE NAVE, LOOKING EAST.

often that we meet with such a combination of intellect and energy. Hexham and Ripon are two only of the many monasteries which he founded, and it is no slight honour to have aided the establishment of such abbeys as Ely and Evesham and Southwell. And though, doubtless, many would blame him for his appeals to Rome, he may be admired for the apostolic energy with which he threw himself into the evangelisation of Sussex—its inhabitants no better than heathens—their land desolated by famine—the emaciated natives so desperate as, grasping hold of each other's hands, to throw themselves from the cliffs into the sea, thus to end their misery. He died at Oundle, but his remains were carried, at his own request, to his old home at Ripon, being entombed at the south side of the altar. The abbey became one of the three great churches in Yorkshire, and the privilege of sanctuary and the right of using the ordeal were among the honours conferred upon it by Athelstan. The boundary of this place of refuge was marked afterwards by eight crosses, sur-

THE EXTERIOR, FROM THE SOUTH-EAST.

rounding the church, where the Archbishop of York claimed that his bailiffs had the right to meet the homicide, and, after oath, to admit him within the privileged jurisdiction. In after-years not the least profitable of the sources whence the fabric fund was derived was the money contributed by pilgrims at the shrine of St. Wilfrid. There has been much controversy as to the final resting-place of his body, but an indulgence of Archbishop Gray's states that it was then perfect at Ripon, and that it was exhibited to the worshipping beholders; and it has been recently conjectured by one of the learned that if one of the walls in the crypt were tapped, the remains of the patron saint might still be found.

But the present building had a Norman predecessor too, now only represented by the chapter-house and vestry, with the walls of the crypt below them, built either by Archbishop Thomas or Thurstan.

With these exceptions the church was rebuilt on an entirely new design by Archbishop Roger of York (1154—1181). He was one of the greatest men of his day, and had been in early life a companion of Becket at Canterbury. Later, however, he espoused the king's side; and it was Roger who gave the last account of Becket's doings to the king which led the four knights to determine on his murder, and though Roger purged himself by oath of all evil intent, he was regarded as a participator in the crime. He was one of the leaders in that great revolution of art which converted the heavy Romanesque into the light and lofty Gothic. The design of the nave and choir can only be partially gathered now from the small remains at either end of the nave, and other portions of the choir and transepts, but it is one of the most valuable specimens which we have of this great transition in architecture.

The next change in the building is attributed to Archbishop Gray, and consisted of the addition of the two western towers surmounted by leaded spires, and of the rebuilding of the façade which connects them—an excellent specimen of Early English. About 1280 the east end of the choir gave way, and was rebuilt. In the words of Sir Gilbert Scott—"It stands high among the productions of this admirable style. Its east window is a peculiarly fine one of seven lights, and all its details are excellent."

The church remained thus until the inroad of the Scots in 1319, who set fire to it, and destroyed some of the inmates. And a century had but just elapsed when it suffered from the attacks of an enemy even more irresistible than man's violence, in the shape of "thunder and lightning"; and the lantern tower became so ruinous that an indulgence was granted for forty days to all who gave towards its repair. The result you see as you walk up the nave—the widest of any cathedral in the kingdom, except those of York, Chichester, Winchester, and St. Paul's, measuring eighty-seven feet. For there meets the eye a strange admixture of Romanesque and Perpendicular in the arches supporting the central tower: a striking picture of time's ravages, preserving also for lovers of art marks of its stages.

The stall-work of the choir, which was begun in 1489, is very beautiful, and the misereres are very quaint. But it suffered much damage by-and-by, for in 1593 the central spire was partially destroyed by lightning, and the remainder of it fell after a time, destroying part of the choir-roof and stalls. Four years afterwards the two western spires were removed, for fear of a like catastrophe.

In 1842 an Order in Council called attention to the unsafe condition of the fabric, and immediate danger was warded off. But in 1861 it became evident that restoration on a large scale was imperative, and Sir Gilbert Scott was set to work. In so bad a state was the fabric found to be, that the sinkage had produced fissures from the base to the top of the towers! Wonderful were the means adopted to render them safe—the application of very powerful shoring to the walls, so that the towers were upheld for the time by artificial means, while better foundations were made. It is to be hoped that some day these restored towers may be surmounted, as of old, with timber and leaded spires. The restoration of the cathedral, which has been so judiciously carried out, at a cost of £40,000, has recently had its effect increased by external improvement in the opening out of the close, under the direction of the present dean.

A word or two about the monuments. In the north transept aisle is one that derives its interest not so much from the knight in armour representing one of the chivalric race of the Markenfields, as from its being the only example existing in England of an effigy bearing the unique collar of a park-pale and a stag couchant, the badge of Henry IV. Then there is close by a stone pulpit, of early Perpendicular character and of unusual form, as it is without a stem. In the nave there is a slab, on which is sculptured in low relief a man on his knees, with a gigantic lion in a grove of trees in the foreground. Tradition says that it covers the body of an Irish prince, who died at Ripon on his return from Palestine, whence he brought a lion that followed him with all the docility of a spaniel. It may have been the custom for the chapter tenants to pay their rents on this stone, as it was in York Minster on Haxby's tomb. Then there is a bust of the last Wakeman, and first Mayor of Ripon, and a statue of James I.

The celebrated bone-house is no more; it required a pit twelve feet deep to bury its contents in the churchyard. But though the dead bones are gone, there is plenty of life in the cathedral services, which are not a little assisted by the tones of a new organ of fine character, whose pneumatic action has to reach the length of 150 feet, and which possesses 44 sounding stops and 2,646 pipes.

H. D. CUST-NUNN.

THE EXTERIOR, FROM THE SOUTH-WEST.

CHICHESTER.

THE history of the Cathedral of Chichester is to be learnt chiefly from the study of its architectural details. Documents inform us only that the see of the Bishop of the South Saxons was removed from the village of Selsey to the city of Chichester in the reign of William the Conqueror; that the church, erected at Chiches- ter chiefly by Bishop Ralph Luffa, and consecrated in 1108, was largely injured by fire in 1114, and that Ralph was assisted by the liberality of Henry I. in the restoration of his building; that a second and far more serious fire, extending through the city, occurred in 1186; that the damage occasioned by this was repaired by Bishop Seffrid II. at great cost, and that the church was re- dedicated to the Holy Trinity with great pomp in 1199. Then we read of a licence from King John to bring marble from Purbeck in 1207. Among the remaining archives of the cathedral I have found that in the year 1234 great efforts were made for the reparation of the church, and that in 1239 a contract was entered into to glaze it "with picture and with history" in some, at least, of the windows. In 1247 there is a note that moneys left by the Bishop, Ralph Neville, to pay his debts to the canons, were devoted, at their instigation,

towards the "completion of a certain stone tower which had remained for a
long time unfinished, and which (it was hoped) would now rise in the form of
an elegant structure." About the same time we find that the canons remonstrated
with the Pope because he had directed that all prebends throughout the country
should remain vacant for twelve months, and their proceeds be devoted to the
church of Canterbury. The clergy of Chichester naturally claimed moneys so

THE INTERIOR, LOOKING EAST.

accruing in Chichester for the repairs of their own cathedral. Once more we
are told that Gilbert de S. Leofard (bishop 1288—1305) constructed from its
foundations the Lady Chapel. Then John Langton, Chancellor of England, and
bishop for thirty-two years after Gilbert's death, erected the great window in
the south transept; simultaneously, no doubt, he cased with ashlar the transept
itself, and built the chapter-room, of which more hereafter. Lastly, in 1411,
we hear of a campanile, as being, like other parts of the fabric, deformed and
ruinous. These are the only records which we have to prepare us for the lessons
which the building itself conveys.

s

These lessons are deeply interesting. They were first read out by Professor Willis, in one of those masterly lectures with which he delighted the members of the Archæological Institute. The Institute visited Chichester in 1853; the memoir was published after the spire had fallen in 1861.

There can be no doubt that the nave of the church was built in two portions. The ceiling originally was flat with the beams exposed. Choir and nave had each a single aisle to the north and south, with triforium galleries over; the transepts had no aisles. So the buttresses of the transepts were slight, for they had no thrust to meet: one may be seen in the present muniment room by the side of a larger buttress which became necessary when the roof of the transept was vaulted. The character of the aisles may be learnt by examining the arches leading into the western towers; they must have had simply cylindrical roofs: the galleries above still exhibit the springing of the arches which sustained their heavier covering. In the nave there was an early subsidence towards the south. Both walls exhibit this. The south is concave in the interior, the north convex, and the string-course of the gallery is far from being level. This subsidence must have preceded the fire of 1186; for it will be noticed that when the vaulted roof was built (as we shall explain ere long), and the vaulting shafts erected, these vaulting shafts did not follow the curvature of the walls, but were packed up behind with additional stonework where the wall of the church had fallen back. This may be seen, too, in the external parapets. Professor Willis showed that the east end was apsidal. He proved this by a marked feature in the windows of the choir triforium, and his statement is corroborated by a curious fragment—a curved stone slab found recently in the floor behind the present reredos. The altar, no doubt, stood in or near its present position, *i.e.*, in the chord of the arc of the apse; and the bishop's throne was behind the altar, as it was at Norwich, the Lady Chapel extending probably for a couple of bays—and so we have the church complete. The windows were all round-headed; one remains in the aisle of the choir, another may be seen blocked up in the passage between the south porch and the transept. The windows of the triforium were small and low. The south and north walls of the transepts must have resembled in great measure the western wall of the church. The passage under the upper row of windows, the clerestory, ran all round the building.

The fire of 1186 gave the occasion for all this to be altered. First it was determined that precautions should be taken against the recurrence of such a calamity, and it was resolved that the church should be vaulted. This entailed the flying buttresses and the vaulting shafts we have spoken of (clearly insertions in the older parts of the building). The height of the interior was necessarily much diminished. In the meantime the famous Council of the Lateran had affected the arrangements of the churches, and all over Europe was seen, to use the words of Guéranger, "the reconstruction of our cathedrals on a plan so mysteriously sublime." At Chichester the apse was removed, and the east end of the church made square—the two bays behind the reredos exhibit the date and character of this change—and the Lady Chapel was prolonged and beautified. But the diligent explorer may still see traces of the fire which gave the opportunity for all this, in the discoloured stones of the arches of the choir triforium. An oak beam over the choir was removed in 1862, which bore substantial marks of having been exposed to the severity of the flames in 1186!

The piers of the central tower were, like the other piers and walls of the church, composed of rubble stone set in mortar and cased with ashlar. This central tower, even after it was partly rebuilt after the fire of 1186, rose only a little above the gables of the roofs, as was discovered shortly before the fall. The building of the grander tower, which was assigned by Professor Willis to the second quarter of the thirteenth century (a date which agrees very satisfactorily with our notice of the "certain stone tower" in 1247), was commenced in ignorance of the extreme weakness of the substructure; and on the summit of this tower, in the same ignorance, was erected in the fifteenth century the beautiful spire. Subsidence followed, and an attentive visitor may observe in the most eastern bay on the north side of the nave an indication of the apprehensions that ensued. The arch is strengthened by an inner arch, diminishing its span. Indeed, the whole of the great works intended to beautify the cathedral increased its weakness. The south-west corner of the tower was weakened by the grand staircase carried up to the chapter-room; the south transept was weakened by the beautiful window of Bishop Langton; the north transept by the large window placed in it. Attempts, producing not very graceful results, were made to prevent the arches over these windows from spreading. Ultimately the weight of the gables was diminished by removing the greater part of the gables themselves. They were replaced by Dean Chandler. But, earlier than this, the bells were removed from the central tower. These were placed, first in the south-west corner of the church; then the magnificent campanile was erected to receive them. But it seems to have been erected for a further purpose. Its massive walls, the strength of its buttresses, and other details show that it was intended to carry a lofty spire. The authorities seem to have despaired of saving the central structure of the cathedral itself.

The history of the last thirty years has exhibited the reasonableness of these apprehensions. The long desire of Dean Chandler (one of the greatest and most far-seeing of cathedral dignitaries) had been to utilise the nave of the church, and the first special services in a cathedral nave were held at Chichester He left some money for the building, and his executors, in conjunction with an influential committee, resolved in 1859 to remove the beautiful but somewhat frail screen which separated the choir from the nave. The committee soon became aware of the danger they had to contend with; the piers of the tower were found to be rotten. There was no adhesion in the core. Every effort was made to renew the piers, but every effort was useless. A heavy gale on the night of Wednesday, February 20th, 1861, precipitated the calamity; and on the next day, at about twenty minutes past one in the afternoon, the writer saw the spire move gently and bodily towards the south-west, then it seemed to recover itself, and spire and tower sank out of sight, with little noise, into the centre of the building. With the exception

THE CATHEDRAL, FROM THE NORTH-EAST.

of the capstone, which fell upon one of the flying buttresses of the nave, every stone fell within the church. The weather-cock alone was picked up in the churchyard, and a heap of disintegrated materials filled the cross of the church up to the level of the triforium.

We need not describe the rebuilding. The work was placed under the care of the late Sir Gilbert Scott, and it never ceased until the church was re-opened in November, 1867. The Duke of Richmond was mainly instrumental in carrying the work to its successful conclusion, as is commemorated in the notes left by Sir Gilbert Scott. Much, too, was due to the bishop and the dean.

But we must proceed to describe the rest of the church. At some early time the height of the aisles was raised by sacrificing the level of the galleries above, and these galleries became practically useless. Simultaneously the arches from the aisles into the transepts were rebuilt in the Pointed style. The nave (almost alone of English naves) appears to have two aisles on either side. A slight amount of attention will show that this appearance is due to the erection of a series of chapels, three upon the south and two upon the north, at dates slightly varying. These chapels opened into the aisles; each had its own altar and its own reredos; in some cases a substantial wall. These intervening walls must have been removed at the Reformation, and the present appearance produced. In consequence most of the early windows in the nave have disappeared. One (as we have said already) may be seen, blocked up, in the passage between the south porch and the transept; another, with its form slightly pointed, almost

CHICHESTER, FROM THE SOUTH-EAST MEADOWS.

immediately opposite. The old string-course may be traced at intervals along the original south wall of the nave aisle, showing that the wall of the church was merely pierced when the entrances to the chapels were formed. There is much interest connected with the western towers. The south tower awaits a thorough restoration, when it ought to be made as beautiful a feature of the cathedral as the corresponding tower at Ely. The north tower needs to be rebuilt entirely. For many years there was a tradition that this tower was battered down by the cannon of the Commonwealth, during the famous siege of Chichester. But the writer discovered some years ago a memorandum of a visit of inspection from Sir Christopher Wren, where it was stated that the tower had *fallen* some fifty years before his visit. The recommendations of the great architect were characteristic of the time and of the man. He said the west end never could have been beautiful or uniform. He advised, therefore, that the remaining tower should be removed, the church cut short a bay, and a fair front erected towards the west. Happily, either he had not influence, or the chapter had not money, to carry out his proposal.   This ruined tower was for many years blocked out from the cathedral, but about ten years ago one of the arches was opened.   It was not deemed safe to open the other into the aisle.   As he proceeds to the east the visitor should notice the perspective looking diagonally across the church.   In the north transept he will see a curious series of paintings, intended to represent the bishops from the foundation of the see at Selsey to the time of Sherborne.   These were all painted by an Italian—one Bernardi—during the episcopate of the last-named benefactor of the church.   The legends attached to the names are interesting.   Then the chapel to the east of this is deserving of inspection.   Its one pillar, supporting the floor above, is characteristic, and the vaulting is well worthy of notice.   Here, too, may be seen, in part, the exterior of one of the original cathedral windows, and further portions may be examined above in the dilapidated chamber which once contained the library of the cathedral, but of which the roof was dropped and the windows almost entirely blocked, within the last two hundred years.   In the present library are a few curiosities, as a genuine Abraxas ring, found on the finger of one of the early bishops, whose tomb it was necessary to remove.   It was above the level of the floor.   Then there is a cross of lead discovered on the breast of another bishop, commemorating his absolution.   His name is not to be seen among the series painted under Sherborne's order.   Another interesting relic is the Litany of the great reforming continental prelate, whose death caused such joy at the opening of the Council of Trent—Archbishop Herman of Cologne.   This was Cranmer's copy, and has his signature on the title-page. There can be little doubt that this very volume furnished the model for the English Litany.   Passing eastward along the aisle of the choir, the visitor will notice one or two monuments of early bishops, then an interesting stone (originally on the platform behind the reredos) of beautiful design—two hands holding a heart-formed vessel, with the legend fast disappearing, " ICI GIST LE COEVR DE MAVDE . . ."   And so we pass to the Lady Chapel.

The Lady Chapel is said to have been built or rebuilt from its foundations by Bishop Gilbert de S. Leofard.   No doubt this bishop repaired and enlarged it.   On the roof may be seen some remains of the original beautiful colouring. In one or two of the western bays—west, that is, of the entrance to the chapel proper—may be seen the motto of Winchester School, the favourite of Sherborne. In the middle of last century this building was said to be a ruin, and the crypt was placed at the disposal of the family of the Dukes of Richmond for a mausoleum.   The floor was raised to give the necessary height below, and then the windows were partly plastered up and partly glazed, and the books which had again begun to accumulate were placed in the building, and a grand fireplace erected against the east window.   So it was when Professor

Willis paid his visit, and good reason had he to lament that the unfortunate position of the sepulchral vault of the Richmond family had robbed the chapel of its due proportions. And so it continued until 1867. The upper part of the walls, which enclosed the library, was then removed, and the beauty of its roof was seen in the choir; and when Bishop Ashhurst Turner Gilbert died in 1870 after an episcopate of nearly thirty years, and the desire was felt to restore to his memory the chapel which had been built by a former Bishop Gilbert nearly six hundred years before, the Duke of Richmond allowed the floor to be lowered, and an immense improvement was effected. The stained glass, commemorating events in the life of the Virgin, has of course been added since.

The visitor, as he passes along, will see the monument of Bishop Sherborne, who held the see during a great portion of the troublous reign of Henry VIII., and the cenotaph of the celebrated Dr. Hook, who was dean from 1859 to 1874. He will notice the two curious panels of carved stone, representing, the one the healing of the blind man at Jericho, the other the raising of Lazarus. They were found behind the panels of the stalls, imbedded in the piers, about fifty years ago, and repieced and placed here. The recumbent figure in the south transept is often said to represent St. Richard of Chichester, to whose shrine pilgrimages were made, much to the benefit of the cathedral, before the Reformation. But his "shrine" was destroyed at that time, and in the cathedral documents this effigy is said to be that of Bishop Robert Stratford (1337—1362). The canopy that was over this tomb was destroyed at the fall. The adjacent paintings were by Bernardi, and were intended to represent, the one the landing of Wilfrid in the seventh century, the other the petition of Sherborne to Henry VIII. in the sixteenth. Under Bishop Langton's window may be seen the remains of his monument, and also the monument of Mr. Abel Smith, of Dale Park. The ancient sacristry is well worthy of attention, as is also its ancient door and lock. A handsome staircase (to the construction of which attention has already been drawn, as contributing to the weakness of the building) leads from the church to the room above. This room is described as the bishop's chapter-house, and the bishop's seat may still be seen in it. The staircase was adapted for grand processions. There is in this room a sliding panel, covering the entrance to a secret chamber, where, doubtless, the chief treasures of the church were kept when not in use. There is a record that, when the cathedral was in the power of the Commonwealth forces, one of the servants betrayed the place where the treasures were deposited. The troops were not likely to have discovered it otherwise. The visitor must not believe that the Lollards were confined here, whatever guides or guide-books may affirm. The "bishop's prison" was in the bishop's gateway.

The choir of the church retains scarcely anything ancient. At some period since Bishop Sherborne's time it had become blocked with pews and galleries, and a clean sweep was necessary, and some of the stalls alone remain of the more ancient structure. These stalls are assigned, as in other cathedrals of the old foundation, to the dean, precentor, chancellor, treasurer, archdeacon, prebendaries, and each officer is installed on his appointment with much ceremony, "staff as to spirituals, loaf as to temporals," but the seat is the only property to which he can now claim a right. One of these stalls was found to preserve its ancient decoration. The bishop's throne is modern. The reredos (not yet completed) was the first, I believe, in England, in which the Ascension of our Lord replaced the figure of the Crucified.

The window of the transept has been recently filled with stained glass, the character of which has been found to raise up the thoughts and aspirations of some as much as or even more than it is found fault with by others. The glass was executed at Bar-le-Duc, being completed at the expense of the family of the late John Abel Smith, Esq., who was anxious to leave behind him this memorial of his attachment to the cathedral church of the city, whose interests he had watched for many years as its representative in Parliament.

We have little space to commemorate the worthies of the cathedral. Most of the bishops of distinction we have named—St. Richard, Langton, Stratford, and Sherborne. Another, Reginald Pecock, fell under the displeasure of the Church. To escape burning he recanted; but he was deprived and banished to one of the abbeys in the Cambridge fen country, where he was allowed to perish by cold. Several distinguished men of later dates have been consecrated to the bishopric of Chichester and then have been translated, as Andrews, Brian Duppa, Gunning, Patrick, and Maltby. The celebrated Chillingworth was buried in the cloisters. His tomb was opened by the Parliamentary forces, who fired into his coffin, "nec sensit damna sepulcri," as his epitaph runs. The famous Edmund Gibson was canon and precentor before his elevation to the see of London. The deanery was rebuilt by another notable of his day, Thomas Sherlock, who became successively Bishop of Bangor, Salisbury, and London. I have spoken of the obligations of the church to Dean Chandler. But the most celebrated of all our deans was Dr. Hook, who, after his retirement from his labours at Leeds, devoted the last fifteen years of his life to Chichester, where he penned his great historical work, "The Lives of the Archbishops of Canterbury." On leaving Leeds he told his parishioners that, if he did not find at Chichester sufficient work for his energies, he should make work. He found work in the renovating and rebuilding of his cathedral; he made work in the library of his deanery.

C. A. SWAINSON.

ST. ALBANS, FROM VERULAM.

ST. ALBANS.

Iᴛ is but recently that this abbey church has been entitled to rank among the cathedrals of England, for the bishopric of St. Albans was only constituted in the year 1877. Previously it had been included in the diocese of Rochester, but when that was limited to the southern bank of the Thames, certain additions were made to the part lying north of that river, and St. Albans gave the name to and became the cathedral town of the new diocese; the Right Rev. T. L. Claughton—at that time Bishop of Rochester—becoming first Bishop of St. Albans. The new-formed diocese has, at present, neither dean nor canons residentiary; but is fortunate in finding ready to hand one of the grandest and the most interesting churches of England as its cathedral.

In few districts are we carried further back in the history of our country than in the immediate neighbourhood of St. Albans. The site of the abbey church was "holy ground" long before the mission of Augustine: on the opposite slope, on the other side of the little river Ver, still remain ruins of the Roman town of Verulamium. Earthworks in the neighbourhood are said to be remnants of the stronghold (*oppidum*) of Cassivelaunus, chief of the Cassii, which

T

was stormed by the troops of Cæsar. Near to or in some part of this was founded the first Roman city built in Britain; whose site is still indicated by fragments of ruined walls and great tree-covered mounds. It was stormed and sacked by the British forces in the revolt headed by Boadicea, and it was again rebuilt when the Iceni had been subdued by the legions of Suetonius Paulinus.

The event which led to the foundation and the fame of the abbey church is said to have occurred about the end of the third century in the Diocletian persecution. At that time a young Roman of good family, named Alban, was living at Verulamium. Though he was a pagan, one of the Christian priests, who were being everywhere hunted down, sought refuge in his house. In the few days of his sojourn Amphibalus, the fugitive, had gained his host as a convert, and when his hiding-place was discovered Alban dismissed Amphibalus, and wrapping himself in the priest's robes, awaited the arrival of the soldiers. On being taken before the prefect, the deception was of course discovered. Alban declared himself a Christian, and was led forth to Holmhurst, the hill across the Ver, to execution.

Miracles, the legend tells us, were duly wrought, but at last the saint's head was smitten off and he was buried at the place of doom. Amphibalus also, before long, was captured and tortured to death at Redburn, a village on the Watling Street Road, about four miles from St. Albans. Time went on, persecution ceased, and the Roman Empire became Christian. The heresy of Pelagius disturbed the peace of the church, and brought to England Germanus of Auxerre and Lupus of Troyes. During their visit the remains of Alban were solemnly exhumed, and a small wooden chapel was built to mark the sacred spot. A synod was also held at Verulamium in the year 401.

But evil times were yet to come, when the heathen English invaded the land. The chapel perished; even the memory of the site was lost. Not till the later part of the eighth century does a continuous history begin for St. Albans Abbey. At that time Offa, King of Mercia, smitten by remorse for a treacherous murder, decided to found an abbey in honour of St. Alban. The martyr's remains were discovered, as chroniclers say, miraculously, by the leading of a star, and a little church was built upon the spot. Offa then departed to Rome, and on his return founded and richly endowed a monastery for monks of the Benedictine order. A little town, as was natural, grew up around the new abbey. Roman Verulamium became wholly deserted, and its ruins the haunts of wild beasts and of evil characters. Shortly before the Norman Conquest it was determined to rebuild the minster. For this purpose Abbot Eadmer and his successor collected materials, using the ruins of Verulam for a quarry. Its accomplishment was delayed by the coming of the Norman invader, whom the

English monks and their abbot resisted to the utmost of their power, and the work did not begin till Paul of Caen, a Norman, was appointed Abbot of St. Albans by William. With the materials already collected and others from the same sources, he erected a great church on the ancient site. Many changes have since been made, as will be described below, but the transepts, central tower, eastern part of the nave, with a few small portions of the choir, were the work of Paul of Caen.

The town of St. Albans is built upon the edge of an upland plateau, and straggles downwards towards the river on the west and south-east. The church is built just at the edge of the plateau, where it begins to round off for the descent towards the valley. On the northern side it was near to the houses of the town, which, since the Reformation, have encroached upon its precincts; on the slopes towards the south stood the monastic buildings. These have disappeared with the exception of the principal entrance, a work—though somewhat altered in later years—of the latter part of the fourteenth century. Only some inequalities in the turf, or some chance scrap of wall hidden in a garden, mark the site of one of the most famous of the Benedictine monasteries of Britain.

A glance at the abbey church shows it to be unique in England. The long ridge line of the nave roof, the massive central tower, the prominent transepts, like it, except for some later insertions, of the simplest Norman architecture and built of Roman brick, and then the great and more varied extension eastward, show that we have before us a building of no ordinary interest and no common design. The western front is obviously new, for it was rebuilt only a very few years since. It is, however, to a great extent a reproduction of the façade which was begun by John de Sella about the end of the twelfth century, and completed, after interruption, by William of Trumpington.

This façade had been defaced in the middle part of the fifteenth century, by the insertion of a huge Perpendicular window of mechanical design, and in the subsequent ill fortunes of the abbey, it had been hacked and patched with the commonest materials and in the most unskilful way, till only the practised eye could recognise the traces of its former beauty. The present façade is composed of a centre, flanked by rather lofty wings ending in turrets—slightly in the style of Salisbury—the latter are to a certain extent screens, as the wall is carried up beyond the level of the aisle roof. Each is pierced by a door in front of which is a deep porch, and the upper part is relieved by a double row of arcades, while in the centre is a fine Decorated window, in design rather later than the rest of the façade, and there is a doorway and porch below. For the lower stage and for the arcades sufficient fragments of early work were left to enable the architect to reproduce to a great extent the ancient design, and some portion of the work of John de Sella still remains incorporated in the porches.   Shortly before the rebuilding of this façade a new and high pitched roof had been placed upon the nave, which is now terminated by a gable pierced with lancet windows, rising behind an open-work stone balustrade.

It may be convenient, while still standing outside the cathedral, to enumerate briefly the main epochs of building or reconstruction which are recorded in its

THE TOWER.

walls.   Paul of Caen, as has been said, was the builder of St. Albans Abbey on its present scale.   He erected, using as his materials, almost exclusively, Roman bricks, taken from the ruins of Verulam, a church whose dimensions, except at the eastern part, corresponded with the present.   Its total length was 450 feet; its plan was a Latin cross with well developed arms, the nave being 285 feet long; the choir as usual having an apsidal termination.   Partly from the nature of the materials, possibly from a desire to gratify the feelings of the brotherhood, the style of Paul's building is of an archaic simplicity. It seems as if it might be a century older than, instead of almost contemporary with, the work of Gundulf at Rochester and of Walkelyn at Winchester.   Rather more than a century later the architects began upon the west front.   John de Sella pulled down, two or three years before the end of the twelfth century, the Norman western towers, and commenced the erection of a grand façade in the Early English style, but, as the chroniclers say, he was one of those who began to build without counting the cost, and the work soon came to a standstill.   It was, however, completed (except the towers) by William of Trumpington, his successor, by whom the four adjoining bays on the northern and the five on the southern side of the nave were rebuilt.   About the year 1256 John de Hertford rebuilt the choir, and began the elaborate group of chapels to the east; the Lady Chapel, by which the whole was terminated, appears not to have been completed till about the year 1320.   Very soon after this, in the year 1323, two of the Norman piers on the south side of the nave fell with a great crash, and caused the ruin of about a hundred feet of the roof. In consequence of this five bays of the Norman work were rebuilt in the Decorated order. After this little was done till nearly a century had passed, when Whethamstede was appointed abbot. He ruled from 1420 to 1440, and then resigned, but on the death of his successor in 1452 he was again elected, and so remained in office till his death twelve years later. In his days great changes, mostly for the worse, were made. The high

pitched roofs were removed from the nave, its aisles, and the transepts, and replaced by structures of a lower pitch. Huge windows were inserted in the west façade, and in the two ends of the transept,* and the older work generally was considerably maltreated. Wallingford, appointed abbot in 1476, erected the grand screen behind the high altar, and with this practically ends the history of pre-Reformation work at St. Albans.

THE CHOIR, LOOKING EAST.

The building suffered severely after the suppression of the monasteries. Incredible as it may seem, this noble abbey, with its historic memories, would have been destroyed by the ruthless barbarians who disgraced the English Reformation, had not the townsfolk of St. Albans come forward and purchased it as their parish church. At this time a passage was driven through the building east of the retrochoir, the arches communicating with the latter being walled up, and the Lady

* Mr. J. Chapple, who was clerk of the works to Sir G. G. Scott, and continued in charge of the restoration after Sir Gilbert's death, informs me that the reckless way in which Whethamstede's architects executed their task of "beautifying" the ancient structure, has nearly brought about its ruin. By cutting away the solid masonry of the end walls, in order to insert their huge windows, they destroyed what was essential constructively in order to bind together the side walls; hence these slowly inclined outwards under the pressure of the roof, and would probably have fallen in no long time had not the late restoration been begun. I am greatly indebted to the kindness of this gentleman for much unpublished information connected with the architecture of the abbey, and the history of its restoration.

Chapel converted into a school.   Visitors who feel inclined to be severe upon the injuries wrought on this and other parts of the fabric, must bear in mind that the townsfolk had acquired a building out of all proportion to their wants, the proper maintenance of which would have been a constant and heavy expense, and that but for this St. Albans would have been now as the cathedral of Coventry or the neighbouring nunnery of Sopewell.   Repairs were undertaken now and again in the later part of the seventeenth and in the eighteenth century : one of them being the restoration of the south transept window, blown in by the gale of 1703, but it was not till the present century that any serious attempt at restoration was made. Mr. Cottingham carried on some important works in 1832, and in 1856 some more was done by Sir G. G. Scott.   Still, on both these occasions the difficulty of raising adequate funds prevented any very systematic restoration of the building.   But in the year 1870 the church may be said to have taken matters into its own hands.   On the 1st of August it became evident "that the central tower was cracking up and falling !"   The architect was at once summoned by his clerk of the works, and quickly saw that the reported danger was only too true.   The tower was shored up by immense balks of timber, but for more than six months the workmen ran a race with ruin, and only won by a neck.   The piers were then strengthened and in part rebuilt, the tower was clamped by iron bolts, and the whole, we may trust, made secure for generations to come.   The passage which cut off the Lady Chapel was closed, the school was transferred to the old gateway, and the restoration of the eastern portion of the church was commenced.   The next step was to lift the roof off the nave and screw back the walls to a vertical position.   After the death of Sir G. G. Scott, it was decided to replace Whethamstede's roof by one of the original pitch, and to rebuild the west front.   This decision gave rise to great controversy, and to the secession of some of those who up to this period had taken an active part in the restoration.   Into this contest it is not within our purpose to enter.   The whole question of restoration is ever a thorny one, and there will always be the two camps.   Our own sympathies are generally with the more conservative, but we must frankly admit that the west front of St. Albans was hopelessly mutilated, and for two centuries at least had been patched with heterogeneous materials of the commonest kind ; Whethamstede's great window being the only mediæval feature in respectable condition, and this, as we have seen, was in itself an intrusion.   The façade was past " restoration ;" the choice lay between the merest repair and reconstruction, and there can be no question that even if critics may differ about portions of the present work, it is one worthy of a great cathedral.

On entering the nave, we have right and left of us the beautiful Early English work of William of Trumpington—arches, triforium, and clerestory.   We find our view is somewhat limited by the stone screen, against which once stood the altar of St. Cuthbert, a work of the fourteenth century ; above this now rises the organ, which, on the eastern side, is supported by a handsome new screen of carved oak. Thus three bays of the nave are now occupied by seats. On the northern side the rude Norman work of Paul of Caen still remains; on the southern is the Decorated reconstruction described above, which harmonises well with the more western part of the nave, but is still more ornate. In the transept and tower, of which two stages are visible from within, we have in the main the original Norman work, and the singular columns of the triforium cannot but attract attention. So archaic are some of their patterns that some antiquarians have suggested that they once formed a part of the Saxon church. The floor of the northern transept is at a higher level than that of the southern; the building also rises eastward by a series of steps till the site of the high altar is reached. The south transept leads into a remarkable, rather late Norman, annexe, which formed the slype of the old monastery. The choir is almost closed eastward by the magnificent screen of Wallingford, which once was adorned by figures, and has considerable resemblance to that at Winchester. It has been lately restored, and figures have been replaced in the numerous niches. The choir has been repaved with embossed encaustic tiles, made from an old pattern, which still remained in the building, but a considerable part of the floor towards the east is covered with marble slabs, from most of which, unfortunately, the brasses have been torn away. The arches which separate the choir from the nave are blocked up for the present, but in the one north of the altar is the magnificent chantry chapel of Abbot Ramryge, who died about 1509, and on the south, that of Abbot Whethamstede; on the floor is temporarily laid a magnificent brass commemorating Abbot de la Mare, the host of John of France. The extreme east of the choir, behind Wallingford's great screen, forms the chapel of St. Alban, in which his relics were preserved. At the dissolution of the monasteries the shrine was destroyed, and for long its only memorial was the Purbeck marble slab in the pavement on which it once stood. But during the late restorations some carved fragments were discovered, which the supervisors shrewdly suspected had belonged to it; careful search was made, under floors and wherever openings had been blocked, with the result that almost the whole of the shrine has been recovered, the pieces have been skilfully fitted together, and this beautiful relic of mediæval workmanship has been replaced in its former position. The style is Early Decorated. Another relic, hardly less interesting, has been preserved intact, this is the "Watching Gallery," a richly-carved oak structure in two stages, placed on the north side of the shrine. The lower part contains cupboards, probably for smaller relics and ecclesiastical vessels. South of the shrine is the monumental chantry—erected by Abbot Whethamstede, to Humphrey the "Good Duke" of Gloucester. Though his rank was only equalled by the love borne him by the people, he saw his wife led in penance through the streets on a charge of witchcraft, and was found dead in his bed, not without suspicions that if the Duke of Suffolk and Cardinal Beaufort had wished it, his life would have been longer. A rude painting represents the condition in which his body was found in 1703. So great was the veneration of our ancestors for everything ancient, that for years visitors to the abbey were allowed to carry away the duke's bones as "curiosities!"

Some restorations have been accomplished, besides its restitution to the church.

ST. ALBAN'S SHRINE.

in the eastern part where the retro-choir joins the Lady Chapel. This was to a large extent effected by the exertions of a committee of ladies, headed by the Marchioness of Salisbury, but the devastation of this part of the building has been fearful, the carved work in many places having been completely hacked away, and even the ashlar now and then stripped from the walls, so that in parts "restoration," in any strict sense of the word, is impossible. During the work considerable fragments of the shrine of St. Amphibalus were found, and these have been fitted together and placed east of the retro-choir. Though the recovery has been less complete than in the other case, we are enabled to form a very fair idea of the original structure.

Of the famous men once connected with the monastery of St. Albans our space does not permit us to write. Kings of England, from the days of the Norman Conqueror downwards, came to pay their devotions at the shrine of the great English saint. Hither was brought Henry VI., a captive after his defeat at the first battle of St. Albans, and here again, released from captivity, he came to offer thanks after the second and far the more fortunate battle. John of France also, after Poitiers, was committed to the custody of Abbot de la Mare. Great men were these mitred abbots; they even disputed priority with Westminster. They had at one time the power of life and death, and held large estates. Towards the end of the lists appears the name of Cardinal Wolsey, who held the office *in commendam*. The members of the foundation were often honourably distinguished for learning. Among them are found the names of Matthew Paris and other chroniclers. Adrian IV., the only English pope, when a young man, in vain sought admission into the order. He was at that time too unlettered for the fraternity. "In the days when an emperor held his stirrup he probably regarded with complacency his failure at St. Albans."

Important changes have within the last few years been made in the process of restoration, or, as some would call it, destruction. The roofs of the transepts have been raised to the same pitch as that of the nave; their ends, north and south, have been to a great extent reconstructed. In the north one a huge circular window replaces the fifteenth-century intruder; in the south one five lancets have been inserted, which internally appear of the same height, and externally rise to the centre light, an arrangement gratifying to those who stickle for truth in architecture. The corner turrets have been "restored;" picturesque formerly, they are now hideous. The old windows had not much to commend them, and were vandalisms in their day; but they had acquired a certain historical interest of which the new are wholly destitute. These are no more congruous with the rest of the architecture, and are rather commonplace as designs. But the worst act of vandalism—for no milder term can be used—is the destruction of the ancient slype. Its mangled remains are now inserted as "curiosities" in the new structure which replaces it,* and underneath the window of the south transept. It is melancholy to see what mischief zeal without discretion has wrought recently at St. Albans. Much as the present rector, Archdeacon Lawrance, has done to save his church from falling down, he will not receive unmixed praise from posterity, and the Bishop of the Diocese cannot be justified for facilitating the indulgence of architectural vagaries in a building of national interest.

T. G. BONNEY.

* That is to say, the remains have been dismembered (after the modern fashion of murdering), and are found in two places.

U

ROCHESTER.

THE see of Rochester is the daughter of that of Canterbury: the first outpost advanced by Augustine from his settlement in the palace of Ethelbert. Its cathedral bears also a strong family likeness to the mother church. Here, and at London simultaneously, he established new sees seven years after his own landing in Thanet. The situation was well selected for a missionary church. Hrofs ceastre—now Rochester—was a fortified station on the line of the great highway of the Watling Street, commanding the point where it crossed the Medway; and the bishopric, of which it was the cathedral town, included the western part of Kent. Justus was the first bishop, one of the band who had come to strengthen the hands of Augustine after his arrival in England; and he, after twenty years of work—at one time troublous, when Ethelbert's son relapsed into paganism—was translated to Canterbury. Paulinus, also the great missionary of the North, after his expulsion from York, undertook the charge of Rochester. Here he died, and was buried in the cathedral, of which his shrine was for long one of the chief attractions.

Of the building in which he worshipped—the church, which according to Bede, was built by Ethelbert himself—no trace remains. The situation by the Medway, which had once been an advantage, became a bane in the days of the Danish rovers. The cathedral fared no better than Canterbury, and when William the Norman came to England it was greatly ruined. After the Conquest, Gundulf—a friend of Lanfranc's and a mighy builder—was appointed Bishop of Rochester. The earliest parts of the present cathedral are his work; to him also the keep of the neighbouring castle as well as the White Tower in London are attributed. Doubts have been expressed concerning his hand in these, and probably most of the cathedral which now remains is of slightly later date, but still the Norman part of Rochester was begun by Bishop Gundulf.

As has been already said, there are many respects in which the material fabric of Rochester proclaims its relationship with Canterbury. In an important one however, it differs; that, though the relics of Paulinus, and still more those of St. William of Perth, brought to it pilgrims and wealth, Rochester never enjoyed that full tide of gifts which flowed into the coffers at the shrine of Thomas, and so does not exhibit that efflorescence of architectural splendour which makes the eastern end of Canterbury in some respects unique in England. The plan of Rochester is simpler; beyond its eastern transept it has only a comparatively short chancel; its architecture is less ornate, its shrines occupied less commanding positions. In another respect also it differs from Canterbury, and that for the worse; it is far more closely hemmed in with buildings, so that it is extremely difficult to obtain a good view of the cathedral, indeed it is better seen from the keep of the old castle than from any position on the ground itself.

Externally the cathedral cannot be called an impressive building. Small in itself, there is nothing in its outline to enhance its dimensions or appeal to the senses by grace of outline instead of grandeur of size. It is without western towers; and the central one is low and squat; at a glance it proclaims itself modern or modernised, and is no better, perhaps worse, than most Gothic of the early Victorian period. We pass from the High Street of Rochester beneath one of the old gateways of the monastery, now almost buried in houses, through a comparatively narrow passage into the precincts of the cathedral. The view, however, of its western part is impeded by the Church of St. Nicholas, which stands immediately to the south of the western end of the nave, and after passing this we reach the little open space in front of the main entrance. Here, if we are readers of Dickens, we may remember how he has interwoven the chief features of the scene with the story of his last and unfinished work, and if it be summer-time, through the open west door of the cathedral we may look "down the throat of old time." The west front is not the least noted part of Rochester Cathedral; in its main outlines it is Norman, although it did not escape the vulgar hands of fifteenth-century "improvers," and was disfigured by the insertion of a commonplace Perpendicular window. This has deprived us, as at Norwich and at so many other places, of a perfect and, as far as we can conjecture, a very pretty piece of Norman work. The design consists of a centre of the width of the nave, flanked with turrets, only one of which remains in its original condition, and two wings formed by the side aisles. It is ornamented by a series of arcades, and has an extremely beautiful though rather small centre doorway. The design of this, according to Mr. Fergusson, is Continental rather than English; two of its shafts are carved with figures, supposed to represent Henry I. and "Good Queen Maud." The nave is in great part Norman, but the fifteenth-century "improvers" rebuilt the clerestory and raised the roof (which is of wood and plain), thereby destroying the harmony of its well-balanced composition. The nave-arches and piers, though simple in design, are good in execution, and the triforium, which is made an important feature, is more richly ornamented than is usual. By a subsequent heightening of the side aisles, the usual gallery above the latter has been destroyed, so that the triforium arches are now visible on both sides from within the church. The two last bays to the east are Early English work, and show the influence of the school of architecture which left so conspicuous a mark on Canterbury. So far as one can judge there seems to have been an intention of rebuilding the nave, but this, we may say, fortunately, was not carried out, as thus a very interesting relic of Norman work has been spared. As the connection between the two cathedrals has always been close—Ernulf, once Prior of Canterbury, having been among the Bishops of Rochester, and a zealous architect at both—it is very probable that in the nave of the latter, begun by Gundulf, and perhaps brought very near completion by Ernulf himself, we can obtain some idea of what the Norman nave of Canterbury

ROCHESTER, FROM THE RIVER.

was like. The Cathedral of Rochester, and especially its nave, has not fared well. Twice in the twelfth century it suffered severely from fire, but exactly how much and what damage was done on those occasions we do not know, or in what parts the flames were most destructive. When the castle was besieged in 1264 by Simon of Montfort, his soldiers plundered and grievously injured the cathedral, converting the nave into a stable, setting an example which the Puritans afterwards followed. These were saved the trouble of breaking the stained glass windows—a favourite occupation, as it gratified both iconoclastic zeal, and the destructive impulse in human nature that makes pelting a bottle so pleasurable a pastime—because they seem to have been smashed or stolen after the dissolution of the monastery. The brasses, however, in which, as we can see from their moulds in the monumental slabs, the church was very rich, disappeared then, and the nave was long used as a carpenter's shop, several saw-pits being dug in it.

Like the two eastern bays, the transepts are Early English, though not all of the same date, and they recall the work of the two Williams at Canterbury. On the southern side of the nave, just west of the transept, is a chapel dedicated to St. Mary, a Perpendicular structure, recently restored; and in the same transept is the monument to one Richard Watts, a local worthy in the days of Elizabeth, whose memory is kept green by the hospital which he founded and endowed for the nightly entertainment of six poor travellers, "pro-

THE NAVE.

vided they be not rogues nor proctors."

As at Canterbury, the choir is to an exceptional degree shut off from the nave. It is enclosed by a stone screen, and approached by a flight of steps, the latter construction being rendered necessary by the crypt beneath the eastern part of the church. In the larger cathedral this arrangement enhances the idea of magnitude, in the smaller it has, we think, an opposite effect. The choir especially seems narrow and cramped. Its architecture is rather heavy, and it produces on the whole an "imprisoned" feeling. The style is Early English, but the exact date is not known; it was, however, completed before 1227. The most marked peculiarity is in the western part of the choir, which is

THE CHOIR.

ENTRANCE TO THE CHAPTER-HOUSE FROM
THE TRANSEPT.

entirely shut off from the aisles, and does not seem to have ever communicated with them, the wall appearing to be perfectly solid up to the clerestory. The stalls are wholly without canopies, and the wall behind is adorned with diaper painting, this being a restoration of ancient work.　On the north side is a rather narrow aisle, interrupted by a flight of steps ; on the southern a much wider aisle, with a curious roof.　From this the crypt is approached, and another flight of steps leads through a doorway into the south-eastern transept. These eastern transepts—entirely open to the choir, and so available during the time of service—with their comparatively broad eastern aisle, give this portion of the choir a spacious aspect, contrasting with the narrowness of the western part, and the architecture in many respects recalls the work of " English William " at Canterbury. Farther east is the short chancel, with its double eastern triplet of lancet windows, one of the late restorations.　Purbeck marble is freely used in the decoration of this part, and the contrast between it and the western portion is very singular.

In the northern choir-transept was St. William's tomb, and on a flat stone in the middle of the same transept his shrine is said to have rested.　St. William was a worthy baker of Perth, noted for his liberality to the poor.　He undertook a pilgrimage to the Holy Land, and intended to visit the throne of Becket on his way, but without going so far as Gadshill he fell among thieves, who were worse than those on the descent to Jericho, for they left him quite dead. His corpse was brought to Rochester and solemnly interred.　Presently miracles began to be wrought at his tomb, and he who had been a pilgrim himself became the cause of pilgrimage in others.　The offerings of the faithful paid for the building of the eastern part of the church.　St. William was murdered in 1201, and was canonised fifty years afterwards.

The pavement of the choir—encaustic tiles—is modern ; so are all the fittings, as well as the communion-table and the handsome reredos.　In fact, the whole of this part of the cathedral was remodelled in Sir G. G. Scott's restoration, which was completed some few years since.　The nave, as we have said, is destitute of monuments of any interest, but several remain in the choir.　Purbeck marble is the material commonly used.　In the north choir-transept is a fine canopied monument, greatly restored, which marks the resting-place of Walter de Merton, once Bishop of Rochester and founder of the earliest college in Oxford, if we decline to accept the mythical story of Alfred and University College.　He was a clear-sighted man for his age—he died in the year 1278—for he ordained in the statutes of his new foundation, that if any member of it took the vows of a religious order he should forfeit his fellowship.

In this transept also are commemorated Bishop Warner and Archdeacon Warner, his son, monuments of the later part of the seventeenth century, and Bishop John de Sheppey (died 1360), whose tomb still retains its ancient colouring.　Glanville's sarcophagus, though much damaged, will attract notice from its unusual form, and the richly-carved canopy of the recumbent effigy of Bishop Lawrence de St. Martin ;

the one belonging to the earlier, the other to the later, part of the thirteenth century.   A plain slab on the opposite side is believed to cover the dust of Gundulf, the builder of the cathedral, and near him is the tomb of one of his successors, Bishop Inglethorpe, who died in 1291.   In the eastern wall of the south-east transept is the noted doorway, leading to the chapter-room, a magnificent piece of Late Decorated work, which is supposed to date from about the middle of the fourteenth century.   The chapter-room itself is a modern building, a narrow, mean room, with no more architectural pretensions than a scullery; indeed, on the first sight of it from the exterior one concludes that it is simply part of the back premises of the deanery.   Its library, however, contains some interesting books.   Some fragments of the original chapter-house are incorporated into the deanery, and the ruined west front, a fine piece of Norman work, together with a portion of the eastern wall of the old cloister, may be seen in the gardens.   The position is an exceptional one, and the doorway already mentioned did not lead to it but to the dormitory of the monks.

We must not omit to notice the crypt, one of the most interesting parts of the cathedral.   As at Canterbury, this is to a considerable extent above ground, and is thus tolerably well lighted; it is approached, as has been said, from the south choir aisle, and extends under the eastern transept and the chancel, and about half of the western or narrower portion of the choir.   The greater part is Early English, of the same age as the choir above.   The western part, however, is massive Norman, and is no doubt the work of Bishop Gundulf, and so rather earlier than most of the nave; for commonly speaking the latter was not begun till the eastern part of the cathedral was well advanced, if not completed.   Unfortunately the hydraulic apparatus connected with the organ has been placed in this portion, so that it is now almost impossible to examine the architecture.

Outside the cathedral there is not much to delay the visitor.   He will wonder at Gundulf's massive and half-ruined tower, more like a part of a fortress than a cathedral, which seems strangely out of place between the two northern transepts. Perhaps the bishop had not quite lost the memory of the Danes, and determined that if ever again plunderers came to his church there should be a safe place of refuge for its treasures.   Mr. St. John Hope, to whom we are much indebted for information, considers that it probably stood eastward of the ruined cathedral of the English bishops, and bears no direct relation to the present structure.   It was after-wards used as a bell-tower.   There are some old gateways connected with the monastic buildings, generally much dilapidated, and from most places the noble keep of the old castle—attributed also to Gundulf, but probably slightly later in date—is a prominent feature in every view.   A seventeenth-century house has replaced the palace once inhabited by the Bishops of Rochester.   In that not a few men of eminence lived.   Several of them have already been mentioned, but there is yet one whose remains indeed found no honoured grave, but whose memory will ever adorn the annals of Rochester, and who was to Cambridge a benefactor no less open-handed than was his predecessor, Walter de Merton, to the sister university.

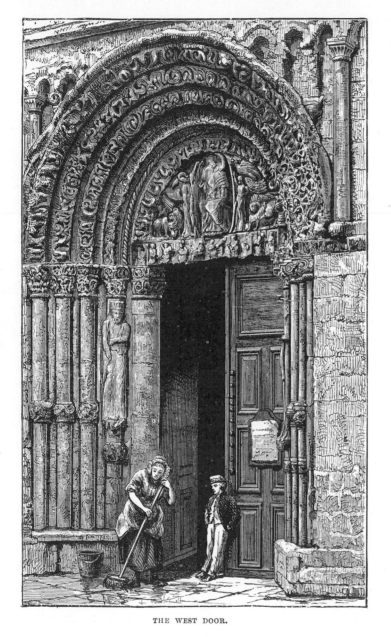

THE WEST DOOR.

This was John Fisher, once chaplain to the Lady Margaret, mother of Henry VII., and for thirty-five years Bishop of Rochester, which in the days of his court favour he refused more than once to quit for better preferment. He was a man of exceptional learning and piety, to whose munificence, as a patron of letters, St. John's College at Cambridge bears witness. It was indeed the foundation of his patroness, but without him for a foster-father might well have perished in its infancy. But like so many men of gentle spirit and deep religious feeling, he clung to the old ways and dreaded the new. Hence after a while he fell out of favour with the king, Henry VIII. He feared change but not death. His conscience forbade him either to consent to the divorce of Catharine, or to take the oath of succession, and for this the tyrant condemned him to die. So the old man went to the scaffold, and as he opened his Bible his eye lighted on the verse beginning, "This is life eternal," and in that belief he laid his hoary head upon the block.

T. G. BONNEY.

BATH, FROM THE RIVER.

BATH.

THE visitor to Bath, whether he catches his first glimpse of the city from the summit of one of the circle of hills in which it lies embosomed, or sweeps through the valley in a Great Western express, will find from either point of view that one building seizes and fixes his attention. There is much in the natural surroundings of the place to awaken admiration; there are many graceful spires and church towers to gladden the eye; and climbing one above another on the hill slopes rise terraces and crescents, the master-pieces of the classic genius of the elder and younger Wood, built of the now beautifully weathered local freestone. But standing forth from all these looms up in the centre of the city the Abbey Church of SS. Peter and Paul, massive and square-built in form, but deriving lightness and elegance from its wealth of lofty windows, its flying buttresses and pierced parapets. The close observer will perceive that it is not ancient in comparison with the cathedrals of England, for it is indeed a most complete specimen of the latest style of pure Gothic architecture. But if his mind is fitly prepared to yield to the charms of the place he will be aware that the present city rises, phœnix-like, actually upon the ashes of a long-vanished predecessor, which flourished before Christianity was the acknowledged religion of Europe. When the Romans came to Britain they found in the hot springs, which still cause Bath to be a favourite place of human habitation, a means of reproducing one at least of the luxuries of their far-distant Italy, and the warm climate of this sheltered valley. together with the magnificent system

V

of baths which they created, rendered their settlement of Aquae Sulis a welcome oasis in the desert of this humid and sunless island. The traveller wending his way hither in those days along the Julian Way would have gazed upon nearly the same spot as that where the abbey now stands, and would have seen in like manner, dominating the public buildings of Aquae Sulis, the magnificent pagan temple dedicated to Sul Minerva, of which nothing now remains but some beautifully sculptured fragments in the Bath Museum.

INTERIOR, LOOKING EAST.

When the country was becoming settled under its English conquerors, Osric, an under-king of the Hwiccii, is said, on doubtful authority, to have founded a nunnery at Bath in 676; about 775 the Mercian king Offa established here a college of secular canons. Archbishop Dunstan procured their expulsion, and the establishment in their place of a Benedictine abbey which continued, through various changes, until the dissolution of monasteries. King Eadgar came to Bath with great pomp, and was crowned in the abbey church on Whit-Sunday, 973, in the presence of a large assemblage of nobles and monks. Leland bears witness that as late as his time it was customary to elect from among the citizens on Whit-Sunday in every year a king of Bath, in joyful remembrance of the crowning of Eadgar.

The period of this church's greatest magnificence, however, began when John de Villula was appointed to the see of Wells in 1088. This great benefactor of the Abbey of Bath was a native and originally a physician of Tours, whence he is also called John of Tours; he had acquired considerable wealth, and by means of it obtained from William Rufus grants of the Bath Abbey, and subsequently of the city of Bath. According to the Continental custom, which was then becoming fashionable in England, of removing the bishop's stool to the largest town in the diocese, Bishop John transferred his from Wells to Bath. In connection with this change he pulled down the old church of the abbey, and set about building a suitable cathedral, which has now completely disappeared, except the bases of some of the pillars, which are to be seen at the east end of the present church and beneath gratings in the nave. Some idea of its size may be gathered from the fact that the present church only occupies the site of the nave. Bishop John died about 1122, and was buried in the middle of the presbytery of his cathedral, where Leland saw his " Image " overgrown with weeds, while " Al the chirch that he made lay to wast and was onrofid." The removal of the bishop from Wells was naturally most unpalatable to the canons of Wells, who in 1218 won the final adoption of the present title of the see, and a few years later induced the bishop entirely to desert Bath, of which, however, he remained titular abbot and drew the principal revenues. The community was thus very much impoverished, and the priors allowed the cathedral to fall into disrepair, so that Oliver King, who was translated from Exeter to Bath and Wells in 1495, found it to be ruined to the foundations.

This prelate was the founder of the present church, to the building of which it is said he was moved by a dream, which he accepted as a divine revelation. Whilst at Bath, musing one night after his devotions, he saw a vision of the Holy Trinity, with angels ascending and descending by a ladder, near to the foot of which was a fair olive tree supporting a crown, and a voice that said, "Let an Olive establish the crown and let a King restore the church." This vision he sculptured on the west front of the abbey, adding the words " de sursum est." Bishop King set about the work in the year 1500, but died three years afterwards, before the south and west parts were covered in or all the walls raised to their proper height. He was assisted by Prior Bird, whose rebus, a W and a bird, is to be seen on various parts of the building. At the dissolution all the glass, iron, bells, and lead were sold off, and the roofless building passed to private owners with the rest of the abbey property, but was presented to the city in 1560. Some years after, by the liberality of private persons, the choir was made fit for divine service and the church was reconsecrated and dedicated to SS. Peter and Paul. Dr. James Montague, who was appointed to the see in 1608, by his liberality and advocacy effected the completion of the church, in which he is buried under a handsome porphyry tomb, with a recumbent effigy.

Flying buttresses were added to the nave and pinnacles to the embattled turrets in the early part of the present century.

In 1860, when Sir Gilbert Scott inspected the church, it was very seriously dilapidated; and between 1864, when the work was commenced, and 1874, when it was completed, a thorough restoration was carried out at a total cost of £35,000. This included, beside the renovation of the fabric, the substitution of fan-tracery vaulting, in completion of the original design, for Bishop Montague's ceiling in the nave. At the same time the entire area was made available for service. The master-spirit of the restoration was the late rector, the Rev. Charles Kemble, whose munificence and energy were alike conspicuous. His health broke down suddenly at the close of the work, and he died in November, 1874, leaving a void in the public work of the city not easily to be filled. The many stained-glass windows are modern and of very varying merit.

The church, following its Norman predecessor, is in the shape of a Latin cross with a central tower. The design has been to give an effect of height, and for this purpose the transepts are very narrow and the clerestory is remarkably lofty, the aisle windows seeming somewhat stunted by comparison. Owing to the narrowness of the transepts the tower is not square but oblong in plan. The east front is plain and the aisles of the choir project beyond it, because the original intention was to

THE ABBEY, FROM THE NORTH-EAST.

build out a Lady Chapel eastward. The east window, which is of seven lights, is square-headed, and probably occupies the position of the tower arch of the Norman cathedral. The north and south transepts have each long end windows of five lights. The nave consists of five bays and the choir of three. The length from the east to the west window is 225 feet; the width from the north window to the south is 124 feet; the width of the church, irrespective of the transepts, 74 feet. The transepts are 20 feet broad, and the tower 162 feet high. Passing to the interior, there is no triforium, the sills of the clerestory windows being brought down to the string-course above the arches. The pointed arches, the vaulting shafts running up between the clerestory windows, all direct the eye upward and minister to the effect of the chief glory of the church, its intricate and beautiful fan-tracery vaulting. This unique feature gives the building a charm peculiarly its own.

The only chantry chapel is that of Prior Bird in the easternmost bay on the south side of the choir, but the work upon it is very beautiful. The same cause which stopped the building of the abbey itself prevented the completion of this chapel by its founder. It was furthermore very much cut about in the succeeding centuries and its exquisite decorations buried beneath successive coats of whitewash. In 1833 it was rescued from this state of neglect and repaired by public subscription, and when the abbey was restored the Kemble family caused the unfinished carvings to be completed with so much skill and fidelity that it is difficult to distinguish the old work from the new.

The abbey was a favourite place of interment when Bath was filled with fashionable visitors in the last century, and interments were crowded into it to an extent which would not now be tolerated. At the same time large monumental tablets were allowed to be plastered over the pillars of the nave and choir and to disfigure the building in all directions. It was this which suggested the well-known couplet—

> "These walls, so full of monument and bust,
> Show how Bath waters serve to lay the dust."

They are now, however, neatly arranged beneath the string-course on the walls of the building, none having been destroyed in the process. There are two monuments by Flaxman, two by Chantrey, and one by Nollekens to be seen here. Jane Lady Waller, wife of the gallant commander who held Bath for the Parliament and fought the battles of Lansdown and Roundway down, has a large tomb in the south transept, with effigies of herself and family. James Quin, the actor, whose praise of Bath as an abiding place for the evening of one's days is well known, has a monument with a good medallion portrait, and a very feeling inscription by Garrick. Beau Nash, the famous King of Bath, who ended his days in poverty and was buried at the expense of the Corporation, also rests here; and so does Rauzzini, the musician, the teacher of Braham, Incledon, and Storace; Dr. Haweis, the founder of the London Missionary Society; Dr. Sibthorp, the botanist; Dr. Caleb Hillier Parry, a well-known man of science in his day, and father of the Arctic explorer; William Melmoth, the translator of Cicero and Pliny; and Dr. Archibald Maclaine, the translator of Mosheim's "Ecclesiastical History;" Lady Miller, whose poetical amusements at Batheaston Villa acquired more than a local fame; Sarah Fielding, the sister of the author of "Tom Jones," and herself a novelist; and Parson Malthus, the author of the "Essay on Population." Sir William Draper is not remembered for any of the virtues set forth in his pompous Latin epitaph, but as the subject of the scathing satire of Junius. John Palmer, M.P. for the city in two Parliaments, established at Bath the first Theatre Royal out of London; he also projected a reform of the mail service, which, notwithstanding jealousy and obstruction, quadrupled the revenue of the Post Office between 1783 and 1798. A grateful nation, however, never paid him the remuneration agreed upon. He and Ralph Allen, also a Bath man, were the two inventive minds to whom the postal service was most indebted before the time of Rowland Hill. Christopher Anstey, the Bath poet, is not buried in Bath Abbey, but there is a tablet to his memory here, as in Westminster Abbey. Physicians not a few have also mouldered into dust within these walls, which will, indeed, afford a more than usually interesting meditation "among the tombs."

HAROLD LEWIS.

WELLS.

WELLS is said to be the smallest city in England, and the reason is not far to seek. It has no history of its own apart from its ecclesiastical institutions; it has no natural advantages as a place of trade; it has never been a seat of manufactures, and has never had a great and powerful family living in its neighbourhood. Apart from what may be said on utilitarian grounds as to the proper place for the centre and origin of the church life of a large diocese, it must be agreed that this sleepy hollow on the south side of the Mendips is a delightful and appropriate home for the calm and uneventful life of a capitular body. On the north side of Wells rise the Mendip Hills, detached outliers of which enclose it as in a basin; on the south, indicating the direction of the "island valley of Avilion," is to be seen the clearly-defined outline of Glastonbury Tor, crowned with the tower of its ancient Church of St. Michael, once an important landmark for miles around.

What we know of the beginning of the city is that about the year 704 King Ina established a college of secular canons by the great natural wells, which may perhaps have acquired an odour of sanctity in pagan times. These wells are still to be seen in the beautiful gardens of the bishop's palace, and feed the moat which surrounds it. Bishop Beckington (1443—1464), who built the three gateways to the close, also granted the citizens the right to supply a conduit in High Street from the wells by a twelve-inch pipe, and therefrom streams of water ripple down each side of the roadway of the principal street of the city, with an effect as pretty as it is unusual. The see of Wells was founded in 909, and Athelm was the first bishop. John de Villula transferred his seat to Bath about 1092. In 1139 it was decreed that the title should be Bishop of Bath and Wells; but Savaric, having obtained from Richard I. the rich Abbey of Glastonbury, which was believed throughout the Middle Ages to occupy the site of the earliest Christian church in Great Britain, transferred his seat thither, and assumed the title of Bishop of Bath and Glastonbury. But in 1218 the monks of Glastonbury obtained their release from a subjection which was very offensive to them, and the prelates have ever since been Bishops of Bath and Wells. Of their number have been Cardinal Wolsey, who held this see *in commendam* from 1518 to 1523, when he resigned it to accept the rich bishopric of Durham, being all the while Archbishop of York; and William Laud, who was appointed in 1626, being also Dean of Gloucester, but he was transferred to London in 1628. The most illustrious Bishop of Bath and Wells, however, was Thomas Ken, a descendant of a very old Somersetshire family, born at Berkhampstead in 1637. He was a Wykehamist, proceeding from Winchester to New College, Oxford, in 1657. He accompanied Mary, Princess of Orange, to Holland as chaplain, and was also chaplain to the king. His refusal to allow Nell Gwynne to lodge in his prebendal house at Winchester is said to have induced Charles II. to give him this bishopric, to which he was consecrated in January, 1685. At any rate, Macaulay says of the king, "Of all prelates, he liked Ken the best;" and on the monarch's death-bed Ken was sent for, after the Archbishop of Canterbury had failed to persuade him to prepare for the end; but it was of no use, though the good bishop's "solemn and pathetic exhortation awed and melted the bystanders." Ken's stainless character won the respect of all his contemporaries, and in his diocese he was in very truth the pastor of his flock. Though Monmouth's men had stripped the lead from the cathedral to make their bullets, and had been guilty of more wanton and inexcusable sacrilege, yet when the Rebellion had failed, and the gaols of Dorset and Somerset were crowded with captives, the best friend of the prisoners was Bishop Ken, who impoverished himself in ministering to their needs, and pleaded eloquently, though in vain, for the king's mercy after the Bloody Assize. Ken was one of the seven bishops prosecuted by James II. for refusing to read the Declaration of Indulgence, and bore himself with the utmost dignity throughout that trying period. His peculiar views, however, made him after the Revolution one of the nonjurors, but he abandoned his palace quietly, and counselled passive submission to the rest of his party. He found an asylum with Viscount Weymouth in the noble mansion of Longleat, where he died on March 19th, 1711, and was buried beneath the east window of the parish church of Frome. His years of retirement were happily spent in study and in writing hymns. His sermons are now read only by the student, but his morning and evening hymns are well known. His successor, Richard Kidder, was, strange to say, killed with his wife in bed in his palace at Wells by the fall of a stack of chimneys during the great storm of November, 1703.

Every side from which the city is approached affords a picturesque view of the cathedral. Fergusson says of it: "Though one of the smallest, it is perhaps, taken altogether, the most beautiful of English cathedrals. Externally its three well-proportioned towers group so gracefully with the chapter-house, the remains of the vicar's close, the ruins of the bishop's palace, and the tall trees with which it is surrounded, that there is no instance so characteristic of English art, nor an effect so pleasing produced with the same dimensions." The present building dates from the time of Bishop Joceline of Wells (1206—1242), who pulled down all the previous building from the west end to the middle of the choir, and rebuilt it, dedicating the building anew to St. Andrew in October, 1239. The present nave, three bays of the choir, the transept, and the central tower as high as the roof, are generally

THE MARKET-PLACE, WELLS.

attributed to this bishop, though there are some indications of an interruption of the work and modification of the original design. The work at Wells cannot be exactly compared with the Early English to be seen at Lincoln, Ely, and Salisbury, because there was evidently a local school of masons here, who continued to work in their own style —which more resembles Norman design, with considerable ornament and having mouldings of special richness—long after the new ideas had been introduced into England. This receives special illustration in the very beautiful north or Galilee porch.

The building was completed during the Decorated period, the crypt of the chapter-house being assigned to the time of Bishop Burnell (1274—1292), and the chapter-house itself to Bishop William de la March (1293—1302). The central tower was finished in 1321, but had to be supported with buttressing arches in 1338. The Lady Chapel was finished before 1326, and the completion of the choir is attributed to Bishops Drokensford and Shrewsbury (1320—1340). Of the two western towers, that on the north was carried up by Bishop Harewell (1366—1386), and that on the south by the executors of Bishop Bubwith (1407 —1424). They also built part of the cloisters, which were finished by Bishop Beckington and his executors, and are therefore Perpendicular in style. We may add here that the total external length of the cathedral is 388 feet; the height of the nave, transept, and choir is 67 feet, and of the central tower 165 feet.

Though there is not here such a perfect close as that in which Salisbury Cathedral stands, yet there is, fortunately, a broad expanse of turf on the west side of the cathedral, so that the grand and imposing effect of the marvellous west front can be fully studied and enjoyed. The wall space, as well as the six projecting buttresses which divide it into five compartments, is covered with statuary as

THE NAVE, LOOKING EAST.

W

with a screen. The figures stand tier above tier, resting upon pedestals, and are surmounted by elegant canopies, supported by shafts of Kilkenny marble. Instead of a great west window there are three lancet-headed lights, and the piers between these are also covered with sculpture. This magnificent work has evoked the enthusiastic admiration of Flaxman and Stothard, and indeed of all who have seen it. There is nothing like it in England, and Fergusson declares that it can only be compared with Chartres or Rheims. Between 1869 and 1876 the chapter spent upwards of £13,000 in levelling the green and in restoring the west front; all the canopies and shafts were then made good, but the figures were wisely left alone; but advantage was taken of the opportunity to photograph them. Much ingenuity has been bestowed upon the task of identifying them, and a very elaborate explanation has been given, but it rests upon no satisfactory foundation, nor does there appear to have been a recorded list of the statues. The modern visitor will probably prefer to the vain labour of endeavouring to name such a list of figures the contemplation of the beautiful effect of the whole work, tinted as it now is by age with a most soft and delicate grey, and to wonder at the skill of the unknown genius which planned out such a masterpiece of art many centuries ago.

The nave consists of ten bays, divided by octagonal piers, with clustered shafts in groups of three. The enrichment of the capitals approximates to Norman in character, and illustrates the influence of the local school. Various curious monsters are placed among the foliage. The triforium extends backwards over the whole width of the side aisles; the solid tympanum which fills each of its lancet-headed openings to the nave is grotesquely carved. The roof has not been altered, though Perpendicular tracery has been inserted in the clerestory and aisle windows. The ribbed vaulting rises from triple shafts which are supported on corbels; the coloured scroll ornamenting it is a restoration from traces discovered when the whitewash was removed.

In the central bay on the south side is the music gallery in three panels, of Early Perpendicular character. In the fifth bay from the west are two corbel heads of a king and a falling child, and of a bishop with a woman and children. Many fanciful stories have been told about them, but they probably formed supports for a small organ.

Under the western towers were two chapels: that on the north was the Chapel of the Holy Cross, the first station in processions; it is now the Consistorial Court. In the nave are two very beautiful chantry chapels. That on the north side is to Bishop Bubwith, who died in 1424. The screen-work and cornices are very beautiful and graceful Perpendicular work. That on the south side is Dean Sugar's, who died in 1489; it is very similar in style, with differences which show its later date. Close by is a sixteenth-century stone pulpit, the gift of Bishop Knight.

The inverted arches which help to support the tower—forming appropriately enough a St. Andrew's cross—are a curious and ingenious device to check the settling of the massive superstructure; but though they are interesting on this ground, it cannot be said that they add to the elegance of the building. It is upon record that a convocation was hastily called in 1338 to consider the serious settlement of the tower, and that this and auxiliary measures—such as blocking up some of the triforium arches to give a lateral thrust—were then resolved upon. The vaulting of the tower is decorated with fan tracery.

The transepts are Early English in style, like the nave, though not of precisely the same date. The carving of the capitals is worthy of note; those on the eastern side are of much later date than those on the west, with which much that is grotesque is mingled. In the south transept, for example, is shown a man in the agony of toothache; another extracting a thorn from his foot; while on the capital of another pier a theft and its consequences are depicted in four scenes. All these sculptures are done with vigour and a keen sense of humour. In the south transept is the late Norman font and the remains of the fine shrine of Bishop Beckington, besides monuments to other cathedral dignitaries. In the north transept is a curious old clock, constructed by Peter Lightfoot, a monk of Glastonbury, in 1325. It has been renewed and repaired until little of the original remains. But it still boasts four figures who dash round in opposite directions, as if at a tournament, when the hours strike, together with some other quaint mechanical movements.

Passing under the Decorated screen supporting the organ into the choir, the visitor sees before him a vista which is one of the most admired features of the cathedral. The first three bays are Early English, those beyond are Decorated work, to which period belong the whole of the clerestory and the rich and beautiful tabernacle work which takes the place of the triforium. The triple shafts of Purbeck marble and the brackets encircled with foliage are very beautiful. The handsome Perpendicular stalls were unfortunately removed between 1848 and 1854, and replaced by forty-one stalls of Doulting stone; the misericords have happily been preserved. The canopied throne is ascribed to Bishop Beckington, but is probably earlier than his time. The east end consists of three arches, resting upon very slender and graceful shafts; above is some very rich tabernacle work, in harmony with the rest of the choir, and then an east window of seven cinquefoil lights, the arrangement of the tracery being unusual. The glazing represents the tree of Jesse, and is of the Decorated period. The unique feature of the choir is, however, the effect of the low diapered reredos, which conceals only the floor and lower parts of the more easterly portions of the church, and reveals the light and graceful clustered shafts of the retro-choir and the beautiful Decorated windows of the polygonal Lady Chapel. The present reredos is entirely modern, but that it is in harmony with the original design is clearly shown by the arrangement of the shafts in the retro-choir, which are placed out of line with those at the east end of the choir, thus giving a delightful maze-like appearance to the eye, suggested perhaps by that of the tree-trunks in a forest glade, through which the sun sometimes shines, just as it beams through the stained glass of the magnificent windows of the Lady Chapel and lights up this scene with curious patches of reflected colour. In the north aisle of the choir is the tomb of Bishop William Button (1267—1274), generally called Bishop Button II., as he was nephew of William Button who filled the see from 1248 to 1267. They took their name from a village close to Bath, now called Bitton. His

THE CATHEDRAL, FROM THE SWAN POOL.

tomb is a coffin-shaped slab, with an incised episcopal figure, and is remarkable as almost the earliest example of an incised slab in Europe. It was once still more remarkable as a place of pilgrimage for those who suffered from toothache, it being believed until long after the Reformation that the sanctity in which the bishop had died was so great that a visit to his tomb was enough to drive away the malady. In the same transept is the tomb of Bishop Beckington, whose benefactions to the city have already been referred to; they were recognised by the mayor and corporation by an annual visit to his chantry to pray for the repose of his soul. The chantry has been removed by modern iconoclasts because it projected into the choir, but the tomb remains, and is of a type which was somewhat favoured in those days. On an upper stage is an effigy of the bishop in all the splendour of his episcopal robes; on a lower a grimly realistic depiction of his corpse in its winding sheet. The tomb of

Bishop Drokensford is very fairly carved, and has a lofty and beautiful canopy. There are several effigies also which have been identified by name with certain of the early bishops, but no reliance is to be placed upon the precise accuracy of the results.

The Lady Chapel is, strictly speaking, an octagon deprived of three of its sides by its forming part of the cathedral. Each of the five sides that are left contains a large Decorated window, with glazing of the same period.

From the eastern aisle of the north transept a fine staircase leads to the chapter-house. The staircase is lighted by two fine Decorated windows on the west side, and the effect of these, with the double arches at the entrance to the chapter-house on the other side of the stair, and the way over the chain-bridge (a covered way from the vicar's close to the church) between, is most picturesque as one looks up the stairs. The chapter-house itself is octagonal; it has a central pier, with sixteen clustered shafts, from which the ribs of the vaulting radiate. The corresponding ribs spring from shafts which are placed at the angles of the walls, between the large Decorated windows, each of which fills a face of the octagon. This chapter-house is one of the glories of Wells Cathedral. The ball-flower ornament is used very freely in its decoration, and the same fancy for grotesque heads at the head of the columns will be found here as in other parts of the building. Beneath the windows runs an arcade with Purbeck shafts and enriched canopies.

The cloisters are on the south side of the cathedral, and are of unusual area, but have only three sides instead of four. The canons of Wells did not need a cloister in the same sense as monks, and this is merely an ornamental walk, enclosing the burial-ground for the liberty of St. Andrew. It leads, however, to the bishop's palace, which was fortified by Bishops Ralph and Shrewsbury sufficiently to stand a severe siege. The great hall of Bishop Burnell (1274—1292) was the largest episcopal hall in England, but it was allowed to fall into ruins in the last century.

HAROLD LEWIS.

PETERBOROUGH.

THE city of Peterborough has grown up round the abbey. Until the changes of this century, which within thirty years have increased the population threefold, it was essentially an ecclesiastical borough. The fortunes of the people varied with those of the church. From the time when the little fen village of Medeshamstead saw the first establishment of a monastic body, to the prosperous and wealthy foundation of Burgh Saint Peter, and thence to its state of diminished wealth but perhaps increased dignity as the city of Peterborough, the church and town have been inseparably connected. The abbey called the town into existence.

The present cathedral is the third minster that has been erected on the same spot. The first was built in the seventh century, founded by a king of the Mercians, Peada, who died before the work was completed. This was entirely destroyed by the Danes in the year 870, in the time of the seventh abbot, Hedda, who was killed in the attack, together with the whole of his monks. It was a century before any attempt was made to remedy this disaster. In the year 971 King Edgar, moved by the story of the desolation of the place—instead of a monastery there being "nothing but old walls and wild woods"—commenced the building of the second church; and when it was completed came to see it with the Archbishops Dunstan and Oswald, and a great company of nobles. This building suffered much in another Danish attack in the middle of the eleventh century, but it was by an accident, in 1116, that it was finally destroyed by fire. A quaint legend, recorded by one of the chroniclers, attributes the calamity to an intemperate invocation by the abbot, who was in a choleric mood because the bakehouse fire would not burn and his meal was delayed. The building we now see was commenced within a couple of years of this time. The work proceeded, as was usual, from east to west, and took in all nearly one hundred and twenty years to complete, being consecrated by the Bishops of Lincoln and Exeter in 1237. The choir was ready for divine service in 1143, in which year the convent is said to have entered into their new church. At times the work proceeded with good speed, and each year saw some considerable addition; at other times it languished, for ten or more years together, from want of enterprise or lack of funds. But it is seldom that we can trace so completely and precisely the gradual advance of the work as we can here. The original fabric remains, with additions, but with no great alterations. At the time of the consecration, much that we now see had not been erected. The bell tower, the western spires, the new building at the east end (often erroneously called the Lady Chapel), and the lantern tower which has been recently reconstructed, have all been added since. With the single exception of Norwich, it will be generally conceded that in Peterborough Cathedral we find the grandest and most complete Norman church left in England. It is true that the original Norman tower has perished, removed (it is believed) in alarm at the fate of the massive Ely tower in 1321; and that the windows in the nave aisles have been enlarged, and in other parts of the church altered by the insertion of late tracery; but it retains its Norman choir and apse, a remarkable series of monumental effigies of early abbots, and wooden Norman ceilings to the nave and transepts, which are unique. The grand western transept and Galilee porch were an after-thought. Originally the building was meant to terminate with two towers, at a distance of three bays east of the present front. Evidences of this are still to be seen in the increased size of the nave piers, which were constructed to support these towers; in the greater thickness of the aisle walls at the same place; and in other indications easily to be detected by close inspection. It is probable, but not established, that these towers were actually erected. One of the main charms of the interior is to be found in the continuity of style which prevails. As the erection of the nave proceeded, the fashion in architecture was changing. The sturdy mass of the Norman pier was giving way to a pillar of lighter and more elegant construction, and the pointed was beginning to supplant the round arch; but happily the nave here was finished in the same style as that in which it was begun, notwithstanding this change of fashion; although in many of the details, such as the bases of the piers towards the west, and the heads in the arcades of the aisle walls, the influence of the later style has made itself felt. In the western transept itself are some glorious examples of the transition period, large pointed arches being covered with the characteristic mouldings of the Norman style.

The finest feature of the cathedral is its west front. This has been described by no mean authority as " the grandest portico in Europe." The date of its erection has not been recorded; but as it is in the best style of Early English architecture, it may be assumed to have been completed a few years only before the solemn dedication of the whole church, already mentioned, in 1237. A south-west tower has never been built, and it is much to be doubted if the general effect of the western façade would be improved by the addition of a second tower. Of the spires, that to the south is by far the more beautiful. It is of early fourteenth-century work, and some feet more lofty than its fellow, which was erected some eighty or one hundred years later. The graceful combination of pinnacles and spire lights at the foot of the south-west spire is, as a work of art, the most beautiful thing to be seen in Peterborough. But glorious as is this western front, it has some blemishes, detected at once by the artistic eye. The central gable is a true one, being the termination of the nave roof; but the side ones are to a certain extent a deception, for they have only smaller roofs built on purpose for the gables. And the insecurity of the

THE WEST FRONT.

whole, built without any buttress on the west, is manifest. This has been in part remedied by the erection of an inner porch with a room above (now the library), which clearly improves the stability of the central arch. This arch is narrower than the others, but the gables above have been ingeniously made of the same angle. Of the thirty figures in the niches, some are of Saxon character, and were carved before any of the stones of the building that we now see were in their present places. Two more figures of the same style are built into the wall of the south transept. The whole of the west front is in a dangerous state. For the last quarter of a century hardly a year has passed without some warning having been given of its insecurity. At one time a piece of a pinnacle has fallen; at another a projecting ornament; at another one of the shafts. A few only of the old marble shafts remain in position; some are wholly gone, some have been replaced by stone shafts from a quarry in the neighbourhood, some by shafts of wood. The northern arch in particular, as can be seen from below, is in a very precarious condition.

The precincts are most picturesque. The old Norman gateway at the entrance

THE CHOIR.

of the close, encased with Perpendicular work; the late Decorated chancel of the chapel of Saint Thomas à Becket, who was held here in high esteem, many relics, such as paving-stones from the spot where he fell, parts of his dress, and drops of his blood, having been brought hither from Canterbury by Benedict, a monk of Christ Church at the time of the murder, afterwards abbot here; the grand early gateway of the abbot's lodge; the enriched entrance to the prior's quarters; and the remains of some thirteenth-century buildings on the south— all ranged round the ample close, give a result not attained elsewhere in England. Passing round the south of the minster we come to the laurel court, where can

x

be traced remains of two different sets of cloisters, of the lavatory, and of a wall of older date than the present church; and so pass on to the ruins of the infirmary, which has arches and arcading of great beauty. What is left of the refectory is now in the private grounds of the bishop. The cloisters themselves have disappeared, as well as the chapter-house and the Lady Chapel. This last formerly stood eastwards from the north transept, where its exact position can be clearly seen.

Of the six effigies of abbots, which form so interesting a series, one only can with certainty be identified. In 1830 some remains were discovered in a stone coffin beneath one of these effigies, and a small piece of lead was found on which were the words " Abbas Alexan." Alexander of Holderness died in 1226. The figure of this abbot has now been placed on a stone plinth, in its original position, under the second bay of the north choir aisle. The latest in date is doubtless that which has suffered most in appearance, owing to its soft and perishable material, while the more ancient ones, being of Purbeck or some other very hard marble, have their mouldings and ornaments, and mostly their features, as clear as ever. One monument, now preserved in the new building, formerly in the churchyard, is of very great interest and importance. It is a coped stone, about three feet long by one foot thick, and between two and three feet in height. By tradition, as well as by description in the annals of the abbey, this stone was erected as a memorial of Abbot Hedda and the monks killed by the Danes in 870. This date is indeed on the stone, but it has been added at a later time. On each side are carved six figures in monastic dress; but one has the cruciform nimbus of the Saviour. The rude ornamentation of the sloping sides of the head is the work of a time some years before the Conquest, though we may hesitate to assign to the stone so early a date as the ninth century. The new building, where this monument is now preserved, is at the extreme east end of the cathedral, and is the latest of the abbey works, being completed only at the beginning of the sixteenth century. It has some fine, rich work, and a stone roof of beautiful fan tracery.

Two Archbishops of York, both of whom had been monks of the house, Elfricus and Kinsius, are interred here, but without monuments. Kinsius had been chaplain to Edward the Confessor. Of ancient inscriptions the church has singularly few. Those that escaped the fury of the Civil War in the seventeenth century fell victims to an indiscriminate zeal for repaving in the eighteenth. Fragments of five or six pre-Reformation inscriptions at most can now be seen, and of these the only perfect ones have been laid bare in the recent work. The abbots were many of them men of influence in the councils of the nation, a race of statesmen and warriors. Four became archbishops or bishops; Leofricus was with the army of Harold at Senlac; Robert of Lindesay, or perhaps a suc-cessor, assisted Henry III. at the siege of Rockingham Castle; Robert of Sutton appeared in arms at Northampton and elsewhere against the same monarch, and was alternately laid under contribution by the king, for his opposition, and by the barons, for granting money to the king. One abbot, Adulphus, had been chancellor to King Edgar; another, John de Caleto, was chief justice, and went on circuit; Leofricus was of near kin to the queen of Edward the Confessor; Brando was uncle to Hereward. On not a few occasions has the sovereign been entertained by the abbey at great cost. Stephen came to see the most precious relic of the house, the famous arm of the sainted King Oswald. Henry III. twice visited the abbey, once with his queen and Prince Edward; and this monarch accepted a present of sixty marks towards the marriage of his daughter with the King of Scotland. In 1273 Edward, now king, paid a second visit to the abbot; in 1302, with his queen, a third; and later on a fourth. The abbot contributed largely towards his expenses in Scotland. Prince Edward, afterwards Edward II., bringing Gaveston with him, was once entertained here. On New Year's Day, 1327, Philippa of Hainault stayed at Peterborough, on her way to be married at York. Twice did Abbot Adam de Boothby receive Edward III. and Philippa; and once the Black Prince and his two sisters stopped eight weeks at the monastery. In 1528 Cardinal Wolsey kept his Maundy at Peterborough, celebrating high mass on Easter Day.

Fourteen bishops lie buried within the church or in the churchyard. No elaborate monument has been erected to any one of them; and a stone on the floor, or a tablet on the wall, with sometimes a coat of arms, and the preferments of the deceased prelate, alone commemorates him. A very comely monument, with an effigy, was erected to the memory of Bishop Dove; but this was destroyed in 1643. Among others here interred are the bodies of Richard Cumberland, the philosophical writer; White Kennett, the indefatigable antiquary; John Hinchcliffe, master of Trinity College, Cambridge; Spencer Madan, the poet Cowper's first cousin; Herbert Marsh, author of many controversial works. Two of the bishops, William Lloyd, afterwards of Norwich, and Thomas White, were deprived of their sees as nonjurors. Of the deans, thirteen were advanced to the episcopal dignity, including John Cosin, of Durham; Edward Rainbow, of Carlisle; Simon Patrick, of Chichester and Ely; Richard Kidder, of Bath and Wells; Charles Manners Sutton, of Canterbury; James Henry Monk, of Gloucester; Thomas Turton, of Ely. James Duport, professor of Greek at Cambridge, and Thomas Nevill, master of Trinity, were also deans here. John Williams, the famous Bishop of Lincoln; John Pocklington, the author of "Sunday no Sabbath," persecuted by the Parliament and deprived of his preferments; John Bridgeman, Bishop of Chester, are among the more celebrated of the prebendaries.

On the west wall of the cathedral hangs a very quaint portrait, with some verses painted on the wall beneath. This is a copy of a picture of Richard

Scarlett, sexton, who died in 1594, at the age of ninety-eight. In the verses we read:—

"He had interd two queenes within this place,
And this townes householders in his lives space
Twice over."

The two queens were Catharine of Arragon, the first wife of Henry VIII., and Mary of Scots, his sister's grand-daughter. The former was interred in the north

THE NORTH TRANSEPT.

choir aisle in 1536; the latter in the corresponding position in the south choir aisle in 1587. At one time handsome hearses were over both these tombs. An account has been preserved of a so-called miracle wrought at the hearse of Queen Catharine; and, curiously enough, the Westminster tomb of Mary of Scots has been made the scene of miracles. For the divorced wife of Henry VIII. a simple table monument was erected. Some persons who defaced it were imprisoned until the damage was made good. There is no need to reject the familiar story that the minster itself is her noblest monument, being spared, when others were sacrificed, because it had become her burial-place. The actual monument was repaired at his own cost by one of the prebendaries, John Taylor, who held a stall from 1685 to 1726. It is said that he cut the inscription with his own hand. All has now been wholly removed, and there is left a plain body stone in the floor, with a small broken brass plate, a few inches long, which when perfect bore the simple words, "Queen Catherine, A.D. M.D.XXX.VI." It is not a little singular that her daughter designed the removal of her body, though the intention was never carried out. Queen Mary of England in her

THE CHOIR, LOOKING WEST.

will directed "that the body of the vertuous Lady and my most Dere and well-beloved Mother of happy memory, Quene Kateryn, which lyeth now buried at Peterborowh," should be removed and laid near the spot where she herself was to be buried. The body of the other queen was removed to Westminster in 1613, by order of her son, James I. A very stately funeral was celebrated for Queen Mary of Scots. An epitaph, expressed in very strong language, was also inscribed on a tablet, and placed near the vault; but this was soon taken down. The remains of the hearse and funeral achievements were destroyed in 1643, though the adjacent piers still show where the canopy must have been. A photograph of the king's letter, directing the removal of his mother's body, is hung in a frame close to the spot.

The same year that witnessed the wanton destruction of these royal memorials saw also much more irreparable loss. The soldiers of the Civil War spared little. The ancient records of the church, with very few exceptions, were burnt; the elaborate altar-screen laid low; the painted roof of the choir defaced; the tombs and monuments and brasses nearly all demolished; the stained-glass windows broken; and the cloisters, which had an unrivalled series of such windows, completely wrecked. Through the influence of Oliver Saint John the building was not sold or demolished, but was assigned to the townspeople for a workshop as well as for worship. It was with difficulty, after the recent mischief, that the inhabitants made the needful repairs. The Lady Chapel was taken down to supply materials for this purpose. One sad memory of this desolation is yet to be seen. At the south of the apse, in the new building, are the remains of a handsome monument, erected by Sir Humphry Orme, as was not unusual in those days, to commemorate himself and his family. He lived to see it destroyed. And it can still be seen as it was left after mutilation by the axes and hammers of the soldiery. Near this is the solitary instance of a monument of any size and pretension; it has a life-size figure in marble of Thomas Deacon, a great benefactor to the town, who died in 1721. The two central windows of the apse contain some of the old glass collected from different parts of the church; but it is in detached fragments only, and has no coherence. From the pieces of text it may be observed that much of it came from windows representing scenes from the life of the patron saint.

About sixty years ago the lately removed fittings of the choir were erected, as well as a stone organ-screen. The original rood-screen was at the third pier of the nave. In the year 1882 the condition of the lantern tower was found to be most perilous. One of the great piers, that to the south-east, had been bound up with iron and other supports for nearly three hundred years. A careful examination made it apparent that no repairs would be of any avail, and that the whole must be removed and rebuilt. This has now been done; except that the corner pinnacles, erected by Dean Kipling at the beginning of the present century, have not been replaced. In process of removal many stones were found which had formed part of the original Norman tower, as well as several of Roman and Saxon workmanship. The most interesting discovery has been the site of the early Saxon church. It was cruciform, its chancel being situated where the south transept of the present cathedral has been built; but its nave was wholly without the existing building. A crypt has been constructed, so that what remains of this early church may be always open to inspection.

W. D. SWEETING.

CHESTER.

THE present Cathedral of Chester was not the earliest episcopal church of the diocese which now bears this name. If we turn to the periods which immediately preceded and followed the Norman Conquest we find Chester, Lichfield, and Coventry co-ordinated as sister cathedral cities, the bishop's title being taken indifferently from any one of them. This is the reason why three mitres appear in the arms of the see of Chester.

The kingdom of Mercia was then one vast diocese, which extended far over the north-west of England, including even part of Wales, and reaching to the edge of the territory of the Bishops of Durham. It is the more important to name this historical fact, because then the Chester Cathedral of this unwieldy diocese was the fine Norman Church of St. John the Baptist, where a great calamity, in the fall of a magnificent tower, has recently deprived the city of Chester of one of its most dignified and characteristic features.

The history of this diocese has been, to a most remarkable degree, a history of successive subdivisions. The first important change of this kind was the creation by King Henry VIII. of a separate see of Chester, the abbey church of the great Benedictine house of St. Werburgh being assigned as the cathedral church to the new diocese, which was made part of the Northern Province. This new diocese, however, though separated off from Shropshire, Staffordshire, and Derbyshire, was still enormous; for besides Cheshire it included the whole of Lancashire and Westmoreland, with parts of Denbighshire, Flintshire, and parts of Cumberland and Yorkshire. Recent changes, indeed, of the most imperative and advantageous kind have been made. It was over this vast area, however, that even Bishop Blomfield was the ecclesiastical ruler; and it must be remembered that we are thinking here not merely of a large extent of country, but of a population rapidly growing and full of energy. The first of the recent subdivisions was the result of the creation of the see of Ripon in 1836, the second resulted from that of the see of Manchester in 1847, the third from that of the see of Liverpool in 1880. Now the diocese is simply coincident with the county of Chester, which has a proud and well-defined history of its own.

It is evident that the building of Chester Cathedral is to be distinguished from its cathedral-history. We must take as our starting-point for architectural description the erection of the Benedictine abbey church. In two respects this erection has a distinguished origin. The foundation of the house was due to the great feudal lord, Hugh Lupus, a kinsman of William I., who was planted here after the Conquest; and at the head of the Benedictine monks, who came for this purpose from Bec in Normandy, was Anselm, who was made Archbishop of Canterbury on his return from Chester. From this time onward the structural changes in this church followed the same course as in other great churches of the country. Each period of architecture can be traced here from about 1100 to about 1500.

If we begin now with the church of the time of King Henry I., its Norman

CHESTER, FROM THE WALLS.

architecture is not, indeed, at first sight very obtrusive; yet, when closely examined, it is quite sufficient to lead us to some important conclusions, and these conclusions have been largely aided by discoveries made during the work of recent restoration. The Norman arches on the exterior of the northern wall of the nave, and the unfinished Norman tower (destined now for a baptistery, for which the preparations are already in progress), show that the length of the nave during the time of the early Plantagenet kings was the same as at present. The size and the form of the small north transept remain as they were at this period. It has been ascertained that the piers of the choir were then, in their massive rotundity, like the piers of St. John's Church. The lines of curvature of the apsidal terminations on the east have been discovered, and special mention must be made of the recently disinterred and restored Norman crypt, which is on the west side of the cloister, and is now one of the best surviving specimens of Norman architecture in this part of England.

The reign of King Edward I. may be taken as our next historical landmark for architectural description. Before his visit to Chester the Lady Chapel was built on the east of the choir; and the architects whom he aided were probably engaged upon the choir and its aisles at the time when he was here. As to the former portion of the cathedral buildings, great ingenuity was shown by Sir Gilbert Scott in discovering the correct form of the buttresses, whereby he was enabled at this place

THE CHOIR, LOOKING WEST.

to effect a forcible and truthful restoration. As regards the latter, the attention of all who walk on that part of the city wall, which is on the east of the cathedral, must be arrested by a singular cone at the eastern extremity of the south aisle of the choir. This also is a recovery of the past, and it is the result of a shrewd observation of facts by Mr. Frater, who was clerk of the works from 1868 to 1876. The evidence on which the rebuilding of this cone is justified was quite certain. There seems no doubt that it was the result of some fancy of a monk or architect from Normandy; and at Norrey, near Caen, may be seen a structural peculiarity of exactly the same kind. In each of these instances the obliteration of ancient features, the happy recovery of which has now been found possible, was chiefly due to the

Y

prolongation of the aisles of the choir in a late period of bad architecture. The south aisle is now arrested at its original point. The change observed in the vaulting of the north aisle tells its own story.

To the Early Pointed style succeeded in due order that which is termed the Decorated; and good specimens are found of each of its subdivisions in the geometrical tracery of some windows and the flowing tracery of others. The former are in the south aisle and in the clerestory of the choir, the latter in the south aisle of the nave and in the east aisle of the south transept. The general impression, however, produced on the eye by these two conspicuous parts of the cathedral is that of the commanding presence of the latest or Perpendicular style of Gothic architecture. This arises from the large clerestory windows of that date. Those of the nave belong probably to the reign of Henry VII. Those of the transept are earlier in date and better in form. It ought to be added that the great central tower and the exquisite woodwork of the choir belong to the earliest and best part of the Perpendicular period. The upper portion of the north transept, recently restored, is of the same general date.

THE CENTRAL TOWER.

The great south transept is so remarkable, both historically and architecturally, that it deserves, and indeed requires, a separate mention. In size it is as large as the choir and nearly as large as the nave. This circumstance constitutes it the most singular feature of Chester Cathedral; and it attracts attention the more because of its contrast with the diminutive size of the north transept. This anomaly, if we may so call it, probably arose in this way, that the Benedictine monks, unable to extend their church to the north, because the conventual buildings were there, pushed it forward to the south, so as to absorb the parish church of St. Oswald. In the end the parishioners recoiled successfully upon the monks, and obtained permission to hold their services within the abbey church on the old ground. The mouldings of the late doorway inserted in one of the windows on the south of the transept combine with other evidence to attest this fact. The parochial rights within the cathedral continued till the close of 1880; and thus St. Oswald's name is still connected with this part of it; and it is to be hoped that this association with the good missionary King of Northumbria will never be lost.

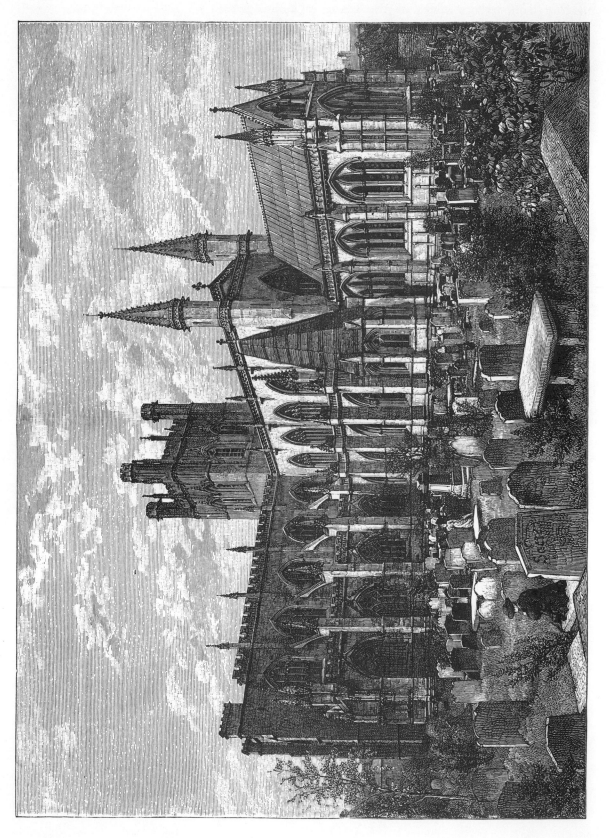

CHESTER CATHEDRAL, FROM THE SOUTH-EAST.

6

This is a good moment for asking attention to the south transept; for, after many delays and disappointments, an effort is about to be made to effect the complete restoration of its great south front, which affords one of the best architectural opportunities that could be afforded. The late Sir G. Gilbert Scott, under whom the general restoration of the cathedral was for many years conducted, looked forward with eager wishes to this effort. The enterprise has now been placed in the hands of his successor, Mr. Arthur Blomfield, whose design is during the present season (1885) in the exhibition of the Royal Academy.

To the mention which has been made of the cloister, a few words must be added. In its mouldering decay it is eminently picturesque; and it is impossible not to regret that the restorative process will soon be inevitable here. The Norman walls on the south and west sides of the cloister have already been named. On the east, where the dormitory used to be, are the chapter-house and its vestibule; both are very fine and unchanged (though extremely different) specimens of the architecture of the thirteenth century. To the same period belong the original parts of the refectory on the north. This noble room has been grievously injured, and it invites and deserves a costly restoration. The pulpit in the south-east corner is unique in its beauty.

This cathedral church has had its full share of association with varied historical incidents, and with recollections of eminent men. The names of two who are distinguished in the literary sense during its monastic period must not be forgotten. These were Higden, the author of the " Polychronicon," and Bradshaw, who wrote a metrical life of St. Werburgh; nor must we leave without mention St. Werburgh herself, the kinswoman of the successive princesses who were abbesses of the great house of St. Etheldreda at Ely. King Alfred's daughter had brought her remains to Chester in the time of the Danish troubles, and founded here a Saxon monastery in her name. To pass to the period of the Reformation, one who suffered in its cause was George Marsh, who was condemned to death in the Lady Chapel, then used as the Consistory Court, and was burnt in one of the suburbs of Chester. The period of the great Civil War was marked here by the severity of Bishop Bridgeman, otherwise an excellent prelate, who caused penance to be done in the cathedral for kind treatment of Prynne, when he came to Chester with his ears cut off, and by the severity of Cromwell's party to Bridgeman himself afterwards. A most remarkable series of men were bishops here between the Restoration and the end of the seventeenth century. The first of these was Bryan Walton, fresh from his labour on the " Polyglot " Bible; the last was Cartwright, who went with James II. to Dublin. Between them came Wilkins, who with Evelyn founded the Royal Society, and especially Pearson, whose remains rest in the north transept under a monument designed by the present architect of the cathedral. In the roof above are the arms of Wolsey. Finally this cathedral is not without monuments recalling, in an animated manner, incidents of the great American War, and of the British conquests in India. Though now the cathedral simply of one English county, it has gathered round itself much interest from a wide circumference, and it will gather more.

J. S. Howson.

ELY, FROM THE FENS.

ELY.

 A SLUGGISH river, fringed by pollarded willows and defined by towing-paths; wide meadows, and corn-fields of rich fertility, intersected by dykes and enlivened by wind-mills; long lines of embankment which defend these prolific tracts from the incursions of winter floods: these are some of the features of the peculiar landscape which surrounds the old city of Ely.

A gentle eminence, adorned in summer with masses of foliage and groups of flowering shrubs; clusters of dwelling-houses, mostly of low elevation and mean exterior, raising their roof-ridges and chimneys amid the greenery; crowning the whole, the central object and single point of attraction, presiding over the humble town spread around it, a church of immense length, its ridge broken by a peculiar octagonal lantern, and terminating in a massive and stately tower, flanked by attendant turrets: this is the general view of Ely and its cathedral presented to the traveller arriving from the south.

From the northern and from the eastern approaches this commanding presidency of the vast church over the secular buildings is still more conspicuous and impressive. At the hamlet of Stuntney, some two miles or less from Ely, a view of the whole group is presented which cannot easily be forgotten; while the huge pile is seen from a curve on the railway, or from the meadows near it, under unexpected conditions which invest it with a grandeur altogether its own.

Mounting the hill after leaving the station, we pass along a street, or rather lane, known as the "Gallery," flanked by low buildings evidently reared in mediæval times, and find ourselves at the west end of the church.

A façade, which might have been magnificent, is manifestly spoiled by the absence of the northern arm of the cross aisle, or western transept, which bears the name of the "Galilee." No record exists of the fall or demolition of this northern arm, and the allusions to the Galilee in the chronicles accessible to us are too obscure to enable us to form an accurate judgment as to its dimensions and builders; nor are we much more fortunate in the references to the porch, which projects from the line of the cross aisle, and, though admirable in itself, certainly contributes to mar the effect of this west front.

Before we pass through the porch into the church, it may be well to carry with us a remembrance of the chief historical facts connected with it. They may be summarised thus:—

A religious house had been founded in 673 by Etheldreda, a queen or princess of East Anglia, remarkable for personal beauty and for gentleness of character. The church which she built, and which was probably of wood, was burnt in one of the Danish irruptions, probably about 870. About one hundred years later—namely, about 974—the buildings were repaired and a body of Benedictine monks placed in them by Ethelwold, a zealous partisan and active supporter of Dunstan, the great champion of monasticism. Another century elapsed; England had passed under the rule of the Normans, who brought with them the love of sumptuous and imposing architecture which has enriched Northern Europe with so many castles and churches. At Ely the newcomers began in 1082 the vast pile before us. We shall keep this brief summary of the local history in our minds as we examine the church; but the times of Etheldreda are too remote, and the chronicles of her life are too largely intermingled with legend and fable, to come within the scope of this work. A fragment of a stone cross, now placed against the south wall of the nave, may perhaps be a relic of her age. "Ovin's Cross" was possibly erected by her steward, Ovini, or Wini, in the neighbouring village of Haddenham, from which it was brought to its present resting-place. We know, however, that the Abbots of Ely before the Conquest were among the most powerful churchmen of their time. Thurstan, abbot in 1066, had been brought up in the monastery, and had become its head by the favour of Harold, whose cause he most strenuously upheld. For five years—namely, from 1066 to 1071—the Isle of Ely formed a Saxon stronghold, or Camp of Refuge, for all the English who refused submission to the yoke of the foreigners. William of Normandy conducted in person the military operations for the reduction of the isle; but he was compelled to retire, and it was only by the voluntary submission of Thurstan and the monks that he obtained possession of the Fen fortress, which he garrisoned with Norman troops. Thurstan died in 1072, the last Saxon Abbot of Ely; and after an interregnum of nine years, the first Norman abbot was installed in the person of Simeon, a relative of the Conqueror, and eighty-seven years of age. The stately church before us was commenced by this energetic old man, who reached the age of one hundred.

Full of these recollections, we enter and stand on the threshold. Under favourable conditions of light and shade, we doubt if a more striking architectural view than this can be presented to the eye. The vista is unbroken as far as the eastern wall, 517 feet from us, save by light screen-work of open design. Three tall lancets, surmounted by five others, ingeniously worked into the curves of the stone vaulting, terminate and close in the distant point in which the long lines of walls, roof, and floor are brought together, with an effect surpassing in solemn grandeur, as we think, any composition in which one vast window, as at York or Carlisle, is the chief feature. Tall and narrow arches carry the eye upwards, and give an impression of loftiness which will bear comparison even with that conveyed by Cologne or Amiens, and to which the narrowness of the central alley contributes.

Above our heads, as we still stand upon the door-step, after passing through the porch, rises the great tower. Its second and third stages are open to the pavement, and are adorned with arcading; its wooden ceiling has been painted with great taste and skill by an accomplished amateur of our own day, Mr. Le Strange, of Hunstanton Hall, in Norfolk. We note that four arches of immense strength and excellent masonry have been built, at some period, beneath the original arches of the tower, sustaining on their shoulders its enormous superincumbent weight.

The nave is of twelve bays, or severies, and as we walk along it we may take note that the arcade of the second stage, or triforium, is of nearly equal height with that of the lower stage, or ambulatory.

The walls and mouldings have been in many places decorated with polychrome, abundant traces of which may be seen, brought to light by careful removal of the coats of yellow-wash with which they had been encrusted in later times; at the tenth bay the chipping away of the piers of the triforium on the north side shows the probable place of one of the "pairs of organs," of which the church possessed three. The aisles are vaulted, and still show traces of rich decoration in colour upon a plastered surface; the great nave itself has

been ceiled in recent times with wood, and on this ceiling, which has a
pentagonal section, a vast picture has been delineated with great skill and
power by Mr. Le Strange, and by Mr. Gambier Parry, of Highnam Court, near

CHOIR OF ELY CATHEDRAL.

Gloucester, who, after the death of his old friend and school-fellow, continued
the half-finished work.

We have said that Abbot Simeon commenced the present church in 1082,
probably by laying the foundations of the south transept. His successor,
Richard, appointed in 1100, prosecuted the work so far that the remains of

Etheldreda, and of three other abbesses, her relatives, were translated into it with great pomp and ceremony, and were laid in shrines immediately behind the chief altar.   This was in 1106.   To understand the magnificent interior as we now see it, we must picture to ourselves Richard's church enlarged and enriched, not only by grand western additions, but also by an eastern extension of no fewer than six bays of most perfect design and workmanship. Abbot Richard had greatly desired the conversion of the abbey into an episcopal see.   On his death in 1107, this change was pressed upon the king (Henry I.) by Hervè le Breton, Bishop of Bangor, who was in temporary charge of the abbey. In 1109 he was himself translated from Bangor, as first Bishop of Ely; and thenceforward, as we shall see, the embellishment of the church became an object of episcopal concern.   It was Geoffrey Ridel, third bishop (1174—1189), who built the great tower and the western cross aisle; and it was Eustace (1198—1215) who is said to have added the western porch, though this statement is open to considerable doubt.

1. THE EAST END.   2. THE ABBEY GATE.
3. THE GALILEE DOOR.

A still more munificent prelate was Hugh of Northwold, Abbot of St. Edmundsbury, consecrated Bishop of Ely in 1229.   Dissatisfied with the plain and even rude architecture of Richard, and probably desiring a more stately lodgment for the sepulchral monuments of the four abbesses, he commenced in 1234 the erection of a new presbytery or retro-choir, which was consecrated in 1252 in the presence of Henry III. and his son, afterwards Edward I., then

z

a boy of thirteen years, and which remains to this day in all its exquisite beauty, unsurpassed and even unrivalled in this country, unless by the "Angel Choir" of Lincoln.

Seventy years afterwards—namely, in 1322—the central tower, which rose above the intersection of the nave, choir, and transept, fell with a mighty crash, not unexpected, however, by the monks, who for some time had not dared to say the offices beneath the tottering structure.

A calamity almost identical in its incidents befell the Cathedral of Chichester a few years ago. A similar disaster has been averted at Peterborough by timely demolition. In both these cases a wise discretion has limited the rebuilders to an exact copy of the original.

The year 1322, however, belongs to an era in which the beautiful craft of the architect and builder may be said to have reached its culmination ; and the Abbey of Ely possessed in its sacrist, Alan, surnamed "of Walsingham," a true artist, who saw his opportunity in the ruin which had overtaken his church, and who availed himself of it to such purpose that we may search Europe without finding a grander example of original design, bold construction, and charming detail than is presented before our eyes in this octagon.

Its history is read at a glance. Instead of re-erecting a heavy stone tower on four massive piers, he threw a canopy of wooden groining over a noble area made by removing the four massive piers altogether; and he filled up the corners of the space so gained by diagonal walls pierced with graceful arches below, and above with large windows of admirable proportions, worked into the curve of the groining by an artifice worthy of a master-mind, and which should not escape the observer. A life of Etheldreda is related in a series of carvings happily uninjured to this day. The carpentry of the roof, strong enough to sustain the great weight of a lantern of lead-covered oak, has been admired by a succession of competent judges, with Sir Christopher Wren at their head.

Alan removed entirely the eastern ruins of Abbot Richard's choir, and united the new octagon to Northwold's presbytery by three bays of remarkable beauty. In these three bays Ely possesses probably the most perfect example extant of the pure Edwardian or Decorated style. In the six bays of Northwold the Early English style is presented, as we have said, in grace and beauty well-nigh unrivalled. Both are marked by a specialty full of interest. It is this :—When Northwold (or his architect) designed the presbytery, he respected the proportions already established by his predecessors, and carried his string-courses forward at the same levels. Alan followed this excellent example in his three lovely bays. Hence the Early English and Decorated styles at Ely differ widely from the types of those styles as existing in perfection at Salisbury and at Lichfield.

ELY CATHEDRAL, FROM THE SOUTH.

7

The lofty triforium must be regarded as a great characteristic and peculiarity of this church, and its treatment has given occasion for the introduction of work of the very highest degree of excellence. The eye ranges with entire satisfaction over the ornamentation lavished upon these nine bays. It is never wearied with admiring the clustered columns of Purbeck marble, boldly carved as to their capitals with masses of foliage, and the long corbels of the same refractory material, each representing a marvellous amount of untiring industry as well as of artistic skill—the low open parapet running along the string-courses; the tracery of the triforium-openings and of the clerestory windows; above, the rich vault.

The changes introduced by successive bishops were not always improvements. Thus Bishop Barnet (1366—1373), unroofing the triforium of the presbytery to the extent of two bays on each side, filled the arches with glass as windows. This was done, probably, with the intention of throwing more light upon the shrines of the abbesses. Happily the bad example was not followed. Bishop Gray, however (1454—1478), thoroughly accomplished as he was, altered for the worse many or most of the windows in the aisles; and it was in his time that the outer walls of the triforia were raised, and the character of the whole structure thereby much altered.

Nor must it be supposed that all the bishops were nursing fathers of their cathedral church. Some were too busily occupied with great affairs of the State to concern themselves much with Ely and its abbey.

The convent had the right of nominating to the see, but its election was often set aside by the Pope. The distinguished sacrist, then prior, Alan, had been elected in 1345, but Thomas de Lisle was intruded by Clement VI. Louis de Luxembourg, Archbishop of Rouen, and afterwards cardinal, was similarly intruded in 1438. That jealousies should have arisen between the bishop, the head of the diocese, and the prior, the head of the convent, can occasion no surprise. Even after the division of the revenues of the abbey on the establishment of the see, the position of the prior was one of high dignity and ample emolument. In 1474 we find that he travelled with a retinue of twenty servants.

To John of Crawden (or Crowden), elected prior in 1321, the church and abbey were largely indebted for judicious administration and personal munificence. Living on terms of close friendship with Bishop John of Hotham, these two distinguished men, aided as they were by royal favour, secured many privileges for the monastery, which may be said to have reached the culminating point of its prosperity under their rule. Crawden greatly improved the secular buildings of the abbey; and he erected besides a beautiful little chapel or oratory, which still, happily, remains.

The cathedral is not rich in monuments. The great bishops, abbots, and priors, to whom the fabric owes its sumptuous grandeur, lie buried, for the most part, under its pavement; but we have to deplore in some cases the displacement or destruction of the tombs which commemorated them. Their true monument is the church which they helped to rear and beautify.

Turning from the choir, fitted now with the beautiful fourteenth-century stall-work of Alan, enriched by modern *alti-rilievi*, and closed in by an oak screen with brass grilles and gates, we betake ourselves to the Lady Chapel.

This superb example of the Decorated style will probably be seen with something like astonishment by those who enter it for the first time. Its erection, begun in 1321, side by side with the vast works entailed on the monks by the fall of their tower, is an instance of indomitable energy characteristic of the times. Bishop Montacute (1337—1345), who succeeded the munificent Hotham, was a large contributor towards its cost, and his body was buried in front of its altar; but it was not actually finished until 1349.

THE WEST DOOR,
INTERIOR.

OVIN'S CROSS.

The sculptures with which the interior is profusely adorned, though the figures are now, with one single exception, headless, are thought to betray an Italian hand, or the influence of an Italian school of artists. In the days of its glory the whole chapel must have been a perfect store-house of statuary and elaborate canopies; no part of the wall-space was left undecorated with diapering, executed in the most brilliant colours or carved in the stone itself, and it is not easy to name any example of old masonry of which the execution is more finished and masterly. Every true lover of art must wish to see this English "Sainte Chapelle" cleared of all which now disfigures it, and reverently restored to its pristine beauty.

The dissolution of the abbey in 1531 fell gently upon Ely. When the prior became dean, and when eight canons, three of whom had been monks, were established in houses of residence near the church; when eight minor canons, six of whom had been monks, with eight singing-men, eight choristers, and the masters of a school for twenty-four poor boys of Ely, were lodged in the old monastic buildings, the change, however important in itself, must have been little more than nominal to those on the spot.

But an end had come to the care and devotion lavished on the cathedral. Bishop Goodrich (1534—1554), the last episcopal Lord Chancellor, and Bishop Cox (1559—1581) were resolute promoters of the Reformation, and cared little for the relics of the past. The Lady Chapel was handed over in the reign of Elizabeth to the parish of the Holy Trinity in Ely as its church, with the usual results. The Parliamentary Survey in 1649, signed " Mr. Cromwell," condemned to destruction many of the conventual buildings which were still standing, though its behests were not always obeyed. The potent Protector is believed to have willingly saved from utter profanation the church with which he was so familiar, for he resided for some years in Ely, and is said to have collected rents, in early life, for the dean and chapter. But the historian and novelist Defoe, in his " Tour Through the Islands of Great Britain," published early in the eighteenth century, speaks of the cathedral as tottering to its fall, and likely, in a very few years, to become a total ruin. From this fate it was saved by timely though tasteless repairs, executed with great mechanical ingenuity by Richard Essex, a builder of Cambridge, in the episcopate of Bishop Mawson (1754—1770); and in 1845 great works of restoration were commenced which have placed the church beyond the reach, we trust, of danger. With these works two names must always be associated: those of George Peacock, dean (1839—1858), and Edward Bowyer Sparke, canon (1829—1879).

W. E. Dickson.

EXETER.

 THE monastic church of the Benedictines, dedicated to St. Mary and St. Peter, served for the episcopal seat of Leofric, the first Bishop of Exeter, on that prelate's translation from Crediton, by King Edward the Confessor, in 1050, and continued to be the cathedral church until the reign of King Henry I. in 1112. This Saxon cathedral seated two bishops—namely, Leofric and Osbern; the latter, dying in 1102, was succeeded by William Warelwast, a nephew of William the Conqueror, after a lapse of years, occasioned by disputes between the Church and Crown concerning investitures. "The 'chronicon' of the Church of Exeter assigns to him (Warelwast) the honour of rebuilding the cathedral. Of that structure we have remaining the north and south towers, forming the transepts of the present church, and some traces in the Chapels of St. Andrew and St. James, and in the south-east door leading into the cloisters."* This cathedral, commenced by Warelwast in 1112, and completed by Bishop Henry Marshall in 1206, may be best described as being a Norman and semi-Norman building, for the change in the form of the arch from that of the semicircular (Norman) to that of the pointed form had commenced in about mid-distance between the eras of these two prelates. Six bishops occupied this cathedral, and during the siege of Exeter by King Stephen in 1136 it was greatly damaged.

"To the same period we may safely ascribe the small quasi-transepts of the choir," now known as the Chapel of St. Andrew, on the north, and that of St. James, on the south; to these may be added the Lady Chapel, and the two adjacent Chapels of St. Mary Magdalene (north) and St. Gabriel (south), all of which have experienced transmutations by later hands. The chapter-house, originally by Bishop Bruere in the thirteenth century, also passed through similar changes under Bishop Lacy in the fifteenth century. Bishop Bruere also originated the capitular body by the appointment of a dean, and by the elevation of the precentor, chancellor, and treasurer to the position of dignitaries.† He also fitted the choir with stalls and seats, amongst them the curious and unique misereres. ‡

The next important event connected with the history of Exeter Cathedral is its entire transformation from the ponderous Norman and semi-Norman character

---

* Dr. Oliver.　　　　　† Dr. Oliver.　　　　　‡ Archdeacon Freeman.

to that of the lightness and elegance of the Decorated period, emerging as it did from the Early English style which it superseded. To Bishop Peter Quivil, an Exeter man, is undoubtedly due the credit of the great design. "To transmute this, without any pulling down, into a structure of the most airy lightness and grace, was a daring project indeed, the realisation of which was destined to be unremittingly prosecuted, through nearly a whole century, by men every way fitted to the task. And Quivil made the first plunge—

> "He was the first that ever burst
> Into that silent sea."

His first work was the transformation of the great transeptal crossing from Romanesque ponderousness to Gothic grace. To appreciate the manner in which he initiated the process of translating the massive Norman-French into elegant Middle-Pointed English, we must take our stand in the transept crossing: say at the south-west angle, looking north-east. The great features are the mazy windows, fluted arches, branched vaulting, and slender Purbeck shafts, and the pierced balconies attached to the massive Norman walls.

Quivil did not, however, as is commonly supposed, originate the pointed transeptal arches. What he did was to enrich the already existing arches and piers, and take down the partition walls, which still extended some way up the towers. But we owe him much more than this. The whole idea of transformation was his; and we may almost be sure that he left behind him the plans for it. And so entire was the metamorphosis as not unfairly to have won for him the title of "Founder of the New Cathedral," which the *Exeter Chronicle* (fifteenth century) has given him.*

Bishop Bitton succeeded Quivil in 1292, and to him is credited the transformation of the choir as his chief work. He also dealt with the Lady Chapel, and those of St. Mary Magdalene and St. Gabriel; in proof of this Archdeacon Freeman quotes the charges for stone, colour, bosses, glass, &c., from the fabric rolls.

Among the great changes made by those "master-builders" were those of the insertion of the present wide windows in the place of the narrow ones of the Norman or transition period. The rolls furnish full particulars of the charges for glass and glazing. In 1299 the sum of £170 6s. 2d. was laid out, and in 1307 a further sum of £156 19s. 1d., for repairs, &c.; great sums when we consider that skilled artisans worked at 3d. per day.

The precentor of Exeter Cathedral, and a native of the county of Devon, was elected to the bishopric in 1307, on Quivil's death. Stapeldon was inducted to the see with great pomp, and became a liberal benefactor to his cathedral;

* Archdeacon Freeman.

for in 1310 the expenses thereon amounted to £383 18s. 8d., and in 1318 to £176 16s. 5d.* Dr. Oliver says of this prelate: "That he vaulted a part of his choir is certain; that he prepared a large stock of materials, glazed several windows, provided a gorgeous canopy over the silver high altar, cannot be questioned; and to him is assigned the erection of the matchless sedilia on the south side of the sanctuary." He probably re-seated the choir, and, in the opinion of the late Archdeacon of Exeter, the magnificent episcopal throne was his work, although

THE WEST FRONT.

usually attributed to Bishop Bothe at a much later period. Bishop Stapeldon's generosity stimulated a corresponding feeling in that of his own church dignitaries, as well as those of other clerics and laymen in his diocese. Dean Lyttleton calculates that from the beginning of the fourteenth century to the middle of the succeeding one, £1,000 a year was expended upon the cathedral.

Stapeldon's successor, James Berkley, occupied the episcopal throne for only the brief period of a few months, and was succeeded by another "master-builder," the famous John de Grandisson,† of royal and noble lineage. Whilst chaplain to Pope John XII. he had obtained that potentate's favourable notice, and at the vacancy was appointed by his Holiness to the see of Exeter in 1327. On taking possession of the see he found the cathedral in an incomplete state, and loaded

* Britton and Brayley.

† The bishop's sister, the Lady Catherine, is the heroine of the romantic story of the institution of the Order of the Garter.

with pecuniary difficulties. These in due time were got rid of, and succeeding in 1358 to the wealthy peerage of his brother Peter, Lord Grandisson, the bishop was enabled to carry out and complete the great design so nobly commenced by his predecessor, Peter Quivil, who vaulted the whole of the nave, including the aisles, inserted their windows, and the great window of the west end. Adjoining the south side of the principal entrance he constructed the chapel of St. Radegundes as his mortuary chamber, on the site of an ancient chapel of similar dedication. Thus, after seventy years from Quivil's time, was the great work completed in its main features. The magnificent façade of apostolic, saintly, and royal personages was probably added by Bishop Brantyngham, or even later bishops, as it possesses many indications of the handiwork of later artists, especially in the Gothic fan tracery of the northern entrance of the west front.

No material injury from fire, sword, or storm was done to the cathedral until the Civil Wars in the seventeenth century, when the city was taken by the Parliamentary forces under Fairfax, and the cathedral sustained much damage at the hands of its Puritan occupants. Extracts have been commonly made from the Rev. Bruno Ryves's paper, the "Mercurius Rusticus," to show the amount of desecration and destruction

THE THRONE.

wrought by these persons; but these accounts are now generally supposed to have been much exaggerated. A partition wall was run up during the Commonwealth at a cost of £150, and the church was divided into two portions, and named respectively East Peter's and West Peter's, for the use of the Presbyterians and Independents. At the Restoration this innovation was removed, by means of an early application to the King and Council by Dean Ward, afterwards bishop of the diocese. Dr. Oliver says, quoting from his biographer: "He accordingly caused the partition to be pulled down, and repaired

A A

and beautified the cathedral; the expenses whereof amounted to £25,000. He next bought a new pair of organs, esteemed the best in England, which cost £2,000."

A correspondent of the *Exeter and Plymouth Gazette* to its "Notes and Queries for Devonshire and Cornwall," in 1855, says: "It would seem that the diocesan Church of St. Peter, at Exeter, was provided with an organ at a very early period, though it is a question with the musical antiquary what was the exact character of the instrument referred to in early records under the title which now bears so distinctive a meaning. In the fabric rolls of A.D. 1286 is a charge of 4s. for work about the organs;" and Mr. Ellacombe, in his paper on "Bells," quotes an earlier case from the Record Office, namely, in 1284, where provision is made for repairs of the organ. Roman authorities say that the organ was used in churches as early as A.D. 660. Dr. Hook thinks organs were introduced into the service of the church in the tenth century.

The organ-screen is supported by four Purbeck stone pillars, from which spring the groins of three depressed arches. Above these is a row of thirteen compartments filled with curious ancient paintings, representing the leading incidents from the Old and New Testament history, as follows, commencing at the north end :—

1. The Creation.	7. The Angel appearing to Zacharias.
2. Adam and Eve in Paradise.	8. The Nativity.
3. The Deluge.	9. The Baptism of Christ.
4. Moses dividing the Red Sea.	10. Descent from the Cross.
5. Destruction of Solomon's Temple.	11. The Resurrection.
6. Building of the Second Temple.	12. The Ascension.

13. Descent of the Holy Ghost.

Archdeacon Freeman is of opinion that the screen, judging of it from its general features, is of the later portion of the Decorated period. Also, during the time of the Commonwealth, the cloisters, then somewhat dilapidated, were finally destroyed, after partial use as a serge market. Bishop Brantyngham (fourteenth century) and his successor, Stafford, renewed the buildings, of which nothing now remains.

In the north tower hangs the great "Peter" bell, said to have been originally brought from Llandaff. Its reputed weight is 14,000 lbs. It is only used as a clock bell.

In the south tower there are eleven bells; ten of these are rung in peal, the heaviest and finest in tone in the kingdom. The tenor ("Grandisson") weighs 7,550 lbs.

Below, in the north wall, is the curious clock erected by Bishop Courtenay (fifteenth century), with its motto, "Pereunt et imputantur."

The dimensions of the fabric are about as follows:—

		FEET.
Length from west entrance to eastern end of Lady Chapel.	. . . .	380
Breadth of nave and aisles	. . . .	72
Length of transept .	. . . .	138
Breadth of ditto	. . . .	28½
Height of vaulting from pavement	. . . .	66
Height of towers	. . . .	130

The great east window and the west window claim a passing notice. Of the former, it will be seen that it does not harmonise in style with this portion of the church, being a stage later in date with the rest of the work; it was enlarged from a gable window to its present proportions in the fourteenth century. The fabric rolls of 1391 show the agreement entered into by the dean and chapter with Robert Syen, the glazier of the church, for filling the window with old and new glass. It is composed of figures of saints and angels, of armorial bearings, architectural devices and borders; and of it Dr. Oliver says that, when reading was confined to the comparatively few, instruction was conveyed to the people by these " lively representations of events recorded in the Holy Bible and ecclesiastical history. An appeal was thus made to the head and heart of the spectators; they became intelligibly reminded of the blessings and graces of the Almighty, were excited to a sense of gratitude, and urged to the imitation of God's servants."

Of the great west window the spectator will acknowledge that its tracery harmonises with the completed façade of the building. As it now stands before us, we have the glazing of it, executed, as recorded on the window, in 1766. The glazier, one William Peckitt, of York, seems to have been unsuccessful in obtaining permanency for his colours, designated by Dr. Oliver as " Wm. Peckitt's diluted tints." The head of the window is filled with armorial bearings of the great families of the county, royal badges and devices, and apostolic figures, with St. Peter in the centre light. An old printed description of this window says of it that it " is 37 feet high and 27 broad, besides the coats of arms, probably adorned with supporters, coronets, crests, and mottoes; the spaces around the figures (which are 5 feet high), between the arms, and in the smaller lights are elegantly filled with mosaic work, Gothic architecture, foliage, &c., the whole together making the most beautiful appearance, perhaps not excelled by any other work of the kind in England."

" The church," observes Dean Lyttleton, " appears to have been newly glazed, or at least a great part of it, about the year 1317, *temp.* Edward II., with both plain and coloured glass brought from Rouen, in Normandy. Thus, in the fabric rolls in that year: ' In 629 peys de albo vitro empt. apud Rotomagensem xv£ xivs. ixd.' This was probably ordered for the Lady Chapel. In the roll of

1323, 12 feet of coloured or painted glass is charged at 8s., and 8 feet of plain or white at 2s. 3d., so that in Edward II.'s time painted glass appears to have been no more than 8d. per foot, and plain glass 4d." *

Looking through the building from the great western entrance, the eye is led from end to end, embracing and attracted by its lofty and intricate vaulting, organ-case, pillars, and quaint carvings in bosses and corbels; also its remarkable projecting minstrels' gallery, with sculptured figures of instrumentalists. The impression that this vista makes is well described by Charles Knight, in his

THE NORTH TOWER.

"Old England." He says of it: "It is hardly necessary to say the interior is in many respects surpassingly noble and beautiful. The delicate and numberless pillars, clustering together into so many solid groups for the support of the nave and choir, always a beautiful illustration of a beautiful thought, the power resulting from union, seem to particularly arrest our attention in Exeter Cathedral."

The entire range of the north side of Exeter Cathedral may be inspected and taken in at one view from the green on this side of the building, while only the nave, tower, and chapter-house can be seen on the south side; and, as Archdeacon Freeman remarks, the plan, "as now completed, exhibits perhaps the most perfect specimen in the world of bilateral (or right and left hand) symmetry. Not only does

* Cooke's "Topography" (Devon).

pillar answer to pillar, and aisle to aisle, and window tracery to window tracery, but also chapel to chapel : St. John Baptist's to St. Paul's, St. James's to St. Andrew's, St. Saviour's to St. George's, St. Gabriel's to St. Mary Magdalene's; while, to crown all, the grand characteristic feature of our cathedral—the transeptal towers—completes this balance of parts, and was, indeed, the primary instance and model of it.

From the north side of the building the visitor will notice the interception of the nave and choir by the two massive Norman towers ; and in the north face

THE MINSTRELS' GALLERY.

of the north tower the insertion of the large Decorated window. Among recent alterations the great window in the north transept has been filled with stained glass by Hardman. It is the gift of the women of Devonshire, and represents famous women in Bible history. That in the south tower was put in to the memory of the late Sir J. Duke Coleridge, father of the present Lord Chief Justice of England. The cloisters have now been partly restored on the south side, and are adapted to the purposes of a library, in which provision will be made for the many valuable MSS. and printed records and books belonging to the capitular body.

It should be added that in 1888 the colours of the 11th Devonshire Regiment (2nd Battalion) were placed in the north aisle of the nave, with a suitable inscription. Those of the 9th Royal Lancers may also be seen close at hand, with the famous bronze relief of Marochetti.

H. E. REYNOLDS.

GLOUCESTER.

THE Church of the Holy and Undivided Trinity owes its present dedication and its distinction as a cathedral to Henry VIII.; but it had existed for many centuries before the Reformation as the church of the great Benedictine Abbey of St. Peter.

Tradition speaks of a bishop and a Christian king at Gloucester in the second century; but there is no trustworthy evidence for the story of King Lucius and his burial in the Church of St. Mary de Lode. It is altogether improbable that Christianity had any recognised position in Britain until the early part of the fourth century; but we can readily believe that after the conversion of Constantine, Glevum, a Roman town of great importance, as commanding the passage of the Severn and one of the principal highways into South Wales, became an episcopal see.

The battle of Deorham, in 577, swept away Christianity from the vale of the Severn; and for many years the Romano-British town of Caer Gleow, or Glou-ceaster, lay desolate and in ruins. Fifty years later the present counties of Gloucester and Worcester, at that time occupied by the Hwiccas, a West Saxon tribe, passed under the sway of the Mercian king Penda. Penda's grandson and successor Ethelred, who was a Christian, made a large grant of land to the Hwiccian ealdorman or under-king Osric, on condition that he built a monastery at Gloucester, and constituted his sister Kyneburg the first abbess. This was in the year 681. Osric was raised to the throne of Northumbria in the year 718, and dying in 729, was brought to Gloucester, and buried before the altar of St. Petronilla, near the grave of his sister Kyneburg who had died in 710. His chantry chapel lies on the north side of the choir, and his effigy bears on its breast a representation of a Romanesque building. It is an old figure—older than the chapel which William Parker, the last Abbot of Gloucester, built in memory of the founder, but of course not so old as the days of pre-Norman Christianity. On the east wall of the chapel, at the feet of the effigy, these words are still legible: "𝕺𝖘𝖗𝖎𝖈𝖚𝖘 𝕽𝖊𝖝 𝕱𝖚𝖓𝖉𝖆𝖙𝖔𝖗 𝕳𝖚𝖏𝖚𝖘 𝕸𝖔𝖓𝖆𝖘𝖙𝖊𝖗𝖎𝖎."

There were three abbesses in succession—Kyneburg, Eadburgh, and Eva—all of them ladies of royal lineage, and two of them queens. Eva, the last of the abbesses, died in 767, and was buried, like her predecessors, before the altar of St. Petronilla. Then followed a period of shame and disaster. The nuns were outraged and driven from their abbey, and Offa, the Mercian conqueror of West Saxons and Britons, would not or could not help them. St. Peter's lay in ruins for fifty years.

Beornulph, the Mercian king who was slain in East Anglia in 825, moved with compassion at the ruined state of his predecessor's abbey, is said to have rebuilt it. Instead of a nunnery he made it a college of secular canons or preachers, who dressed and lived as though they were laymen, and who were for the most part married.

In 862 Burgred, King of the Mercians, confirmed all his predecessor's donations to St. Peter's, and freed the canons from all lay service, on condition that they should pray for his soul and the souls of his ancestors.

In course of time a rival minster arose at Gloucester. Æthelflæd, the brave Lady of the Mercians, founded another college of canons in honour of the Northumbrian king, St. Oswald, and translated his bones to Gloucester from Bardney. Æthelflæd's foundation was known as the New Minster, whilst St. Peter's was "Ealdanhame," the old home.

Canute the Dane is said to have driven out the secular canons, and to have substituted for them monks of the order of St. Benedict in 1021. This change, which was destined to be reversed more than five centuries later, was unacceptable to the citizens of Gloucester, and the followers of the portreeve, Wulphin le Rue, fell upon seven of the monks and slew them near the banks of the Severn. Wulphin was compelled to make a pilgrimage to Rome, and only obtained pardon for the crime on condition that he gave two of his best manors—Highnam and Churcham— to the abbey, to provide maintenance for seven monks, who should daily say masses for his soul.

The first abbot of the new order was Edric, one of the secular canons, who took the tonsure and the monk's cowl in order that he might enjoy this honour. But Edric's heart was ill at ease. The Benedictine monks were imbued (so the memorial says) with no saving knowledge, nor were they under the restraint of a just conscience; so troubles came upon them—St. Peter's was spoiled by the Danes, and the monks were driven out. Edric went away disgusted and disheartened, and died, and was buried elsewhere.

In 1051 there was a great meeting of Edward the Confessor and his nobles at

THE CATHEDRAL, FROM THE NORTH-WEST.

Gloucester. Godwin, Earl of Kent, came there with his sons and a large force, and complained of the wrong done to his people, the burghers of Dover, by Eustace of Boulogne. Two years later there was another meeting at Gloucester to organise a raid on the territory of a Welsh prince. The position of Gloucester as a frontier town gave it an importance in the eleventh, twelfth, and thirteenth centuries that was only inferior to that of London, York, and Winchester.

During the reign of Edward the Confessor the style of architecture which we call Norman was introduced into England, and soon after the foundation of Westminster, Aldred, Bishop of Hwiccas, commenced a new abbey in this style at Gloucester. By the seventh year of the Confessor's reign the under-croft, the choir.

and the chapter-house were completed, and dedicated to St. Peter. The new church was not exactly on the site of Osric's. About this time the boundaries of the town of Gloucester were extended to the north and north-west, and the north-west angle

THE SOUTH PORCH.

of the old Roman wall was demolished. Aldred seems to have availed himself of the materials and to have occupied the site with his new monastery.

In 1062 Aldred was translated from Worcester to the archiepiscopal see of York, and he retained, as security for expenditure out of his private purse, several manors belonging to St. Peter's Abbey and St. Oswald's Priory. Wulstan, the second Abbot of Gloucester, went away on a pilgrimage to Jerusalem, and his abbey was left in charge of two monks and eight young boys. The old conventual buildings had been destroyed with the church, and the work of restoration was arrested before a new day-room, dormitory, and refectory had been erected. Moreover, the treasury of the abbey was impoverished by extraordinary expenditure and by the cupidity of Aldred. Such was the state of things at Gloucester when William the Norman, in 1066, won for himself the crown of England at Hastings.

About 1067 Gloucester fell into the hands of the invaders, and Aldred's church was seriously damaged by fire, whether by Normans or Saxons we cannot tell. It is not unlikely that the foundations of the new choir were defective, for Aldred had chosen a site that was full of springs of water. This led to faults in the arches and groining of the crypt. King William recognised the importance of Gloucester as a frontier town, and held his court here at Christmas more than once. In 1072 Serlo, William's chaplain, was installed as abbot, and so destitute was he of funds, that he was driven to seek, and he obtained, pecuniary assistance from the neighbouring Abbey of Evesham. Serlo was a man of determination and energy, and under his rule the fortunes of St. Peter's rapidly improved. William bestowed on the monastery the manors of Barnwood and Brompton, and the Church of St. Peter, Norwich; his sons Robert, William, and Henry were also generous patrons. The Norman knights, who were encouraged by the Conqueror to seize the lands of the Welsh in the counties of Monmouth, Glamorgan, and Brecknock, quieted their consciences by donations of Welsh lands and churches to Serlo and his successors.

Thus the means were provided for the restoration of Aldred's choir and the addition of a nave and conventual buildings. Serlo's first work was to case and strengthen the arches of the crypt and repair the choir and chapter-house. In 1089 he laid the foundation of the nave, and in 1100 the church and monastery were re-dedicated with great honour by Sampson, Bishop of Worcester, and by Gondulf and Henry, Bishops of Rochester and Bangor. Aldred's work may be distinguished by its lack of ornament; Serlo's workmen used zigzag or chevron moulding, and their masonry was more solid and imposing than that of the earlier structure. It requires more than a glance to realise how much of the Norman work still remains. At first sight the choir and the transepts seem to belong to the fourteenth century, but on further examination it is found that the Perpendicular work is only skin-deep. The panelling has been skilfully attached, as though with cement, to the Norman arches, which have been cut away to receive it.

In 1092 William Rufus held a great Witenagemot, or council of his wise men, in St. Peter's Abbey, and Anselm was compelled, notwithstanding his entreaties to be spared the honour, to accept the vacant Archbishopric of Canterbury. Mr. Freeman says that almost everything that happened in the reign of William II. somehow contrived to happen at Gloucester. In 1100 the king was slain in the New Forest, but not without a warning reaching him from Abbot Serlo that some such calamity was overhanging him.

All this time, under the sway of Serlo, the abbey was rapidly approaching completion. Two years after its re-dedication a fire is said to have consumed the town and church of Gloucester. The same story is frequently told in the abbey chronicles. We must suppose that on such occasions only the flat wooden roof or the wooden bell-towers perished; the walls and pillars, which still bear the marks of fire, remained comparatively uninjured.

In 1104 Serlo passed away, and was buried on the south side of the choir, where a bracket monument was in later times erected to his memory.

Serlo's successor, Abbot Peter, was distinguished for his love of the fine arts. An example of his taste is preserved in the South Kensington Museum—a latten candlestick, bearing the following inscription:—

"ABBATIS PETRI GREGIS ET DEVOTIO MITIS
ME DEDIT ECCLESIE SANCTI PETRI GLOECESTRE."

This candlestick was probably sold many years after the death of Abbot Peter, when the religious houses were called upon to give up part of their treasures to ransom Richard Cœur de Lion from an Austrian prison.

The next event of any great interest at St. Peter's was the burial of Robert, Duke of Normandy. He died in Cardiff Castle in 1134, was brought to Gloucester, and reverently buried in front of the high altar. There is some difficulty about this statement of the chronicle; for immediately below the tiled floor of the choir is the groined roof of the crypt, and an inscription on the wall of the chapter-house says: "Hic jacet Robertus Curtus." But the effigy of Duke Robert, carved in Irish bog-oak, which now lies encaged in Abbot Boteler's chapel on the north side of the north choir aisle, formerly rested on an altar-tomb in the middle of the choir, and ought to be replaced where Sir Gilbert Scott has laid a parallelogram of red tiles to receive it. During the Civil Wars the effigy was broken in pieces by the Parliamentary soldiers; but Sir Humphry Tracy carefully preserved the fragments, and at the Restoration had them fastened together, repainted, and taken back to the cathedral. The bodies of many other Norman knights were laid to rest in the chapter-house. There are inscriptions in the arcades to Roger Fitz-Milo, Earl of Hereford, Richard Strongbowe Fitz-Gilbert, Earl of Pembroke, Walter de Lacy, Sir Philip de Foye, Bernard Newmarch, Pagan de Cadurcis, and Adam de Cadurcis, all of whom were patrons of the abbey.

In 1168 a Christian boy, named Harold, was murdered by Jews at Gloucester.

This was followed by the burial of the martyr, as they called him, in the crypt of the church, and the performance of miracles at his grave.

On October 28th, 1216, the young sovereign, Henry III., was crowned in the choir of St. Peter's by the Bishops of Winchester, Bath, Worcester, and Exeter.

SHRINE OF EDWARD II.

Six years after this coronation the building of the great central tower was commenced, and the work was completed in 1239, when the abbey church was re-dedicated by Walter de Cantilupe, the patriot Bishop of Worcester. No trace of the Early

THE CLOISTERS.

English tower remains—in fact little work of this period is to be found in the cathedral. The vaulting of the nave, completed by the monks in 1242 with their own hands, the reliquary, if it be one, in the north transept, the arches of the ruined infirmary next the palace garden, and the north-east doorway of the cloisters, are the principal examples. Yet at one time the great tower, the flanking towers at the west end of the nave, the Lady Chapel of the De Willingtons, the stalls in the choir, and much more, were Early English.

In 1283 Gloucester Hall was founded at Oxford by the Giffards of Brimps-field, on the site of Worcester College; and in 1298 and 1301 we read of monks of St. Peter's proceeding to their doctor's degrees in the presence of abbots, bishops, and nobles. Thus Gloucester took its part in the great revival of learning.

The examples of Decorated or Edwardian architecture which may be found in Gloucester Cathedral are the windows of the south aisle, with the characteristic ball-flower moulding, the vaulting and buttresses of the same aisle added to the Norman work by Abbot Thokey in 1318, the windows in the aisles and chapels of the choir, and the beautiful tomb of Edward II. The murder of that king in Berkeley Castle, and his subsequent burial in St. Peter's Abbey, did more than anything else for the welfare of that monastery. The tide of popular feeling that

THE CLOISTERS, FROM THE CLOISTER GARTH.

turned the weak and misguided sovereign into a saint and a martyr swept thousands of pilgrims laden with offerings to his shrine at Gloucester. Then there began to rise, in the new architectural style which Professor Willis in 1860 so plainly showed to have been invented at Gloucester, and of which the south aisle (1329—1337) is the earliest known example, that marvellous adaptation of earlier work, so perfectly unique, the choir of Gloucester Cathedral, and the beautiful cloisters, with their roofing of fan tracery.

The flying buttresses in the choir, between the piers supporting the tower, deserve special attention. They were designed for the capitals of the vaulting to rest upon, and do not give any real support to the tower. The east window was erected about 1350. The architect of that date removed the Norman chapel, and widened the sides of the eastern termination of the choir; then he threw up a vast network of vertical and horizontal mullions, and filled the compartments with painted glass, representing Apostles, saints, kings, and ecclesiastics, as well as the heraldic shields of many of Edward III.'s nobility. An interesting article on this window by Mr. Winslow appears in the *Archæological Journal*, vol. xx.

The same architect took down and rebuilt the Norman gallery which spanned the choir, using over again the Norman ashlar work and chevron moulding.

The "Whispering Gallery," as it is called, is pointed out to visitors as one of the most striking features of the cathedral. So ingenious is its construction that the faintest whisper at one end is heard distinctly at the other.

The cloisters were commenced in 1351, and completed in 1412. The south walk has twenty carols, or cells with windows, where the monks wrote and studied. The north walk has a large trough, which the monks used as a lavatory. Opposite the trough is a recess for the towels. Very few traces are left of the great dining hall or refectory, which occupied the space on the north side of this cloister walk.

The chronicles of St. Peter's terminate with the fourteenth century, and from this time to the Reformation we are almost entirely dependent upon what Leland, the great itinerant antiquary of the reign of Henry VIII., "learned of an ould man made lately a monke of Gloucester." about the later additions and alterations in its structure. In 1421—1437 Abbot Morwent rebuilt the west end of the nave, removed the western towers, and commenced the transformation of the Norman arches into Perpendicular, a work which his death happily arrested when he had completed the western bay. In 1460 the great eastern tower was begun to be rebuilt, and was finished in 1482. In the latter half of the fifteenth century, nearly at the close of the reign of Edward IV., the present Lady Chapel was substituted for the earlier structure of Ralph and Olympias de Willington. The abbey was now complete, and with its window tracery and painted glass, its frescoes and encaustic tiles, its sculptured monuments and vaulted roofing, was the glory not only of Gloucestershire, but of all the west. Alas! all this was soon to be changed by the hands of the spoilers, with Thomas Cromwell at their head. On the 4th of January, 1540, the king's commissioners visited the abbey, and demanded its surrender. Abbot Parker was probably dead, though it is not known where he died, or whether he was buried in the chantry chapel that he had built for himself at the west end of the tomb of Edward II.; but the prior and the monks were there to sign the fatal deed and receive their pensions. The next year the abbey church was converted into a cathedral; and again, after a lapse of a thousand years, Gloucester had its own bishop.

John Wakeman, the last Abbot of Tewkesbury, was raised to the new see, and when he died was taken back to his abbey church, and buried beneath a hideous effigy representing his body in the last stages of dissolution. His successor, John Hooper, who ruled the united sees of Gloucester and Worcester, died a martyr in front of the old abbey gate. It was he who, in 1553, stripped the cathedral church of its "goods, money, jewels, plate, vestments, and ornaments," and only left the chime of bells, which is still the glory of the city, and "one chalys without a paten" for the celebration of the Holy Communion.

On entering the triforium of the choir from the spiral staircase, which ascends from the south transept, the attention of the visitor is arrested by a painting of the "Last Judgment," which was discovered in 1718 behind some wainscoting in the nave. There is the usual contrast between the lot of the "blessed" and that of the "cursed." The interest lies in the date of the painting. The classic architecture of the "New Jerusalem," and the absence of the Virgin Mother and St. John the Baptist from our Lord's side, are internal proofs that the painter was influenced by the Renaissance and the Reformation.

Laud was Dean of Gloucester, 1616—1621, but he left no trace of his rule. In 1657 the cathedral church was vested by the Parliament in the mayor and burgesses of the city of Gloucester. The younger Pury had a lease of the deanery, and resided there. The present cathedral library had been founded by Bishop Gabriel Goodman in 1629 for the use of the diocesan clergy, who, in fact, gave the books. Pury, with the permission of the corporation of Gloucester, refounded it in 1648, and induced his friends to join him in munificent donations of books and money. At one time, during the rule of the great Protector, scaffolding was placed against the Lady Chapel, with a view to taking it down and selling the materials; but it was saved by the influence of Pury. In 1660 the cathedral and its possessions were restored to the dean and chapter. In 1665 the organ, which has lately been renovated and improved, was constructed by Thomas and Renatus Harris, a large part of the cost being borne by Anne, Duchess of York, and daughter of Clarendon.

Robert Frampton, Bishop of Gloucester, 1681—1691, was distinguished as a nonjuror. He lost his bishopric, but retained the living of Standish, where he died, and was buried in 1708. Warburton, the distinguished author of the "Divine Legation of Moses," was Bishop of Gloucester, 1759—1779. Josiah Tucker, of whom Bishop Warburton once said that "he made trade his religion," was dean from 1756 to 1799.

To this period belongs a very beautiful monument in the nave, designed by Flaxman, to the memory of Mrs. Morley. The sculptor has represented the mother rising from the sea with an infant in her arms. Mrs. Morley died in 1784 during a long voyage, soon after the birth of her child, and was buried at sea.

In 1836 the sees of Bristol and Gloucester were united in the person of James Henry Monk. The present bishop, Charles John Ellicott, succeeded William Thompson on his translation to York. He is a distinguished theologian, and has taken a leading part in the revision of the New Testament, as his predecessor, Bishop Wakeman, did 340 years ago.

During the rule of the late Dean Law the cathedral was carefully restored under the direction of Sir Gilbert Scott, and a very beautiful reredos was subscribed for by the freemasons of Gloucestershire. The Lady Chapel is still ruined and desolate; but there is not wanting in Gloucestershire either the enthusiasm or the wealth to restore it to its former short-lived grandeur.   W. BAZELEY.

THE CATHEDRAL, SHOWING THE NEW WESTERN TOWERS.

BRISTOL.

A STRANGER reaching Bristol by the Great Western Railway, and driving from the station to the cathedral, may notice that he crosses two bridges—Bristol Bridge, over the Avon, by which he enters what was once the walled city, and the drawbridge over the Froom, by which he leaves it. Before he reaches the steep ascent that leads to Clifton he finds himself in "College Green," an open space some thirty feet above the level of the river Froom, whose grass and sheep and avenues of lime-trees contrast pleasantly with the crowded streets of the old city.

Nearly the whole of the south side of College Green is occupied by the cathedral, and behind the cathedral the whole of the sloping ground down to the river was in ancient days occupied by the various buildings and gardens of the Augustinian abbey. This abbey was founded by Robert Fitzhardinge, son of the chief magistrate of Bristol in King Stephen's reign. Bristol Castle was the stronghold of Robert, Earl of Gloucester, the greatest scholar and warrior of his time, and the commander of his half-sister the Empress Matilda's army. Hither he brought Stephen prisoner after the battle of Lincoln; and here he gave shelter to Matilda and her son the Prince Henry, who was educated by one Matthew in Baldwin Street. Henry never forgot the kindness he had received in Bristol, and enriched Fitzhardinge with the confiscated lands of the Lords of Berkeley when he came to the throne, so enabling him to complete his abbey on a grander scale than he had at first intended.

Of these abbey buildings there now remain: (1) the abbey gateway, a Norman archway of singular beauty (recently restored with turret-stair by Mr. Pearson, R.A.); (2) a yet older Norman archway, leading out of Lower College Green to the abbot's lodging; (3) some remains of the abbot's lodging, preserved by Bishop Butler when he re-built the Palace; (4) through a covered passage, what was once the lower cloister, now the choristers' playground, which should be visited for the sake of seeing the south side of the fifteenth-century refectory, the north face of which, in the upper cloister garth, has been modern-ised; (5) the upper cloisters, and, opening into their eastern alley, the chapter-room, one of the finest specimens of a Nor-man chamber in England (ac-cording to Mr. Street), with a vestibule of Romanesque ar-cading that will well repay study.

THE ABBEY GATEWAY.

Entering the graveyard, a charmingly secluded garden, from which the south side of the cathedral, with its various jutting chapels, may be seen to great advantage, the visitor will look down on the blackened ruins of the bishop's palace, burnt by the rioters in 1831. The story may be read in Southey's Diary. It was Sunday morning, October 30th, and Bishop Gray had insisted on preaching as usual, notwithstanding the expostulations of the minor canon, who feared violence. "My young friend," the bishop said, laying his hand on his shoulder, "these are times when we must not shrink from doing our duty." As the service proceeded his palace was fired, and reduced to a ruin ere the day closed; and the cathedral was only saved by the heroism of the sub-sacrist Phillips, who wrenched an iron bar from a foremost rioter and kept the mob at bay until the door was closed and bolted behind him. The bishop had voted for

C C

the rejection of the Reform Bill in the House of Lords, and was as unpopular as Sir Charles Wetherell, the Recorder of Bristol, who had strenuously opposed it in the Commons.

It was in this palace that a long line of bishops had lived during the three centuries from 1542 (when the monastery was dissolved, and the bishopric, with dean and canons, founded) to 1831. Among them were:—Paul Bush, who was required by Queen Mary to resign his see or his wife Edith, and loyal to the latter, retired to Winterbourn: his *cadaver* monument may be seen in the north aisle of the cathedral; Richard Fletcher, father of the dramatist, whose importunities had troubled the Queen of Scots on the scaffold; Trelawny, one of the seven imprisoned bishops in James II.'s reign, best known by the lines so often quoted—the refrain of a spirited ballad by "the Cornish Bard" of the last generation, Mr. Hawker, Vicar of Morwenstow—

> "And shall Trelawny die? And shall Trelawny die?
> There's twenty thousand Cornish boys will know the reason why;"

Secker, for a few years Bishop of Bristol, translated to Oxford and Canterbury; and then (1738—1750) his friend, most illustrious of all, Joseph Butler, the author of the "Analogy of Religion" and those wonderful sermons on Human Nature, who was buried beneath the throne of our cathedral, as an eloquent Latin inscription bears witness, and a no less eloquent English inscription from the pen of Southey. The "Butler Tower" (the northern of the two west towers, designed by Mr. Street, and completed by Mr. Pearson) is dedicated to his memory. Conybeare was Butler's successor; and a little later (1761—1782) came Newton, the author of the Dissertations on Prophecy. In 1836 the sees of Gloucester and Bristol were united by Act of Parliament; in 1884 another Act was passed to disunite them, which will take effect so soon as the required endowment is provided.

Having thus made the tour of the cathedral precincts, we must take our visitor back to College Green, and ask him to examine carefully the long north front before him. The first thing that will strike him will be the great apparent length of the church. And yet the real length is only 300 feet; but an effect of much greater length is given to it by the want of height, and the want of height is due, as he will soon find out, to the distinguishing peculiarity of the church, the absence of any clerestory. At first it will appear as if the church had no side aisles, but was one long aisle, lighted by lofty windows throughout its length, like a college chapel, or rather like two college chapels placed end to end, with a tower and transept to mark their juncture. But if he walk to either end he will find out his mistake, and perceive that the church has the full complement of three aisles of spacious width, but of co-ordinate height and under one roof. The question will then force itself upon him: What was the motive for this most unusual design, making the church stand altogether alone among our cathedral churches?

Returning to his first point of view, a practised eye will see at once that the long eastern limb is ancient and Edwardian, while the western limb, or nave, with its western towers, is a modern work, similar in style, only in its details more beautiful. The central tower (whose parapet and pinnacle, removed for safety, he must kindly restore in his mind's eye) the visitor cannot fail to admire, stately in its proportion and richly arcaded, all its details dating from the fifteenth century, but in its general design clearly Norman. On enquiry he will learn that the eastern limb is the long and spacious choir which, in Edward II.'s reign, Abbot Knowle built up against the Norman tower then standing. He will then see at once that to have added a clerestory would have dwarfed the effect of the stately old tower, and that Edmund Street, the architect of the present nave, was right in repeating Edmund Knowle's peculiar design, only enriching the details, and so leaving the central tower in perfect harmony with the rest of the church. In my "Early History and Architecture of Bristol Cathedral" (Chillcott, Bristol), I have given reasons for believing that the Norman church had two western towers.

And now, in explaining one problem we have solved another. If the church date in style from Edward II.'s reign, why those transoms in the windows? A little thought will remind one of the difficulty of constructing windows so far more lofty than the side windows of any other cathedral he has ever seen, without the additional strength derived from transoms. Then, again, why those buttresses of such unusual projection, almost hiding the intervening windows from one who looks at the church obliquely? A moment's reflection suggests their necessity to counteract the lateral thrust of a roof of more than 70 feet in total width. Thus, even before we enter the church we have almost forgiven Knowle for the audacious originality of his work. When we enter we more than forgive, nay, we rejoice that our greatest modern architect has completed, and by completing interpreted, Abbot Knowle's design. The internal effect is very striking. Standing at the west end, we have before us a lengthened avenue of arcading, as remarkable for its solemnity as for its beauty. Though the vault is only 52 feet above the floor, there is no feeling of depression. This is due perhaps to the form of arch chosen for the vaulting, not flattened, as at Lincoln and York, but boldly pointed, and springing directly throughout the whole length of the church, not from a triforium, but from the pavement. The lofty side aisles, of equal height with the central aisle, are not seen in the perspective. But the light that streams through the arcade on either side traverses the shadows of the roof wonderfully. The visitor should pause for some time ere he leave his station at this west door. Whenever a cross view is obtained, as he proceeds eastward, the side aisles, with their lofty windows, give the effect of spaciousness; and the purity of the arches between the piers, reminding him by their graceful lancet form of Westminster Abbey rather than of York—the only English churches that have arcades of equal height—will go far to compensate the eye for the want of the familiar triforium and clerestory of our English cathedrals.   Not that the purposes of a triforium are unfulfilled.   A passage on the level of the window-sills traverses the walls from end to end, giving access to every part, for the convenience of the servants of the church.

The visitor who is interested in principles of construction will admire the way in which Abbot Knowle and Mr. Street have carried the thrust of the central vault across the side aisles, by what is, in fact, a flying buttress, to the very massive external buttresses already noticed.   These flying buttresses, or transoms, rest on

THE CHOIR.

the crown of the transverse arches of the side aisles, and from the centre of each, over the crown of the arch below, there springs a cluster of vaulting shafts.

As the visitor moves up the nave, the extreme beauty of Knowle's east window should be observed.   The arms of Edward III. in the apex show that it was finished in that reign, about 1330.   The elder Pugin thought its tracery worthy of comparison with that of Carlisle.   Nor must we omit to turn round and gaze at Mr. Street's rose window over his west portal.   He made drawings before he died for all the painted windows of the nave, and begged that they might be executed by Messrs. Hardman.   This round window represents in its inner lights the heavenly host adoring our Lord in glory, while the outer circle depicts all the several industries of Bristol, which contributed to the building of this nave for the glory of God.   The side windows are to illustrate the power of prayer, the upper lights by incidents from the New Testament, the lower from the Old.   The silvery crispness of Hardman's glass will give pleasure to every eye.   The windows do not enter into competition with oil paintings (the greatest fault stained glass can have), nor are they too dark, but fulfil the true function of a window in transmitting abundant light, and are carefully subordinated to the general architectural effect of the church.

Passing through the modern screen, the visitor will be painfully aware of the need of re-arrangement of the choir.   When the nave was removed the altar was pushed up to the east end to gain room, and the fourteenth-century stalls followed it.   It need hardly be said that this will be set right so soon as funds are forthcoming.   The altar will be brought down to its old place (where the cusping of the vault marks it), leaving an eastern Lady Chapel and processional path behind the reredos.   The side aisles will thus be restored to their proper purpose, and the oak stalls and choir will be brought down to the screen.   The organ too may then be removed from its present unsightly position.

While standing outside in College Green the visitor may have noticed an Early English chapel, and wondered how it came to lean against Abbot Knowle's later chancel aisle.   If he visit this from within he will see the explanation.   It was an elder Lady Chapel, of graceful design, opening into the north transept, at a time when this north transept was also of Early English style, still indicated by the shafts of its northern triplet window.   As there was sufficient space between this chapel and the Norman church for the widening of the side aisle, Knowle left it standing; and removing its high-pitched roof (of which the lines are discernible on one of the pinnacles), he made it lean (as now) against the widened Edwardian church.   At a later date the double wall that separated it from the church was cut away and its arcading mutilated, to admit the insertion of one of the costly altar-tombs of the Berkeley family.   The knight is clad in conical skull-cap or helmet, attached to a hawberk or tippet of mail; the armour is partly mail and partly plate, after the manner of Edward II.'s and Edward III.'s time.   The dress of the lady by his side is also that of the fourteenth century: coif, hood or veil, and wimple cover head, neck, and chin.   A late inscription describes it as commemorating Maurice, Lord Berkeley, ninth baron, who died 8th June, 1368, and the Lady Margaret, his mother (daughter of the infamous Roger Mortimer, Earl of March), who died 5th May, 1337; but the lady is more probably Elizabeth, his wife, daughter of Hugh Despenser.

Three other tombs of the Berkeleys are to be seen in the south aisle, under the stellated monumental recesses (peculiar to the churches of Bristol, Berkeley, and St. David's).   In the easternmost of these recesses, opening into the Berkeley Chapel, lies the second Thomas, Lord Berkeley, who died 1321, and further west the first Lord Thomas (his legs crossed), who died 1243.   This effigy and the adjoining one of the second Lord Maurice (died 1281) must have belonged to the older Norman church.   In similar monumental recesses in the sacrarium we have effigies of Abbot

Knowle, the great builder, and next below him Abbot Newberry in full canonicals; on the south side, adjoining the beautiful sedilia, Newland (or Nailheart), the "good abbot," who built much of the fifteenth-century work.

Knowle's love of natural forms is remarkable. On these stellated recesses we find sculptured the oak-leaf and oak-apple, the vine-leaf, the mistletoe, the thorn, the ranunculus-leaf, with snails carrying their shells over it, and in the vestibule of the Berkeley Chapel the Ammonite of St. Keyna taking the place of the usual ball-flower. The fourteenth-century glass of the sacrarium windows is of great value, and should be carefully examined.

It may perhaps assist the reader if we now give briefly the principal epochs of the church's architectural history, so dating the several parts of the present structure.

1142.—The abbey founded by Robert Fitzhardinge, chief magistrate of Bristol, in whose time Robert, Earl of Gloucester, gave shelter to his half-sister the Empress Matilda, in her struggle with the usurper Stephen; and here Prince Henry spent his boyhood. The church was consecrated on Easter Day, 1148.

1154.—Henry II. bestowed the confiscated estates of Roger de Berkeley on his old friend Robert Fitzhardinge, who, thus enriched, completed his abbey in the more sumptuous style of the chapter-room. He was the founder of the family of the Berkeleys, Lords of Berkeley Castle, so many of whom are buried in this church. The only portions of the Norman church now remaining are the walls and buttresses of the transepts north and south. The line of the old high-pitched roof of the latter may be traced on its south gable, and a small round-headed window in the gable.

1216—1234.—Abbot David is believed to have built the elder Lady Chapel still standing, opening into the north transept, although Mr. Godwin ascribes it to his predecessor, Abbot John. The east window of this chapel (Geometrical or Early Decorated) was inserted about 1290.

1306—1332.—Abbot Knowle began rebuilding the church in the Decorated or Middle Pointed style, completing the choir, but leaving the Norman or Romanesque tower and nave still standing, and laying foundations of a wider nave, discovered in 1865. Berkeley Chapel and Newton Chapel added after Knowle's death, late Decorated.

1481—1515.—Abbot Newland (or Nailheart) remodelled the central tower, reconstructing the roof and windows of the transept in the Third Pointed or Perpendicular style, with rich *lierne* vaulting.

1542.—Dissolution of the monastery and endowment of the church as a cathedral church, with dean and six canons. The ancient Norman nave of Fitzhardinge removed as unsafe.

1866—1874.—The present nave built on old foundations.

1887—1888.—Western tower completed.

It may be well, in conclusion, to put on record the reasons which determined Mr. Street not to attempt to restore the Norman nave removed in Henry VIII.'s reign, but rather to build such a nave as Abbot Knowle would have erected in Edward II.'s reign had he lived to complete his work. In the first place, no traces were left of the ancient Norman nave to guide a restorer except two fragments of the wall of its narrow south aisle; whereas of the nave designed and actually commenced by Abbot Knowle very interesting remains were left. We found, on excavating, the foundations which he had laid for the wall of the north aisle, with deep buttresses (like those of the choir), and for a north porch. We found also the spring of the first arch embedded in the buttress which stood against the north-west pier of the central tower; and built into the prior's lodging (removed in 1867) there was a portion of the south-west angle of the south aisle, where the work was carried up to some height, showing how a triforium gallery was intended to be carried round the nave, as in the choir at the level of the window sills. From these remains it was possible to design a nave substantially such as Knowle intended to build, yet sufficiently differenced in detail to make it no mere servile copy of the choir. It will be noticed that the axis of the nave is inclined to that of the choir at a very perceptible angle, as in so many ancient churches. The total length of the church is 300 feet, the width 73 feet; height from pavement to ridge of vault, choir 50 feet, nave 52 feet. By the two western towers of noble dimensions which Mr. Street has added, the church is now more distinctly marked as the cathedral in distant views of the city.

J. P. NORRIS.

CARLISLE.

UNTIL the other day, when the Church of St. Nicholas became the Cathedral of Newcastle, Carlisle was the most northern of our English cathedrals, and it is still the nearest to Scotland. Being the church of a border city, "the bulwark of England against the Scot," the cathedral has not escaped the perils of its position. It fell into the hands of those who destroyed most of the ancient cathedrals of Scotland, in whose eyes the defacing of churches was a pious work, and they have left their mark upon it to this day. As seen from a short distance outside the city, the peculiarity of its outline must at once strike the observer. It rises in the centre of the town, high above all the other buildings, except the tall chimneys of the factories. The long and lofty choir is a noble object, and the tower, though low by comparison and unworthy of the choir, is not dwarfed by the steeple of any other church. But the beholder looks in vain for the long nave, which is so characteristic of a cathedral church. To the west of the tower only a short piece of the roof is visible, much lower than the choir, and looking not unlike the chancel of a parish church turned round from east to west.

A walk round the outside will enable us to comprehend the general outline of the history of the building. It has been originally a Norman minster of moderate size, but of this Norman church nothing apparently remains, save the south transept and a fragment of the nave, its eastern limb having been replaced by a vast and magnificent choir of the thirteenth and fourteenth centuries, on a scale far exceeding the dimensions of the earlier church. It is easy to distinguish the portions of the original structure from the alterations and additions of later times, the Norman builders having used for the outside a grey freestone, whereas all the later work is of the new red sandstone of the district.

There is little known about the church beyond the general outline of its history, and in the absence of any fabric rolls there has been much doubt and difference of opinion on many points connected with the architecture.

According to the commonly received account, a Norman follower of William Rufus, named Walter, whom he had left at Carlisle to superintend the

CARLISLE CATHEDRAL, FROM THE SOUTH-WEST.

A. W. SCOTT. Sc

8

building of the castle and the fortifications, founded within the city a college of secular priests, but died before the church which he intended to build was completed. Henry I. then took up the work, and in the year 1101 founded a house of regular canons of St. Augustine, and made his English confessor and chaplain, Athelwald, the first prior of the new society.

At this time Carlisle was in the diocese of Durham, and it was not until

CARLISLE, FROM RICKERBY PARK.

1133, when Henry I. founded the bishopric, and made Athelwald the first bishop, that the priory church became a cathedral.

The canons of St. Augustine, or Austin canons, as they were called, were not, strictly speaking, monks, though they lived together under one roof according to the rule (*regula*) of their order, and hence were known as regular canons, to distinguish them from the secular canons of the old foundation cathedrals and other collegiate churches, who lived in separate houses, and moved about in the world (*seculum*) as the canons of cathedrals do now. The Austin canons had a number of priories in England, but only one of these—that of Carlisle—was a cathedral church, and in this respect, therefore, Carlisle stands alone, all the other cathedrals of the new foundation having been the churches of Benedictine monasteries before they were changed by Henry VIII. into chapters of secular canons. From their habit, which consisted of a long black

D D

cassock, a white rocket over it, and over all a black cloak and hood, the
Augustinians were called Black Canons. They also wore beards, and a cap upon
their heads, which distinguished them from monks, who went bareheaded and
shaven. In many Austin foundations the church of the priory was also the
church of the parish, the canons occupying the choir, which was hence called
ecclesia conventualis canonicorum, and the parishioners occupying the nave, which
formed the *ecclesia parochialis*, so that there were two churches within one.
This was the case at Carlisle, and it explains some matters connected with the
history of the church which otherwise it would be difficult to account for. Until
a few years ago this double use of a building which was architecturally only
one church was an existing fact. What remained of the nave was partitioned
off from the choir and transepts, and formed the Church of St. Mary; and notwithstanding the improvement that has been effected by throwing open the
nave and building a new parish church, it is impossible not to feel some regret
at the abolition of an arrangement which had lasted for upwards of seven
centuries and a half, and was essentially a part of the history of the place.

In the arrangement of their domestic buildings the Austin canons followed
the plan of a Benedictine monastery, and grouped them on the south of the
church. At Carlisle some of these buildings are still to be seen, but none of
them are of the same date as the Norman church. What that church was like
when complete we can only tell from a comparison of what remains with other
churches of the same period. The nave was originally eight bays long, instead
of only two as at present, but it was always shorter than the existing choir.
No doubt originally there was a handsome Norman doorway at the west end,
but no drawing or description of the original west front remains. In the centre
of the Norman church was a tower, probably low, of which the piers are still
in situ; and east of the tower was a short choir, supposed to have extended as
far as the end of the present stalls, and to have terminated in a round apse.
Opening out of each transept by an arch in the eastern wall was a small
chapel. The archway can still be seen in the south transept, and it leads into
St. Catherine's Chapel, now used as a vestry, and which, though of thirteenth-
century date, is built on the foundations of a pre-existing Norman chapel.

Such, in outline at least, was what we may call the Norman church of
Athelwald, a plain massive building, with little ornamentation except in the
doorways and windows, but with a certain grandeur in its stern simplicity.
This Norman church is believed to have remained pretty much as it was when
completed in the reign of Henry I. throughout the rest of the twelfth century;
and it was not until Henry III. had reigned some thirty years, and half the
thirteenth century had passed, that the bishop and canons set themselves to
the great work of rebuilding the choir of the cathedral on a vastly larger scale.

Judging from the Early English style of the existing aisles, the work must have been begun about the middle of the thirteenth century, probably under the auspices of Sylvester de Everdon, who was bishop from 1246 to 1255, and there is good reason to believe that it was roofed in before the death of Bishop Irton, in 1292. The new choir was built with very little regard to the old Norman church, and perhaps it was the intention of the bishop and canons when they had finished the choir to rebuild the nave as well. Possibly this was never done for lack of funds, but it is just as probable that the canons considered it was not their business to improve the nave, and that the parishioners might be left to restore their own church. Very beautiful indeed are those parts of the present choir which date from the rebuilding in the second half of the thirteenth century, and the whole, if ever it was completely finished, must have been a noble work. Little is now left beyond the north and south external walls, with the beautiful lancet windows of the aisles, and the exquisite cinquefoil arcade beneath them. Scarcely was the work finished when, in 1292, there was a dreadful fire in Carlisle, which consumed a great part of the city. The priory suffered much. The new choir was left a mass of ruins, the east end, and all except the side aisles, being destroyed. The north transept was also greatly injured, and the conventual buildings perished almost entirely.

The rebuilding of the choir progressed only slowly, probably owing to the disturbed state of the country during the Scottish wars, and it must have been quite unfinished when Edward I., who had been detained at Lanercost by sickness throughout the winter, came to Carlisle in the last year of his reign to meet his Parliament, and to organise an expedition into Scotland. At this time the cathedral was the scene of two important ceremonies. In it the Papal legate preached to the many strangers whom the presence of the court and parliament had brought together, and then proceeded to solemnly excommunicate Robert Bruce, and to pronounce a terrible curse against the usurper of the crown of Scotland.

A few months later Edward came to the cathedral, and there offered up to God the litter in which he had been forced by failing health to make his journey to the north. At the door, as if in token of his complete recovery, he mounted his horse for the first time after many months' illness, and rode away through the gateway of the priory to lead his army into Scotland. But he was destined never to reach it; and at Burgh-by-Sands, on the Solway, within sight of the Scottish coast, he died.

After the fire of 1292 the choir was partially rebuilt, but during the reign of Edward II. the work stood still for want of funds.

It was not until 1352, when Gilbert Welton was bishop, that the work was resumed in good earnest. By him and by his successor, Bishop Appleby, great efforts were made to complete the choir; and by the help of Edward III., and by subscriptions from the Lucies, the Nevilles, the Percies, and other gentry of the north, the church was at length finished. At this period the triforium and the

THE NAVE.

clerestory, which are in the Decorated style of the fourteenth century, were added to the choir, the east end was raised to its present height, and the whole was roofed in and finished in the interior by a wooden ceiling, resplendent with colour and gilding. Portions of this ancient ceiling were discovered at the late restoration, and the present ceiling is a reproduction of the old, in design at least, if not in colouring.

Its east window is the one point in which Carlisle Cathedral stands unrivalled, and on which its architectural fame chiefly rests. Of its kind it is the grandest window to be seen in England, or even in the world. It is not only unsurpassed in size, it is also unmatched in beauty. Those windows that come next to it are a window at Perugia, said to be as large, but not so beautiful in design; the great window at York, which is not so large, nor so elaborate in the tracery; and the east window of Selby, which, though it has very fine tracery, is smaller. The window in the lower part is divided into nine lights by eight mullions, of which the two central ones are thicker than the others, and the tracery, it has been computed, is composed of no fewer than 263 circles, and contains as many as thirteen quatrefoils. As to the glass, the lower portion is modern, but that in the head of the window is ancient, and well deserves careful inspection. The subject is what is called a "Doom," and forms one connected picture, in which are seen the resurrection from the dead, Christ seated on the throne of judgment, the procession of the blessed to the new Jerusalem in Heaven, and the casting of the lost into the place of torment. A minute examination of this old glass has recently led to discoveries which go to prove that it was not inserted until about forty years after the tracery was finished, and that its date is from 1380 to 1384.

The carvings on the capitals of the main pillars of the choir represent the different occupations of each month in the year, and no more interesting or perfect series of the kind is known to exist.

In the choir should be noticed also the fine tabernacle work of the stalls, supposed to

THE EAST WINDOW.

have been put in by Bishop Strickland (1400—1419). It was once painted and gilded, and the numerous niches filled with images, but these have been removed, and the angels which formed the pendants have been roughly sawn off. The backs of the stalls are decorated with a series of paintings representing the legends of St. Augustine, St. Anthony, and St. Cuthbert, executed in the fifteenth century.

In 1540 the priory was dissolved, but it was done without violence. Lancelot Salkeld, the last prior, became the first dean, and two of the old canons regular became prebendaries, or canons, of the new chapter, which was founded by Henry VIII. the year after the priory was suppressed. There was not, as far as is known, any damage done to the cathedral or its ornaments, and the king's charter shows that the services were continued according to the rites of the old religion. The king, however, changed the dedication of the church, and what had been the Priory of the Blessed Virgin Mary became henceforth the Cathedral Church of the Holy and Undivided Trinity.

A good deal of damage must have been done in the reigns of Edward VI. and Elizabeth by the destruction of stained glass, and the defacing of all that might remind men of the old religion. But the mischief done by Protestant enthusiasts, and in later times by neglect or ignorance, has been trivial as compared with the great act of vandalism which was committed in 1646, when Carlisle was besieged and taken by a Scottish army in the name of the Parliament of England.

Once again, in 1746, Scottish soldiers filled the cathedral, but they were of a different race from the destroyers of the nave, and they were there not as conquerors, but as prisoners. When Carlisle surrendered to the Duke of Cumberland, the Highlanders who had been left to garrison it laid down their arms in the market-place, and then went, according to the terms of surrender, to the cathedral, where a strong guard was placed over them. Some mischief may have been done at that time, but it was probably not equal to the damage of 1764, when "a general repair was commenced in the choir, and a great amount of ancient work was destroyed." These repairs consisted in breaking up the fine oak ceiling, and inserting plaster groining beneath it, in removing the screens between the choir piers, together with the ancient bishop's throne, and in replacing them by modern work of poor design. Throughout the last century and the early part of the present one the same destruction of old work went on, but at length, under Dean Tait, better times set in, and the restoration, which was so much needed, was begun. Upon the whole the work was judiciously carried out; and though the archæologist of these more modern days may not approve of all that was done, those who can remember what the cathedral was previously will own that a vast improvement has been effected.

Looking at the building as a whole, its parts are too unequal in scale to make up together one noble and perfect church, and even if two-thirds of the nave had not been destroyed, the Cathedral of Carlisle would not have taken high rank amongst the old cathedrals of England. Nevertheless, it has its noble features, and standing in the lofty choir and looking at the great east window, it is possible for the moment to forget even the destruction of the nave.

W. NANSON.

MANCHESTER.

 THE present Cathedral Church of St. Mary the Virgin, St. George, and St. Denis in earlier times was only a parish church, which first became collegiate in the year 1422, when Henry V. granted a charter to Thomas De-la-Warre, the rector of the parish, who, though a priest, was also lord of the manor. Before that time, as early as William the Conqueror's reign, there had been a church on the wooded rock at the junction of the rivers Irwell and Irk, for in the Doomsday Book we find the following record: "The Church of St. Mary and the Church of St. Michael hold one carucate (about a hundred acres) of land, quit of all taxation except the Dane-gelt." Several traces of a church built of stone about the year 1220 have been found during the recent restorations, yet an author, writing in the year 1650, says that before the collegiation of the parish Church of St. Mary in 1422, the structure was entirely of wood. During the sway of the early barons of Manchester the church was held by some fifteen rectors, including William de la Marcia (1290), afterwards Bishop of Bath and Wells; Walter de Langton (1299), a great architect, subsequently Bishop of Lichfield; John de Verdun (1313), later on Dean of St. Paul's; and Thomas De-la-Warre (1373), the last rector, who endowed the college and procured the first charter. Provision was therein made for a warden, eight priest-fellows, four deacons, and six boy choristers. The first warden was John Huntingdon (1422), a man of great benevolence and piety; his rebus, a hunting scene and two tuns of wine, may be seen on either side of the choir arch, which he completed, together with the upper portion of the arcades. A fine brass to his memory exists, but is hidden in the vaults. The third warden, John Booth (1459), became Bishop of Exeter; while the sixth (1481) was James Stanley, a scion of the Derby family, and afterwards Bishop of Ely. The Derby Chapel, a large building to the north of the choir, was erected to his memory. The bishop lies buried in the wall of this chapel within a pretty little chantry. On his tomb is a brass representing him in full episcopal vestments.

Wardens Walton and Chaderton were respectively raised to the sees of Exeter and Lincoln during the earlier part of Queen Elizabeth's reign, towards the end of which John Dee, a layman and a celebrated alchemist, was appointed their successor.

Warden Dee, who professed to see visions in crystals, and who was deeply imbued with the superstitions of the age, retired in the early years of James I.'s reign, and died a poor man at Mortlake.

The cathedral consists of a nave and aisles, equal in length to the choir and

THE CHOIR SCREEN.

ambulatory; a chapter-house; a lofty west tower; and the following chapels:—the Lady Chapel (*circa* 1313), with a beautiful screen, at the extreme east end of the church; the Jesus Chapel (1506), to the south of the choir, now used as a library; St. Nicholas' Chapel, the oldest chantry in the building (*circa* 1220), to the south of the nave, and St. George's Chapel to the west of it; St. John Baptist's or Derby Chapel (*circa* 1510), with the Ely Chantry to the north of the choir;

St. James' (*circa* 1440) and Holy Trinity (*circa* 1500) Chapels to the north of the nave: north and south porches are now being added. While the beautiful par-close screens still remain around the choir chapels, they have been removed from those in the nave, thereby increasing the area and making in reality a five-aisled church, the widest in the kingdom with the exception of St. Helen's, Abingdon. This great width, however, is not unpleasantly noticeable, owing to the lofty height of the nave arcades, whose clustered pillars of delicately-moulded red sand-stone support elaborately-carved spandrels, and bold five-light clerestory windows of the Perpendicular order. Between each window is an angel of carved oak playing some ancient musical instrument—there are seven with wind instruments on one side, seven with strings on the other, a most unique and beautiful set. The roofs, of solid oak, are almost flat, and panelled with moulded beams and purlins, each intersection being covered by a carved boss.

Entering the choir by the richly-decorated organ-screen, we find the interior small and narrow, but filled with exceedingly beautiful stalls, fifteen on each side. They are surmounted by the most elaborate canopies it is possible to imagine. There are niches for over a hundred saints, and the crockets and finials, cuspings and pinnacles, are bewildering in their variety and multitude. Nor less interesting are the quaint groups of the subcellæ or misereres. Tavern incidents, hunting scenes, fabulous monsters, combats, legends, all find a place, carved with the most elegant minuteness, and fortunately little damaged by the hand of time. The choir is divided into equal portions by two steps, the lower part being called the Radcliffe Choir, from the family which used it as a cemetery: their brasses once covered the floor, but are now replaced by encaustic tiles. In the upper portion of the choir stands the bishop's throne, a sad contrast to, though an imitation of, the stalls by its side. Little need be said of the sanctuary, which is at present enclosed to the eastward by a stone screen, as an elaborate plan of restoration is in contemplation. It should, however, be mentioned that on the death of Bishop Fraser, the space between the octagonal chapter-house and the east end of the south choir aisle was filled by a monumental chapel, separated from the main building by a handsome oak screen. In the middle of this chapel rises a beautiful alabaster altar-tomb, upon which lies the full-length effigy of the deceased prelate; the likeness is an admirable one. On the opposite side of the choir a handsome altar-tomb and effigy of Mr. Hugh Birley has been erected. The nave has also been recently enriched with many stained-glass windows of various merit, among which is one to the memory of the late General Gordon.

We may add that the dimensions of the cathedral are: length, 215 feet; width of nave, 112 feet; height of tower, 140 feet; and area, 18,340 square feet.

Ernest F. Letts.

E E

LIVERPOOL CATHEDRAL, FROM THE NORTH-EAST.

LIVERPOOL.

MANY of the recently-formed bishoprics have found already existing churches, either old collegiate institutions or ancient parish
churches, to afford not unworthy centres for the new diocesan
work. With Liverpool, by far the most important of the new
sees, the case has been very different. No observant visitor to
the modern Tyre can fail to be struck by the exceeding poverty
of her ecclesiastical buildings. The cause of this is to be found
in the very recent date of the city's growth. The inhabitants
speak of the "good old town," with this partial justification, that a charter
of incorporation was granted so long ago as the reign of King John. But,
ecclesiastically, Liverpool was only a chapelry of the parish of Walton-on-the-
Hill down to the end of the seventeenth century. In 1699 an Act of Parliament was passed, by which, subject to certain valuable consideration granted
to the Rector of Walton-on-the Hill, Liverpool was made a separate and independent parish. At a town's meeting held soon after the Act had been obtained,

it was resolved to build a new church to be thenceforth the parish church of Liverpool. Plans were approved and the work begun on a site which was then on the very limit of the inhabited part of the town. The church was completed in 1704, and then consecrated under the name of the Church of St. Peter. In this building the throne of the first Bishop of Liverpool is set up.

A rectangular, box-like structure, with a western annexe in the form of a tower, and an eastern annexe which serves as the sacrarium, presents externally no features of interest. Internally the case is little better. Galleries, north, west, and south—the last containing the organ—take away from whatever effect the open space might have had. The font is almost hidden away under the western gallery, and the eastern end, with oak carving of very good quality, but of altogether un-churchlike design, is partially concealed by the state *cathedra* of the bishop. The next most noticeable points of the interior are the gilded and decorated stands in which on high civic occasions the insignia of the mayor and the corporation are brought to rest. It is, indeed, as the parish church of one of the largest parishes in England, not in any way as a building, that St. Peter's Pro-Cathedral can have any interest to the visitor. To understand what " Peterses " is to the middle and lower classes of Liverpool, one should be there about three o'clock almost any afternoon and see the endless train of babies brought to be christened; or, better still, in the street outside (Church Street), between the hours of eleven and twelve on New Year's Eve. Thousands of men completely block the street, and wait there till " Peterses " has struck the hour. Then, and not till then, can they believe that the New Year has actually come.

The scheme for providing Liverpool with a worthy cathedral was for several years under the consideration of a committee, but it failed to rouse general en-thusiasm, and was at last reluctantly abandoned by its promoters. For a time, therefore, possibly for this generation, Liverpool churchmen will have to be content with the building of which a sketch heads this notice. It is some com-pensation, however, to know that the bishop and the honorary chapter, headed by the Rector of Liverpool as quasi-dean, have not been prevented by the difficulties arising from the construction of the church, or by the still greater difficulty of complete lack of endowment for the purpose, from organising and bringing to a high degree of excellence the special cathedral services. With a good organist and a well-trained choir, and with the constant attendance of some members of the chapter, the best that can be done is done to set before the clergy and laity of the diocese an example of what the services of the Church are when properly rendered.

J. PULLIBLANK.

TRURO.

THE history of the cathedral in Cornwall is of peculiar interest. Christianity was probably introduced there early in the third century. Soon after the Saxons landed in Britain, and as their conquests spread from east to west, " the Cornish purchased by an annual tribute from Cerdocius permission still to exercise the rights of the Christian religion."* Solomon, King (or Duke) of Cornwall, professed Christianity about the middle of the fourth century. Probably the see of Cornwall commenced about the year 614. Cornwall then and until 927 extended to the River Exe, in Devonshire. In 927 Howel, the then King of Cornwall, resolved not to own the supremacy of Athelstan, gave battle to the Saxon king, and was defeated near Exeter, probably on Haldon Hill (Howeldon?), and Cornwall became subordinate to the crown of England; but it was not till nine years later that Cornwall was really conquered: Athelstan then passed with an army from end to end, and to the Scilly Isles; and one of his acts was to nominate Conan, a native Cornish bishop, to the Cornish see in the Church of St. Germans, on December 5th of that year, and from that time Cornwall was an English, not a British diocese. On the death of Burthwold, the last bishop at St. German's, the see of Cornwall was added to that of Crediton; Lyfing, the nephew of Burthwold, Bishop of Crediton in 1027, also Bishop of Worcester in 1038, became also Bishop of Cornwall in 1042. He was succeeded by Leofric in 1046 in the sees of Crediton and Cornwall; and in 1050 the two dioceses were united, and the see was fixed at Exeter.

Leofric was installed in St. Peter's Church, Exeter, by the Confessor and Editha, his queen, in person, and the union of the sees remained till the passing of the Truro Bishopric Act in 1876, when the new see was founded and the parish Church of St. Mary was assigned as the cathedral church.

The first bishop, Dr. Edward White Benson, Chancellor of Lincoln, was consecrated at St. Paul's Cathedral on the festival of St. Mark, 1877, and was installed May 1st of that year by Dr. Temple, Bishop of Exeter, a voluntary restorer (with £800 a year out of his own endowment) of that see which had been taken as one with Exeter by his predecessor Leofric.

The new bishop found his cathedral a dilapidated parish church, of no special architectural interest, and the building of a new cathedral was one of

* Perranzabuloe, " The Lost Church Found," p. 6.

the first necessities.   Mr. J. L. Pearson, R.A., was selected as architect, and on the 20th of May, 1880, two foundation stones were laid by the Prince of Wales.

The design of the cathedral is Early English in style, simple, without pretence of much ornamentation, but very striking and beautiful, not only as a

DESIGN OF THE CATHEDRAL, SOUTH-EAST VIEW.

whole, but in detail.   Skill is specially shown in the interior arrangements; all had to be adapted to a limited area, and the power of producing the effect of length, height, and proportion, in the choir, side aisles, and transepts, is here illustrated in great perfection.   The natural sloping of the ground towards the east has been turned to advantage for the building of the spacious crypt under the choir, with access by skilfully-formed staircases and archways north and south to the choir above, the southern staircase entering into a narrow aisle, or ambulatory, which unites the new building to the restored south aisle of the old Church of St. Mary. The crypt has been divided by thin wall partitions into various chambers for temporary accommodation, such as a chapter-room, vestries for the bishop and the clergy respectively, a choir vestry, a singing school, and vestment and muniment rooms. These chambers sadly mar the effect of the original design, with its vaulted roof and solid pillars open from end to end. A good chapter-house within the precincts of the cathedral area is included in the unfinished portion of the architect's design. The beauty of the crypt may, therefore, be some day restored by the demolition of some of its present disfigurements. The old south aisle of St. Mary's is the low part with the seven windows east of the south transept porch, shown in the print. At the west end of this a small tower is added for the reception of bells until the large central and western towers are built. West of the south porch of the transept is a handsome baptistery, erected as a memorial to Henry Martyn, the missionary, a native of Truro; and the southern part of the large transept commemorates the episcopate of the first bishop of the new see, and is called Bishop Benson's Transept.

It will be seen from our engraving that a grand central tower, a small clock tower or campanile, and two western towers, and structural lines of Early English architecture, are the leading characteristics of the design of the cathedral. The entire length is to be 303 feet, the height of the central tower 217 feet from the nave floor, of the western towers about 204 feet, of the clock tower 135 feet. The spire of the clock tower—the only one completed—is covered with copper; and the parish bells and a clock with two dials are in place in it. So much of the central tower only has been built as is level with the apex of the choir roof. The completion of this tower, with the whole of the western towers and the nave, with the exception of portions of the two bays adjoining the transept, is now in abeyance.

It is estimated that the completed portion—the area of choir and transept —affords accommodation for about 1,400 worshippers, and that, when the nave is added, the building will seat 2,500 persons. The exact amount spent, including the purchase of houses and land for additional site, consecration expenses, and internal fittings, has been £114,081 11s. 9d. There is no permanent provision for the maintenance either of the fabric or of the services.

On the removal of Bishop Benson to the archiepiscopal see of Canterbury, the great work which he had organised passed into the hands of Dr. George Howard Wilkinson, who was consecrated at St. Paul's on the festival of St. Mark, and installed on the 15th of May, 1883. By him the completed portion of the edifice was consecrated on the 3rd of November, 1887.

EDMUND CARLYON.

NEWCASTLE.

THE new diocese of Newcastle is fortunate in the possession of a church which is not unworthy of the name of a cathedral, though it can never be converted into a cathedral of the ordinary type. It is above all things the chief church of a great town. It stands in the centre of that town's busy life. It bears clear traces of having grown with the prosperity of a growing centre of commerce. It owes everything to the munificence of wealthy burghers. Its structure is plain and solid, telling of the severity and sternness of northern life in bygone times. The church itself is a symbol of the attempts to keep pace with the needs of a growing population which led to the formation of a see of Newcastle.

The original Church of St. Nicholas was consecrated by Bishop Osmund of Salisbury in 1091. It does not seem to have been a place of much ecclesiastical importance, for Henry I. granted it to the canons of Carlisle. It was burnt down in 1216, and there are still remains of the early transitional work which mark the first attempt at rebuilding. The chief part, however, of the present structure of the nave dates from 1359. In 1368 the transepts were added. The choir was soon afterwards proceeded with, and the east window was due to a citizen, Roger Thornton, who died in 1429. Another citizen, Robert Rhodes, who died in 1474, finished the tower which rises at the west end of the church, and built the spire which is the distinguishing ornament of the structure.

From these dates it will be seen that the architectural style of the church is flowing Decorated, rapidly passing into Perpendicular. The chief features of the church are those which mark the Early Perpendicular style. The entrance at the west end has three doorways admitting into a spacious vestibule, which is separated from the body of the church by a plain wooden screen. The church is seated throughout, and is impressive through its massive simplicity. Its pillars have no capitals, and the plain chamfer of the arches ends in a simple bevel. One step only raises the level of the chancel above the nave, and there are no choir stalls. The aisles of the chancel are as broad as those of the nave. Behind the high altar is a chapel, which is used as a choir vestry. The large organ stands in the north transept, and blocks up an old chapel of St. George. The church is rich in side chapels. It contains nine of these chantries, which were built by citizens as burying-places for their families, and had separate endowments that masses might be said for the dead.

The plainness and simplicity of the church is accounted for by the early intercourse between Newcastle and Antwerp, and the consequent influence of Flemish models. But this plain massiveness of structure characterises most of the churches of Northumberland, and probably expressed the feeling of northern taste

NEWCASTLE CATHEDRAL, FROM THE SOUTH-EAST.

in a land where constant warfare led to a wish for security rather than ornament. The citizens of Newcastle erected a strong and spacious building. Their church was a solid and substantial shell, to which decoration might afterwards be applied. The numerous chantries gave scope for the exhibition of individual taste. The church was eminently a civic building. It grew little by little, and is a monument of the public spirit of the citizens. It was conceived in no niggard spirit, being 245 feet long, and as at present arranged can seat 3,000 people. The actual appearance of the church is due to a restoration conducted by Sir Gilbert Scott, between 1873 and 1877. Before that time the chancel was surrounded by a screen, and the nave was left unoccupied during service. Now the entire building scarcely suffices to contain the congregation. The need of the church is additional decoration, which its plain structure was evidently intended to receive. Already the decoration of the chancel has been begun by the erection of a reredos, a dignified structure of alabaster, designed by a Newcastle architect, Mr. R. J. Johnson, at the expense of a citizen of Newcastle. A bishop's throne has also been set up, and plans have been formed for a choir-screen and choir-stalls.

Externally the Cathedral of Newcastle does not appeal to the eye by an imposing mass of buildings. The west front and part of the north side lie along an open square and show their smoke-blackened features; but the east end is surrounded by other structures which hem it in. The south side of the chancel is concealed by a large vestry-room and library, built in 1736, a good example of the Classical style. The growing trade of Newcastle has absorbed the open space which once surrounded the church, and has thereby stamped still more distinctly a local significance upon the building.

The chief architectural feature of the church is its flying spire. On the top of the square tower flying buttresses rise from the four corners and meet to support an elegant tapering spire, which rises to a height of 200 feet. The motive of such an ornament seems to have been the figure of a crown rising on the summit of the building. Other instances of the same treatment are to be found in the spires of St. Giles', Edinburgh, and at St. Dunstan's-in-the-East, London. But the lantern, or flying spire, of the Cathedral of Newcastle surpasses all others in its grace of proportion and elegance of form. Structurally such an ornament is indefensible. It can only be maintained by iron supports. It has little power of resistance either to the wind or to the action of the smoky atmosphere. It needs constant care and frequent repairs. But it is, and has been, the chief feature of all views of Newcastle, and gives picturesqueness to the aspect of the city on whichever side it is approached. All else may be hidden in the blue-grey mist which rolls westwards along the valley of the Tyne; the cathedral spire still points upwards, borne on its soaring buttresses, which seem to cleave the mist and force it to reveal some of the proportions of the tower below.

M. CREIGHTON.

F F

SOUTHWELL.

THE great collegiate Church of St. Mary the Virgin at Southwell is in every respect worthy to be advanced to the rank of a cathedral. In size and stateliness it excels more than one of the churches long occupied by a bishop's chair, and it is also in plan and character a true cathedral rather than a large parish church. Neither is it wanting in strong individuality and peculiar beauty. Approaching from the west, which, though not the most picturesque, is the best point for a first general view, one of these beauties will be found in the massive four-square appearance of the building, a character given by bold horizontal lines carried completely round the nave, by the squareness of the centre tower in outline and ornament, and by the bands of moulding and arcading which cut the western towers into rectangular divisions. Something of this unity of impression is now lost by the crowning of the west towers with spires, instead of the parapets and pinnacles which, poor and mean in themselves, repeated the square finish of the centre tower in a manner very pleasing to the eye. Pointed caps, with eaves over the corbel-tables, were probably the original coverings of all three towers. The massive, fortress-like aspect once presented by the west front is much impaired by the enormous Perpendicular window, which, as by a fissure, divides the towers, and by the round-headed windows with which their lowest storey has been pierced. The west portal, now dwarfed by the window above, should be the chief feature of this front. It is fine in itself; the arch is of five orders of well-grouped mouldings; the inner one is not divided by the abacus. The doors are early fourteenth-century work, strengthened by iron-work of singular and beautiful design.

On the south side of the nave the Norman windows are modern copies of the original form. The Perpendicular windows are good examples of their time—late fourteenth century. The lower of the two string-courses which encompass the building in firm bands has been brought down to admit these deeper windows, and eked out with the jambs of the old Norman windows. The roofs no longer come down over the corbel-tables, which are surmounted by parapets of later work. The round windows of the clerestory are unique in this place, forming one of the special features of the church. On the north side of the nave is a beautiful and uncommon porch, made one with the building by a bold and skilful arrangement of the string-courses. The outer arch has plain mouldings, the inner one is much enriched. The doors are somewhat later than those of the west portal, and are carved and without ironwork.

The transepts retain the original Norman windows, and show a rare variation of cable moulding. The zigzag and other string-courses are continued round the transepts; the former is curiously bent over the small door in the south transept. The gables of the transepts are filled with a kind of herring-bone ornament; the upper parts are a restoration to the original roof-pitch. The bear on the north gable is the original creature returned to his watch after many wanderings. No trace was found of his companion, so a lion was carved to match him on the south.

The grave and massive central tower fitly sums up the Norman church, with which it is in admirable harmony. The story of the stones of the parapet tells that they came from the transept gables, probably soon after the roofs were lowered, and it is conjectured that the curious pinnacles once flanked these same gables. The Norman church was completed by apsidal chapels east of the transepts, and by a short choir having apsidal terminations to the aisles, but ending in a square chancel, or sacrarium, a very uncommon form for this style. The date of the Norman building is 1100—1150. It is not known when the roofs were first lowered; they were raised again, and the present spires placed on the west towers, 1879—1883.

The exterior of the Early English choir is marred by the low-pitched roofs, not yet restored in this part of the church; the Gothic requires the steep roof more than the Romanesque. This part of the building is as perfect and beautiful an example of its style as the nave and transepts, with which it not only contrasts, but subtly harmonises. Instead of presenting the unequally yoked appearance that is often found on the Continent when the two styles meet, as at Aix-la-Chapelle, where the effect both within and without is grotesque, here it shows as a noble and perfect marriage. The great beauty of proportion in the choir is more easily felt than pointed out; few of the details are uncommon—their singularity lies in happy grouping and exquisite finish. As in the nave, the string-courses and corbel-tables are emphasised and very complete, adding much to the solidity and unity of the

---

An Early English chapel, opening into the north transept, very interesting in its details, fills the space beyond the chapter-house.

To enter the church, it is best to return to the west portal, as the interior is thus better appreciated. The first impression is of too much light, the massive pillars and low arches giving a desire for deeper shadow and more gravity and mystery; but the huge west window lets in the broad daylight in a way the builders did not intend, and we must be content with the warm tint it gives to the yellow stone, and notice the soft shadows taken by the great round piers, the simple strength of the arches and of the aisle vaultings. The piers have broad square bases, the capitals are round, with little projection, and the ornament is flat and without emphasis. The triforium arches are low and wide; some filling-in seems to have been planned but never executed. Above, the light from the semicircular clerestory windows is admitted through small arches, having a passage between them pierced in the wall. The pavement, relaid, retains at the west end portions of the old herring-bone floor. The new barrel roof replaces a flat wooden ceiling. The four lofty arches to the tower have engaged semicircular pillars. These arches are very beautiful; the bold cable moulding around them has

THE NAVE, LOOKING EAST.

peculiar features and should be compared with the cables of the transept windows. The transepts have three tiers of windows; below them, at each end, there are two arches in the wall resting in the middle on a round pillar, set close to the wall, but detached from it. The entrance arches only remain of the destroyed apsidal chapels east of the transepts. The Early English chapel opening into the north transept deserves examination; it is below the level of the present pavement, and was built for two altars. The sharply-pointed arches of entrance are oddly proportioned, and have an exuberance of moulding. A stair to the triforium and tower is in the north transept. Over the door is a tympanum stone, much older than the existing church. It is said to represent St. Michael; but the curious Byzantine character of the design and the subordinate figure of David suggest Psalm xci. 13 as a probable interpretation. The parvise, or sacrist's chamber, over the porch, is reached by this stair. In the north transept is now placed the beautiful alabaster monument of Edwin Sandys, Archbishop of York. His figure is recumbent on an altar-tomb; the widow and seven children kneel below. The vestments show the form worn by the archbishop, who died 1588.

The rood-screen is a fine example of Decorated work, date about 1340, of intricate and singular construction and profuse ornament. The open spandrels of the vaulting, the arches opening west, the stairs right and left of the east arch, are the more uncommon features of this screen. On the east side are six canopied stalls, one of them lined with very good diaper work. The place of the rood is now occupied by the organ.

The interior of the choir is a very fine construction, of extraordinary purity and beauty of proportion. It was cleared from whitewash a few years ago, and there is a glorious difference between the warm living surface of the stone and the dead limewash, with its lead-coloured shadows. The rosy-tinted perspectives into the nave are often very beautiful. The six great arches on each side the choir rest on piers of eight clustered shafts, to which the mouldings above are specially well adapted. The fillet of the succeeding period is just indicated on these shafts, while the base mouldings have an earlier character. All but three of the arches have a bold variety of dog-tooth carried between the mouldings. The triforium and clerestory are here included within one tier of tall lancet arches, having clustered shafts; here the dog-tooth runs between the shafts as well as over the arches; most of the capitals are plain, except those of the chancel windows. These last have a deep interior splay, and are grouped under hood mouldings. The small transepts of the choir have a very good effect within; they are about as deep as the width of the aisles, and repeat their square terminations; like them, also, they had each an altar on the east, making five in the choir. The vaulting is simple throughout; the great centre rib is carried down between the east windows to a small shaft with peculiar and excellent effect. The side springs of the vault come low down between the main arches on triple shafts; these are clasped by the great string-course which runs round the choir under the triforium arches. The bosses are of varied and boldly carved foliage, and the ubiquitous dog-tooth is carried along the centre and eastern ribs.

The sedilia are an uncommon piece of rich Decorated work, with curious details, added to the chancel. A pavement of variously coloured Derbyshire marble has recently been placed in the sacrarium.

From the north aisle a fine Decorated doorway, with a thick wreath of foliage over the arch, divided by a carved marble shaft under a trefoil, leads by a short cloister passage to the chapter-house. This cloister has an arcade of trefoiled arches on one side, and on the other a beautiful row of pointed arches, once open to the court, resting on double pillars, the capitals and connecting bars delicately carved with natural foliage. This cloister, court, and vestibule are full of interest in design, in construction, and in picturesque effect, which should not be overlooked in the admiration excited by the chapter-house itself and the splendid doorway leading into it. The first impression of this arch is that it is perfectly new, and it is hard to believe that nearly 600 years have passed since the last strokes of that most skilful chisel were given. Its beauty and purity have been its defence against friend and foe; it has lost nothing but the marble jamb shafts, now replaced, and has never been touched by paint, whitewash, or the scraper. Two wreaths of foliage are carried round the arch, one over a hollow and one over a filleted moulding; this moulding and the bells of the capitals here and through the building are as perfect under the foliage as if the latter had been laid on as an after-thought. The doorway is divided by a slender stone shaft, the head is fitted by a quatrefoil between two cusped arches, and a rare and lovely leaf ornament is set round these arches. There is no appearance of a door having actually filled this exquisite arch. Within, the varied ornament of foliage, very slightly conventionalised, and relieved by heads, birds, and grotesques, that profusely adorns the arcade, is of spirited and original treatment; with the doorway it seems to be the independent work of one artist carver, who has, however, subordinated this last finish and adornment to the architectural construction of the beautifully-designed building. It is octagonal in form, having six large windows in the disengaged bays, and a fine vault springing from between the windows and following the octagon form; the ribs meet in a particularly fine boss. The string-course under the windows connects the terminations of the crocketed arcades with the same firm and bold effect seen in the earlier parts of the church, which, with many details too minute and technical to be pointed out here, show that each builder has studied and caught the spirit of his predecessors, in a manner that makes the cathedral of many periods a single and perfect building, telling its one story in many voices, and a fit type of the Church of Christ in every age of the world.

E. GLAISTER.

WAKEFIELD.

THE Cathedral Church of Wakefield, although not very ancient in the structural sense, has been raised on an old foundation. The site is believed to have been originally occupied by a Norman edifice, of which, however, there is but scant mention, although it is known to have remained until the beginning of the reign of Edward III., when John, last Earl of Warren, was tenant of Wakefield for life. Under what circumstances it was demolished there is no record to show. Wakefield was now, however, coming into prominence as a cloth-producing centre; and it is not unlikely that the Norman church had become too small for the growing population of the parish. The church that took its place was consecrated in 1329 by William de Melton, Archbishop of York. With the exception of the tower and spire, this church was, for some unknown reason, demolished about the middle of the fifteenth century. Another church, which Leland, who visited the town in 1538, speaks of as a new building, was then erected, and it is this building which, with many additions and alterations, has become the Cathedral of Wakefield. The structure may be said to have been in process of restoration since early in the eighteenth century. About a third of the spire was blown down in 1715; and after this had been rebuilt it became necessary to restore the south side of the church, which was done in 1724. About seventy years later the same course had to be taken with the north side and east end. The spire was repaired a second time in 1802, but it was subjected to the merest patchwork—a little "pointing" here and there, with protecting iron bands at intervals. In 1823 the bands were removed and the spire re-topped and left smooth along its fine vanishing lines. The present spire, which is crocketed and octagonal, was erected as part of a scheme of restoration begun about 1860 by Sir Gilbert Scott, R.A., and continued to a recent period. More than £30,000 has been spent in the improvement of the fabric during the last thirty years.

Situated in Northgate, the Cathedral of Wakefield occupies a central position on high ground. The spire from the base of the tower runs up to 247 feet. It is the highest in Yorkshire, and a conspicuous feature over a considerable area. The cathedral stands clear of buildings, and it is possible to study the Decorated and Perpendicular features of its style on all sides. The western door leads through the tower, and, once entered, reveals the composition of the

church—a nave and chancel with side aisles that extend the whole length of
the building. The nave and chancel are under a continuous flat roof, and both
are clerestoried. On the south side is a fine porch with a parvise vestry. The
building is 186 feet in length and 69ˑ in breadth, and has accommodation for
1,500 worshippers. The stonework of the interior, except in the accessories, is
almost entirely free from adornment. The church makes a fine show, how-

THE INTERIOR, LOOKING EAST.

ever, externally. The bold crocketing, which is so conspicuous a feature on the
lines of the spire, is repeated elaborately on pinnacles rising from arcaded and
panelled parapets over a fine series of four-light windows along the whole length
of the edifice and at the east end. Over the east window, and in the centre
of the parapet, is a fine canopy containing a figure of William de Melton, and
surmounted by a cross. The sides and tower are buttressed in gabled stages.
The refacing gives the building a fresh look externally, and contrasts curiously
with the signs of age on the bays of the nave and the internal walls. The
stained glass is modern, and has been introduced for memorial purposes.

Dividing the chancel from the nave is an elegant screen of floriated oak
of the Jacobean era; and the stalls in the chancel show some fine tabernacle
work. A Percy badge—the crescent and manacles—is found carved on the stall-
work, but when or for what reason introduced does not seem to be known. The

G G

ceiling of the nave and chancel aisles shows carved bosses, some of which per-
petuate the arms of Wakefield, and others the badge of the House of York. The
organ case, like the chancel screen, belongs to the time of Charles I. It was the
gift of the ill-fated Earl of Strafford. The octagonal font, which rises from a
slender shaft, bears the date 1661 on one of its faces; on another are the
initials of Charles II., the remaining faces bearing the initials of churchwardens.
The east end of the south aisle, formerly called " Our Lady's Quire," is the burial-
place of the Pilkingtons. It has been thoroughly restored at the expense of Sir
Lionel Pilkington, Bart., of Chevet, and is now known as the Pilkington Chantry.
It was founded by Sir John Pilkington under authority of letters patent from
Edward IV. There are numerous Pilkington monuments in the little chapel, the
most elaborate being one to the memory of Sir Lyon Pilkington, who died in 1714;
it shows a full-length figure under a canopy, with a long inscription in Latin.

The church generally is rich in monumental features. None of the slabs
or tablets go beyond the seventeenth century; but traces of old memorials
were found during the Scott restoration. On clearing off the colour-wash from
the walls of the chancel, traces of black-letter inscriptions were discovered beneath
the stucco. Mr. James Fowler, in a paper on the subject, expresses the opinion
that these inscriptions were probably of the beginning of the seventeenth century. But a still more interesting discovery was made. On the removal of the
incrustations it was found that all the surface had once been painted, and on
lifting a sheet of plaster from off the south-west spandrel of the choir-arch there
was seen the figure of an angel in an attitude of adoration, supposed to have
been part of a large picture filling up the whole of the space above the arch.
Mr. Fowler, after a careful study of the pigments, assigned 1470 as the probable date of the picture, this being the year in which the body of the church,
including the choir, was rebuilt. Numerous presentations were made to the
church during the period of the last restoration, amongst the articles being a
very fine reredos of Caen stone and white marble.

The original grant of the church was made by William Rufus to the second
William de Warren, and was transferred about the close of the eleventh century to the monastery at Lewes, in Sussex. During the reign of Edward III.
(1325) it was allotted by the monastery to Hugh de Spencer the younger. From
the Spencers the church passed to the Crown. The next trace is a grant of the
church to the Dean and College of St. Stephen, at Westminster, and in the hands
of this body it remained till the Dissolution, when it reverted to the Crown.
The living then continued in the gift of the Sovereign until 1860, when the
patronage was transferred to the Bishop of Ripon and his successors. It has now,
of course, passed to the Bishop of Wakefield. The value of the living is £400.

American and other readers of Goldsmith's famous story frequently make their way to the vicarage of Wakefield, only to be bereft of the pleasing fancy that they have discovered the starting-ground of the English classic. Dr. Primrose is purely a creation of the brain, and there is no reason to believe that Goldsmith ever visited Wakefield, or that the choice of title was more than a coincidence.* But though such visits have an element of disappointment, the tourist will not repent the pilgrimage. Wakefield is itself an interesting spot, and the neighbourhood abounds with antiquities and historical associations.

The Order in Council founding the Diocese of Wakefield was issued on the 17th of May, 1888. This was the result of a movement extending over twelve or thirteen years. The see has the peculiarity of being almost wholly cut out of another not much more than half a century older than itself. In the year preceding the accession of the Queen the greater part of the West Riding and a portion of the northern division of the county received episcopal privileges apart from York, the ancient Bishopric of Ripon, dormant from pre-Reformation times, being revived for the purpose. In its resuscitated form the diocese of Ripon had some three hundred livings and a population of about eight hundred thousand. By the time the Queen attained her Jubilee, this population had doubled, and the number of livings had gone up to about five hundred. It has been estimated that the amount of money spent in the diocese during the fifty years for church restoration and building must have been close upon a million and a half; and it is officially known that over a million of this generous total was raised in sums above five hundred pounds. So that with the increase of population there was a corresponding development of Church work. Even in area—over a million and a half of acres—the see was a heavy one to administer; and as it was an area embracing many large towns in which church extension had been taken up with spirit, the question whether something could be done to lessen the growing burden on the diocesan began to press for consideration long before relief was found.

Dr. Walsham How, the Bishop Suffragan of Bedford, was nominated to the new see early in 1888. Soon after, All Saints, the parish church of Wakefield, was made the cathedral for the diocese; and here, on June 25, 1888, the bishop was installed by the Archbishop of York. Wakefield was then elevated to the dignity of a city. The diocese has an area of 235,000 acres; the population, which at the census of 1881 was 663,235, will now run well up to 900,000.

W. S. CAMERON.

* An enthusiastic student of Goldsmith (Mr. Edward Ford) holds a different opinion. He gives a Yorkshire application to the novel nearly all through, and states that Kirby-Moorside was the scene of many of the incidents. It has been stated also that if Goldsmith had his mind on the actual Wakefield when he wrote the book, the vicar he introduces could be none other than the Rev. Benjamin Wilson, M.A. Mr. Wilson, who acquired some reputation as a Greek scholar, began his career in Wakefield as Master of the Grammar School, was appointed to the vicariate in 1751, and died in 1764, two years before the "Vicar of Wakefield" was published.

THE EXTERIOR, FROM THE SOUTH-WEST.

BANGOR.

THOSE who regard the historic monuments of Welsh antiquity from a general standpoint must be content to find fewer evidences of power, wealth, and lavish taste in the principality than on the other side of the English border. A more ancient yet scantier civilisation, the natural poverty of moor and mountain, the long struggle for independence, the isolation of a distinct race and language, have tended to produce this result, which is nevertheless in some degree atoned for to the sight-seer by the beautiful setting of the jewels which remain in Wales, and to the church (in North Wales at least) by its continued possession of nearly all those rectorial rights which elsewhere became first the appanage of religious houses, and next the prey of the spoiler. In the first rank of these monuments stands Bangor Cathedral, the seat of one of the most ancient among existing British sees, dating as it does from the time when Christianity seems first to have gained a permanent footing in Venedotia or North Wales, and to have rooted itself in certain definite localities. St. Daniel, or Deiniol, made the first settlement here about 550. His church was doubtless of timber, but built on the still existing site, and of structure and dimensions entitling it to a name indicative of high excellence. It was Bangor, the place of the Fair Choir. There were several such places within Celtic limits and similarly designated. Three survive in history, one of them, Bangor-is-coed, with familiar but melancholy interest connected with Saxon encroachment; Bangor in Carnarvonshire alone retains an ecclesiastical significance.

The cathedral as it now stands has all the appearance of a large and hand-some parish church. Parish church indeed it is, for the vicars of the church are

INTERIOR, LOOKING WEST.

parish vicars also, and parish services still alternate in it with those of a cathedral; nevertheless we have here not indeed a mediæval church throughout, but one of Sir Gilbert Scott's choicest restorations. The centre and transepts are specially effective, though the former is seemingly incapable of bearing the weight of a tower (once designed to crown the building) by reason of cracks in each one of the supporting arches. The style adopted for the new work is the Early Decorated, which was suggested by the foundations and other structural remains of the cathedral of 1292, the later-built walls furnishing a perfect quarry of stonework (often richly wrought) of that period. In particular the great windows of the north and south transepts are almost exactly what they must have been more than 500 years ago, being in a great measure formed of the old material put back in its original place. Both outside and inside of the south transept plain evidences are given of side chapels commenced at the same early period. In the choir or chancel the more modern details, such as the roof and woodwork, are specimens of modern introduction in the same Decorated style, but the original work of the fifteenth and early sixteenth centuries abounds, and is left untouched in all its naked simplicity. The east window is a fair specimen of its period, but there are no cusps or other ornaments in the plain Perpendicular windows facing north and south, which have a general correspondence with the style of the nave arcade, and in point of time just preceded it. As witnesses to a still earlier building, there remain outside the choir on the south a Norman arch and a Norman buttress; and during the late restoration traces could be seen of the Norman apse, both in a semicircular line of foundations very considerably abridging the length of the existing choir, and also in the curvature of the outside masonry of the choir eastward from the south, now barely if at all perceptible. The nave with the western tower is of very late Perpendicular, the work of Bishop Skeffington continued by him till as late as 1532, and not wholly finished till Bishop Rowland's time, 1611. Here the columns and clerestory windows are poor, scarcely worthy of the good modern roof surmounting them, but the windows of the nave aisles are of late Edwardian design, surviving when nearly all else except a portion of the south end of the south transept perished by fire. The walk round the cathedral (233 feet in extreme length with breadth at transepts 96 feet) shows no further special features. Palace, deanery, canonry, all modern, are pleasantly embosomed in trees, and the group of cathedral buildings receives no accession but from the restored chapter-room, which is also a library containing one great treasure, " The Bangor Use," otherwise called " The Pontifical of Bishop Anian," of the date 1291, a book lost and recovered more than once by the cathedral authorities.

Something of an historical sketch is needed to render the structural changes in the cathedral intelligible. King Edgar (959—1017), an early patron of the Church of Bangor, must have left that church a wooden erection, for though recent research has revealed three several foundations of the cathedral at its centre, none of these point to a stone building existing before the Conquest. As late as 1102 stone seems first to have been used, when a new cathedral rose on the ashes of an earlier building destroyed in 1071. The few remaining Norman features are of this period. This Norman cathedral again was destroyed in the wars of King Henry III. and Prince David, but the accession of Edward I. brought with it the subjugation of Wales, the establishment of a line of fortresses along the Welsh coast, the nomination to the bishopric of Edward's friend, the

Anian above mentioned, and the rebuilding in the Early Decorated style of the cathedral about 1291. This is that cathedral whose design the restoration in our own times has endeavoured to follow out, while preserving later existing features. Here in Bangor (as Shakespeare has it) the archdeacon (a chimney of whose house is still exhibited) mapped out England and Wales into three parts, for Mortimer one, for Glyndwr one, and one for Harry Hotspur. Yet in the end Glyndwr figures as the ravager and burner of this and of St. Asaph Cathedrals, many of whose dignitaries suffered outlawry for the support they had rendered him. The work of destruction took place in 1402, and now for ninety years through the long Wars of the Roses the church waited for the quiet times of Henry Tudor. Then Bishop Deane, or Denis, took up the work of rebuilding, himself completing the choir, and building into his walls the old material which offered itself for use, and now has seen the light again. For, long after the storms of the Reformation had subsided, and chantries and vestments and even bells had disappeared, and successful rebellion had come and gone, and the church had slept out her long sleep through periods of peaceful revolution and Georgian indifference, in this latter age good people were again minded to beautify this ancient centre of religious life. Twice their efforts were called forth; choir and transepts, as we now see them, are the result of the former, nave of the second effort of this happy inspiration.

Bangor cannot lay claim to many notable men. Kings did not pension their State officers with Welsh preferment. Possibly the notoriety of Bishop Hoadley (1716) may entitle him to a passing word. Appointed because of political considerations, he was travelling to his diocese; but when at Chester, anticipating a reception the reverse of pleasant, he turned tail and never again attempted to visit Bangor through a seven years' occupancy of the see. He it was who gave rise to the well-known Bangorian controversy.

One word to the antiquarian who prefers what is really old to any amount of successful imitation. The south transept retains its three original buttresses; they are worth examination, and further valuable as corresponding with the work in the Lady Chapel of Chester Cathedral, whence it may be inferred that Edward I. drew his masons and chief designer.

R. H. HILL.

THE CATHEDRAL, FROM THE RIVER.

ST. ASAPH.

THE fine position of the old Cathedral Church of St. Asaph has often proved its ruin. You see nothing of St. David's till you are quite upon it; hills command Llandaff and Bangor all around. No one would occupy them for defence, except so far as the mere walls would protect those who took refuge within them.

But in troublous times the tongue of land which runs down between the rivers Elwy and Clwyd was a position to be occupied at once. The only building of any strength upon it was the cathedral. Even in the early days, when it was constructed of wood, its position made it somewhat difficult to take by assault, when weapons of offence were not brought to any great degree of efficiency. But when once entered it was easily destroyed.

It is curious how little we can learn about it from history or tradition, nor can we infer much from earthworks, architectural remains, or monuments of any kind.

For all the early part of the history of the cathedral, we can only begin with "they say," referring to the old Llyfr coch, or the later writers Browne Willis and Pennant, and various scattered notices, most of which are mentioned in the carefully-compiled history of St. Asaph, by Thomas.

If St. Asaph was ever a fortified position, as is stated in one old document, the vallum probably ran just within the palace grounds, and turned up across the hill, so as to include the corner of the kitchen-garden on the

THE INTERIOR, LOOKING WEST.

(From a Photograph by F. Bedford, by permission of Messrs. Catherall and Prichard.)

south side of the cathedral—as there is certainly an artificially made terrace or rectangular earthwork along those lines.

The story goes that Kentigern, driven from somewhere in Strathclyde about the year 560, went to St. David's, from which he organised a missionary expedition into the vale of Clwyd, and having overcome the opposition of Maelgwyn, or Maelgwn, erected a church, with monastic buildings attached, at what is now known as St. Asaph, but very likely may have been known as Llanelwy long before the time of St. Asaph. As was usual in those days, they were all constructed of wood.

H H

Century after century rolled by, and in the church of Llanelwy, whether the solemn chant may have arisen from day to day, and the monks have lived a life of contemplation in its quiet cloisters, or whether its precincts may have often witnessed the clash of arms and the drunken revelry of victorious troops, we know not. The first record of it is a story of fire and sword, when the soldiers of Henry III. occupied it in 1247. The earliest relic is a silver penny of Henry III., found with sawn antlers of red deer and various bones of domestic animals in cutting a drain through made-ground in the palace stable-yard. In 1282, also, we read that it was burnt down. It must be noted, however, that when the cathedral emerges from the mists of those troublous story-less times, it is not as a newly-founded institution, but one that had been long exercising wide influence and jurisdiction, for Bishop Anian having quarrelled with Prince Llewelyn in 1274, appealed to the English archbishop and to the king to support his claims, and met with the usual reward of such conduct; for the English came, and Anian and his neighbours suffered more from his new supporters than from his old opponents.

Now we begin to find definite records of a building, some of the stones of which at any rate remain in the cathedral of to-day; for we learn that Edward I. made very liberal offers, on condition that the cathedral and its staff were removed to Rhuddlan, but that this was strongly opposed, and that the cathedral was rebuilt on the old site. There is a small capital of a shaft preserved in the north transept, which was recently found built into the wall of the nave. This seems to belong to the Norman period. Though it is not improbable that the early English style did not get down into Wales till late, we can hardly suppose that a church was erected in the Norman style after the time of Edward I.; and it seems more probable that there had been an earlier building partly of stone. If so, all records of that Norman church have been swept away save this one stone.

Nor have we much evidence left as to the early English church. When the cathedral was being restored some few years ago, it was not until the work had gone on for some time that Sir Gilbert Scott found sufficient evidence of the character of the early English work to enable him to satisfy himself as to the general features of the chancel windows.

There was, as we read in a writ of Henry VI. (1442), another destruction of the cathedral and its surrounding buildings, "in the last werre tyme of Wales," when all that the fire could seize "was brent and utterly destroyed" by Owen Glyndwr in 1402, and "no styk laft."

In 1482 Bishop Redman repaired the walls which had not been destroyed, re-roofed the church, and placed carved oak stalls and an episcopal throne in the choir. The present stalls do in part represent the original work, having probably been to some extent preserved by the successive coats of paint laid on in former years, and only removed during the late restoration of the cathedral. They have of course been restored from time to time, as for instance after the storm of 1714, when part of the tower was blown down, and breaking through the roof of the choir beat down the tabernacle work. The fifteenth-century east window was replaced in 1780, and a window, said to be a copy by Egginton of the east window of Tintern Abbey, was inserted in its place. The throne was broken down in the Civil War, and used for feeding cattle in, but after the restoration Bishop Griffith built a new one. It is not improbable that some portions of the cathedral may have got worked into the old parish church from time to time, either in the progress of so-called improvements, or when the cathedral ruins were used as a quarry. There was formerly a chapter-house in the north-east angle between the chancel and the north transept.

Any one who examines the walls of the cathedral will see such a mixture of stones of various kinds and different colour that he will readily admit the probability of there having been several successive cathedrals, constructed out of the material of pre-existing buildings, with new stones introduced each time.

The walls show a not unpleasing mixture of the light grey of the mountain limestone, with the bright red of the new red sandstone, the pale claret colour of the stained carboniferous rocks, the unstained beds of which have furnished the yellow or grey stones so largely used in the interior, while the massive battlemented tower, 93 feet in height, the most conspicuous feature in the building, is of white limestone for three-quarters of its height, finished off above in bright red sandstone. This may have been done in 1638, when "greate timber trees were carried out of Jannian Wood, in Beraigne, for and towards the making of a new steeple-lofft or belfrye," or later when the tower was repaired after it had been injured in the great storm of 1714. Through such changes the cathedral came to be what it is, a cruciform church, 182 feet in length, 108 feet across the transepts, 45 feet high in the nave, and 40 in the chancel, with a tower rising out of the intersection of the transepts and nave. The transepts are, however, cut off by the oak stalls of the choir. Part of the north transept forms a robing-room for the choristers, above which the organ is placed. The soft-coloured reredos of alabaster is somewhat lost in the rich setting of pink and red sandstone, and the architecture did not admit of its being well defined.

The south transept is the chapter-room. In this there is an interesting old library, which contains many ancient versions of the Bible and Prayer Book, both in Welsh and English, and other rare and valuable documents.

The most striking feature inside is the manner in which the arches between the nave and the two aisles rest on pillars with no capitals, so that the mouldings run down uninterruptedly from the top of the arch to the base of the pillar, as we often find in Flemish churches. The clerestory has been restored on the north side, so as to correspond with that which still remained on the south.

The glass in the east window was put up in memory of Bishop Carey in 1865. The armorial bearings of Bishop Bagot's window, which are now placed in the chapter-room, were taken from the chancel when this memorial window was put in, while the central subject was carried off to a small church at the south end of the vale. The rest of the glass is modern. The organ is a fine-toned instrument by Hill of London, added to in later years. There are one or two ancient monuments. In the north transept lies a monumental slab, on which is carved in low relief the representation of a hare pursued by a greyhound, and a shield bearing a lion gardant and four fleurs-de-lis. Unfortunately there is no inscription to tell us any more about it.

Another slab was found during the course of the same excavations, on which was carved a floriated cross, but no inscription. Underneath it was a circular leaden object, on which was roughly cut the figure of a hand, with two fingers raised as in blessing. On the south wall of the nave is a monumental tablet to Felicia Hemans, the poetess, who was a resident in the neighbourhood.

Except the monument of Bishop Davydd ap Owen, a great benefactor to the cathedral, who died in 1502, there are very few memorials of the former occupants of the see. Yet this was the cathedral church of Bishop Morgan, who translated the Welsh Bible of 1588, and contributed to Queen Elizabeth's version of the English Bible; of Davies and Parry, also translators of the Bible into Welsh or English; of Lloyd, one of the seven bishops; of the devout Beveridge; of Owen, and Hooper, and Halifax, and Horsley. A plain tombstone in the churchyard marks the resting-place of Bishop Isaac Barrow, uncle of the more celebrated Dr. Isaac Barrow, whom he helped to educate. In the south transept there is a full-length figure of Dean Shipley, in white marble, by Ternouth, a pupil of Chantrey. This was put up by subscription in 1829.

The chancel is paved with encaustic tiles, set in bands of mottled grey Anglesey marble. Some of the tiles are exact reproductions of old ones found in excavating for the new work.

There is nothing to suggest any architectural connection between the cathedral and any of its immediate surroundings. The palace grounds adjoin those of the cathedral on the west, but there is no part of the palace now existing which is known to be of any great antiquity. The east front, or that seen from the cathedral, was built by Bishop Bagot in 1791, and the west front, or that which faces the river, was built by Bishop Carey in 1831.

There are remains of a very pretty chapel over a holy well near Wigfair, about two miles up the Elwy, which seems to have been served by one of the vicars choral.   The great territorial extent of the cathedral dependencies and property in all probability points more to the wide range of the episcopal jurisdiction than to the wealth and importance of the cathedral church.   The diocese extends over nearly the whole of Denbighshire, Flintshire, and Montgomeryshire, and over a considerable part of Merioneth and Shropshire.

There are only two bells, the same that are mentioned by Browne Willis; an inscription states that they were cast out of the material of three older ones.   Metal is likely to be scarce in this poor old church, fought over so fiercely for thirteen centuries by troops to whom a bit of metal was an object for which it was worth risking a battle.   Of recent years the structure has with pious care been adapted for the services of our day, along the lines of the ancient building, as far as data could be gathered for the task, and it now stands a small but impressive monument, suggesting rather than telling us its past eventful history.

THOS. McKENNY HUGHES.

GENERAL VIEW OF THE EXTERIOR.

(From a Photograph by Poulton and Sons, Lee.)

ST. DAVID'S.

THERE are few more interesting spots in Great Britain than "Dewisland," or the "halidom" of St. David. The wanderer in search of the picturesque may well hesitate whether to award the palm to the magnificent church and its dependent buildings, or to the rugged cliffs with their far-reaching views over the great ocean. The student of history may try to picture to himself the swarm of Irish saints who were taught in the famous school of St. David, or the throng of mediæval pilgrims hastening to pay their devotions at the shrine of the single Welsh saint who has found a place in the calendar of the Western Church. The antiquary will find plenty to occupy him in the cromlechs and other ancient monuments which abound in North Pembrokeshire, and may spend much time in unravelling the intricate architectural history of the cathedral buildings. Each will be fully repaid for his long journey to this remote corner of Wales, for even now St. David's is sixteen miles from the railway at Haverfordwest, and is reached by an interesting drive under the remains of Roch Castle, past Newgale Sands, and across the deep-cut Boscastle-like hollow of Solva, during which the modern pilgrim in his carriage may recall the mediæval proverb that two journeys to St.

David's were equal in merit to one to Rome, so long and difficult was the way thither in the olden time. Yet to this distant shrine came not only all true Welshmen, but their Norman conquerors as well, and among them the three greatest of the mediæval kings of England, viz., the Conqueror in 1081, Henry II. in 1173, and Edward I. in 1284. Indeed it was by a Norman bishop that the present church was mainly built, so that the shrine of St. David formed a bond of union between conquerors and conquered, so widely separated in all other points.

The traveller will naturally approach the church from the south-east, passing through the market-place of the little city, with its ancient cross restored by the care of Bishop Thirlwall. A steep lane paved with rounded stones (hence known as the "Popples") leads down to the Tower Gate, flanked to the north by an octagonal Early English tower, which does not seem to have been ever completed, and to the south by a circular one coæval with the portcullised doorway. A few steps more and the first extended view of the cathedral buildings is gained. The spectator looks down on them nestling in the narrow green valley of the Alan, while beyond the stream rises the fine bishop's palace (now in ruins), backed by the crags of Carn Llidi and of Penberry. It is a most striking scene, and grows on one more and more every time one sees it.

The eye will at once be caught by the massive central tower, the restoration of which ranks among the late Sir Gilbert Scott's most successful and daring feats. For the western piers were so shattered that the tower had to be supported by gigantic balks of timber for months while they were being rebuilt under circumstances of the greatest difficulty and danger. No one, too, can fail to be struck by the fact that the roofed-in part of the church east of the tower is higher than the nave, and by the very complicated ground-plan of the roofless eastern chapels. The church is mainly built of sandstone from Caerbwdy, one of the neighbouring bays, and its rich grey, reddish, and purple hues add to the picturesqueness of the scene, especially in the recently-restored parts of the building.

The architectural history of the church may be briefly summed up thus. The nave, central tower, transepts, and presbytery were commenced in 1180 by Bishop Peter de Leia, in the transition style between Norman and Early English; but the lower part of the tower and the presbytery were reconstructed after the fall of the tower in 1220. Bishop Gower added the Decorated second stage of the tower in the fourteenth century, and Bishop Vaughan the Perpendicular third stage in the early sixteenth century. Many changes were made by Bishop Gower (such as the raising of the aisles of the nave and presbytery, and the insertion of windows in the former), so that the general appearance

of the exterior is Decorated. The Lady Chapel was built by Bishop Martyn during the great burst of devotion towards the Blessed Virgin which characterised the thirteenth century.

Descending a flight of steps which passes through a cemetery on the hillside, we enter the church by the rich southern door, and get our first view of the interior standing at the west end of the nave. And a most wonderful view it is! The stately rise of fourteen feet from the west door to the high altar, the gorgeous roof of the nave, the heavy but very ornate rood-screen, the peculiar treatment of the clerestory and triforium which form but one main division, the massive piers (on several of which are traces of ancient paintings), combine to produce a profound impression on the mind of even the much-travelled visitor.

The splendid roof is of the early sixteenth century, and is a flat timber ceiling, apparently supported by a series of segmental arches, from the intersections of which the most delicately carved pendants drop "in a style of almost Arabian gorgeousness." The nave itself has been repaved, and is used for the parish services, as well as for the choir services on Sundays. Passing up it, we may linger for a moment to admire Bishop Gower's rood-screen, in the southernmost compartment of which is the tomb of Gower himself. A new organ has within this decade been placed on the rood loft: in order to diminish the weight and to avoid blocking the view up and down the church, Mr. Willis has, by an ingenious arrangement, placed the bellows in the south transept at the back of the choir stalls.

Passing by the altar used for the services in the nave, through a richly-groined passage of two bays, we enter the space beneath the tower, which forms the ritual choir, and is used for the week-day services. It is filled with twenty-eight fifteenth-century stalls, some of the misereres (or movable seats) of which are carved with unusual subjects. One stall belongs to the Sovereign, who holds a cursal prebend, though this arrangement may not date farther back than the Reformation. The ceiling, which is of the same date as that of the nave, was slightly raised by Sir G. Scott so as to clear the whole of the four lantern windows. It has been repainted, and emblazoned with the arms of some of the more distinguished bishops of the see. The canopy of the bishop's throne has considerable dignity, but the excellent work of which it is composed is of two dates. But the chief object to be noticed is the light wooden screen which separates the choir from the presbytery, for though the division is clearly made in all great churches, there is no other case known where the screen remains in position. Through its open lattice-work we catch a glimpse of a great tomb standing in the midst of the presbytery, before the high altar. But it is disappointing to find that it is only that of Edmund

Tudor, Earl of Richmond, the father of Henry VII. by his wife Margaret (foundress of Christ's and St. John's Colleges at Cambridge, and of divinity professorships at the two universities). The tomb has occupied its present position since the dissolution of the monasteries, when it was brought hither from the house of the Grey Friars at Carmarthen. For the shrine of St. David is in a position unusual except in Wales, and is on the north side of the presbytery. The stone base only remains, the relics of the saint and the portable

THE CHOIR.

shrine having disappeared at the Reformation. It is one of the four examples still surviving in England, and was constructed in 1275.

The roof of the presbytery, which was in a very insecure state, has been thoroughly repaired, and the original colours and blazonry on its ceiling carefully renewed. The masonry of the east end is singularly rich. It consists of three noble lancets, with four smaller ones above. The former (now filled with fine mosaics by Salviati) have been blocked since the early part of the sixteenth century, when Bishop Vaughan erected on the vacant space between the east wall of the presbytery and the Lady Chapel the very beautiful chapel (dedicated to the Holy Trinity) in which he was buried. The pierced cross which is seen just over the altar is lighted from Bishop Vaughan's Chapel; below it, in a recess in the east wall, there were lately discovered a number of human

I I

bones embedded in mortar, which were probably placed there for safety at the Reformation, and may possibly include the relics of St. David himself. The cross aisle east of Bishop Vaughan's Chapel forms the vestibule to the Lady Chapel, and is roofed; but the Lady Chapel itself, and the aisles connecting this part of the church with the aisles of the presbytery, are now in a ruinous condition, though it is hoped that they may speedily be restored.

Retracing our steps to the western end, we may leave the church by the north door. A few steps to the left and we find ourselves before the west front of the cathedral. This was rebuilt in 1793, by Nash, of very perishable stone. In memory of Bishop Thirlwall it has now been entirely remodelled after a design by Sir G. Scott, who, with the help of the drawings preserved in the library of the Society of Antiquaries, has endeavoured to bring the whole front back to what it may originally have been. It consists of three one-light windows, over which is a range of five smaller ones, while above the west door is a statue of Bishop Thirlwall, seated, and in the act of delivering a charge. It is a modest west front, but probably quite as rich as is consistent with the simplicity of the exterior of the church.

Returning to the north door, one is surprised to see on the right a huge building, with a graceful tower. This is the chapel of St. Mary's College, founded in the fourteenth century, for a master, seven fellows or chaplains, and two choristers, the whole being under the control of the precentor. And if we pass by this ruined building, and go to the east side of the north transept, a fresh surprise is in store for us; for here is a lofty building overtopping the north transept, to the eastern wall of which it is joined, though separated by a narrow slype from the main mass of the church. The lower stage is the Chapel of St. Thomas, added during the rebuilding of the central tower after its fall in 1220, the very year in which the body of St. Thomas was translated to its final resting-place in the choir of Canterbury. St. David's was clearly determined not to be behind the rest of the world in honouring the martyred archbishop. In the fourteenth century two upper stages seem to have been added, the former being the chapter-house, the latter the treasury. The floor between these two stages has long since disappeared, and the lofty chamber which has been the result has received a new roof, and has become the chapter library, while St. Thomas's Chapel is now used as the chapter-house.

The restoration of the church has been in progress for the last twenty years, and (with the exception of the eastern chapels) is now nearly completed. It has been zealously watched over by the present dean (to whom the thanks of all architectural and historical students are specially due), much of the cost being defrayed by various special gifts, particularly those of the late Rev. John Lucey, and the munificent bequests of Mr. and Mrs. Montgomery Traherne, of Coedriglan.

ST. DAVID'S CATHEDRAL, FROM THE NORTH-EAST.

9

The original settlement at St. David's was monastic, but since Norman times the chapter has been composed of secular canons, and now consists of a dean and four canons residentiary. The bishop, by a vague tradition, ranked as dean, and even now he occupies the stall which in other cathedral churches is appropriated to the dean. By virtue of 3 & 4 Vict., cap. 113, and of 6 & 7 Vict., cap. 77, the precentor was given the title and authority of dean, and occupies the corresponding stall on the north side.

St. David himself flourished in the sixth century, and the Celtic church in this district kept aloof from the Norman church till the consecration in 1115 of the Norman Bernard to the see by Ralph, Archbishop of Canterbury. One of the most remarkable persons connected with the church was Gerald de Barri (or Giraldus Cambrensis), who in the twelfth century made several attempts to secure his election to the see. He was the great champion of the claims (for which there is no real evidence) of St. David's to be the metropolitan see of Wales, and has left many lively and interesting narratives and descriptions of St. David's and of Wales generally. Among the more distinguished successors of St. David we may name Peter de Leia (1176—1198), the founder of the present church; Henry Gower (1328—1347), its second founder; Henry Chichele (1408—1414), translated to Canterbury; Lyndwood, the canonist (1442—1446), Barlow (1536—1549), the chief consecrator of Archbishop Parker; Laud (1621—1626); Bull (1705—1710), the great theologian; Lowth, the Hebraist (1766); Thirlwall (1840—1878), the historian of Greece; and the present bishop, William Basil Jones, who in 1856 completed, in conjunction with Mr. E. A. Freeman (the historian of the Norman Conquest), a most exhaustive history of the see and of the district. It is impossible to quit St. David's without a mention of the ruined Chapel of St. Non (St. David's mother), on the cliffs near Caerfai Bay, which is of very early date, and that of St. Justinian (rebuilt in the sixteenth century, but now roofless) on those opposite Ramsey Island. There has been talk of transferring the see to some more central and more conveniently situated place, but to do so would break that long chain of historical associations which runs back to the sixth century, and is a witness to the identity (in all essential points) of the Church of St. David with the English Church of the nineteenth century.

W. A. B. Coolidge.

THE NAVE AND CHOIR.

(From a Photograph by Mr. F. Bedford. By permission of Messrs. Catherall and Prichard.)

LLANDAFF.

ALTHOUGH the Cathedral of Llandaff cannot be compared with any of the English cathedrals, either architecturally or historically, nevertheless it is one of the most interesting spots in Britain, for here we witness not merely a noble restoration "reflecting undying honour upon all concerned in it," but an actual resurrection, not of the material fabric only, but of the spiritual fabric as well. It is almost impossible for those who have not witnessed it to realise from what a depth of degradation this charming cathedral has arisen. From its completion in mediæval times till late in this century, its only history has been one of "Decline and Fall." So that though Llandaff claims to be one of the most ancient sees, if not the most ancient, yet practically its bishopric, its cathedral, and its cathedral body are all alike new. No bishop had resided there for about three hundred years. For something like six centuries there had been no dean.

The chapter was merely a nominal one, "for as no special residentiaries were ever appointed, the duties falling upon all alike were avoided by all alike." Of the cathedral itself, half of it had become a roofless ruin, and the other half was hideously disfigured into the similitude of some pseudo-classical temple. The choral service had been suppressed, and the daily service had ceased; "the practical ecclesiastical establishment consisted of a single vicar; the choral establishment consisted of a single fiddle.' The late Bishop Ollivant describes his cathedral on the day of his enthronement on the 13th March, 1850, in these words:—

"When the present Bishop of Llandaff presented himself at the cathedral to demand installation into his sacred office, the western portion of the building, through which the procession had to pass, was, as it had been for 127 years, a roofless ruin. The beautiful window in the western façade was dilapidated and unglazed. A lofty fragment of what had once been a south-west tower frowned haughtily upon the desolation below, threatening at any moment still further destruction. Thick branches of ivy had forced themselves into the joints of the noble columns of the arches

LLANDAFF CATHEDRAL, WEST FRONT.

which had so long been exposed to wind and weather. One solitary portion of the ancient clerestory had survived, a model of exquisite beauty, which, in the event of any future restoration, the most fastidious architect would feel himself constrained and delighted to copy. Beyond the three roofless bays stood an Italian temple, terminated at the west by a wall which crossed the nave and side aisles from north to south. Its western front exhibited on its summit two Grecian urns. The inside of it was lighted with round-headed windows; rosettes of plaster of Paris adorned its ceiling. The choir and stall-work of painted deal were in keeping with the style of the building. The floor had been raised by a considerable accumulation of rubbish, beneath which the plinths of the noble columns lay concealed. The doorway of the crossing wall transmitted to posterity the date (1752) of the completion of the Italian building, which, by those who erected it, was regarded with intense satisfaction.

"The demand of the bishop to be admitted to his throne was responded to by the late excellent and highly respected vicar choral, the only ecclesiastic at that time in residence, having all the cathedral, parochial, and pastoral duties of Llandaff resting upon him. There were at that time no residentiary canons, nor houses of any kind for canons, residentiary or minor, nor even for the dean. There had been no choir since 1691, when the archdeacon and chapter placed upon record in their Act Book that, 'considering the small revenues of this church, and the irregular management of the choir by the singing-men and singing-boys, the choir singing should be put down and discontinued,' in lieu of which the schoolmaster was appointed to give out the singing Psalms, and four pounds a year were allowed him for doing it.

"On the opening of the door, in reply to the bishop's summons, the musical arrangements of 1691 were found to be still in force. The national schoolmaster, heading the procession, gave out a Psalm, which was sung by about a dozen of his scholars, a bass viol being the only instrument then in the possession of the cathedral. In this way the bishop was conducted to his throne; and, after installation, to the Lady Chapel, in which divine service was then ordinarily performed, the body of the cathedral having been for several years disused, as it continued to be for many that followed them, from its unfitness for the celebration of public worship." (*Charge*, 1869.)

It is only by bearing in mind this apparently hopeless dilapidation and humiliation into which the cathedral had been suffered to fall that one can duly appreciate the contrast exhibited by its present architectural condition, the beauty of its services, and the efficiency of its staff.

There is something exceedingly picturesque in the situation of the cathedral as it is usually approached through the little village-city. It stands on low ground near the river Taff (hence its name Llan-daff—the church by the Taff);

but on the south and west the ground rises abruptly from the very doors of the cathedral; and from the lych-gate above we look down upon the cathedral through the intervening trees, and on to the Caerphilly hills beyond. From this point the great defect of the cathedral is very evident—the want of transepts and a central tower. With the exception of the beautiful west front, which is not visible from this point, there is no cathedral character about the exterior—it is nothing more than a village church upon an enlarged scale. The most beautiful portion of the cathedral is the west front, extremely simple in its parts, yet of exceeding dignity. It consists of a gabled centre, divided into three stages, and flanked on each side by a tower, that to the south having a spire. The central part is pure Early English, and fortunately at the restoration needed hardly more than the glazing of the windows. The western doorway, with its round-headed arch, is peculiar and hardly pleasing. Its position explains the reason of the round arch instead of a pointed one; but owing to the two arches in the lower part of the tympanum, it has all the effect of a mutilated doorway, wanting its central shaft, though it never could have had one. The west window consists of three broad lancets, the central one being higher than the others. The whole arrangement of this stage and of the one above it is most effective.

"There is no place from which one can get a distant general view, but this is quite counterbalanced by the singular and striking approach from the deanery; the steep descent coming down almost immediately upon the grand western portal."

The tower on the north is Perpendicular, and is massive and simple. It was built by Jasper Tudor, uncle to Henry VII., and replaces an Early English one, of which a portion still remains. During the last century the battlement and pinnacles were blown down in a great storm, so that the present beautiful work is new. On the south side the tower, with its graceful spire, is entirely new. Originally there had been an Early English tower, but it had become a complete ruin, and there was evidence to show that it was bare and poor, and quite unworthy of the rest of the beautiful west front; so Mr. Prichard, the architect of the restoration, considered that in this case he was quite justified in replacing it by one of altogether different design. Consequently he has built a tower, which is strikingly effective; and to this he has added a lofty spire, crocketed, with a handsome open parapet, and a variety of pinnacles at the juncture of the tower and spire, which harmonise well with the rich open-work of the Tudor tower. Mr. Prichard has been blamed for not rebuilding the former tower, no matter how poor it may have been, and also because the general design of the spire and its adaptation to the tower are foreign rather than English, reminding one strongly of the churches in Normandy. But he certainly has given to the cathedral its most striking feature, and the golden colour of the stone is beautiful.

On the north and south sides are two late Norman doorways, the latter being the more highly enriched, though both are of very considerable ornamentation. The south door has an outer moulding "closely resembling the ordinary Etruscan scroll—a circumstance," Dean Conybeare believes, "without any other example in our Norman ornaments." The north door is remarkable for having the dog-tooth moulding, which shows its late character.

WEST DOOR

NORTH DOOR

THE WEST AND NORTH DOORS.

The internal view from the west door is very striking. There is nothing about the exterior to raise the expectation of such dignity and grace. As one stands on the steps, which descend from the door into the nave, the eye is led along the dignified arcade to the choir and lofty presbytery arch, and on to the well-raised altar, with the splendid Norman arch behind opening into the Lady Chapel beyond. From this point the transepts are not missed, and though the scale is small, yet there is a cathedral dignity which is unmistakable. Beautiful as is the exterior of the west end, its internal treatment is still finer; for the fall of ground allows a great increase of height, which adds immensely to its effect. It is thus Dr. Freeman describes it: "The height thus gained allows the triplet itself, with a rich array of arch mouldings and jamb-shafts, to occupy the whole width of the church . . . without the width of each lancet being made disproportionate. The skill with which the internal and external arrangements, each the better suited for its own position, are adapted to each other deserves our best study and admiration." It is almost incredible that it was the intention of the cathedral mutilators in the last century to take down the whole of this west front, together with the three western bays of the nave! The style of the nave and choir is pure Early English, but of a type which is almost peculiar to South Wales and Somersetshire, a stiffer form which has not quite worked itself free from Norman influence. There is no marked structural difference between nave and choir. The eye of the visitor is naturally attracted to the great Norman arch behind the altar, with its unique exterior moulding. This arch, together with a reredos of the fourteenth century, had been concealed by lath and plaster till the restoration. The reredos, being considered too mutilated, has been removed into the north aisle, and a new reredos takes its place, the arches of which have been filled with three very fine paintings by Rossetti. But however excellent they may be in themselves, they are not effective in a reredos. It would be here impossible to enter into the differences of opinion as to the origin of the Norman arch, and the singular remains of unfinished work on the south side of the presbytery; but the following theory of Mr. Freeman's seems to be the most probable, though it is not without its difficulties :—

When Bishop Urban, in the twelfth century, removed the British church of St. Dubricius and St. Teilo, his cathedral, which replaced it, must after all have been of very small size, though highly ornamented. The Norman arch would be the chancel arch, and the present presbytery the nave of what must have been an aisleless building. In all probability Urban's church did not extend further than one bay beyond the present presbytery, and the vaulted vestibule now leading into the chapter-house may have been the porch. In the fourteenth century this Norman nave, which up to this time must have remained without any alteration, was altered into the present decorated presbytery, the existing arches being cut through the Norman walls.

There are some interesting monuments of the thirteenth and fifteenth centuries. One, on the south side of the presbytery, is the tomb of St. Teilo, the second bishop; on the north side, a very fine one, by Armstead, has lately been erected to the memory of Bishop Ollivant, during whose episcopacy the restoration took place. The Lady Chapel is an early example of the transition from Early English to Decorated.

About 1836 it was seriously proposed to unite Llandaff to Bristol, which would have given the *coup de grâce* to the unfortunate see; but from this it was saved, and under its last two bishops, Copleston and Ollivant, the new era began. In 1840 and 1843 two important Acts were passed, which resuscitated the dean's office; and fortunate, indeed, has Llandaff been in its deans—the first three, Bruce-Knight, Conybeare, geologist and archæologist, and Williams, successfully carrying out the restoration to its final completion. They gave their whole energies to the noble work of raising their ruined minster from the ground. It has well been said: " There may be other churches which in some points come nearer to ideal perfection, but then there is none which has in the same way risen to a new life out of a state of such hopeless ruin."

E. A. FISHBOURNE.

J J

RUINS OF ST. GERMAN'S.

(From a Photograph by Messrs. Poulton and Son, Lee.)

ST. GERMAN'S.

RISING, as it were, out of the rock, at the entrance to the harbour of Peel, on what was formerly St. Patrick's Isle, but now united to the mainland by a solid causeway, stands the picturesque ruin of St. German's, for centuries the cathedral church of the ancient diocese of Man. Like the sister church of Iona, it is no longer the centre of religious life and activity, whence the minister of God went forth to carry on his mission of salvation in the adjacent isles. Its life, its usefulness seem gone. The restorer has done some little with its roofless walls to stay destruction's hand. But its precincts are only now the resting-place of the shipwrecked mariner, its stones an object of curiosity to the tourist. Yet even in their ruin they may still be said to do a work for God; for standing in their desolation at the harbour's mouth, they cannot but remind the hardy Manxman, when he puts to sea, to pray for a blessing as his fathers did.

What the date was of the original structure it is impossible to say, but no doubt from very early times there was a church on this spot. And if there is truth in the tradition that here Germanus was consecrated by St. Patrick in 447 the first bishop of the Sodorenses, or Southern Isles, we may conclude that this was the seat of the Bishops of Sodor and Man. But however this may be, the cathedral as it now appears was cruciform in shape, built of coarse grey stone from the neighbourhood, and coigned with red sandstone, and consisted of a chancel with crypt underneath, transepts, central tower, nave, and south aisle. The length of the chancel is 36 feet 4 inches; of the nave, 52 feet 6 inches; of the base of the tower, 26 feet; and of the whole, about 114 feet. The width at the intersection of the transepts measures 68 feet 3 inches; height of chancel walls, 18 feet; thickness of walls, 3 feet. The architecture, which is a mixture of the Early English and the Edwardian or Decorated period, gives distinct evidence of the alterations which have been made in the building at various times. In the gable of the north transept, for instance, the doorway is of a very late date, while on the inside there are traces of three windows belonging to three different periods; and in the south transept the windows are of two different periods. The choir, however, which is the oldest part of the present structure, is generally acknowledged to have been rebuilt by Bishop Simon (1226—1247), while the nave and transepts belong to a later period.

Of the church itself there are not many circumstances of interest to relate. Within its walls the bishops were enthroned until the close of the last century, when its roofless condition rendered the ceremony impossible. Some few of the occupants of the see are here interred. Wymundus (1151) and John (1154) are stated to have been buried in St. German's, which proves that the present was not the original cathedral. Simon was the first to be interred within the new building; and in 1871, when the chancel was being cleared with a view to restoration, what are supposed to be the remains of this bishop were discovered, with this remarkable circumstance: near his feet were found the remains of a dog, the jaw-bones and some of the teeth being quite perfect. Bishops Mark (1303), Huan Hesketh (1510), John Philips (1633), and Richard Parr (1643), all lie within the sanctuary. But the only tomb of interest is that of Bishop Samuel Rutter. He was the staunch friend as well as the able counsellor of the heroic Charlotte de la Tremouille, and took an active part with her in the memorable defence of Lathom House against the Parliamentary forces under Fairfax. There is also buried here the child of Bishop Wilson, aged but six months, of whom touching mention is made in his private diary: "June 3, 1703, my little Alice died." And we should add that in the nave there is a Runic stone much defaced, but on which there is still decipherable "—raised this cross to his wife Astrith, the daughter of Utr" (Ottar).

The most interesting feature of the cathedral, however, is the crypt beneath the chancel, entered by a steep narrow staircase in the wall, opening from the south side of the choir.   It is clearly not part of the original work of Bishop Simon, or if built by him it was at a later date, as it is evident that the construction of the crypt led to the raising of the floor to its present level.   In length 34 feet, and in breadth 16 feet, it has a curiously ribbed roof, with thirteen groins springing from pilasters on the solid rock, and it is lighted by a small aperture under the east choir window.   Till 1780 this damp and dismal dungeon was used as the ecclesiastical prison, and at times also as a place of confinement for civil offenders.   It was certainly within this wretched cell that Eleanor Cobham, the haughty wife of Humphrey, Duke of Gloucester, Shakespeare's "presumptuous dame—ill-nurtured Eleanor," dragged out fourteen weary years of imprisonment for witchcraft.   It was here that, during the persecution of the Quakers in the Isle of Man, several of them were imprisoned between 1656 and 1662.

But a very practical question remains for our enquiry.   Why should the old Cathedral of St. German's still remain a ruin?   Why should the diocese of Sodor and Man, with an historical interest of more than a thousand years, be lacking in that great centre which it once possessed, and which is the privilege of the most recent English bishopric?   There was no doubt some good reason for Bishop Wilson acting as he did when he stripped the lead off for roofing the church of the adjoining parish.   He was devoted in his love to the Church and diocese. But he was thoroughly practical.   He foresaw, perhaps, in the altered circumstances of the times, when St. Patrick's Isle had ceased to be the residence of the lord and the governing body, that the use of the cathedral where it stood was now impracticable, and that the services of the Church could more efficiently be carried out on the mainland.   That his heart was with the hallowed pile we may be sure, from his making it the resting-place of his little babe.   But no doubt what pressed most on those concerned — the patron and the bishop — was the lack of money.   The bishop would hardly have consented to a restoration that was unworthy of the former edifice.   The Earl of Derby has recorded the hope, that a benefactor might be one day raised up to complete the work. But more than a hundred years have passed away since Bishop Wilson's time—the Church has multiplied in wealth, and her shrines have been restored on every hand, yet still St. German's stands a ruin on the rock by Peel.   She waits the benefactor to arise.   She asks the zeal of Churchmen to make her what she was.

R. SODOR AND MAN.

EXTERIOR OF HENRY THE SEVENTH'S CHAPEL.

WESTMINSTER ABBEY.

THE CORONATION
CHAIR.

K K

THE Abbey of Westminster, to use the words of the late Dean Stanley, "is not only Rheims Cathedral and St. Denys both in one, but is also what the Panthéon was intended to be to France, what the Valhalla is to Germany, what Santa Croce is to Italy." *Siste, viator, calcas heroa*, is nowhere so apt as within its walls. Every stone within the building seems incorporated into the fabric of our national history, every slab of its pavements tells of those who have played their part, often for good, sometimes for ill, in the making of England.

The date of the first foundation of Westminster Abbey is uncertain. Its earlier history is inextricably entangled with legend. At any rate, before the Romans came—when a British village marked the future site of London city—there was higher up, on the left bank of the Thames, an island or peninsula among the marshes, formed by the confluence of two tributary brooks with the main river. We may well doubt the tale which states that a Roman temple stood on the site of St. Peter's Abbey, although a stone sarcophagus of that age has been dug up near the north buttresses. Time passed; the Romans left, the English came. The land became more populous, and this spot—the isle of Thorns, as it was called — attracted attention. Being raised slightly above the surrounding fen, and supplied by springs—of which one was till lately indicated by "Dean's Yard Pump"—it came to be selected as a settlement, possibly monastic from the first. The grave of Sebert, king early in the seventh century, is still shown in the Abbey, and he is claimed as its first founder; but, at any rate, a community of Benedictine monks was established here in the reign of Edgar. It is, however, to Edward (commonly called the Confessor) that we must look as the originator of the greatness of St. Peter's Church at Westminster. Before coming to the throne he had vowed a pilgrimage to Rome, but had been absolved from this obligation by the Pope on condition of establishing a monastery in honour of Rome's patron saint. Westminster had now become a royal residence, though its palace had not the fame or splendour of after days. The little Abbey near its gates was already of some repute, for it had been dedicated to St. Peter, as the tale went, by the saint himself. This Edward resolved to rebuild. During the later years of his reign he reared, at a vast cost, and by the help of Norman architects, a church almost coextensive with the present building.

The Confessor's Minster was no doubt far more elaborate in design and execution than any other church in Britain. St. Stephen's and La Trinité, at Caen, though both of slightly later date, may perhaps give us an idea of its main features. It was cruciform in plan, with three towers, two western, one central, capped by short spires, and with an apsidal east end. No trace of it, however, now remains above ground, though here and there in the monastic precincts a few fragments of wall may be seen, some of them actual remnants of the Confessor's work, others built not long after his death, and in continuance of his plan. The church was only ready for dedication at the close of his reign; and he was unable to be present at the ceremony. On Innocents' Day, 1065, he was just able to sign the Charter, the new building was consecrated in the Queen's presence by the hands of Stigand, and on Sylvester's Eve Edward passed away, and a troublous time for England began.

WESTMINSTER ABBEY.

10

Thus the inaugural events for the Abbey of Westminster were the funeral of its founder and the coronation of his successor—both of them events significant of its future history. But we will only dwell upon this so far as it affects the fabric itself. That remained with little change for nearly two centuries. One of the first acts of Henry III. was to add a Lady Chapel east of the Norman apse. A quarter of a century later (A.D. 1245) he undertook a far greater work, the rebuilding of the whole Abbey. To him we owe a large part of the present structure; and to his eclectic tastes many of its peculiarities are due. The new church was the outcome both of his religious fervour, which was exceptional, and of his personal feeling towards the English side of his ancestry. It is no less a memorial of another trait in his character—his lavish expenditure; for "the royal Abbey, as in the Confessor's time so in Henry's, is absolutely a royal gift." At his death the building was carried westward only one bay beyond the transept. It was continued three bays further by his son, Edward I. For some two hundred years the work progressed slowly, the nave being gradually replaced; but at the time of the Civil War the western towers were still unfinished. After the Restoration they fell into the hands of Wren, who completed the western façade of the building. Of his addition to the Abbey, we can only say that it is an excellent piece of masonry, and might easily have been yet more incongruous. His design for the finished building will be found on page 287. He also disfigured the details of the front of the north transept. Here, however, a recent restoration, directed by Mr. (afterwards Sir) G. G. Scott, has effaced the traces of Wren's unsympathetic hand. But, while the old faith yet prevailed, and before the old style of architecture had yielded to the reviving classic spirit, one great alteration was made in the eastern part of the Abbey: the Lady Chapel—the third Henry's earliest work—was taken down by the seventh Henry, and replaced by one of larger and statelier proportions. It was designed to quiet his conscience by enlisting on his side the Virgin, in whom he had always had "most singulier trust and confidence," to secure that masses should be said, and alms distributed for the welfare of his soul "perpetually for ever, while the world shall endure"—that is, for some thirty years; perhaps, also, in consciousness of the weakness of his title to the throne, to set his mark on this which was already one of the most truly national among our edifices, and to make his grave in one of its most sacred places.

The Abbey suffered less than might have been expected both at the Reformation and during the Civil War. As the tomb-house of so many kings, it was dealt with tenderly at the former epoch. There had been no contumacious churchman, whose memory was an offence, in what had been almost a chapel royal. He whose relics were enshrined in its holiest place had been an English king. On the second occasion, when crown and mitre went down before the Puritan, the Abbey had become nationalised. No more striking testimony to this can be quoted than the fact that the great Protector, with other magnates of his age, was laid to rest in the easternmost part of its Lady Chapel. So the hand of the iconoclast was to a great extent withheld. Natural decay, and the dull contempt for mediæval work which characterised the last century, have wrought mischief enough; nevertheless, many of its choicest relics have suffered but little. Disfigured as it is in many parts by incongruous and often hideous monuments, overcrowded with such memorials as it is in all, "the Abbey" still remains one of the most beautiful among our churches, the most interesting

THE NORTH TRANSEPT.

THE SOUTH TRANSEPT.

historic building in the whole of the United Kingdom.

Let us enter the Minster by its western door; for this is the best way of apprehending at a glance its most characteristic features. One, as seen from this point— with Wren's work at our back, and that of Henry VII. hid from view—is the uniformity of the design as a whole. Though, as we have said, almost the whole of the nave is later than the reign of Henry III., it produces the impression of a building belonging to the earliest part of the Middle Pointed, or Decorated, Period. Another feature is, for an English Minster, its exceptional height. Its architecture has, from the first, been slightly exotic. Both the English Edward and the English-born Henry made use of French architects. Westminster Abbey is not only actually the loftiest ecclesiastical structure in England, but also the highest in proportion to its breadth; the ratio of the one to the other being 3 to 1, while in most of our cathedrals it varies from 2 to 2·5 to 1. Another characteristic, not common, though not unique, is its chevet, or apse. This, too, is French rather than English. The last feature we will notice is its high ornamentation. Though, as is usual in buildings of this date, the tracery of the windows and the capitals of the columns are not especially rich in design, the walls are covered with elaborate diapering up to the base of the clerestory. If we may venture on a criticism, the height is almost disproportionate, making the building look a little narrow, and the triforium, beautiful as it is in itself, rather detracts from the effect of the clerestory. An arcade of simpler design, as at Rheims, produces a more harmonious whole. The ritual choir now occupies three bays of the nave. It is enclosed by a

SHRINE OF EDWARD THE CONFESSOR.

stone screen; of this the inner stonework dates from the thirteenth century, but the façade is of the nineteenth. Right of the doorway and beneath an arch is the monument of the first Earl Stanhope; left, that of Isaac Newton, the mathematician and physicist. The organ, not long since re-arranged and enlarged, is grouped on each side of the screen so as not to obstruct the view.

The monuments in the nave, numerous as they have become, are comparatively modern, few interments, at any rate of note, having taken place here before the beginning of the last century. Yet there is now but little room left in the floor for graves, or on the walls for memorials. Under the north-west tower, around the cumbrous monument of Fox (removed from the north transept, where the great orator was buried), are grouped those of other eminent Liberals, so that this "has been consecrated as the Whigs' Corner." Over the west door is the statue of Pitt. Under the south-west tower, in the baptistery, was the consistory court; a figure in the window is said to represent the Black Prince. Here is a monument to Addison's friend Craggs, with an epitaph written by Pope. Here, too, are memorials of William Wordsworth, John Keble, Frederick Maurice, and Charles Kingsley—all buried elsewhere.

The north aisle shows us the stone beneath which "rare Ben Jonson" is buried in a standing position; the last resting-place of the great surgeon, John Hunter; the graves of Spencer Perceval, the murdered statesman, and Charles Lyell, great in geology, near that of Woodward, founder of the professorship of that science at Cambridge. John Herschel, the illustrious astronomer, is not far from the monument of Newton, and in fit proximity to the latter is Charles Darwin, hardly less great among naturalists than he among mathematicians.

In the south aisle we must not forget to notice the curious Abbots' pew above the Dean's door. Its pavement, as its walls, tells us of Atterbury, divine, statesman, and conspirator, who was buried in this familiar spot "as far from kings and Cæsars as the space will admit of." Friend's memorial is appropriately near. Congreve, the dramatist, favourite of a duchess, is here; and, in congenial company, Mrs. Oldfield, whom the pomps and vanities of the world accompanied to her coffin. Admiral Tyrell deserved better of his generation than to be commemorated by so hideous a monument, which has, however, now assumed less offensive proportions. Many other brave soldiers and sailors have memorials here. Some of the monuments record those whose graves are in the central part of the nave. Among these are several who in our own days have attained to repute. Here rested for a few days the body of George Peabody. Toward the eastern part lie, in one row, G. E. Street, G. G. Scott, and Charles Barry. South of these are placed Lord Lawrence, Colin Campbell (Lord Clyde), and Outram, the Bayard of India. Not far away rests the body of David Livingstone, brought to the African coast from the central wilds by the loving care of his native attendants; and Cochrane, Lord Dundonald, the prey of faction, has here met with tardy justice. Here is a brass to Robert Stephenson, who is interred in St. Andrew's Chapel, and one to Sir Robert Wilson; the former ugly in its realism, the latter ridiculous in its mediævalism. The General is represented in full fourteenth century armour! North and south of the Choir the aisles continue to be crowded with monuments. On the north side we note memorials of Blow, Croft, and Purcell, of Arnold, of Wilberforce, and of Stamford Raffles, and the new altar-tomb of the late Sub-Dean, Lord John Thynne. On the south side are memorials of Watts and the Wesleys, of Kneller and Paoli. The murder of Thomas Thynn is " writ in marble ;" and among many other brave men is Sir Cloudesley Shovel, " a very gallant man."

The north transept, after the interment of Lord Chatham, became "the states-man's aisle." No part of the building is more crowded with monuments, especially with monuments of modern date. It might be compared to a petrified Madame Tussaud's. In several cases the monuments are only memorials, but Chatham, Fox, Grattan, George Canning, and his son, the Viceroy of India, are actually buried here. On the west side, under the arches, are three large monuments: one, the " Great Commoner;" another, three captains in Rodney's fleet ; the third, Lord Mansfield. Near these are the statues of Castlereagh and Palmerston and Follett. In the adjoining aisle Lord Aberdeen ("the travelled Thane"), George Cornewall Lewis, Warren Hastings, Jonas Hanway, Francis Horner, and Richard Cobden, are commemorated ; also Herbert Edwardes and Vice-Admiral Watson, both of Indian fame, with many more " mighty men of valour." Newcastle, " the loyal Duke," and his literary Duchess, occupy places under the arches on the north side, and east of these is the monument to Sir Peter Warren. The statues of the three Cannings are side by side ; south of them stands Sir John Malcolm, and then Beaconsfield. At the corner is Peel, absurdly clad in a Roman toga. Behind these are the chapels of St. Andrew, St. Michael, and St. John the Evangelist, now thrown together by the destruction of their screens. They, too, are crowded with monuments. The kneeling knights supporting the upper slab of Sir Francis Vere's tomb are admirably executed, as Roubiliac himself testified. That sculptor's ghastly memorial to Mrs. Nightingale is familiar to all. Norris, made fatherless by Anne Boleyn's fondness, with his wife—Queen Elizabeth's " black crow"—rests in St. Andrew's Chapel. Sir George Holles has displaced the altar of St. John ; Sarah, Duchess of Somerset, that of St. Michael ; and among others recorded on the walls we can only name Mrs. Siddons, Admiral Kempenfelt, and Sir John Franklin.

The south transept has become the Valhalla of literature. The eastern portion has long borne the name of " Poets' Corner." The western wall " was early called the 'learned' or the 'historical' side." We cannot attempt to enumerate the names of all those who are buried or commemorated here. The paragraph would become a mere catalogue. We can only mention some of those for whom it is the actual resting-place. Chief is Chaucer, who ended his life in the Abbey precincts. The monument was erected a century and a half later. Close by are Dryden's tomb and Beaumont's grave. Here, too, lie Michael Drayton and Edmund Spenser, Abraham Cowley and Matthew Prior, Thomas Campbell and John Gay. In or near this transept also are laid Isaac Casaubon, William Camden, Henry Spelman, Isaac Barrow, David Garrick, Samuel Johnson, Thomas

Babington Macaulay, and Connop Thirlwall. The large allegorical monument of
the Duke of Argyll and Greenwich, whom readers of the "Heart of Midlothian"

THE CHOIR.

will remember, disfigures this transept, but his body was laid in a vault beneath
the Chapel of Henry VII.

In the Choir the fittings are modern, as are the altar and reredos; the marble
pavement is only of interest as the gift of Busby, the great schoolmaster of

his age. But that within the rails is, for England, an exceptional work; the materials, in great part spoils of classic structures, were brought from Rome by an Abbot of Westminster, and the mosaic was executed by workmen from that city about the year 1268. The sepulchral memorials around us here go back to earlier times. A beautiful tomb north of the altar commemorates Edmund Crouchback, son of Henry III., and founder of the House of Lancaster. Beneath the next arch is the monument of his wife, Aveline, together with that of Aymer de Valence, nicknamed by Gaveston, to his sorrow, "Joseph the Jew." On the south side, behind the sedilia, is the reputed tomb of Sebert, but not, of course, a contemporary work, and beneath the next arch rests the "great Flemish mare," Anne of Cleves. The portrait of Richard II., "the first contemporary painting of an English Sovereign," now hangs in front of some curious tapestry. The beginning of many an epoch in English history is brought to mind as we regard this part of the Abbey, for here the Sovereign is crowned, the throne being placed in front of the altar. The homage of the peers is received on another seat, erected beneath the lantern. Each one who

INTERIOR OF HENRY THE SEVENTH'S CHAPEL.

can be said to have really reigned over England has been crowned in the Abbey of Westminster, from the days of William the Norman to those of Queen Victoria; and it has also been the scene of many another act of national worship, such as the Thanksgiving Service on the completion of the fiftieth year of her present Majesty's reign.

East of the transepts, north and south, are two little chapels. The northern bears Abbot Islip's name, and in the chantry above are preserved the remains of the waxwork effigies which used to be carried at royal and other great funerals, and in former days were among the chief attractions of the Abbey.

L L

On the south side is the chapel of St. Benedict. In the north ambulatory are those of St. John the Baptist and St. Paul: in the south, of St. Edmund and St. Nicholas. All are crowded with monuments — mostly of Elizabethan and Jacobean times, though among them are some of earlier date. The most interesting (in the chapel of St. Edmund) is the tomb of William de Valence, half-brother of Henry III., "the only existing example of an effigy in Limoges enamel work in England," but it has been sadly mutilated. In the same chapel is the effigy of Elizabeth Russell, who, according to the old legend, died from the prick of a needle, "a martyr to good housewifery."

The place of chief interest is the Confessor's Chapel, which occupies the remainder of the Choir behind the high altar, and is thus raised considerably above the level of the ambulatory. In the centre of the ancient inlaid pavement stands the magnificent shrine erected by Henry III. to contain the body of his sainted predecessor. Though the golden casket which enclosed the coffin has been replaced by a humbler fabric of wood, though the Purbeck marble of the lower part has crumbled, and the glass mosaic has in many places been chipped away, this is still the most perfect monument of its kind in Britain, for to such as these the Reformation proved exceptionally fatal. A memorial hardly less interesting stands in front of the old screen which backs the reredos. This is the Coronation Chair. It was made by order of Edward I., and first used at his son's coronation. It has served the same purpose without interruption for six hundred years. Beneath it is the stone of Scone, a relic yet more venerable— though we discard the legends of its having served as Jacob's pillow at Bethel, and of its subsequent wanderings—for it was the Palladium of Scotland, and the throning-stool of its kings. The second chair was made for Queen Mary at the joint coronation of herself and William III. Between these are placed the huge sword and shield of Edward III. "Longshanks" lies beneath the third bay to the north, his strange order as to the disposal of his body having been thus violated. Beneath the next arch is the stately tomb of Henry III., enriched with slabs of Egyptian and Spartan "porphyry," the spoils of Rome. Next comes the monument of Queen Eleanor, ending the line of memorial crosses. Then, beneath a stately chantry, which is extended eastward to overarch the ambulatory, stands the tomb of Henry V., the victor of Agincourt. The body of his wife, Katherine, after many vicissitudes, is now placed near. Opposite to Eleanor lies Queen Philippa; then comes the monument of her husband, Edward III.; and lastly the ill-fated Richard II. and his Queen, Anne. All are memorials of the highest interest, on account of their execution as well as of their antiquity. They have not wholly escaped the hand of the iconoclast or of the relic-hunter. Still, as a rule, the injuries are comparatively light, and it has been deemed needless, happily, to invoke the aid of the restorer. John of Waltham, favourite of

Richard II., has been admitted into this august fellowship. Edith, wife of Edward the Confessor, rests near her husband's shrine. Queen Maud lies on the south side, while Elizabeth Tudor and Thomas of Woodstock complete the company of monarchs and their kinsfolk.

After the entombment of Henry V. there came a break in the royal

WREN'S DESIGN FOR THE COMPLETION OF THE ABBEY.

funerals. Henry VI., though, as graphically described by Dean Stanley, he chose him a place near the Confessor, rests at Windsor, as does his rival, Edward IV. But the union of the Houses of York and Lancaster is commemorated by the building of a large tomb-house. Henry VII. took down the original Lady Chapel, and erected that which now bears his name. This, though not the largest, is the finest piece of "Tudor" work in England. Although we may hesitate to apply to it Leland's courtly phrase—*orbis miraculum*—the roof, at any rate, is a marvel of elaboration. The building has side aisles, and is terminated by a chevet of four chapels. The stalls, of contemporary work, are adorned with the banners and marked by the armorial bearings of Knights of the Bath—of which order the Dean of Westminster is *ex officio* dean. Near the eastern end is the stately monument of the founder, Henry VII., and of his wife. The figures are of bronze, the tomb is of marble, adorned with alabaster and with medallions in copper. It is the work of Torregiano, Renaissance rather than Gothic in design. The grille, however, wrought by English artists, is more in harmony with the chapel. Henry the VII.'s grandson, Edward VI., was interred on the site of the altar at which masses were to be perpetually said for his grandfather's soul. No monument marked the boy-king's grave, but a re-

DEAN STANLEY.

storation of the altar, including two pillars from the original, now serves as a memorial. From his time till the reign of George III. this chapel was the usual burial-place for members of the royal house, but the line of royal monuments closes with the reign of James I., whose body was laid within the founder's vault. A stately monument in the south aisle covers the corpse of his mother, transferred hither from the cathedral of Peterborough. By this is a tomb not less worthy of note than the founder's: that of his mother, the saintly Lady Margaret, also the work of Torregiano. In this aisle also lie Margaret Lennox (grandmother of James I.), numerous members of the Stuart family, and other illustrious personages, including General Monk. At the eastern end of the same aisle lie

Charles II., William III. and Queen Mary, Queen Anne, and Prince George of Denmark; west of the founder's vault are George II. and Queen Caroline, with not a few of their children and grandchildren. In the north aisle a splendid monument commemorates the national mourning for Queen Elizabeth, and in the same grave is buried her less lamented sister Mary. Two children of James I. lie near, and in a small sarcophagus are placed the bones, discovered in the Tower, which were supposed to be the remains of the murdered sons of Edward IV.

Few members of any royal family are buried beneath the chapels of the chevet. One is encumbered by the vast monument of George Villiers, Duke of Buckingham, King James's "Steenie;" another, no less by that of Ludovic Stuart, Duke of Richmond and Lennox. In the north-eastern chapel lies John Sheffield, Duke of Buckinghamshire, with his fantastic wife. In the south-eastern is placed the Duc de Montpensier—brother to Louis Philippe—who died an exile in England, in

1807; and the late Dean, Arthur Stanley, rests by the side of his beloved wife. Over their graves a beautiful altar-tomb has been erected. The easternmost chapel has no monument, but a glance at the inscriptions on the floor is enough. In the vault beneath were laid the Protector Cromwell, with some of his family and friends, chief among them being Ireton, Bradshaw, and Admiral Blake. After the Restoration these were all ejected; most of them were reinterred

THE CHAPEL OF THE PYX.

outside the Abbey, but the corpses of Cromwell, Ireton, and Bradshaw were dragged to Tyburn for mutilation and insult. The vault afterwards received some of the illegitimate progeny of the second Charles, but was saved from utter dishonour by the subsequent interment in it of the Duke of Ormond, and of Bentinck, Earl of Portland. What satire could be more bitter than to place a bastard of that Charles who brought England so low among nations, in the very grave from which Blake had been ejected as unworthy!

Full of interest as is the exterior of the Abbey, our space forbids us to linger there. Notwithstanding three centuries of change, much still remains of the old Benedictine monastery. There are the venerable cloisters, black with the smoke of London; there is the exquisite chapter-house, built by the second founder, and now, after so many years of misuse, restored to something of its pristine beauty; there is the massive door which closes the old Norman Chapel of the Pyx, with its grim history, and the dark passage which retains portions, at least, of the Confessor's work. Fragments of the Norman dormitory can be discerned in the great schoolroom where generation after generation of scholars has been reared since the days of " Good Queen Bess." At the back of Ashburnham House are some remnants of the ancient Norman refectory. The present house is attributed to Inigo Jones. If it be his design, which is doubtful, it has been greatly altered. Some of the internal decoration is good, but it is difficult to understand, on grounds purely æsthetic, the outcry which was raised a few years ago when the house was transferred to the school. Great Dean's Yard is bordered on the eastern side by a row of houses which still retain many traces of the old monastic buildings. In the Abbots' Hall, built by Littlington, the Queen's Scholars of Westminster School dine, at tables made, it is said, from captured ships of the Spanish Armada; and between this and the Abbey is yet another hall of the same date—the Jerusalem Chamber. Here—who needs to be reminded of it?—Henry IV. died; here the Westminster Confession was drawn up; here Convocation has often assembled; here, also, the revisers of the Old Testament held their meetings.

In the future, as in the past, changes must come to the Abbey of Westminster. Two are imperatively necessary, and cannot long be delayed: a thorough repair of the fabric, and the addition of a building to serve as a tomb-house. Let us hope that in carrying out the former, the hand of the restorer will be as far as possible withheld. Better the crumbling stone, so long as it does not endanger the fabric, than the new-carved capital or tracery; better, in many cases, even the alterations of an unwise age than the modern imitation of what the original architect may have wrought. Incrustations and excrescences might, indeed, here and there be removed with advantage, but even in this it is better to err on the safe side. Still, as the Abbey is already overcrowded with monuments, it is to be hoped that before long the desire of the late and of the present Dean will be accomplished, and an addition be made to the buildings in the form of a cloister or tomb-house, into which some of the most modern monuments might be moved. Beyond this we do not wish to look, though the times are ominous of changes, and there is reason for fear as well as for hope. We part, however, from the Abbey, trusting that Dean Stanley's words may be prophetic: " Here, if anywhere, the Christian worship of England may labour to meet both the strength and the weakness of succeeding ages, to inspire new meanings into ancient forms, and embrace within itself each rising aspiration after Truth and Justice and Love."

T. G. BONNEY.

SHERBORNE: THE CHOIR.

THE lines of the black-robed Benedictines who, for exactly four hundred years, sang their masses in the noble abbey of Sherborne, were indeed cast in pleasant places. The little town, once the seat of a powerful bishop-stool which comprehended the greater part of Wessex, and thereafter the home of a rich and

P P

flourishing abbey, lies retired and silent now among gardens and orchards, backed by lovely wooded hills; yet still the great monastic church dominates the place as it did seven centuries ago, and still the tenor bell given by Wolsey rings out the hours high above the red-tiled roofs. The first view of Sherborne is delightful. The narrow, winding, ruggedly paved streets are lined by ancient houses of grey stone, solid, comfortable, and picturesque. A stone-built town always gives this impression of solidity. At the foot of the principal street, which, as in so many old towns, is built on the slope of a hill, stands a squat, heavily buttressed conduit, formerly part of the monastic buildings, and looking for all the world at a first glance like one of the market crosses that are so plentiful in the west. There is an air of prosperity about Sherborne which is no doubt justified by circumstances; for it lies in a rich, productive country, brisk and bracing, yet so sheltered from extreme rigour that in monastic days its hill-sides were clothed with vines. Eight hundred years ago Sherborne fell from its high estate as the metropolis of a powerful bishopric; for more than three hundred, no monk has entered the choir of its abbey.

It is only from the south that a clear view of the minster can be obtained, since, upon the other sides, it is very much built around. The effect is exceedingly massive, but not heavy. This impression of massiveness is largely produced by the low central tower, which rests on thick Norman piers. The church is really Perpendicular; but it contains some good Norman and Decorated work. Standing at the end of the nave, the visitor receives the same impression of massiveness which is so striking outside, corrected, however, by the exceeding loftiness of the roof, and the effective uniformity of the whole. No church of such antiquity was ever in better preservation. Within the present generation the building has been renovated—not "restored"—from end to end, and every corner is rich, reverend, and seemly. The pillars of the nave bear a very unusual ornamentation, in the shape of trefoil-headed panels, which follow the bend of the arches, where, in the centre, they meet and are finished off by shields of arms. Other shields bear the rebus of Abbot Peter de Rampisham, who commenced the rebuilding of the nave in 1475, and finished it in 1490. There is quite a feast of early heraldry in Sherborne Minster. Upon the bosses of the nave roof are many badges, devices, and ciphers; among them the H and E, connected by a true-lovers' knot, of Henry VII. and Elizabeth of York; St. Michael and the Dragon; and the "Pelican in her piety," to use the picturesque expression employed in heraldry to describe a pelican feeding her young. It is to the fine vaulted roof of its nave that Sherborne Abbey owes much of its beauty. It adds height to the entire church, and bestows grace and lightness where they were most needed.

The choir of Sherborne Abbey is very fine and interesting. So large a sum —£18,000—was spent upon its restoration by the late Earl Digby that it was inevitable it should bear traces of sweeping and garnishing. It leaves the impression of being a little too "smart;" but no violence appears to have been done to the ancient features. The beautiful roof is famous for its grace and elegance, and for the wealth of its enrichments. It is a groined roof with cinquefoil panels; and the bosses and badges have been coloured, and the compartments picked out with gold and brown. The fan-vaulting is sown about with lilies, the emblem of St. Mary, to whom the church is dedicated. Some portions of the walls still bear obvious marks of the fire which destroyed a great part of the church in 1436. The miserere-carvings are among the most interesting things in the building. The work is rude, no doubt, but it is bold and effective, difficult conceptions, such as the fantastic figure of Christ upon a Rainbow, being graphically executed with a few vigorous lines. There are some grotesque heads, and an ascetic-looking face, reputed to be a portrait of one of the abbots. One of the misereres is carved with foliage, very freely and delicately. But the most curious of these carvings is one wherein a schoolmaster or mistress is administering the *dorsi disciplina* to a scholar whose facial contortions are exceedingly expressive. In the Chartres "Book of Hours"—"Les Petites Heures à l'Usage de Chartres"—printed in 1526, there is a very similar illustration.

By far the finest piece of painted glass in the church is the "Te Deum" window, so called from its subject, in the south transept. It was designed by Mr. A. W. Pugin, and its harmony and limpidity of colour have rarely been equalled in modern work. When the setting sun falls upon it the effect is such as you rarely see. Beneath this window is a tablet commemorating Robert and Mary Digby, children of William, Lord Digby, who died, the one in 1726, the other three years later. The greater part of the slab is filled by an epitaph written by Pope, who sometimes visited Lord Digby. It differs curiously from the versions of it printed in Pope's works; but the merit of all the versions is singularly small. In the beautiful vaulted ambulatory behind the choir are reported to have been buried two famous Kings of Wessex; and a small brass of recent fixing thus records the tradition, which, be it said, is well founded: "Near this spot were interred the mortal remains of Ethelbald, and Ethelbert his brother, each of whom in his turn succeeded to the throne of Ethelwulf their father, King of the West Saxons, and were succeeded in the kingdom by their next brother, Alfred the Great."

From the roof of the central tower there is a pleasant view over the picturesquely broken ground which extends for many miles around Sherborne. In the ringing-chamber below hang the ten bells—a sanctus bell, a fire bell, and a peal of eight. The tenor is the smallest of seven sweet-toned bells imported from Tournai, and, as has been said, was the gift of Cardinal Wolsey. It is a little under three tons in weight, and, although it has been twice recast, it still bears the inscription :—

> " By Wolsey's gift I measure time for all,
>   To mirth, to grief, to church I serve to call."

The allusion to the measurement of time is explained by the fact that it is this bell which strikes the hours, with a deep but sweet and melodious note. The fire bell was recast in 1652, and is of such unusual shape that it makes an

unspeakably hideous clangour. It is still rung when there is a fire in the town. The inscription upon it is an odd mixture of piety and practical exhortation :—

> " Lord, quench this furious flame !
>   Arise ! run ! help ! put out the same."

DORCHESTER, WITH THE ABBEY, FROM LITTLE WITTENHAM.

Sherborne has seen some strange ups and downs of fortune. In early ages alternately splendid and inconsiderable, it has for more than three centuries lived a quiet, unchequered existence, broken only by Fairfax's siege of the castle in 1645. The town first emerges from obscurity at the beginning of the eighth century, when Ina, King of Wessex, dissociated Cornwall, Devon, Dorset, Somerset, Wilts, and Berks from the see of Winchester, and erected those counties into a separate bishopric with its seat at Sherborne. The sainted Aldhelm, who in learning and knowledge of the arts was centuries in advance of his time, was the first bishop. He it was who first translated the Latin Psalter into Saxon; for him was made the first organ which ever pealed forth a litany in England.   Aldhelm, indeed, was one of the most energetic men of his age.   He founded three monasteries, and suggested the building of Glastonbury. His learning in theology was as remarkable as his accomplishment in poetry and music.   A line of five-and-twenty Bishops of Sherborne followed him, but shortly

DORCHESTER: THE CHOIR.

after the Conquest Sherborne ceased to be a bishopric, Herman, the last bishop, removing the see to Old Sarum, where he commenced the building of the cathedral.

For something more than half a century after the removal of the bishopric the prosperity of Sherborne languished; but in 1139 Roger, Bishop of Sarum, founded an abbey here, and assigned the cathedral to be the church of the monastery.   For three hundred years after its foundation the records of the abbey are of the most meagre.   But about the middle of the fifteenth century there happened a tragical event which could hardly escape the pen of the chronicler. The ill-feeling, common enough before the Reformation, between the secular and

DORCHESTER: THE SOUTH AISLE.

the regular clergy had lasted for some four centuries; during the fourteenth century it began to grow more acute, and it ended at last in the almost total destruction of the beautiful minster. The monks removed the abbey font from its proper position near the porch, and did other things which so grievously annoyed the townspeople that they complained to the bishop, who ordered that the font should be restored to its ancient place. In the meantime a new one had been placed in the parish church. This the monks endeavoured to displace; whereupon there was a riot, the new font was smashed, the abbey was set on fire, and only the bare walls were left standing.

The minster was thoroughly restored in the second half of the fifteenth century by Abbot Peter de Rampisham, whose penultimate successor, John Barnstaple, surrendered the abbey in 1535 to the Royal Commissioners. The days of the abbey's glory had then long been over; for of the three hundred Benedictine monks who once daily took their seats in its choir, eighteen only now remained. It happened, fortunately for posterity, that the parish church was at this time much decayed; and the parishioners decided to pull it down and to purchase the minster from Sir John Horsey, to whom it had been granted. The price they paid for this beautiful example of Decorated architecture, with its memories of centuries of devotion, was £230! For over thirty years the church was under restoration; and the works were only completed in 1885. Remains of the old monastery may be traced among the buildings occupied by the King's School, raised by the late master, Dr. Harper, to a very high position.

It is a far cry across three counties from Sherborne in Dorset to Dorchester in Oxfordshire; yet, in heptarchical times, both were bishop-stools in the great kingdom of Wessex, which extended from Cornwall to Berkshire. To-day Dorchester is a pretty village of three or four streets, standing upon slightly elevated land above the flat meadows in the neighbourhood of Abingdon, and principally known to boating-men, and to a few antiquaries who come to visit the majestic abbey. Dorchester is a charming spot, with its glimpses of well-wooded country, and with the round-headed Sinodun Hill rising ayont the swooning waters of the Thames, where

" Beauteous Isis and her husband Thame
With mingled waves for ever flow the same."

The long, low nave of the ancient abbey, with its sturdy conical-roofed red tower and its background of trees, is a very picturesque object as seen from the river.

Vast indeed have been the changes in the fortunes of Dorchester. Not only was it the seat of a bishopric, but, according to Bede, it contained many fine churches, no vestiges of which now remain. It was in 639 that Birinus, the afterwards canonised apostle of the West Saxons, converted Cynegils, King of Wessex, and baptised him into the Church at Dorchester. About that time the bishopric was founded, and the emissary of Pope Honorius was consecrated first Bishop. It was always a very extensive diocese, and in the time of Edward the Confessor it stretched from the Thames to the Humber, and was the largest diocese in England. The bishopric was held by a long succession of learned and energetic prelates; but, as not infrequently happened in the early days of the Church, the mitre of Dorchester was sometimes worn by men who were destitute alike of learning and of piety, and lived unseemly and scandalous lives. Of such was Bishop Ulf, a Norman, appointed to the see in 1049 by Edward the Confessor, who had a bad habit of giving bishoprics to foreigners. Ulf seems to have been the most unfit of men for a prelate; indeed, the chronicles of the time record that he "did nought bishop-like." So intense was his ignorance that he could hardly read the Psalter or sing a mass. When he went to Rome Pope Leo was beside himself with anger that such a man should have been set over the greatest diocese in England, and he went very near to depriving Ulf of his see. But Ulf was a master of the art of judicious bribery, and some portion of his great episcopal revenues, artfully spent among those who surrounded the Pope, made him safe in his bishopric. Before this time the see had been removed to Sidnacester; but after a while it was restored to Dorchester, whence it was ultimately transferred, in 1086 or 1088—authorities vary as to the precise date—to Lincoln. Of all Dorchester's state and consequence, nothing now remains save the abbey. Henry of Huntingdon places it fourteenth in importance upon his list of the twenty-eight British cities; but its population is now little more than a thousand.

It is impossible to assign a date, or even a period, to Dorchester Abbey, for it forms a picturesque, and, architecturally, a most interesting mixture of styles, ranging from Norman work, which may perhaps date from a few years before the Conquest, to Tudor. The finest near glimpse of the church is to be obtained from the lych-gate at the western end of the churchyard, which is overshadowed by a chestnut-tree remarkable for its magnificent proportions even in a neighbourhood famous for the luxuriance of these trees. This tree, with the massive grey walls of the abbey beyond, forms one of the "bits" which artists love. The south porch is a peculiarly handsome example of Tudor work in stone, with a timbered roof. Viewed from the southern entrance, the interior of the abbey is heavy and sombre, the nave being divided into two parts by the tower. But this impression of heaviness wears off so soon as the eye begins to appreciate the fine proportions of the church. The roofs, in particular, are exceedingly beautiful. That of the nave is supported upon graceful clustered columns. The lightness and elegance of the groined roof of the Lady Chapel are famous. The abbey is somewhat smaller than that of

DORCHESTER: THE CHANCEL.

Sherborne. It stands 119th upon Lord Grimthorpe's list of great English churches, and is, without the tower, 187 feet long, with a superficial area of 10,000 square feet. Just inside the south door stands the ancient leaden font, which dates from Norman days. The figures of the Apostles—minus, of course, Judas—are cut in high relief round the bowl. Beyond the tower is the Lady Chapel, of the roof of which I have made mention. Formerly there were a great number of altar-tombs in this chapel, but four only now remain. Two of them are tombs of Crusaders, their feet resting upon lioncels.   One represents a knight of the Segrave family ; on the other the Crusader, whose countenance is hardly prepossessing, is in the act of drawing his dagger.   In the floor near by is the brass of Richard Bewforest, who in 1554 purchased the abbey church from the grantee for £140, and presented it to the parish.   A plain brass in this chapel to one Thomas Day, who died in 1693, bears an inscription which deserves a place in any list of curious epitaphs :—

"Sweet Death he came in Hast
  & said his glass is run ;
Thou art ye man i say,
  See what thy God has done."

The altar here is a memorial to Bishop Wilberforce of Winchester.

One of the best of the few remaining brasses is in the choir, and commemorates another member of the Bewforest family, who is vested with a cope, and bears a crozier in his hand.   The famous "Jesse Window" is on the north side of the choir.   It is a pedigree in stone of the line of Jesse. The genealogical tree has its root in the body of Jesse, and each of the progenitors of Christ is represented by a small figure in stone ; but the figures of Christ and His mother have unfortunately been destroyed.   The ancient painted glass in the window contains figures of the chief members of the line of David. Notwithstanding that the window—one of the most remarkable of our ecclesiastical antiquities—is fourteenth century work, it is in very good preservation. Dorchester Abbey, indeed, is richer in old painted glass than most of our churches.   The building has long been intermittently under restoration.   The work was commenced by Sir Gilbert Scott; but much yet remains to be done.

With the exception of the National School, which is believed to have been the refectory of the abbey, no vestige of the monastic buildings remains ; but some sculptured stones, which are conjectured to have formed part of the enrichments of those buildings, have been removed from a house in the village, and are to be built into the fabric of the church.   J. PENDEREL-BRODHURST.

Q Q

HEXHAM.

A BORDER ABBEY.

A DISTANT view of Hexham is always charming : whether it be from the woods of St. John Lee on the north, the steep banks on the south, the long, level sweep of the Tyne valley on the east, or the bold rise of Warden Hill on the west, the prospect is one that cannot fail to delight the traveller. The old town nestles down at the foot of an amphitheatre of surrounding hills, and the broad Tyne sweeps past it, always changing and always beautiful. In summer a clear and occasionally shallow stream, in winter often a mighty, roaring flood, but still the same old river which has seen so many changes on its banks, from the days when the Romans carried their Watling Street up to its southern bank and crossed it with a fine long bridge, to the days when the dreadful floods of 1771 swept it clear of all bridges save that at Corbridge.

The most conspicuous building in the town is the Abbey Church, a battered and sombre-looking edifice ; but the hoary appearance of its time-worn walls gives it a romantic interest not shared by many more beautiful southern churches with their tall spires and rich traceries. Its one tower is low, broad, and spire-less ; its roofs long and flat, their somewhat monotonous outline being broken only by a few rugged pinnacles. East of the church two sturdy and stern-looking towers are to be seen rising above the general level of the houses : the silent evidences that in former days the offices of religion had often to be protected by force of arms. On a nearer approach the old town reveals more of its character. Its streets are narrow and irregular, and in some parts steeply inclined. They all lead to the market-place, which occupies the centre of the town, and contains the shambles, a hundred and fifty years old, with stone colonnade and moss-covered roof. Many of the houses are small and ancient, with dates and the initials of former owners, long since dead and forgotten, cut on the lintels of the doorways ; and there still remain a few heather-thatched roofs, now green with moss, and fast decaying.

Richard, Prior of Hexham from 1142 to about 1160, was a man of considerable literary ability, and, amongst other works, he wrote a history of the church over which he ruled. He tells us that in his day the town was "moderate in size and thinly inhabited, but formerly ample and magnificent, as the vestiges of antiquity testify." In 674, Queen Etheldreda, the wife of Ecgfrid, King of Northumbria, gave to St. Wilfrid land which had formed a portion of her dower. This comprised the district known as Hexhamshire, and included the parishes of Hexham, Allendale, and St. John Lee. St. Wilfrid founded a monastery and built a church, which, according to the old chroniclers, must have been one of the largest and most beautiful to be found in England at that time. It had a crypt and underground passages, porches, towers, and winding staircases, as well as galleries in the walls at various heights. There were many chapels,

THE EXTERIOR.

both on the floor and in the galleries above, and these contained altars dedicated to Apostles, Martyrs, Confessors, and Virgins, all the altars being most sumptuously furnished with vessels and vestments, while the walls were covered with paintings and carvings in relief. In 681 Hexham was made a see dependent on York, and its beautiful church became a cathedral, with the right of sanctuary. The old stone seat, called the "Fridstool" or "seat of peace," still remains. It was probably the bishop's throne of the Saxon cathedral, but up to the time of the abolition of sanctuary it was used as the goal to which the fugitive criminal directed his steps in order that he might be under the protection of the Church; and being seated in it, none dared molest him. The sanctuary extended for a mile from the church in all directions, and four crosses were erected at the four points of the compass to mark its boundaries. The sites of two of these crosses are known, and a fragment of one of them is in existence. The north cross was at first placed in the river, in mid-stream; but we are told that Walter Biwell, chaplain to Bernard de Balliol, had arrested many persons, with their substance, while crossing the river, and these complaining to the archbishop, he had the cross placed on the northern bank of the stream.

St. Wilfrid was a man of mark in his day, and was consecrated archbishop of the northern province. His haughty manner and determined disposition made him many enemies, and he was twice exiled from his diocese; but he lived long enough to survive his troubles, and died peacefully at Ripon in 709. Eleven bishops followed him, and then the see of Hagustald, as Hexham was then called, came to an end; why, we know not, nor does Prior Richard seem to have known, for he says that it had ceased fifty years before the devastation of Northumberland by Haldane the Dane in 875.

The beautiful cathedral was destroyed by the Scandinavian marauders, and the priests and people were either murdered or driven from their homes. At this time someone buried a large bronze vessel containing about twelve thousand of the small bronze coins used by the Saxons, and called stycas. This treasure lay concealed until 1832, when it was found, eight feet from the surface, in digging an unusually deep grave. After a time, peace and order again prevailed in Northumbria, but the church of Hexham was left a battered shell, which its one poor priest repaired as well as he could so that he might say mass in it. In this miserable condition it remained until after the Norman Conquest had changed the affairs of the nation, and the monastic system had become a great power. In 1113, Thomas the Second, Archbishop of York, founded here a priory of canons-regular of St. Augustine, or black canons, as they were commonly called. They were at first miserably poor, and few in number; but wealth, lands, and many privileges soon fell largely to their share, and their numbers steadily increased till the close of the thirteenth century, when Hexham was one of the largest and most influential of the monastic houses in all the Border country.

The Austin Canons at first repaired the old church of St. Wilfrid's day, and built domestic offices of wood. It is evident that from the early days of their establishment at Hexham, the canons saw how hazardous was their position, close to the wild borderland; for the first of their new buildings was a strong gateway on the north side of their enclosure, which was surrounded by a thick, high wall. These erections still to a large extent remain, and from their style we may conclude that they were begun directly after the Battle of the Standard, fought at Northallerton in 1138. In marching southwards, on this occasion, the Scots had halted at Hexham, and though they pillaged the town and neighbourhood, King David had interfered on behalf of the abbey, and no harm befell it; but the canons had learnt how necessary it was that they should have some strong means of defending themselves against such troublesome neighbours. Some years before this event Hexham had had a narrow escape when King Malcolm was in the neighbourhood. Being enraged by the murder of some of his emissaries, he determined to sack the abbey, and sent the fierce men of Galloway to carry out his evil purpose. Poor Eilaf, the priest, prayed to be delivered from their

TRANSEPT AND DORMITORY.

hands, and dreamed that he saw St. Wilfrid, along with St. Cuthbert, riding to his rescue. St. Cuthbert promised to spread a net to catch the Scots; and on the morrow such a dense fog filled the valley of the Tyne that they lost their way and spent days in fruitless wanderings among the hills; and when the fog rolled away they found that the river was so swollen with flood-water that they could not cross, and so Hexham was saved.

Even before the close of the twelfth century the abbey had become a wealthy and influential house, and the old Saxon buildings of St. Wilfrid's time were superseded by an entirely new church, with all the usual domestic offices. Prior Richard tells us how the canons had at first repaired and "built upon the ruins of many edifices which waste and devastation have destroyed." Inasmuch as all the documents which may have mentioned the rebuilding of the abbey have perished, we can only tell the story of its rise from the stones themselves. As the crypt of the earlier church is under the present tower, we suppose that the new church occupied the same ground as its predecessor, and furthermore we can discern that the old church was maintained as long as possible while the new one was being built. About 1175 the aisle walls of the choir were raised, and no doubt their foundations were laid outside St. Wilfrid's Church, which would be somewhat smaller than the new building. Then the foundations of the great pillars would be laid, and the new and spacious choir carried on till the clerestory was reached. All this would take many years to build, for the upper portion of the choir cannot well be earlier than 1210. Then followed the long and noble transepts, with all their fine arcades and boldly designed flanks and end walls. Then, where the wings meet each other in a common centre, the tower rose to a height of a hundred feet, and the new church was ready for dedication. The choir, in which the high altar stood, served for the frequent services of the canons; the transepts, for the smaller altars and for the parish sermon; for there was no nave, it being left to future years to complete the great church according to the plan laid down. The chapter-house, common-house, and dormitory were all built on the east side of the cloister garth; the fratry, or dining hall, and the kitchen, on the south; and the great guest-hall and cellars for stores, on the west. On the north side a thick and high wall was built to serve as a shelter from the cold winds, and to form the lower portion of the nave wall when it should be carried on. The prior's house stood on the west side of the cloister, and the infirmary on the east.

The canons now enjoyed a period of rest and peace. Their buildings were extensive and convenient, and we can picture them pacing the alleys of their cloister in calm contemplation; or attending the constant services in their choir; or dining in the long and lofty fratry, with its beautiful windows of rich tracery; or warming themselves over the common-room fire while they discussed the passing events of the day. Ever and anon they would leave the quiet cloister and go out into the town on some errand of mercy, or up to their chapel of St. Oswald on the Roman wall, or down the Tyne to their dependent cell at Ovingham. But this period of quietude was only the forerunner of a terrible calamity which was to overwhelm both abbey and town, and all the surrounding villages and homesteads, and lay them waste and desolate.

The large and handsome fratry and the exquisitely beautiful lavatory—the parts left to the last—were hardly finished, when the cruel Scots came rushing down the valleys of the Rede and Tyne, burning and destroying all that lay in their path. The little nunnery at Lambley, on the South Tyne, was utterly destroyed, and the nuns butchered. The beautiful priory at Lanercost, on the Irthing, was fired, and its inmates compelled to fly for their lives. Then Hexham was reached, and terrible were the destruction and desecration, and horrible were the cruelties, which the savage men of Galloway perpetrated there. The abbey and church were burned and rifled from end to end; all the shrines and the altar were stripped of their valuables, and the much-prized relics of the saints were thrown into the flames. In the grammar school, which seems to have been within the precincts of the abbey, two hundred poor scholars were roasted alive; for, with fiendish glee, the barbarians fastened up the doors and fired the buildings. The library and muniments, and everything that could be burned, shared a similar fate.

In the following autumn another inroad was made under William Wallace, when everything that had been left was destroyed or carried off. Two canons, who had ventured to return to Hexham, had a narrow escape of their lives as they celebrated mass in their church; and the ruffians even seized the chalice and mass-book from off the altar.

The palmy days of the abbey seem to have passed away for ever, for during the first half of the fourteenth century the inroads of the Scots were frequent and disastrous. During the reign of Edward II., the weakest of English monarchs, they ran riot over all the northern province, and the resources of the abbey were drained away till the poor canons were reduced to the most absolute poverty. After the battle of Nevill's Cross in 1346, when David of Scotland was taken prisoner and his army completely routed, the power of the Scots was broken, and a period of peace followed. The Abbey of Hexham recovered itself to a great extent, and many grants of lands were made to it. The church was repaired, and a new roof added to it, and in the course of the next century many things were done to beautify its interior. The nave appears to have been begun about this time, but was again abandoned for lack of means to carry out so large a work. Though the abbey held up its head and maintained its proper position among other northern monastic houses, its revenues were much more straitened than in former years, and were not sufficient to allow of any extensive building.

Scarcely had the troubles brought on by the Scots been passed by in the ceaseless roll of time, and forgotten, when dangers from another source threatened the canons. The sixteenth century had hardly begun when the popularity of the monastic system commenced to wane. The influence of the monasteries had gradually declined during the last century and a half, and when the final blow which terminated their existence was struck by the strong hand of Henry VIII., the greater portion of the people were not unwilling to see them fall. Hexham showed singular vitality to the very last, and instead of a tame official statement of surrender, which is all we know of the last days of many of the monasteries, we have an exciting story, bristling with incidents which read like a romance.

In April, 1536, Archbishop Lee wrote to Mr. Secretary Cromwell to plead hard the cause of Hexham, and begged that it might be spared, both on account of its ancient renown, and also on account of its position on the Border, whereby it was of great use in serving as a house of call and entertainment for all persons passing into Scotland.   He pleaded in vain, for on the 28th of September four commissioners were sent to Hexham with power to suppress the abbey. When they came to Dilston, two miles further down the Tyne, they heard that the abbey at Hexham was garrisoned by the canons, who, with the Master of Ovingham as their leader, were ready to offer a most determined resistance. Two of the commissioners thought it were well to remain behind, but the other two rode on.   When they entered the market-place a strange sight met their eyes.   The town was full of people, many of them armed with such weapons as they had, while the gates and doors of the abbey were fast shut, and the canons, all arrayed in harness, with bows and artillery, were standing on the leads of the church and on the steeple, and when addressed by the commissioners, they boldly answered: "We be XX[ti] brethren in this hous, and we shall dye all or y[t] shall ye have this hous."   The commissioners replied advising them to consider well and take counsel together, and then answer them again.   So the canons went into the abbey for a time, and then again appeared on the roof and repeated their determination not to surrender.   With this answer the commissioners retired to Corbridge, while the canons with their servants and tenants marched out of the abbey "to a place called the Grene," where they remained till the commissioners were out of sight.

Such resistance was sure to end in serious trouble to the poor canons, but they might even yet have been pardoned had it not been for "the crafty devyse and subtile way conceyved by John Heron of Chipchase, otherwyse callyd Litle John Heron, to have the inhabitantes of Tyndall and Hexhamshyre to breyke."   This scoundrel, who was a Border robber, exercised himself untiringly, and used every artifice, to persuade the canons of Hexham to maintain their defensive position; he knowing that such was the surest means to bring about a rising in the north, by which he hoped to profit in the matter of booty, and to revenge himself on the Carnabys, who were devoted adherents of the king.   Heron pretended to mediate between the canons and Carnaby, but by delivering false messages to both sides he achieved his wicked purpose of maintaining the canons in rebellion, along with the men of Tynedale and Hexhamshire.   Early in the following year the prior of Hexham was hanged at Tyburn, and six of the canons appear to have suffered in a similar manner.   In 1538 the site of the priory was granted to Sir Reginald Carnaby, who died, without an heir, in 1543.

The abbey church was kept in repair, but was not used as the parish church of the town until a century or more after the dissolution, as St. Mary's church was then in existence.   Latterly large sums have been spent on so-called "restoration," in which numbers of the ancient monuments, and many of the most interesting features in and about this grand old church, have been wantonly destroyed.

CHARLES CLEMENT HODGES.

MONKWEARMOUTH AND JARROW.

THE VENERABLE BEDE.

————◦⊶◦————

IT may fairly be said that there are no buildings in England which can exceed in interest the sister Abbey Churches of Monkwearmouth and Jarrow. We have fragments of older buildings in the walls of churches still in existence, as at Dover, Canterbury, and elsewhere; but their earliest history is irrecoverably gone —blotted out by the pagan barbarians from whom the Anglo-Saxon race sprang. At Monkwearmouth and Jarrow, on the other hand, we have remains so considerable of the earliest buildings that we can see with very fair certainty what they were like. In the tower-porch at Monkwearmouth and in the chancel at Jarrow we stand within the walls which Benedict Biscop reared more than twelve hundred years ago; we are in the actual churches in which Ecgfrith, King of the Northumbrian Angles, worshipped; we are on ground traversed by the little feet of Bede when he served as a boy at the altar, and paced over by his graver steps when he had become the most learned man and the most voluminous writer in Western Europe. In the parish churches of to-day we are in the Abbey Churches of 674 and 682.

There can be no doubt that we owe this to one cause which stands out beyond all others. The time never came when the development of these twin monasteries demanded the erection of buildings of greater magnificence; and thus it never became the business of anyone to pull down the old walls, and obliterate the traces of the original buildings, to make way for others on a larger scale. How much this means, anyone will understand who goes into the marvellous crypt of York Minster and sees there, far within the bounding-walls of the vast cathedral of to-day, the ancient herring-bone work of the modest Anglian church, built round the oratory where Edwin, the first-fruits of the kings of the North, was baptised. In the course of such vast enlargements as most of our ancient cathedral and abbey churches have undergone, all external trace of the original building has of necessity disappeared. Monkwearmouth and Jarrow had the less splendid but more happy fate of being made "cells" of Durham by the early Norman bishop, and so the churches as they stood were enough for the wants of the monks; and there, in considerable part, they are standing yet.

The present church of Monkwearmouth has a tower on the porch. The lower part of this tower and the porch are taken to be the original work of Benedict Biscop. The same may be said of the west wall, with its curious window from the tower, ornamented at the sides with baluster-shafts. The upper part of the tower was taken down by the late vicar, and built again with the same stones, set in the same places. The openings in the tower, of the nature of windows, divided into two arches by a central baluster-shaft, are of the same character as those commonly known as Saxon at St. Benet's, Cambridge, St. Mary Wigford, Lincoln, and in other well-known examples. The string-course with cable edging, divided into panels bearing the representations of various animals, is unlike any of the other early string-courses which have been preserved;

MONKWEARMOUTH.

and there are no examples elsewhere of the flat stone jambs, carved with inter-lacing serpents, on the sides of the door leading into the nave, surmounted by two baluster pillars on either side of the doorway. The north wall of the original church was in existence when the repairs of a few years ago were com-menced. All trace of the monastic buildings other than the church has disappeared.

It was in 674 that the pious servant of Christ, Benedict Biscop, began to build a monastery in honour of "the most blessed Peter, chief of the Apostles," on the north side of the mouth of the Wear. The venerable and devout King of Northumbria, Ecgfrith, gave him a site and helped him in the work. That is what Bede tells us. Bede was only a baby at the time, it is true, but he passed his early boyhood in the monastery, and at Jarrow he lived and died, so that he had personal knowledge of what he wrote about.

Benedict, as Bede tells us further, went to France and procured stone-masons who could build him a church of stone in the style of the Romans, which he greatly admired—a Romanesque church, as we should say. When Benedict's Gallo-Roman stonemasons had nearly finished their work, he sent to France for workers in glass to fill the windows of the church, the porches, and the upper chambers. From these workmen the English learned the art of making glass, Wilfrith, for his great churches, having only imported it. Within a year from laying the foundations, Bede tells us—evidently implying that the rapidity with which so large a work was done by the foreign masons appeared remarkable to the Angles—the roof was on and masses were celebrated. The fabric of St. Peter's Church, Monkwearmouth, was thus completed.

As for the fittings of the church, the sacred vessels, the vestments, the decorations, Benedict procured such as he could at home; for others he went to France, and even as far as Rome. On his fifth and last visit to Rome he procured pictures to hang like a crown round the church of " the blessed Mother of God " which he had built in the monastery. This leads us to suppose that before the Romanesque church of St. Peter was built he had erected for the immediate use of the monks a much humbler building, probably of wattle or timber (the Scottish fashion) and of a circular form, dedicated to the Virgin Mary. It was on this visit that he procured pictures for St. Paul's, Jarrow, which King Ecgfrith had begged him to build as soon as he had finished St. Peter's, Monkwearmouth.

The fourth abbot, Ceolfrid, did a great deal for the monastery. Among other things, he made a number of oratories, one of which, that of St. Laurence, is specially named. He doubled the library which Benedict had given, and thus made Bede's extensive studies possible. The Church of St. Mary was still in use in his time, as well as St. Peter's, for on the day on which he resigned the abbacy and left for Rome, mass was sung at early dawn in both the churches.

There can be no real doubt that a considerable part of Biscop's work remains to this day, practically the west porch and west wall of the church. His Romanesque church was a rectangular building with a " porch " at the west end—the " porch of entrance " of which Bede speaks. The foundations showed, when the modern enlargement took place, that the original building was 68 feet long and 22 feet 8 inches wide, measured on the outside. This is a symmetrical arrangement, the length being exactly three times the width; no better proportion could have been chosen. If the rule of " three cubes " was observed, the height of the side walls of the nave would be 22 feet 8 inches. The porch was half the width of the nave. The windows in the main building were no doubt small on the exterior and placed high up, with a wide splay of the jambs and a steep slope to the window-sill, that the light might spread like a fan and come down into the body of the church. The window in the west wall, looking from the tower into the nave, will show us what the windows were like.

The west porch remains. It is square, and its width is half that of the nave—11 feet 4 inches. We cannot doubt that it and the storey above it are Biscop's work—the "porch of entrance" and one of the "upper chambers" mentioned by Bede. Whether the tower was originally higher than these two storeys we must leave to others to settle to their own satisfaction; the arguments, in our opinion, are decidedly against it. But we may fairly say that part of the "porch" is gone. The people would enter through the north and south openings in the porch; the west opening is for another purpose. It led, in all probability, from the porch into a smaller chamber, either square or semicircular, where the font was, so that a person entering by the south door of the porch would turn to the right to enter the church, and to the left to enter the baptistery.

At the east end of the main building there was, no doubt, a corresponding "porch," entered by a Romanesque arch. This chancel would be either semicircular or square; if square, it may have had a semicircular projection or apse to the east. Over it, too, there may have been an upper chamber. There may well have been other porches—"side chapels," as we should call them. Bede speaks of porches in the plural. They would be entered by Romanesque arches from the church.

We can determine the use to which the numerous baluster pillars found at Monkwearmouth and Jarrow were put. Two would be wanted for the sides of each window, as shown in the window in the west wall—a very curious arrangement which we should not have expected. Four would be wanted for each of the more ornamented archways, as shown in the present western entrance. If any of the porches had a storey above the upper chamber, clear of the gable end of the nave, each would require four, or—as at Jarrow—eight, for the central support of the arcade in the opening on each of the four sides. Nineteen balusters were found built into the wall of Jarrow Church when it was being restored. It is unnecessary to give a list of examples of these "Saxon" balusters in England. The largest of all are found in the transepts of St. Albans, where they are believed to be the surviving representatives of the original work of Offa, King of Mercia, about 793.

It was among these surroundings that Bede passed his early years. He was one or two years old when Benedict began to build; and at seven years of age he was placed in the monastery, under the charge of the founder. The sister monastery of St. Paul, at Jarrow, to which we must now pass, was built by Benedict in the year 682, and Bede went there as a boy with Ceolfrid, its first abbot. Here he remained for the rest of his life. He was ordained deacon at nineteen, some years before the usual age, and priest at thirty. He was either fifty-nine or sixty six at the time of his death, according as one view or another is taken of the statement made by one of his disciples. He tells of himself that he spent all his years in the monastery, intent upon the study of the Scriptures, and that in the intervals between the duties enjoined by the disciplinary rule and the daily care of chanting in the church, he took pleasure

JARROW: THE TOWER.

in always learning, teaching, or writing. There can be no doubt that what he chanted was the Gregorian chant, for it was now eighty years since Gregory, who sent Augustine to England, had remodelled the severe Ambrosian chant.

Bede's life was sufficiently uneventful, so far as outward circumstances went, and yet there were crises in it. When he was a boy, a great pestilence raged in the north of England. It carried off almost the whole of the Wearmouth brethren, so that there were only left one man and one boy to carry on the services. This boy can scarcely have been other than Bede. Again, a time came when he was brought face to face with a grave question, affecting seriously the course of his life. His brethren would make him abbot. Bede, we are told, declined the office because he did not wish to deprive himself of leisure for study. A comparison of his life and labours with the life and labours of the canon of a cathedral of to-day might be a useful lesson to some members of some Chapters.

It is sometimes asked, Where could Bede have got his knowledge of much that it might have been supposed no one in England knew? The bishop who ordained him was John of Beverley, a pupil of the learned and wise Archbishop Theodore; and it may well be that Bede owed to Bishop John much of his learning, especially his knowledge of Greek. Theodore had introduced the knowledge of Greek into England shortly before Bede's birth, and it had flourished so greatly that, in Bede's time, there were many who spoke Greek as readily as English. Still, explain it as we will, it is a startling fact that the son of some seventh-century Angle who was probably born a pagan, should have reached so high a place among the most voluminous and learned of Christian writers.

Bede's death seems to have been due to the stooping attitude so constantly maintained by one who wrote many books in days of slow writing, especially in a climate such as that which probably prevailed in the parts where the Don winds in and out on its course to the Tyne.   About a fortnight before Easter he was greatly troubled with shortness of breath, and on Ascension Day he died.   We have a beautiful account of his last illness, written by an eye-witness. His continual giving of thanks to God is a point much insisted on.   His determination to work to the very last moment is another characteristic feature.   And

JARROW : THE CHANCEL.

when he felt that the end was really come, he begged them to turn his face towards his little oratory ; and propped thus on the floor of his cell, he sang glory to God, and singing, died.

Of the domestic buildings of the monastery in which Bede lived and died, we have probably nothing remaining.   Such of the stones of the present ruins, on the south side of the church, as have any sculpture are of early Norman date.   There can be little doubt that the earliest parts of these ruins go back to the time when Aldwin and his two companions from Evesham went north and rebuilt Jarrow under Bishop Walcher, murdered in 1080.   There is a very remarkable triangular-headed doorway in one of the walls of the monastic ruins, which it is tempting to call pre-Norman ; but it has an almost exact counterpart in a doorway at Westminster.   It is otherwise with the chancel of the

v v

church, which we may take as, in the main, Benedict's original building. Its quaint little windows, its exceedingly narrow north door, and the indications in the east wall of an apse relatively wide, tell their own tale of early work. The tower is a puzzling feature, both in itself and in its relation to the other parts of the church. It is very far from square, being 21 feet 3 inches from north to south, and only 13 feet from east to west. The arches into the chancel and into the present nave are relatively very wide—11 feet 6 inches. It has not been sufficiently noticed how nearly these dimensions reproduce some of the Monkwearmouth measurements. The shape of the tower points decidedly to an arrangement resembling that in the porch at Monkwearmouth, the north and south sides being the sides of entrance. It will be seen on careful examination that at Jarrow the monks entered from their dormitories, through the south wall of the tower, into a sort of upper chamber, and came down into the chancel itself through a doorway, which is now represented by the smaller of two arches in the east wall of the tower, looking into the chancel. The considerable width of the arch from the tower into the present nave, as compared with that from the Monkwearmouth porch into the nave, may be due to the fact that there it is at the west end, while at Jarrow it is at the east. The remarkably lofty Romanesque arch from the tower into the nave of St. Benet's, Cambridge, is yet another element in a problem which has still to be solved.

In the vestry at Monkwearmouth and in the porch at Jarrow are a number of very interesting fragments of sculptured stones, which are generally allowed to be of Anglian type and date. They show complicated interlacements and very careful foliage-work; on one of the Jarrow stones two birds are remarkably well sculptured among the foliage, and there is also a graphic contest between a man and a beast. One of the very earliest inscribed Christian gravestones in England is in the vestry at Monkwearmouth—*Here rests in the body the priest Hereberecht.* But of all the sculptured treasures of Jarrow the most precious is the dedication stone. Put into English the inscription runs :—" The dedication of the basilica of St. Paul on the 9th of the Kalends of May, in the 15th year of King Ecgfrith, and in the 4th year of Ceolfrid, abbat and under God founder of the said Church."

G. F. BROWNE.

CHRISTCHURCH AND ROMSEY.

HAMPSHIRE ABBEYS.

THE county of Hampshire, peculiarly rich in antiquities of every kind, contains within its borders many valuable specimens of early churches. The Priory of Christchurch is so ancient that we have no authentic record of its establishment, though some authorities hold that it was founded in the reign of Edward the Confessor for a dean and twenty Austin canons. The town undoubtedly derived its name from this church. There is, however, a legend of monastic origin which suggests more specific derivation. The story runs that during the building of the church a massive oaken beam, when hoisted to its place, was found to be a foot too short; but when the workmen after an interval for rest and refreshment returned to their work, the timber had been lengthened to its proper proportions by miraculous intervention. On this account the church was dedicated to Christ. This, as the reader may perhaps have noticed at odd times, is a type of tradition that has been often met with before, being, in short, merely an old friend in a dressing adapted for local uses. Near Christchurch, and in the surrounding neighbourhood, Roman earthworks point to an occupation by our original invaders. Connoisseurs in such matters have unhesitatingly pronounced certain remains to be a Roman camp and entrenchments, tumuli and barrows, the latter containing human bones. A Roman station here would be almost a matter of course. The Avon would make the position one of strategical importance, and the Romans were not far east of the spot when they sailed their galleys up Southampton Water and pitched at Clausentum.

The first clear mention of Christchurch is in the Saxon chronicles of about the year 900, and it arose from the fighting for the crown which was going on about that time between Edward the Elder and Ethelwald. In the Domesday survey it appears as a burgh and royal manor under the name of Thuinam. These scraps of ancient history, however, do not enlighten us respecting the priory with which we are immediately concerned; but, striking a balance between this and that probability, we may reasonably assume that the great house for secular Augustinian canons was founded by Ethelstane.

The church of modern times, picturesquely planted on the banks of the Avon, and justly accounted a magnificent structure, was the collegiate church of the priory, of the establishment of which there are no authentic records. Camden states that it was founded in remote English times on the ruins of an ancient heathen temple. In the reign of Edward the Confessor there were known to be a prior and four-and-twenty canons of the Order of St. Augustine. The church and convent were given to Flambard, Bishop of Durham, by William

Rufus, and this prelate rebuilt the church on a larger scale, and dedicated it to Christ. The revenues of the establishment received substantial support from de Redvers, Earl of Devon, to whom the manor was granted, and who built the castle which commanded the passage of the Avon. Close to the church, as

CHRISTCHURCH, FROM THE RIVER.

we see it in its restored condition, a wall covered with long-established verdure and an old-world section of causeway mark the whereabouts and solidity of the priory. Portions of the castle keep, more than ten feet in thickness, are also well preserved. On the banks of the river a remarkably good specimen may be seen of the Norman house of the twelfth century, with loopholed walls, chimney-shaft, and windows, of a purity of style rarely to be met with in this country.

At the Dissolution the church was granted to the parish, the abbey lands, according to the custom of the high-handed monarch who carried out the work, being apportioned to private individuals. The last prior was one John Draper, suffragan Bishop of Naples, who was consoled for his deposition by a pension, and has been passed down to posterity as a very honest and comfortable person. In the south aisle the memory of this dignitary, who died in 1552, is perpetuated by a chantry and stone screen, erected by himself twenty-three years before his death; and his grave-slab forms part of the pavement. Vast sums of money

B B B

have been expended on the restoration of this beautiful church, and the principal work was carried out under the superintendence of Mr. Ferrey, by whom a memorial window was placed in the south aisle in memory of his father, Benjamin Ferrey. The church is in the form of a cross, and, in size and richness of exterior and interior, is superior to some English cathedrals.

Much of Flambard's original Norman work has been preserved. The principal example is the nave, 118 feet by 58 feet, used at the present day as the parish church. The basis is of course Norman, but the clerestory is Early English, and the high-pitched roof was ceiled in comparatively recent times by Garbett. Prior Flambard, it may be remembered, after his elevation to the rank of bishop, continued his architectural enterprises with great effect in Durham Cathedral. Admirably in harmony with the main structure is the Early English north porch, which is entered by a recessed gateway. The north aisle, also Early English, is a hundred years later than the southern aisle, where there is a Norman arcade, with Early English windows. There are, moreover, the remains of a staircase which led to the dormitory, the conventual buildings having joined the church on this side. The nave, with its double row of massively squared pillars, demi-columns, and semicircular arches springing between them from grouped pilasters, is considered to be one of our best extant specimens of the Norman style. There are evidences of the same style, with Perpendicular insertions, in the north transept, which has undergone, however, more alteration than the nave; and there are two chantries projecting eastward, instead of aisles. Where the transept joins the north aisle a two-storeyed stone building, known as the governor's rooms, once stood, recalling the departed days when there was a Christchurch Castle, and an appointed governor.

William Eyre was elected prior of Christchurch in 1502. The letters "W.E." in the Perpendicular arch of the south transept, which is Early English, are his initials, and they are also to be found in the choir. This is 70 feet by 21 feet, mainly of Perpendicular character, and retaining traces of the ancient colouring. The roof, of four bays, is much admired. Most curious are the stalls and seats of the choir. The stalls are thirty-six in number, and are probably as old as the latter part of the fifteenth century; the chancel and the whole of the eastern portion of the church being of more recent date than the transept and nave. The carvings of the stalls are quaint, even grotesque; and the fox, geese, and monkey chiselled in the oak are thought by some to be symbolical, if not satirical. The high altar bears an inscription to Baldwin de Redvers, who was lord of the Isle of Wight; he died in 1216, and the crypt beneath is reported to have been his place of burial. The old altar-piece is finely sculptured, and the reredos is, like that of Winchester, in three storeys, the subject being the Jesse tree.

Apart from its architectural beauties and handsome proportions, the church abounds in interesting memorial and other features. One of the most popular, perhaps, with modern visitors is the monument in the tower at the west end of the nave to the poet Shelley. It was sculptured by Weekes, and erected by the poet's son, Sir Percy Shelley, in 1854. The subject, which cannot be said to be felicitously treated, is the recovery of the body by the sea-shore, and the inscription is from *Adonaïs*. The mortuary chantry on the north side of the altar was erected by the Countess of Salisbury, who was mother of Cardinal Pole, and who at the age of seventy was beheaded by Henry VIII. The chapel fabric is well preserved, though the finer surface ornamentation has been destroyed. According to one historian, the escutcheons on the ceiling were defaced by the direct order of bluff King Harry. On the south side of the altar there is a good piece of sculpture by Flaxman, and in the vicinity are two ancient tombs of former priors. Elsewhere is a Perpendicular chapel with memorial to John Cook; a smaller Decorated chapel with a monument by Chantrey; and a chantry and stone screen to one Robert Harys, who died in 1525. The vestry was an ancient chapel in the Early English style.

The Lady Chapel, of the Late Perpendicular period, is one of the most beautiful portions of the church, with its delicate screen, carefully preserved altar, and ancient monuments. St. Michael's loft, over the Lady's Chapel, once the chapter-house of the priory, in modern times became a school-house, which was approached by a winding staircase outside the church. An altar-tomb in the north aisle has effigies of Sir John Chydioke and his wife. The knight was killed in the Wars of the Roses, and his helmet has been preserved. The defacement of the effigies is attributed to the vulgar superstition of a past generation, who believed that the scrapings of Chydioke's tomb would cure certain diseases.

The Abbey Church of Romsey in South Hampshire has made the pretty municipal and market town on the river Test famous for many generations. Some antiquarians, indeed, used to maintain that it was the abbey that gave birth and growth to the town, but it is now more generally accepted, largely on the authority of Stukeley, who devoted much time and labour to the study, that we must go back farther if we would fix the origin of Romsey. The contention of Dr. Stukeley is that here stood the Roman city once named Arminis, but subsequently changed to Romana Insula. The river Test, and a tributary stream which joins the main river near Broadlands, virtually place Romsey and its venerable abbey upon an island, and in the opinion of some this natural conformation gave to the place its earliest Saxon name of Rumes-ey, the broad island. Dr. Stukeley's views have been supported by Mr. Spence, a more recent writer, who points out that the situation of Romsey makes it nearly equidistant from Sorbiodunum, or Old Sarum; Brige, or Broughton; Venta Belgarum, or Winchester; and Clausentum, near Southampton; and that as these were Roman stations of acknowledged importance, the Romans must have passed through Romsey on their marches from one camp to another. The discovery of a number of Roman coins at Abbotswood, near Romsey, in 1845, was accepted as strong evidence in favour of Dr. Stukeley's contention.

The Abbey Church of Romsey, like the Church of Christchurch, was thoroughly restored by Ferrey in modern times, and it is valued by archæologists as presenting more fully than any building of equal size in England the out-line and general aspect of a Norman conventual church, and the manner in which architectural styles became merged. Whatever changes may have been introduced, as in the nave, which is of a later period than the oldest portions of the structure, the dimensions and broad proportions of the original architects have been in the main preserved. A perfect window, of the somewhat common arrangement of Norman clerestory windows observed at Waltham Abbey, Essex, and Christchurch, Oxford, is worthy of special study, and there is a clearly defined apse, of the kind which was characteristic of the Norman style. The lofty arched recesses, carried up over the actual arches and the triforium, though suggesting supplementary work over the original building, are nevertheless characteristic of the first design, of which they form a part. Fortunately, the general character of the stately abbey, which has always been architecturally famous, has not suffered in the careful restoration it has undergone. In Romsey Abbey, the student of ecclesiastical architecture has a most attractive course of investigation open to him from the Norman to the Pointed, and from the Early English to the Decorated, since definite examples of each are there.

The Norman portion of the nave of the abbey, cruciform in design, was the work of Bishop Henry de Blois, and may be dated somewhere between 1129 and 1169, but the remainder is Early English. As the abbey was a minster church to an ancient nunnery, it lacks the great west doorway for which one naturally looks in a building of such important dimensions; and the north and south aisles were raised above the level of the nave, probably to afford accommodation for the stalls of the nuns. The choir is so short as to be peculiar, and the apsidal chapels attached to the east side of the transepts form a feature of the Norman work which should not be overlooked. The three-light windows are Early Decorated additions, but in the north aisle are several windows of four lights, some Perpendicular, others earlier. A gracefully bold Early English arch spans the west front of the nave, and no purer examples could be desired than are furnished by the Early English doors, chastened by slender shafts and foliated capitals.

The Lady Chapel, in Early Decorated style, stood at the east end of the choir, but this has long disappeared, and the discovery of the foundation is due to the untiring zeal of the vicar, the Rev. E. L. Berthon. The chapel was probably built about 1305 A.D., but the only remains are portions of the shafts and groinings of the old walls, and the two restored windows which had been inserted in Norman archways. The excavations which led to this discovery brought to light, within the foundations of the Lady Chapel, the foundations of the smaller and rectangular original Norman chapel. The southern entrance to the abbey, which has been reopened in modern times, formed the old communication with the cloisters. The transepts, which are distinctively Norman, are 121 feet long and $61\frac{1}{4}$ feet high. The total length of the abbey is $240\frac{1}{2}$ feet. The nave is 134 feet long, $72\frac{1}{2}$ broad, and 80 feet high, and a general idea of the squat appearance of the heavy Norman tower may be formed from the statement that it is only $92\frac{1}{2}$ feet high, and some 26 feet square.

Reference has been already made to the nunnery associated with the abbey, and one of the most interesting of the abbey relics is a cope, afterwards converted into an altar-cloth, supposed to have been the handiwork of some of the Romsey sisterhood. The material is green brocaded velvet, spangled with golden stars and figured with lilies, finely worked into the fabric. This altar-cloth was apparently made about the year 1450, or perhaps a quarter of a century earlier. The nuns are closely associated with the earliest history of the abbey, which was founded in a small way by Edward the Elder about 910 A.D.; and it must have been very soon converted to the purposes of an insignificant nunnery. This at first was only poorly endowed, but Edward's grandson, Edgar, able to turn his attention from the alarms of war to the arts of peace, pushed its fortunes, aided by Archbishop Dunstan of Canterbury, along with those of other churches throughout the recently distracted country. In Edgar's reign, Romsey Abbey was accordingly enlarged and rebuilt under Ethelwold, Bishop of Winchester, and was opened by the king in presence of his nobility on Christmas Day in the year 974.

High patronage without stint fell to the share of the abbesses of Romsey, some of whom were themselves of the lineage of Saxon kings. Marivanna, a lady of noble blood and exemplary piety, was the first abbess, and her days were those of peace. Stormy times disturbed the reign of her successor Elwina, for the troublesome Dane and his warlike marauders pushed up the Test as far as Romsey, and pillaged the abbey. The abbess and her nuns, having received, as the

ROMSEY.

legend goes, supernatural forewarning of the attack, fled in the nick of time across country to Winchester, taking with them such holy relics as were portable.

Matilda, queen of Henry I., was educated at Romsey Abbey under the charge of her aunt, the abbess Christina. Later, a daughter of King Stephen was head of the nunnery. This abbess was Countess of Boulogne, and it may not have been forgotten that she was the occasion of a great mediæval scandal by defying the Pope and marrying a son of the Count of Flanders, in defiance of monastic vows, and without troubling his Holiness the Pope for a dispensation. The high-handed proceeding was doubtless instigated and helped on to its *dénouement* by Henry II., as a telling point in his course of opposition to the troublesome Thomas à Becket. For ten years the count and his abbess wife survived excommunication and the bitter denunciation of the Church, but the Church was in the end too strong for them, and they separated. An abbess, in the reign of Henry III., petitioned and actually obtained royal letters patent for the restitution of the privilege of condemning and hanging, that function of the abbesses of Romsey having then become obsolete. On the whole the abbey of Romsey was strictly, virtuously, and liberally managed, and enjoyed high repute for sanctity and learning. Towards the close of the period to which the Dissolution put a sudden stop, the vices which had eaten into the ecclesiastical establishments of the kingdom had, however, tainted even saintly Romsey.

The abbey church shows boldly above the charming valley in which it is built, and the view from the square flat tower is typical of the richest English pastoral scenery. Within easy walking distance of the town is Broadlands, the seat of the late Lord Mount-Temple; and Westmacott's monument in the abbey to the memory of Frances, Viscountess Palmerston, reminds us that this was the ancestral home of one of the most popular of English Prime Ministers. The epitaph was written by Lord Palmerston's father. Amongst other tombs in the church should be mentioned the canopied monument and effigy ascribed to the abbess-countess who married the Count of Flanders; and a lettered stone to the memory of Sir William Petty, who, the son of a Romsey clothier, became physician-in-chief to the army of Ireland, and died in 1687, the founder of the Lansdowne family.

W. SENIOR.

THE CHURCHES OF LEICESTER.
THE LAST HOURS OF WOLSEY.

LEICESTER, once a city and the home of a mitred abbey, and now a busy, thriving manufacturing town, is a very quaint mixture of the old and the new. It possesses in plenty the traditions of antiquity, and some of its streets—such as

RUINS OF LEICESTER ABBEY.

Gallowtreegate and Belgravegate—bear names which sufficiently indicate their olden origin; but, with the exception of its churches and the exceedingly scanty ruins of its abbey, few outward and visible signs of that antiquity remain. To the archæologist and the student of town-lore, the narrow, tortuous streets speak plainly enough of their history; but it is to be feared that the ordinary casual visitor regards Leicester merely as a busy, inelegant town. As a matter of fact, few Midland towns have a longer or more interesting history; and, at all events from an architectural point of view, several of its churches are very curious and attractive. Leicester, moreover, was the scene of the death of Cardinal Wolsey under circumstances so dramatic, not to say tragic, that it was inevitable they should take a strong hold upon the imagination. It was in a chamber of the abbey of St. Mary de Pratis that the Cardinal Thomas Wolsey,

Legate a latere and Archbishop of York, expired, upon a dreary November day in 1530; and long before dawn on the following morning the disgraced prelate was buried by torchlight in the abbey church. That church has long since entirely disappeared; and the day came when even the dust of the proud Chancellor was scattered to the winds.

The Abbey of Leicester was founded in 1143 by Robert, second Earl of Leicester of the de Bellomont creation for Augustinian Canons Regular. In expiation of his rebellion against the sovereign, and of the harm he

ST. MARGARET'S: THE PORCH.

ST. NICHOLAS.

had done to the town of Leicester, the earl entered the monastery of his own foundation, and died there. Leicester Abbey was wealthy

from the first. It counted thirty-six manors in Leicestershire alone among its endowments, and was able to maintain the whole of the poor in its neighbourhood. A few crumbling walls are all that now remains of Earl Robert's rich foundation. These ruins are romantically situated in the centre of the Abbey Park, which is a tastefully laid out and well-kept pleasaunce belonging to the town. The little river Soar flows sluggishly near the scanty vestiges of the building in which was ended one of the most remarkable careers in history. Few men whose names have resounded through the world have left so few visible personal traces as Thomas

C C C

Wolsey; for he has neither tomb nor monument, and even the stone coffin which contained his body is traditionally said to have been used as a horse-trough after his disinterment.

As was the case with most monastic foundations of any importance, many odd legends were current regarding Leicester Abbey. The buildings were enlarged by Petronilla, daughter-in-law of the founder; and it is said that after her death a plait of her hair was used to suspend the ever-burning lamp of the sanctuary. Another anecdote has a more genuinely monkish flavour about it. Gilbert Foliot, the first abbot, who was afterwards successively Bishop of Hereford and of London, one night left the presence of King Henry II., with whom he had been conferring relative to the monarch's differences with Thomas à Becket. As he went along he heard a voice, which he took to be that of the devil, reproaching him: "O Gilbert Foliot, dum revolvis tot et tot, Deus tuus est Astaroth." But the holy man was not to be daunted, even by the devil in person; and he answered proudly and severely: "Mentiris Dæmon! Deus meus est Deus Sabaoth."

Of the five churches of Leicester which possess any historic interest, St. Nicholas's is at once the oldest and the quaintest. It is small and low, with a fine square arcaded tower, containing herring-bone work on the north and south sides; and is constructed of granite, sandstone, and Roman tile. Some of these materials, it is conjectured, were taken from the old Jewry Wall close by. The style is mixed, for we find Saxon, Norman, and Early English. The south porch is an interesting piece of brick and ancient timber work, and the doorway to which it gives access has a Norman arch in good preservation, with dog-tooth mouldings. The Saxon church was a plain, rough, barn-like building, with narrow lights, two of which are still to be seen in the nave. The Norman building was cruciform. The church now consists of nave, Early English chancel and south aisle, Norman tower and nave, a modern north aisle and north transept. The roughness of the interior masonry gives the building a curiously bare and unfinished appearance, little relieved in other ways. The pulpit is a semicircular stone gallery running partly round one of the massive supports of the tower. The church contains three good windows of modern stained glass, the best of which is the richly coloured one representing Christ raising Jairus' Daughter. The east window represents the Crucifixion, and is somewhat weird and striking. There are a few flat tombs, consisting mainly of slabs of slate. In the churchyard are two mutilated pillars of red sandstone, which are conjectured to have formed part of the Roman forum. They were dug out of the street close by. The church, with its low roof and fine tower, makes a striking appearance as seen from the street which commands it.

If St. Nicholas be the most curious, the formerly collegiate St. Mary de Castro is assuredly the most generally interesting as well as one of the most architecturally handsome, of the Leicester churches. As its name indicates, it is close to the castle; and is a fine large church, of great length and of very varied architecture. The ancient square pinnacled tower, from which rises a tall and slender Decorated spire (rebuilt in 1783), imparts a noble and elegant appearance to the exterior. There is evidence that a church existed upon this site in Saxon times. A portion of St. Mary's was built by Robert de Bellomont, first Norman Earl of Leicester, father of the founder of Leicester Abbey. He founded in it a college of twelve canons, to which he granted ample endowments and privileges, among them being the patronage of all the other churches in Leicester, with the exception of St. Margaret's.

The church consists now of two naves of equal length, and a narrow north aisle, said to have been built by John of Gaunt. The tower and spire, which rest upon arches, stand independently of the walls of the church. The interior is exceedingly handsome; and although the building contains examples of so many different styles, the work harmonises excellently, and all the details are fine in themselves as well as exceedingly interesting to the architectural antiquary. The Norman work presents some unusual features. The buttresses of the chancel walls are characteristic of the early forms of that style; they are " of the same breadth and thickness from the ground to the top, and die into the wall with a slope immediately below the parapet," and are ornamented with dog-tooth and billeted mouldings. The sedilia are likewise Norman, but of somewhat later date, which has been conjectured as about 1150. They have double rows of pilasters, and are adorned with lavish chevron-work.

At the east end of the aisle is the chapel, or choir, as it has sometimes been called, of the Trinity Guild, founded in the time of Henry VII. by Sir Richard Sacheverel, Knight, and the "good" Lady Hungerford. On the south side of the chancel the stout Norman walls still remain. The chief beauty of the chancel is in the very fine Perpendicular screen, which dates from about 1450. This is a very elaborate piece of work, richly bossed, panelled, and foliated. It contains an abundance of the characteristic Perpendicular quatrefoil work, deftly varied and harmonious. This handsome screen is happily still in very good condition. In the chancel is a monument, conceived in by no means the best taste, to the Rev. Thomas Robinson, the author of " Scripture Characters "— a book which once enjoyed a popularity as great as it now seems amazing. The character of the monument may be gathered from its date—1813. The rich clerestory dates from the thirteenth century; and the font is of about the same period. The handsome and richly carved roof of the chancel is a fine example of

Norman work; and many of the windows, particularly the two east windows, contain good modern stained glass. St. Mary's forms a richer and more harmonious whole than any other church in Leicester.

ST. MARY'S: THE TOWER.

St. Margaret's is a fine church of somewhat later date than those we have been considering, and occupies the site of the Cathedral of the Saxon Bishopric of Leicester—a see which endured only from A.D. 680 to 870. Its most striking external feature is its embattled Perpendicular tower, more than one hundred feet high. The building is, indeed, mainly Perpendicular, and contains some admirable work of that period. When the pious Robert de Bellomont endowed the collegiate church of St. Mary de Castro, we have seen that he granted to it the patronage of all the other churches in the town with the exception of this, which was almost simultaneously erected into a prebend to Lincoln Cathedral by the bishop of the diocese. St. Margaret's consists of nave and side aisles, with an unusually large chancel, and is a church of fine and ample proportions; but the whiteness of the internal stone-work gives the building a somewhat cold appearance. The church is in exceedingly good condition, and is very well kept, which is unfortunately more than can be said for one or two of the other ancient fanes of Leicester. I have said that the chancel is of considerable size; and it is almost as interesting as that of St. Mary's. It contains the very finest ancient tomb existing in the town, which is, oddly enough, singularly destitute of interesting sepulchral memorials.

This is the tomb of John Penny, for many years abbot of the monastery of St. Mary de Pratis, and afterwards Bishop of Bangor and of Carlisle, who died in 1520. It is a chaste and beautiful monument of alabaster, with a recumbent figure of the bishop in episcopal vestments, executed with all the taste and more than the simplicity of the time. It is happily still quite perfect. The chancel is entirely Perpendicular, and is closed by a handsome modern Perpendicular screen, noticeably excellent in itself, but naturally neither so rich nor so elegant as that of St. Mary's. The chancel windows, which are likewise Perpendicular, have some modern stained glass. Some well-carved poppy-head stalls and two or three *misereres*, which have been figured in more than one book upon ecclesiastical architecture, were removed early in the century; and some of them now enrich the church of Aston, Birmingham. In the side aisles are several slabs to the memory of members of the Burnaby family, an old Leicestershire house which has achieved conspicuous distinction in very recent times. The churchyard contains the very plain tomb of Andrew, fifth Baron Rollo, who died at Leicester in 1765. Lord Rollo was one of the most distinguished members of a military and Jacobite family, which seemed at one time to have an insatiable taste for fighting. He obtained well-deserved laurels for his share in the reduction of Canada, and in the capture of Martinique in 1762. Robert Grossetête, who, after St. Hugh of Avalon was the most famous of Lincoln's bishops, once held this benefice.

WOLSEY.

Notwithstanding that the church of All Saints dates from the fourteenth century, and was no doubt once interesting and sightly, it is now in many respects a disappointment. Even the roof of the chancel is whitewashed, and the chancel itself, which was rebuilt in the worst days of ecclesiastical architecture, is an eyesore; but steps are being taken to improve its appearance. The side aisles are match-boarded, which necessarily produces a cheap, commonplace effect that is sadly out of keeping in a church. The benches, too, are painted and grained; and there is not a single pane of coloured glass in the building. Still the church, which was founded in the middle of the twelfth century, is not without some interesting features; and it is to be hoped that as the restoration proceeds care will be taken to preserve them. The lower section of the tower and the west doorway are Norman. There is a fine and well-carved hexagonal oak pulpit, of Perpendicular work, very much smaller, of course, than most modern pulpits. The windows are of that Decorated curvilinear fashion which is so often found in Leicestershire churches. The roofs of the side aisles are handsome pieces of Perpendicular woodwork. The font, too, is a beautiful example of Early English carving. There is still preserved in the church part of a curious old clock, having a painted representation of Time and two human figures, or "Quarter Jacks," which formerly, when the clock was over the west door, outside the church, struck the quarters with hammers. The only noticeable tomb the church seems to have contained in recent times was that of William Norice, whose claims to remembrance were that he was twice Mayor of Leicester, was thrice married, was ninety-seven years of age when he died in 1615, and that, according to his epitaph, his

> "—grave from all the rest is knowne
> By finding out the greatest stone."

This tomb has disappeared. Close to the west door is a holy-water stoup, with two iron links for the chained bowl still remaining. In the south aisle two piscinas and a bracket-pedestal for a statue indicate that there were formerly side altars. Under the communion table are some ancient tiles, and near the font are the remains of the old screen, unhappily covered with paint. The church was partially restored in 1877, when the beautiful Early English arch between the north aisle and the tower was opened. In 1887 a new organ was erected in commemoration of the Queen's Jubilee.

St. Martin's (or St. Cross, as it has sometimes been called) is the largest church in Leicester, and has been the most intimately connected with the history of the town. It is a cruciform church, of great width, having three aisles, two on the south and one on the north; and it has a fine central tower supported upon arches, and an elegant spire put up in 1867 from the designs of Mr. R. Brandon. The body of the church is Early English, but the existing windows were inserted in the Decorated period. The chancel was rebuilt about the beginning of the sixteenth century. In the great south aisle, which is almost as wide as the nave, the archdeacon holds his court. This aisle contains two chapels or oratories—the chapel of Our Lady at the east end, and that of St. George at the west end; but neither of them is now used. The altars of these chapels, together with the high-altar, were destroyed at the Reformation. These oratories were the chapels of the two powerful guilds that were long attached to the church: the Guilds of St. George and Corpus Christi. The confraternity of St. George possessed many peculiar privileges; and the "Ride of St. George," which it annually performed, was a gorgeous pageant. There was formerly in the church an effigy of a horse decked in the brave trappings that were used on the yearly festival day of the confraternity; but at the

Reformation it went the way of the three altars, and is recorded to have been sold for a shilling. The Guild of Corpus Christi was the more ancient of the two, and was invested with an odd mixture of civil and religious jurisdiction. There were two joint masters of the confraternity who were empowered, in association with the mayor, to impose fines upon members of the corporation who misbehaved themselves.

The roofs and woodwork of St. Martin's are very fine; and the church happily still retains its Norman piscina. There is also a creditable "Ascension" by Vanni, formerly used as an altar-piece, which was presented by Sir William Skeffington, Bart. Here is the unpretending tomb, bearing the date of 1710, of Abigail Swift, mother of the Dean of St. Patrick's. Of the several tombs of members of the Heyrick family, none is of especial interest. The church has unfortunately now finally lost the ancient font which was removed during the Usurpation. It was sold in 1651 to one George Smith for seven shillings, and a new one erected near to the reading-desk, as was common in Puritanical times. But nine months after the Restoration a parish meeting was held, at which it was "agreed that the font of stone formerly belonging to the church shall be set up in the ancient place, and that the other now standing near the desk be taken down;" and a little more than a year later the font was repurchased from George Smith's widow for the same price that had been given for it eleven years previously. St. Martin's suffered much during the civil wars. A Parliamentarian garrison, that was driven out of Newark, took refuge in it, and converted it into a barrack. The church was stormed, and many of the soldiers were killed within its walls, while others were cut down in the market-place near by.

In 1729 a violent and unseemly dispute broke out between the Rev. Mr. Carte, the Vicar of St. Martin's, and Mr. Jackson, a Confrater, who afterwards became Master of the Wigston Hospital. Mr. Jackson disbelieved, or affected to disbelieve, the doctrine of the Trinity; and on several occasions when the Vicar in his Sunday morning sermon had upheld that doctrine, scandalous scenes were caused by Mr. Jackson going into the pulpit in the evening and denying the Vicar's teaching. Upon one occasion the churchwardens commanded him in the middle of his sermon to leave the pulpit; and at another time he was stopped on the steps of the pulpit by the sexton. A judicial decision was at length obtained to the effect that the Confrater's action was illegal.

The tendency of time is always to raise the level of the streets in an old town; and at Leicester several of the more ancient churches are considerably below the street-line, and are entered by a descent of two or three steps.

J. Penderel-Brodhurst.

WALTHAM ABBEY AND BATTLE CHURCH.

MEMORIES OF HAROLD.

WALTHAM CROSS.

MUTILATED as it is, a fragment only, and that a damaged one, of a once splendid conventual church, the Abbey of Waltham is one of the most interesting buildings in Britain. It was a church wherein was lodged the Holy Rood, a worker of miracles in its day hardly less famed than the coat of Treves or the "true cross" of Jerusalem. It was the one great gift of Harold to the Church, and even this was a foundation for secular priests, for "he loved not monks." It is believed to be his building. That Waltham Abbey was practically founded by Harold is beyond dispute; that he built the church which now remains, or that it was his place of burial, is less certain. A religious community, but on a very small scale, had indeed been established in the valley of the Lea at a yet earlier date than the days of Harold. The Holy Rood was discovered at Montacute in the reign of Canute. Its hiding-place was revealed by a vision, and it was brought to Waltham by a team of oxen, as legend says, unguided by any driver. Miracle followed miracle; and the lord of the district, one Thoni, made a foundation at Waltham for two priests and other clerks, to keep the sacred charge. In his sons' days the lordship of Waltham was acquired by the Crown, and granted to Harold. He determined to build a grand church, and to transform the little fraternity of the Holy Rood into a great foundation, and carried out his design about the year 1060, the charter of confirmation bearing date 1062. His motive in selecting Waltham for his munificence is unknown. Legend states that he was cured of a paralysis by the touch of the Holy Rood; but for this explanation there is no foundation. The college flourished, became a monastery, underwent various changes, some of which can still be traced in the fragments which remain, was finally suppressed, and the greater portion of it, together with the monastic buildings, except a gateway and one or two fragments, utterly destroyed. "The nave of the Romanesque church is all that remains. The addition of a large decorated chapel to the south, and of a debased tower to the west, the destruction of the eastern part of the church, and of the whole conventual buildings, have between them converted the once splendid church at Waltham into a patched and mutilated fragment." Too true; but a fragment of no small grandeur, of no little interest.

But was Harold buried in Waltham Abbey? On this point there is a conflict of testimony. As to his final resting-place, there are three accounts at least. The

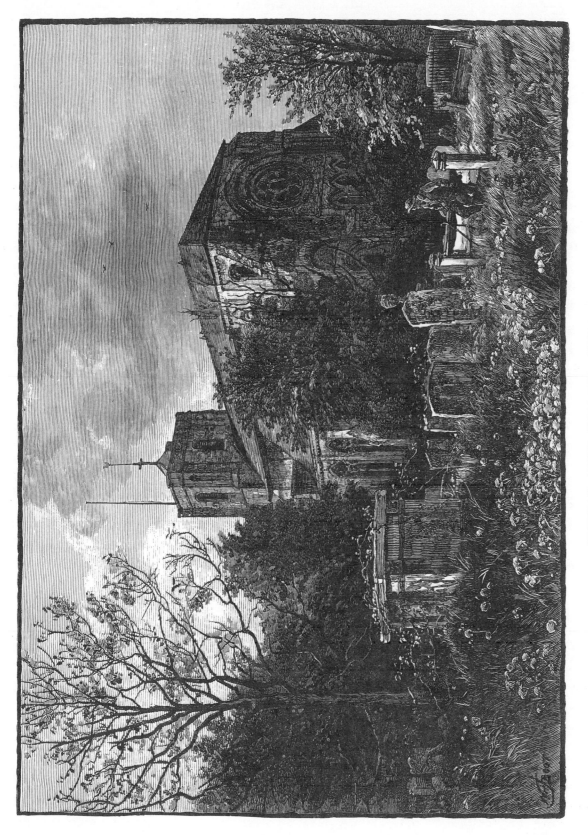

WALTHAM ABBEY, FROM THE SOUTH-EAST.

one declares that he did not fall on the field of Senlac, but, escaping under cover of the night, made his way to Chester, and there, after living some time as an anchorite in a cell near the city walls, which is still pointed out, died and was buried. This theory is by no means of modern growth. It is mentioned, but of course not favourably, in "Liber de Inventione Sanctæ Crucis," the author of which, a canon of Waltham Abbey, wrote in the reign of Henry I. On this story, however, we need not dwell, nor on the variation of it which makes him end his days as a monk at Waltham. As the best authority on the subject informs us, nothing is more certain than that Harold fell on the field of Senlac. Still, granting this, it is doubtful where he was buried. Upon this point the earliest authors are not agreed. Some say that his body was given up freely by the Conqueror to his mother, by whom it was conveyed to Waltham Abbey and there entombed; others that William, though offered for the corpse its weight in gold, sternly refused an honourable burial for him through whose doing so many lay unburied. "Place him," he said, "between the land and the sea, since madly he has oppressed both." On the former side are Ordericus Vitalis, William of Poitou, and Guy of Amiens; on the latter, William of Malmesbury, Wace, and others. With such a conflict of early authorities, it is hard to come to a conclusion. Professor Freeman suggests, as a possible solution, that William may have first pronounced the harsher sentence, and shortly afterwards, when he was adopting a policy of conciliation towards the English, may have permitted Harold's relations to exhume the body and bury it at Waltham. It is certainly difficult to understand how a false tradition of Harold's burial at this abbey could have sprung up within a century of the date of his death, and during a time when the possession of his tomb would not have been a passport to the favour of the king or of his courtiers. Waltham was too near to London to be a suitable centre for reactionary sentiment in the time of the Norman monarchs.

There is yet another question of the highest interest for the archæologist. Is the oldest part of the present church a remnant of the one built by Harold? As a rule, such a question would not be difficult to answer. In this case it is by no means easy. The style of the Romanesque work in Waltham Church, though indicative of an early date, seems too advanced for a building erected soon after the middle of the eleventh century. Still, it appears to be rather earlier in design than the transepts of Winchester and the nave of Durham, which are among our earliest Norman work, and certainly the style is less developed than it is at Ely, Peterborough, or Norwich, with all of which cathedrals it has many points in common. It resembles the nave of St. Stephen's at Caen, which was built by William the Conqueror in commemoration of his victory, and was consecrated eleven years after the death of Harold, or within twenty years of the asserted building of Waltham. Hence we may explain the architectural difficulty by supposing that Harold, like King Edward at Westminster, entrusted the building of his church to Norman architects, as he had personal knowledge of the superiority of their work to that of the men of his own land. Negative evidence, for a discussion of which we are indebted to Professor Freeman, is

CRYPT

WALTHAM ABBEY.

LADY CHAPEL

strongly in favour of the claim of Waltham Abbey to be the actual work of Harold. There are two early chronicles: the "Vita Haroldi," which was written shortly after the year 1205, and the "Liber de Inventione Sanctæ Crucis," already mentioned. Now, whatever be the date of the Romanesque work at Waltham, it is certainly much earlier than the end of the twelfth century. The foundation was indeed remodelled by Henry II., who removed the "seculars" and brought in "regulars;" and this would be a likely occasion for a rebuilding; but we can hardly believe the architecture to be so late as 1177. We may go further, and say that early in this century is the latest date which we can assign to the nave. It is therefore improbable that a church of exceptional splendour would have been rebuilt within little more than half a century without some cause—such as a fire—which would certainly have formed an epoch in the annals of the abbey and have been well known to the above authors. Yet, although Henry's alterations and sundry changes in the monastic buildings are mentioned by the author of the "Vita Haroldi," not a hint is dropped in either work of a reconstruction of the church. It seems, therefore, safe to conclude that

GATEWAY OF BATTLE ABBEY.

in the nave of Waltham Abbey we have a fragment of Harold's church, and a building in the most advanced style of Romanesque architecture, as it then existed, in the north-western part of Europe.

The Abbey of the Holy Rood (for so we may now call it) was placed on the meadows in the level valley of the Lea, between the river and the slopes which rise gradually to the gently-swelling uplands of Epping Forest. There, though perhaps the situation was in early days somewhat marshy, the brethren would not have far to go· for their dinner of fish on a day of fasting, or for a fat buck to grace the table at a high festival. At the present time there is little to attract, either in the situation or in the exterior of the abbey. From the railway station a level road leads us through scattered houses and a poor-looking street up to a mean and rather low tower, which stands full in view at the end. Houses or gardens prevent any examination of the northern side of the church; the road passes close to the western front, but on the south is a fairly spacious churchyard, in which are some large elms, one, opposite to the south door, a huge stump, mutilated like the church itself, but evidently of a very great age.

In a few words we may describe such parts of the exterior as can be seen by the ordinary visitor. The western tower was built in 1556, some years after the suppression of the abbey; it is a paltry work, rendered yet meaner by a "restoration" in the last century. By this addition a rather fine Late Decorated western front, the doorway of which yet remains within the tower, and portions of which may still be seen flanking it, was utterly defaced. This façade, like that of St. Alban's, had no towers; but the Norman church was designed for western towers, indications of which may still be seen, at any rate on the south side, though it is very doubtful whether they were ever completed. This side also shows us the original Norman work, still comparatively intact; the aisle lighted by round-headed windows of simple design, with circular windows above, indicative of a triforium, and a clerestory of windows generally similar to those below. There is a south door (restored), and against the two bays east of it has been erected a Late Decorated chapel with large but not very satisfactory windows. It has a separate entrance, and its floor is on a higher level than the church. Beneath it is a vaulted crypt, half-sunk in the ground, and lighted by small windows; this is now occupied mainly by a warming apparatus. Evidently this addition blocked the side lights of the southern transept, but it has led to the preservation of the wall, from which we see that, as in St. Stephen's, Caen, the transepts were short, consisting only of two bays from the crossing, and without aisles. Beyond this wall all has perished; the western tower arch, of course, still remains, and is blocked up, the windows being evidently a modern restoration. Of the choir not a trace remains, and on the northern side even the western wall of the transept has been obliterated; the churchyard occupies the site of these buildings, and beyond it are gardens. Probably Harold's abbey had only a short choir, like the original one at St. Stephen's, Caen. That at first consisted of two bays only, and was terminated by an apse; but inasmuch as a reconstruction of the nave at Waltham was taken in hand in the fifteenth century, it is very probable that the original choir had been previously removed, and had been replaced by one more suited to an elaborate ritual. A church which in its plan still retained some remembrance of the primitive basilica was rarely suffered to remain unaltered during the latter part of the Middle Ages. The oldest choirs which have come down to us were, I believe, in all cases built after a distinctly cruciform plan had been adopted. In most instances we find the older Norman work in the nave.

Seven bays form the nave of Waltham, six of the bays being arranged in pairs;

the middle pillar of the easternmost pair has a spiral ornament, that of the next pair a chevron ornament. Both these types occur at Durham and Dunfermline; that of the westernmost pair is plain. The capitals are rather flat. There is a large triforium arch in each bay, which is not divided, as at Peterborough and at Rochester, and a fairly high clerestory window of one light, with a small subsidiary blank arch on either side. A zigzag ornamentation is rather freely used. In short, the design and proportion have a general resemblance to those in the naves of Ely, Peterborough, and Southwell, and the old work, except in the western bays, has escaped from later alterations. There is a flat wooden ceiling, a restoration, painted, and a copy of that at Peterborough. The aisles are open to the roof, now a modern half-barrel in wood, so that there is no triforium gallery. They do not appear to have been vaulted, but there seem to be some indications that, as we should expect, the triforium was formerly a reality, and was cut off by a flat ceiling. This, however, must have been removed at an early period, probably in the fourteenth century, when the ill-advised alterations were made in the western bays. These may be briefly designated as a very clumsy attempt to reconstruct the nave, after the manner of William of Wykeham at Winchester. But at Waltham the architect merely cut away the pier arch, replacing the mouldings of the triforium arch by very mean Late Decorated work, leaving the original Norman piers both in the one and in the other. Anything more hideous and incongruous than the result it is difficult to conceive. The blunderers had spoiled two bays, and had just begun upon the next triforium arch on the north side when fortunately their work was stopped. Except for the Lady Chapel on the south side, and the insertion of a fairly good Decorated and of a poor Perpendicular window on the north side, the original work still remains, even in the walls of the aisles.

The church has undergone a very careful restoration, the most noteworthy addition being a carved and painted reredos, which harmonises well with the rest of the buildings. Except for a large Elizabethan monument, and a marble tomb, on which the bust of the departed Mr. R. Smith, who died in 1697, stands as if on a sideboard, there is little to notice in the details of the church. The tomb of Harold, with others of note, was in the choir. These have all perished, but to examine such a precious fragment of the earlier Romanesque is well worth a long pilgrimage.

In association with this foundation of Harold, we may briefly notice the church—which has survived the abbey that was built to commemorate his defeat and death; though with these events the church had only an indirect connection. On the spot where Harold fell, at the foot of the Royal Standard of England, the Conqueror placed the high altar of his votive abbey. Its stately buildings rose upon the plateau, overlooking the slopes which had been drenched with the blood of the combatants. That church, however, has been levelled with the ground; only portions of the monastery remain; the parish church of Battle is an offshoot of later date. At first the people of the village worshipped in the conventual church. This was soon found inconvenient by the monks, so that one Ralph, Abbot of Battle from 1107 to 1124, built a parish church, to the north of the monastery, on the opposite verge of the plateau, which was served by one of the monks as chaplain-vicar. The present structure is of various dates. The older part is Early English, but the pillars of the nave may perhaps be a little more ancient. Considerable additions and alterations were made, in both the Decorated and the Perpendicular styles, the western tower being a late example of the latter. There are several monuments, anterior to the Reformation, which are interesting, and so are other details, on which want of space precludes us from dwelling. The church, which has been restored, is in excellent order, and should not be left unvisited by pilgrims to the field of Senlac. The latter affords little pleasure. Once only in a week is admission granted to one of the most interesting spots in England, the scene of the greatest crisis in our national history; and then the accumulated throngs are conducted along like flocks of sheep. Doubtless anything like admission on easy terms might be annoying to the owner, but if so, steps should be taken to make the field of Senlac national property.

One characteristic of the church must be noticed. As the abbey was free from episcopal jurisdiction, so also was the church. Previous to the Reformation its minister was one of the *decani* or deans of the abbey, and after its suppression the immunity and the title still remained; thus the rector continued to bear the title of Dean of Battle. His parish formed what was called a Peculiar, and so late as 1844 the Bishop of Chichester, when confirming in the church, protested that he acted not by his episcopal authority but with consent of the dean. To this day similar immunity is claimed by the Dean of Westminster, who guards his rights by a formal protest when the abbey is used for an episcopal function; but the only Deans of Peculiar now remaining in England, besides Battle, are at Stamford and at Bocking.

T. G. BONNEY.

HARROW AND NEWSTEAD.

MEMORIES OF BYRON.

—◆◆—

ARMS OF HARROW
SCHOOL.

THE association between Newstead Abbey in Nottinghamshire and the great public school of Harrow in Middlesex is entirely Byronic; and we may at once premise that the two are brought into combination in these pages on that account. As a matter of chronology, Byron went to Newstead before he went to Harrow. The wicked Lord Byron, his grand-uncle, whom he succeeded, having gone to his account, to the regret apparently of none, except his pet crickets, which are said to have marched out of the hall, never to return, on the day of the disreputable old peer's death, there appeared one summer day in 1798, at the fine entrance to the park on the Mansfield Road, a vehicle from Nottingham, containing a stout, common-looking woman, a fat boy of ten, and a second woman, his nurse. The boy was the young Lord Byron, brought to see his inheritance. But the house was almost uninhabitable. Decay and ruin had made alarming encroachments everywhere, and short, therefore, was the stay made by the visitors.

The mother and son had up to this period been residing on a slender income in Scotland, and the hermit peer who despoiled Newstead was wont to speak of the heir as " that young brat of Aberdeen." On receiving news of their change of fortune, the poor widow, who had been shamefully reduced to poverty by a handsome and blackguardly husband, sold up the modest household goods and set off on a southerly journey to Nottinghamshire. For a while Mrs. Byron and the podgy lad, who had been made a ward in Chancery, resided in the county town; then in London, where George Gordon was taught by Glennie of Dulwich; and then briefly at Cheltenham. How often Byron had visited Newstead during the four years covered by these wanderings one can only conjecture; but it is evident that even when he went to Harrow he had possessed himself of all the traditions and spirit of the dreary abbey down in the Midlands.

Lord Byron was at Harrow from 1801 to 1805, passing his holidays principally at Southwell, which in these later days has been made an episcopal see. Newstead Abbey, for the major portion of Byron's minority, was rented by Lord Grey de Ruthen, but the schoolboy owner was always welcome there, and a room was set apart for his use. Harrow, since Byron's residence at the school, is altered in most respects, save in its magnificent situation. No march of progress can improve that away. As seen from the main line of the London and North-Western Railway, and from the level country extending on the other side to Epsom and Windsor, the slender spire rising above the elm tops must often recall to the mind of the wayfarer the scriptural illustration of a city set upon a hill. Truly it cannot be hid.

The church of St. Mary at Harrow was founded by Lanfranc, Archbishop of Canterbury, in the reign of William the Conqueror; but he did not live long enough to consecrate it, and Anselm, his successor, had an undignified squabble with the Bishop of London's agents when, on a winter morning in 1094, he passed through the grand western doorway to perform, with the florid ecclesiastical pomp of the age, the consecration ceremony. It used to be believed that the circular columns which divide the aisles from the nave, and a part of the tower at the west end, were actual remnants of Lanfranc's building. But it has now been demonstrated that the columns are of a later period, and it is doubtful whether anything is left of the original fabric. The date of 1150 has been mentioned as agreeing with the character of the western doorway. The church was substantially rebuilt in the early part of the fourteenth century; and a hundred years afterwards the giving way of the tower resulted in the varied and massive buttresses which are a marked feature of Harrow Church. The slender spire of wood covered with lead was added later. The elegant doorways (north and south) of the Decorated period are good specimens of the work done at this time. It is probable that the font is truly a relic of Lanfranc. For many years it had been used as a trough in the vicarage garden, no one appearing to suspect its true character; but when the discovery was made, the large circular Purbeck marble basin was rescued, its rudimentary carvings were restored, and, with added rim and base, it was placed in the church as it may now be seen.

HARROW: THE SPIRE AND THE PORCH.

The existing church of Harrow-on-the-Hill, consisting of a nave, chancel, aisles, and transepts—not forgetting the famous tower and spire—is the result of a complete restoration, undertaken in 1840 by Sir Gilbert Scott. Previous to that time the additions and renovations of successive ages could be read in the solid handiwork of their diverse builders; but the vestiges of antiquity left are, as already suggested, few; and, such as they are, confined to monuments in stone and brass. The visitor, however, is likely to devote greatest attention to the churchyard, from which an incomparable prospect may be enjoyed. The hill upon which Harrow is built is an abruptly swelling bosom of land, rising from comparatively level ground on every side. On a superlatively clear day, such as probably few persons have found, thirteen counties, it is asserted, are within ken from the church tower. Ten miles to the east, but normally obscured by haze and smoke, is Hyde Park; west and south-west—the glorious landscape commanded from the terrace seats outside the churchyard—Buckinghamshire and Berkshire lie outspread, rich in English homes, in woodland and pasturage; the Surrey hills change the prospect in another direction, with Knockholt Beeches, Hayes Common, and Shooter's Hill trending eastward.

The churchyard brings us back by a cherished tradition to the association of Harrow with Lord Byron. Within a few yards of the church tower is a flat monumental stone, to which the poet, two years before his death, in one of his letters to Murray, the publisher, thus referred:—" There is a spot in the church-yard near the footpath, on the brow of the hill, looking towards Windsor, and a tomb under a large tree (bearing the name of Peachie or Peachey) where I used to sit for hours and hours when a boy. This was my favourite spot." From sundry entries in his journals, and from his poems, we get glimpses of Byron at Harrow, engaging in the athletics of the playground. He recounts his

HARROW: VIEW FROM THE CHURCHYARD.

battles, and his prowess at cricket and swimming; yet he admits that he was " a most unpopular boy, but led latterly." We know also that for two years and

P P P

a half he hated Harrow. From some of his contemporaries it may be gathered that at Harrow, as at Cambridge, he did not excel as a scholar. The spirit of poetry was burning within him, nevertheless, and the "favourite spot" in the church-yard doubtless was the throne of the dreamer, productive of more delight to his precocious genius than the rough contests of the playground, in which he was physically unable to share with enthusiasm. Only a few of the published poems were produced during the Harrow period, but there is one written the year after he left, directly bearing upon the stone slab, which was called "Byron's tomb" by his comrades. The verse is well remembered:—

"Again I behold where for hours I have ponder'd,
    As reclining at eve, on yon tombstone I lay,
Or round the steep brow of the churchyard I wander'd
    To catch the last gleam of the sun's setting ray."

This tomb was repaired, and enclosed in a strong iron railing—to remain a Byron memorial for all time—a few years since by some admirers of the poet, foremost of whom was Mr. John Murray, who was a witness of the burning of the Byron memoirs in his father's drawing-room, and who inherited, with the great publishing business of the Albemarle Street house, an admiration of the author of "Childe Harold."

Byron carved his name along with the rest of the Harrovians in the fourth form room, the largest and most typical of the scattered buildings which make up the great public school at Harrow. A brass in the chancel arch of the church perpetuates the memory of John Lyon, yeoman, who died in 1592, and of the manner in which he founded "a free grammer schoole in this p'she;" and two years before his death the founder, amongst his orders, statutes, and rules for the government of the school, announces his intention of providing, besides con-venient rooms for the schoolmaster and usher, "alsoe a large and convenient schoole house, with a chimney in it." The fourth form room, with its ancient master's seat, usher's chair and desk, plain benches and form, and almost black oak wainscoting, is Lyon's original "schoole house." On the wainscoting Byron cut his name, and so in like manner did Peel, Palmerston, Lord Ripon, Lord Aberdeen, Lord Normanby, R. B. Sheridan, and Sir W. Jones.

The building now used for school examinations was the old speech room, erected after Byron's time, and this was replaced by the handsome tercentenary memorial, a semi-circular building opposite the site of the old college chapel. The picturesque Gothic chapel at the northern end of High Street, with an aisle and stained-glass windows in memory of the Harrow boys killed in the Crimea, was built by Gilbert Scott in 1855, replacing a temporary building; and in the Vaughan Library, a typical specimen of Gilbert Scott's Decorated Gothic, are, amongst other reminders of the past, portraits of Byron and of his distinguished contemporaries. When, in after years, Byron was living in Italy he sent the body of his natural daughter to Harrow, with a marble tablet setting forth, " In memory of Allegra, daughter of G. G. Lord Byron, who died at Bagna Cavallo in Italy, April 20, 1822, aged five years and three months. ' I shall go to her. but she shall not return to me.' " The interment, however, took place elsewhere.

Lord Byron often made Newstead Abbey the poetical subject of happy and accurate descriptions of the building, grounds, and park; and it would be easy to compile a chapter of quotations that, with very trifling links to indicate and explain recent changes, would still, for all practical purposes, serve as a guide to the visitor of to-day. Walpole described Newstead before the poet-peer succeeded to the inheritance. It was then in the hands of the wicked lord, who seemed to be deliberately bent upon ruining the estate; he destroyed its oaks, and, by a sudden whim butchered the deer so that the shambles of Mansfield Market were at one time glutted with venison. Walpole writes loosely, speaking of the beautiful west window of the old abbey church as the east. But he stints not his admiration of the abbey and all its surroundings. An Edinburgh reviewer, subsequent to the publication of " English Bards," criticising the cynical critic Walpole, declares Newstead to be one of the noblest mansions in England, and prophesies that, whatever may be its future fate, the Abbey must henceforth be a memorable abode.

Byron evidently looked upon Newstead with the gloomiest of forebodings, dedicating it in impassioned verse to sure decay, to the whistling of hollow winds, to hemlock and thistle. The Edinburgh reviewer above quoted, quite as anxious probably as the poet to get as much literary effect as possible out of the dilapidations, conceived no future better than possession by vulgar owners. Happily these predictions have been splendidly falsified. Byron, in 1809, vowed in the strongest language that, come what might, Newstead and he would stand or fall together; that no pressure, present or future, should induce him to barter the least vestige of the inheritance; and that if he could exchange Newstead Abbey for the first fortune in the country, he would reject the proposition. Three years later the place was put up to auction at Garraway's, and only £90,000 being bid, it was withdrawn. Next it was sold to a gentleman who failed in his contract, and Newstead once more came back to the poet. In 1818, however, Byron being then thirty years of age, it passed finally from the family which had held it for nearly three centuries, and was purchased by Colonel Wildman for some £100,000.

This was the turning-point of the fortunes of Newstead. The new owner, who had sat on the same form with Byron at Harrow, was a gallant soldier; he had served with distinction in the Peninsula wars; and he devoted himself from the moment of taking possession to repairing, restoring, and beautifying Newstead, without interfering with its character. To any but an enthusiast the work must have appeared hopeless. It is said that Colonel Wildman spent over a quarter of a million of money in the restoration and decoration of the abbey. On the

NEWSTEAD.

death of this gentleman the property was acquired by Mr. W. F. Webb, a famous African traveller, and by him, no less than by his predecessor, the good work has been continued, and the utmost care taken in the preservation of every object of interest associated with the unfortunate poet who loved it, and lost it. Thanks to Colonel Wildman and Mr. Webb, Newstead has risen nobly from its ruins, and is, at the present moment, a lovely domain, with abbey and grounds in perfect preservation; further than this, the most liberal facilities are afforded to visitors desirous of seeing the rooms in which Byron slept, revelled, and worked, or of wandering amidst the gardens and groves trodden by his footsteps.

The Newstead Abbey of to-day, notwithstanding the vast sums of money laid out in its improvement, is, to a greater extent than might be expected, very much what it was when young Byron, a boy of ten years of age, bearing the title of sixth Baron, was taken to see it. The greatest change is that caused by the addition, at the south-west corner, of the square Sussex tower by Colonel Wildman, who named it after the Royal Duke whose equerry he was. Byron's own term—"Mixt Gothic"—very adequately touches off the rest of the architecture of the front of the abbey. Some portions are Early English Gothic of the best type, and the Norman tower at the end, though not in harmony, seems to give a tone of completeness which was formerly wanting. At the other end of the façade are the stately remnants of the west front of the abbey church, the ivy climbing over the ancient stonework with graceful profusion.

In approaching Newstead by the high road from Nottingham, a drive of at least a mile intervenes between the lodge gates and the abbey, and a sharp descent and curve bring the traveller somewhat suddenly before the famous objects of Newstead, namely the lake, the mimic forts, the cascades, the picturesque window of the ruins, and the light and graceful architecture of the front. In his desire not to mar the scene with any incongruous addition, the present owner has built a block of stables near the castellated affair jutting into the lake, of pure Gothic, and all in harmony with the surroundings. The ivy which grows plentifully at Newstead has already given an air of romantic antiquity to buildings erected within thirty years.

Entrance to the pile is obtained through a small strong oaken door, upon which hangs an antique Italian knocker. The crypt of the old abbey is gloomy enough, and now and for the remainder of the time spent under the groined roofs, and amidst long echoing corridors, narrow, winding stone staircases, grim galleries and passages, the explanation of all the ghost legends attached to Newstead must be obvious. In the hall, amidst the twelfth-century masonry of the crypt, are arranged on the floor various trophies of Mr. Webb's prowess amongst the game of Africa, with fishing-rods and other modern articles of the chase, and, in many a corridor, cases of brilliantly plumaged birds, shot by the present owner in Africa and India, are intermingled with relics of the Middle Ages.

Presently you are conducted to Byron's bed-room and dressing-room, where everything remains as it was left by the poet. What few habitable rooms were in the abbey during his brief ownership were in this portion; the rest were barely weather proof. There still are the Byron bedstead, with its gilt and coroneted posts, the dressing-table, and chairs; the portrait of Fox; of Joe Murray, the favourite factotum, with the churchwarden pipe painted in at his own desire; and the portrait of a portly gentleman, who turns out to be Jackson, the prize-fighter.

Byron wisely chose this bed-room, with its recessed window and magnificent view to the west. Again and again in his poetry he betrays inspiration drawn from this particular prospect—the lake, in which he swam, sailed, and tested the courage of his dog Boatswain; the miniature fortress which the mad lord, who butchered the deer, built to amuse him what time he put his toy fleet in action; the cascade making music near the house; the swelling wooded knoll across the water in the direction of Annesley, where Mary Chaworth lived. With the tumbling water and shrubbery close to the house, and rookeries all around, the stillest night would give to the poet in his bed mysterious sounds innumerable.

The library now shown was not used by Byron as such, and some suppose that it was originally an aisle of the chapel. Many valuable and ancient pieces of furniture and paintings are here; the abbey throughout, indeed, is peculiarly rich in well-preserved furniture, paintings, and decorations of the Stuart period. The tapestry in the room used once by Charles II., and in other apartments, was brought by Colonel Wildman from Spain after the Peninsula war. There are few old country houses in England offering such perfect examples of carved oak panelling and mantelpieces. Edward III., if not Edward I., and Henry VII. visited Newstead Abbey in the olden times, when the abbots ruled; and the apartments they are supposed to have used, down to the minutest detail of ornamentation, have been carefully preserved by Colonel Wildman and Mr. W. F. Webb.

The south corridor has been largely devoted by Mr. Webb to the relics of Livingstone and Stanley. The visitors are, towards the close of their round of the abbey, shown the room in which Livingstone, on his last stay in England, wrote his work on the Zambesi, and in the corridor the battered consular cap he wore at the time of his death is preserved. At the other end of the corridor—cases of gorgeous Himalayan birds shot by Mr. Webb intervening—are the Byron relics, and amongst them the piece of beech tree upon which Byron, on his last visit to the abbey (20th September, 1814), carved his name and that of his sister Augusta. A small revolving table is pointed out as that upon which the poet wrote his "English Bards" and part of "Childe Harold." Boxing gloves, foils, candlesticks, inkstand, the arms worn in Greece, and the sumptuously-bound copy of the early poems, recall the stormy career of the peer whose memory has been so sacredly preserved by his successors in the ownership of Newstead Abbey. The largest rooms at Newstead are the Grand Saloon and the Great Dining Hall, now richly furnished and decorated, but in Byron's time wreck and ruin. The breakfast-room, once the Lord Abbot's parlour, was used by Byron as a dining-room.

The cloisters of Newstead are famous for their excellent condition, and in the quadrangle still plays the old Gothic fountain, brought into the court at some remote time from the front of the abbey. The chapel, formerly the chapter-house, has been exquisitely restored and decorated by Mr. Webb in the Early English style. In the gardens, which are liberally maintained, the same anxiety has been manifested as in the interior to cherish every memorial of Byron. The oak he planted; Boatswain's tomb, in which at one time the poet himself wished to be buried, between the dog and Joe Murray; and the satyr's and devil's woods, which belong rather to the wicked lord, are amongst the notable sights outside the abbey.

W. SENIOR.

IVY SCAR ROCK

PRIORY CHURCH

CHOIR - PRIORY CHURCH

PRIORY GATEWAY

GREAT MALVERN: THE PRIORY CHURCH AND THE NEIGHBOURHOOD.

GREAT MALVERN AND TEWKESBURY.

HILL SIDE AND RIVER BRINK.

THE Priory Church of Great Malvern, often miscalled " Abbey," stands on the eastern slope of the Malvern Hills, with the Worcestershire Beacon and North Hill rising behind it. It is very seldom that so fine a church is found in the immediate proximity of so fine a range of hills. From the west it is approached by two long flights of steps, commanding a magnificent view of the northern side and of the stately central tower. The southern transept and the lady chapel (which extended on a lower level than the chancel to the hedge now bounding the churchyard) were demolished when the Priory was suppressed.

Of the other monastic buildings, only the gateway, which admitted into the precincts of the monastery, remains; it is of about the same date as the chancel, and very near the west end of the church. Some fragments of the stonework of the refectory have been preserved. The priory (Benedictine) was founded in the eleventh century, soon after the Conquest. A hermit here, Aldwine, desiring to visit the Holy Land, consulted Wulstan, the good Bishop of Worcester, and was advised by him to form a cœnobitic community of the solitaries* in Malvern Chase, instead of making his pilgrimage. The priory was subject to the abbey of Westminster, the dean and chapter of which still retain property in the diocese; but there were frequent disputes about the control of it between the abbey and the see of Worcester. In the peace which followed the Wars of the Roses, the church was rebuilt under the skilful guidance of Sir Reginald Bray—a favourite counsellor of Henry VII., and designer of the chapel named after Henry in Westminster Abbey—the Norman columns in the nave being left as they were. Apparently it was intended to span the choir with a vaulting of stone; probably the wooden roof was substituted for economy's sake. The commencement of this vaulting is seen on either side. Sir Reginald is represented with his pupil, Prince Arthur, in the north window of the transept. At the Reformation, Latimer, Bishop of Worcester, interceded strenuously with King Henry for the priory, that it should be made a school, and bore his testimony to the good character of the prior and the brethren. But it was in vain. The priory was confiscated, to the advantage of the Knotsfords and others. The whole church would have been destroyed† had not the parishioners purchased it for £300, to be their parish church, in place of a much smaller building then standing to the north of the priory church. In 1852 the priory church, having lapsed into a deplorable condition, was thoroughly repaired at great expense under

* Some fugitives from Deerhurst, when the monastery there was sacked by Danes, are said to have settled in the upper part of the wild forest, which stretched from the hills to the Severn.
† Probably much damage was done then to the painted glass.

the direction of Sir G. G. Scott. The porch, forming the north-west entrance, is lofty and spacious, of the time of Henry VII.; over this is the "parvisum," the old vestry, approached by a winding stone staircase.

The special charm of the interior is in its brightness and cheerfulness, owing to the great size of the windows at each end and in the clerestory. The height, too, of the building, and the loftiness of the chancel arch, while enhancing the solemnity of the interior, prevent what would be the depressing effect of the low, massive Norman piers. From the Norman font at the west end the view is magnificent. The proportions are excellent: six bays in the nave, three in the chancel; there is no chancel screen to interrupt the view.

The arches in the nave are singularly beautiful in their simplicity—semi-circular, and quite unadorned with mouldings, with the exception of the last capital eastward on the north, which seems to show that the monks began to embellish, but stopped immediately. A narrow arched recess, five or six feet from the ground in the pillar nearest the porch, was perhaps for holy water. The smaller aisle, with a doorway, now closed, which marks the entrance into the cloisters of the priory, retains its original dimensions. The northern aisle is wider. The three very small apertures in the western wall were probably in a gallery, to enable the prior, or some other official, to look down into the nave. There are traces of Norman work in the vestry behind the organ, as well as in the south aisle of the nave, and in a beautiful arch over the door from the southern aisle into the vestry.

As one passes from the nave under the tower into the chancel, the contrast of style is remarkable. The walls are panelled with Perpendicular tracery; the slender shafts rise like pines from floor to ceiling. It is supposed, from some indications in the masonry, that the Norman tower fell, as at Gloucester and elsewhere, those ponderous structures being especially liable to such a catastrophe. Under the lower part of the tower on the north side are placed the lectern (an eagle in brass by Hardman, in memory of the late General Eardley Wilmot), the reading desk and the pulpit, both of carved oak. The old monastic stalls are very curious, and resemble those of Worcester Cathedral in the grotesque figures on the misereres. Several gently sloping steps lead up to the sacrarium, which is fenced by a low brass rail of rich workmanship: two doors (an unusual thing), one north, one south of the Holy Table, admit through the reredos into a little sacristy, from which the prior or his deputy could see through three "hagioscopes" into the chapel.

A very beautiful mosaic of the kind which may still be seen in the house of the Faun at Pompeii, forms the centre of the reredos. It was made by Messrs. Powell, Whitefriars, and is the munificent gift of the Rev. E. Peek, of Lyme Regis. It represents the Holy Family, with the Magi on the one side and the shepherds on the other. The details show much care and thought. At each end is mosaic scroll-work, with the emblematic corn and grapes; beyond these are some of the old tiles.

The south aisle of the choir is called St. Anne's Chapel,* of the same date as the choir. The side windows are filled with old Belgian glass representing some of the events recorded in the Book of Genesis and the accompaniments of the Passion of our Lord. The drawing of the figures is grotesque, but the colours are gorgeous, especially the ruby and purple. The chapel is used as a choir vestry, and for lectures, &c. A curious old folio, the Prayer Book with commentary, is chained to an oak desk. The north choir aisle is called the Jesus Chapel.

Few churches or cathedrals in England are so rich in old painted glass. The east window is made up of fragments arranged promiscuously, but the effect is very good. The clerestory windows tell the story of the foundation of the priory. In the transept window, above the kneeling figures of Prince Arthur and his tutor, are two exquisite groups, one of the Nativity and one of the Visitation; above these is the Feast at Cana. In many of the windows are angels,† as if the church, dedicated originally to St. Mary the Virgin, had been rededicated, possibly after civil strife or bloodshed within its walls, to St. Michael and the Holy Angels. From the shape of many of the windows, it seems that the architect had proposed making them even larger than they are, but had been restrained by fears of instability.

There are a few old monuments: one in St. Anne's Chapel of Prior Walcher, noted in his day for learning and science; a recumbent figure of a knight of the name of Corbet, north of the sacrarium; and several on the south side belonging to the Knotsford family; there is also in the Jesus Chapel a very graceful representation in stone of a Mrs. Thompson. There are memorial-brasses of the Rev. G. Fisk, vicar, in the nave; of E. Chance, Esq., in the transept; of the Rev. J. Dyson in the chapel. Under the west window is a costly memorial, by Scott, of Sir H. Lambert, Bart., consisting of an elaborate canopy in stone over a mural brass, with the Evangelists on either side. The organ, by Nicholson, is a very fine instrument.

The noble abbey of Tewkesbury is rich in reminiscences of the past. The name is probably from Theoc, a missionary monk, who is said to have Christianised this corner of Mercia subsequently to the conversion of the rest of the midland kingdom. It has been supposed, from his name, that he was a Briton; but the Britons generally held aloof from intercourse, even in this way, with the invaders. The legendary story of the foundation of the abbey by the brothers

* The famous spring on the hill-side is called St. Anne's Well.
† These have the body covered with plumage, not the wings only.

Oddo and Doddo, Dukes of Mercia, is apocryphal; and, perhaps, was suggested by the names of Earl Dudda in the eighth century, and of Earl Odda in the eleventh. Originally a "cell" or dependency of Cranbourn Abbey in Dorsetshire, the monastery here became an abbey, and shortly before the Conquest the relative position of Tewkesbury and Cranbourn was reversed.

Robert Fitz-Hamon, kinsman of William Rufus, "Lord of Gloucester, etc. etc.," was a great benefactor to the abbey; he commenced the rebuilding of the church, which was completed by Earl Robert of Gloucester, brother of the Empress Maude, a great church-builder in his day. In 1123 the church was dedicated in honour of St. Mary the Virgin; of this building great portions remain now. The monastery flourished under the fostering care of the De Clares,* the Despensers, the Beauchamps, etc., till the Dissolution. Though not mitred, the abbots were often summoned to Parliament. The abbey was rededicated in 1239 by the famous Bishop Walter de Cantilupe, after additions and alterations. The choir was rebuilt about 1350, probably to introduce the new style of architecture then coming into vogue.

Henry VI., always munificent to religious foundations, gave to the abbey the patronage of Deerhurst Priory, in the immediate neighbourhood, the oldest monastery in this part of England. After the battle of Tewkesbury, the abbot, standing at the great door of the church, crucifix in hand, like Ambrose at Milan, repelled Edward IV. pursuing fugitives into the sanctuary.

The revenues of this powerful and wealthy abbey were about £40,000 of our money when it fell into the rapacious hands of Henry VIII. and his courtiers in 1539. It was the last in the county to be surrendered; the abbot, Wakeman, was made Bishop of Gloucester; the monks (only 38 remained) were pensioned. The domestic offices were preserved; the conventual for the most part destroyed. The Gate House, a remarkable edifice, about forty feet high, near the west end of the church, is standing now, with some buildings near the Avon. There is a fine oriel window in the "Abbey House" (probably the infirmary), near the west end. The nave of the church was already in use as the parish church; the rest of the structure was rescued by the parishioners from demolition for £483.

MISERERE, MALVERN.

After undergoing, from time to time, unsightly reparations in the last century and in the early part of this, the church has now been thoroughly

---

* The "Red Earl," late in the thirteenth century, was a De Clare.

restored at great expense; Sir G. G. Scott superintended the work in its commencement.

The old saying "As sure as God is in Gloucestershire" was meant to signify

TEWKESBURY: THE WEST FRONT.

the number and importance of monastic institutions in that county. Tewkesbury had rank among the foremost. The site is remarkable; the two great rivers, Severn and Avon, with two tributary streams, meeting here, almost insulate the town. The church is cruciform, with apsidal chapels grouping themselves, as at Westminster, round the choir. In general character, as might be expected, it resembles Gloucester Cathedral and Pershore Abbey Church. Almost every style of our English Gothic is represented. The total length is 286 feet. The nave is 165 feet by 110; the transepts are 120 by 33. The height of the nave is 58 feet; of the tower, 132. The Lady Chapel was 100 feet long, due east of the choir; it, as well as the cloisters, has been demolished. Only three English churches, not cathedrals, are longer. This church comes next in size to Hereford Cathedral; the nave would stand within the nave of Gloucester, it is said, as one box within another.

The tower, which is Norman except the battlement and turrets, rests on four huge piers; the interior of it is rich in ornamentation, and resembles the tower of Pershore Abbey Church. It was originally a "lantern tower," and was closed in order, perhaps, to render the voice more audible. A wooden spire, erected on

R R R

the tower by Robert, the celebrated Earl of Gloucester already mentioned, fell on Easter Day, 1559. There are eight bells and chimes to the clock. The campanile or bell-tower, a building of no great pretensions, was pulled down in 1813.* The west front, with a lofty and spacious arch in a deep recess (62 feet by 34), is not unworthy to be named with the west fronts of Lincoln and Peterborough. The design appears to have been executed imperfectly. The porch is very plain. The west window was destroyed by a storm in 1661. The nave is Norman, with fourteen columns unusually tall, and with a triforium dwarfed in proportion. In the choir, on the contrary, the columns are short, surmounted by large windows. The font is partly old. The pulpit, octagonal, in stone, was given in 1881. The nave is vaulted with stone, richly groined and sculptured; the bosses have been regilt and recoloured under the direction of Mr. Gambier Parry, of Highnam Court, Gloucestershire. Probably the stonework replaced an original roof of wood. As in the "stanze" of the Vatican, a mirror is useful in enabling one to appreciate the beauty of it.

The choir, with a sexagonal termination, is surrounded by an "ambulatory" or "procession-path." The tracery of the roof is very fine. The most interesting of the chantries, which cluster round the choir, are, on the north, the "Warwick chapel" (1421), and, adjoining it eastward, the "Founder's chapel" (1397) and the chapel of St. Mary Magdalene (1439). The exquisite erection now used as the choir-vestry is supposed by some to have been the chapter-house, but was probably a chapel with ante-chapel. Over this was the treasury of the monastery. The sedilia and the monks' stalls, with their misereres curiously carved, are noteworthy. The history of the organ is remarkable. It was moved from Magdalen College, Oxford, to Hampton Court by Cromwell, and finally placed here in 1737. The rose-window, at the east end, is fine, and contains portraits of benefactors in their baronial costumes.

There are many interesting monuments. The oldest is of Abbot Alan, friend of Becket, prior of Canterbury before coming here. There are monuments also of other abbots, with a cenotaph of Wakeman, the last of them, constructed for him at his request during his lifetime. Then there are a graceful alabaster monument of Sir Guy de Brien (Brienne, Normandy), and a kneeling figure in armour, Sir E. Despenser. In 1796 a brass was laid in the floor in memory of Prince Edward, murdered here after the battle (1471). The Duke of Somerset, who was executed at Tewkesbury after the battle, and Lord Wenlock, who was killed in the fight, are interred here; also the Duke of Clarence, "false, fleeting, perjured Clarence," with his duchess. The general effect of the interior of the church is stately but sombre.

I. GREGORY SMITH.

* By some accounts in 1817.

THE CHOIR.

ST. GEORGE'S CHAPEL, WINDSOR.

THE ENGLISH ESCURIAL.

COMPOSITE, heterogeneous, an organic growth rather than a premeditated construction, such is Windsor Castle; at once a palace and a barrack, a bede-house and a college ecclesiastical. It is no solitary stronghold of military power, no secluded abode of luxurious ease, but is almost a town within a town, inhabited by folk of diverse ranks and callings, who are associated by one common bond of loyal service to the Crown of Great Britain. Thus, like this, it is in touch with the nation; it is the history writ in stone not only of English kings, but also of English men, who in their day have drunk of life's cup of pleasure and of pain within its walls, and now sleep beneath the shadow of its chapel.

As this is an integral part of the castle, the history of the one cannot be wholly dissociated from that of the other, and a few words must be devoted to the early days of the castle before proceeding to the details of the chapel. When the Norman Conqueror first landed in England, neither walls nor towers

T T T

were standing here.   The site of Windsor was but a wooded, chalky hill overlooking the Thames, on the margin of a forest which extended southward from
the river for many a mile.   It was a long undulating mound, running for a space
parallel with the water.   On this side it fell steeply, on the other it shelved
down more gently.   This part of the forest had been bestowed by the Confessor on
his Abbey of Westminster; it pleased the Conqueror, who acquired it by exchange
from the abbey, and ultimately decided to build for himself a castle on the hill.
Thus Windsor has been a royal residence from the days of the first of the
Norman· kings.

The Conqueror's castle, doubtless, was much inferior in size to the present
great group of buildings.   It was enlarged by Henry I., and then probably corresponded in area roughly with the present Lower Ward, being terminated by the
Round Tower as its keep.   Doubtless there was already a chapel, though probably
a small one; but of this nothing remains.   The first on record was erected
by Henry III., the builder of the abbey at Westminster.   This — a building
about sixty feet in length—stood to the east of the present chapel, nearly on
the site of the Tombhouse, otherwise Wolsey or Albert Chapel.   Edward III.,
when establishing the Order of the Garter, erected a chapel in honour of
St. George and for the use of the knights, and founded, in the year 1348, a
college of priests, named after that saint.   The building is gone, but the institution remains, though modified by change of creed and change of circumstances;
and it now consists of a dean, four canons, and the usual establishment of
minor officials, with which were connected certain bedesmen called the " Poor
Knights of Windsor."

At that time the king abandoned the old royal residence west of the
keep to the clergy and garrison, and erected east of it a new palace for
himself, which is represented by the present Upper Ward.   This chapel of
St. George probably stood on the ground now occupied by the eastern part of
the existing chapel.*   Apparently it was not a good piece of mason's work; for
when Edward IV. reigned, it was in such a state of dilapidation that the king
determined to rebuild it on a scale more worthy of the palace and of the great
order of knighthood.   Richard Beauchamp, Bishop of Salisbury, had the oversight of the work, which was commenced about the year 1474, and was pushed
on vigorously, so that in about five years the building appears to have been
ready for roofing.   At first most of it was covered with wood.   The choir and
probably the nave were vaulted in the reign of Henry VII.   As the former
was completed in 1505, the present building, allowing for sundry minor alterations and for restoration, is a record of the latest period of the so-called Gothic
architecture, its style being very late Perpendicular or Tudor.

* On this matter, however, authorities are not agreed.

The chapel is rather peculiar in its plan ; it is a long, square-ended building with aisles, forming an ambulatory at the east end, crossed by two very short transepts with apsidal terminations. At the eastern extremity of the south aisle is a tall projecting chapel which, to some extent, repeats the form of the transept. At the western end and elsewhere are other side chapels. The hill-top slopes down westward, so that the great door at that end of the chapel is high above the level of the ground, and is approached by a flight of steps, which add much to the dignity of the façade. This looks down into the Horseshoe Cloister, a most picturesque group of buildings in red brick and timber (a restoration or rebuilding by Mr. G. G. Scott), which occupies the site of the cloister built by Edward III. in the form of a fetterlock, one of his badges. The southern flank of the chapel lies open to the Lower Ward, but the view of the northern is more or less interrupted by buildings, while the eastern end is almost blocked by the Tomb-house. But as the architecture, as is usual in buildings of this period, is rather monotonous in conception, the visitor will probably frequent the southern side if he wish readily to comprehend the design, but the northern if he be in search of the picturesque, for on this side will be found some delightfully quaint nooks and corners.

As is the exterior, so is the interior of St. George's Chapel—ornate, but monotonous. There is hardly a square yard which is absolutely free from decoration ; but the architect seems to have concentrated his whole faculties on the design of one bay, and then to have written upon the drawing, " Repeat this so many times." St. George's Chapel is larger, but less ornate, than that of Henry VII. in the Abbey of Westminster ; it is smaller and inferior in its design to that of King's College, Cambridge, which was commenced by Henry VI. Still, it is no unworthy rival of the latter ; for if this claim superiority in the greater richness and grace of its vaulting, and in the grandeur of its huge windows, St. George's may put forward its more varied plan, due to the use of aisles and of transepts.

The nave of St. George's Chapel, were it not for some monuments of interest, would be distinctly monotonous, notwithstanding its architectural enrichment ; so that we may pass on into the choir, which is markedly divided from the remainder of the chapel by the rather massive organ-screen and the unusually lofty canopy-work of its stalls. Few places in England are richer in interesting and impressive associations than this ; for on every side we are surrounded by memorials of the most illustrious of our own nation, of not a few among the rulers over foreign countries. The massive dark oak seats, which rise as usual on either hand, lead up to a row of stalls, above which are richly-carved canopies. These are terminated by high spire-like pinnacles beautifully wrought in wood. On the top of each is placed a gilded helmet, from which depends a gilded sword, and over each, projecting forward from the wall, hangs a richly-blazoned banner. For this choir is the chapel of the knights of the Order of the Garter, to each of whom a stall is allotted. His name is inscribed on a brass plate, his crest is on the helmet, his arms are blazoned on the banner. At his death, helmet, sword, and banner are taken down; the plate is moved to a higher position on the panelling, thus indicating a vacancy in the Order.

As we pass along through the choir we read the names of men "such as did bear rule in their kingdoms, men renowned for their power, giving counsel by their understanding;" men who "were honoured in their generations and were the glory of their times." Curious, too, sometimes are the collocations into which the names are brought; but over these details we must not linger, though some of the older plates are in themselves interesting as pieces of ancient metal work. At the present time the return stalls at the western end of the choir are occupied by members of the Royal House of England, and those next to them, as a rule, by foreign sovereigns. A handsome modern reredos of richly-carved alabaster and marble has been erected beneath the great east window; and this, which was formerly occupied by very ugly stained glass and debased tracery of the Georgian era, has recently been restored and filled with admirable modern glass, the work of Messrs. Clayton and Bell, as a memorial to the late Prince Consort.

But St. George's Chapel is not less interesting as a place of burial than for its memorials of the Order of the Garter. In this respect it is second only to Westminster Abbey, though the interments are far less numerous, and the tombs of members of the royal houses bear a larger proportion to those of illustrious subjects; for the position of the chapel renders it a natural resting-place for the one, but an accidental resting-place for the other. The memorials of greatest interest lie in the eastern part of the chapel. In the nave they are not numerous. On the southern side, near the west end, a handsome altar-tomb commemorates the late Duke of Kent; and in the curious Beaufort Chapel, near to it, are monuments of the Somerset family *—among others, the Marquis of Worcester, noted for his brave defence of Raglan Castle against the Parliamentary forces. On the opposite side, against the western wall—the great window is filled by stained glass, much of it ancient, collected together in 1774 from various parts of the building— is a statue of the late King Leopold of Belgium; and near it, affixed to the wall, an ornamental brass plate, which commemorates "Alamayu, the son of Theodore," who fell into the hands of our forces at the capture of Magdala, and before the completion of his education in England, though not until he had given

* That to the first Duke of Beaufort, which formerly encumbered the chapel, was removed some years since to Badminton.

proof of bright intelligence, and an amiable disposition, died from an attack of inflammation. In an adjacent chapel is a monument to the Princess Charlotte.

ST. GEORGE'S CHAPEL, FROM THE RIVER.

This is interesting as a specimen of a class of memorials which a century since evoked superlative admiration, but now are more commonly condemned. It is a sculptured group in white marble, on which artfully-tinted glass sheds a golden light. Mourners watch a bier on which a veiled corpse is lying; above it, from between a pair of curtains, a female figure soars upwards, supposed to represent the spirit of the Princess quitting the tomb; on either side is an angel, one bearing in its arms her infant. To insert this monument a very interesting screen, erected by the founder of the chantry, Dean Urswick, was, again in strict accordance with the spirit of the age, removed into one of the choir aisles. Against the wall in the north aisle is a sculptured tablet which commemorates the late King of Hanover. To obtain a place for this, the least felicitous in design of the more modern monuments, the stone-work of the wall has been defaced.

The northern transept, or Rutland Chapel, contains numerous memorials, frequently of canons and others connected with the place; but the effigies of Lord Roos and his wife, niece to Edward IV., are of greater interest. In the south transept, also, or Braye Chapel (named after its founder, Sir Reginald Braye, Knight of the Garter in the reign of Henry VII.), are several memorials, the most conspicuous being the beautiful white marble cenotaph to the late Prince Imperial of France, which, as will be remembered, was originally intended for Westminster Abbey.

Monuments of early date are more numerous and more interesting in the eastern half of the chapel. A chantry in the northern aisle commemorates Lord Hastings, Chamberlain to Edward IV., the tale of whose summary execution is familiar to all readers of Shakespeare. From the Wars of the Roses till the days of Elizabeth illustrious heads parted so easily from illustrious necks that one would think the "due conduct" on the scaffold must once have been as needful an item in the finished education of an English nobleman as was formerly the correct performance of *harakiri* to a Japanese. Further east is the tomb of the founder of the chapel, Edward IV. A short inscription commemorates him and his wife, "Elizabeth Widvile." Some very elaborate iron gates, reputed to be the work of Quintin Matsys, which once formed a screen to the tomb on this side, are now placed so as to be visible from the choir; and above it is the "royal pew," occupying two bays, with oriel openings projecting into the choir. On this screen were formerly suspended the king's coat of mail and his jewelled surcoat, but these are said to have been stolen by the Parliamentary troops.

In St. George's Chapel "blended lie the oppressor and the oppressed," for in the southern aisle a black slab covers the remains of Henry VI., removed hither from Chertsey. Pilgrims for a time came to this, as to a shrine, and found a cure for the headache in putting on an old red hat which the king had worn. Near to his grave another slab covers the remains of Charles Brandon, Duke of Suffolk. The tall apsidal chantry at the east part of the aisle bears the name of the Earl of Lincoln, Lord High Admiral to Queen Elizabeth; and near his grave lies Richard Beauchamp, Bishop of Salisbury, under whose care the chapel was built. At the western end of the aisle a richly-adorned monument has been erected by the Queen to the memory of the late Duchess of Gloucester, and other members of that branch of the Royal Family. Opposite to this is a little chantry which projects into the Lower Ward.

But a plain slab, which intercepts the chequered pavement of the choir, marks a place of yet greater historical interest. In the vault beneath rests the body of Henry VIII., by the side of Jane Seymour, the best-beloved of his many wives. In this vault—at an epoch widely different—without ceremony and without funeral rites, another corpse was laid, that of the ill-fated Charles I. Fain would he—a Stuart—have reigned as a Tudor king; but the effort only gave him a share in a Tudor's tomb. Such is the irony of fate.

The castle was the last place where Charles was imprisoned before he was removed to London. He quitted it shortly before Christmas, 1648, and on the 7th of February his body was brought back for interment. There it remained all through the next day, while search was made for a resting-place—not an easy task, for the Puritan lambs had been at play in the chapel, and the familiar landmarks were all but effaced. A townsman, however, according to Clarendon, was able to indicate the vault of Henry VIII. Within this the coffin was entombed by a few faithful friends, in the presence of the Bishop of London, who, however, was not permitted to read the service of the English Church. Men did not fail to notice that as the coffin was borne to the chapel the white flecks of snow fell lightly on the black pall, and saw therein

THE PRINCESS CHARLOTTE.

Nature's tribute to the innocency of the "martyr." At the Restoration a loyal Parliament voted a large sum — £70,000 — for the removal of the remains to Westminster, and the erection of a fitting monument. Neither the one nor the other was done—for which neglect various reasons were assigned. Clarendon states that the spot where the body was buried could not be identified by the surviving witnesses. This seems very strange, for the position of the Tudor vault could not well be mistaken, as it is in the middle of the choir. Some said that Charles II. was not anxious for the discovery of the coffin, because of a rumour that it did not really contain the royal corpse. This hardly seems a reason for not erecting a monument, and we have never read that he returned the money. The coffin was found and opened in 1813, and an inspection of the corpse left no doubt that this was really the grave of Charles I.

Some distance further east is another royal vault—that constructed by George III. This is really excavated beneath the Tombhouse or Wolsey Chapel; but as its main entrance is from the eastern part of the choir, it may fittingly be mentioned here. In it, according to the list given in "Marshall's

THE PRINCESS CHARLOTTE MONUMENT.

Guide to Windsor," are deposited the bodies of George III. and Queen Charlotte, George IV., William IV. and Queen Adelaide, with several other members of the Royal Family, among them being George V., ex-King of Hanover, whose remains were brought from Paris in June, 1878. Here also the body of the lamented Prince Consort rested for a time, until the magnificent mausoleum at Frogmore was completed.

The Tombhouse, Wolsey Chapel—or Albert Chapel, as it has been named since the restoration—is parted from the east aisle of St. George's Chapel by a narrow passage. This structure has had a chequered history. It was begun by Henry VII., as a place of burial, nearly on the site of Henry III.'s Chapel, the remains of which can be traced in the north wall. The King, however, changed his mind, and erected instead the sumptuous chapel at Westminster. The unfinished structure was granted by Henry VIII. to Cardinal Wolsey. By him the work was completed, and the erection of a sumptuous monument of marble and bronze was commenced. But before this was done came the "nipping frost," and the disgraced favourite was laid in the earth with scant ceremony at Leicester. Nothing more was done till the Parliamentarians sold the bronze for old metal.* Then, as the pendulum swung from Puritan Protector to Papist King, the ceiling was decorated by Verrio, and mass was celebrated in the chapel in the reign of James II. The building was again defaced in a popular tumult, and it remained unused until, as said above, the great royal vault was excavated beneath it during the reign of George III.

Of late years the Tombhouse has been magnificently restored. Venetian mosaics are inlaid in the compartments of the roof and window-space of the western wall. The eastern and side windows are filled with stained glass, the wall below is adorned with serpentine and coloured marbles, in which are framed beautiful examples of "pictures in marble" by the late Baron Triqueti, and medallions. Beneath these an ornamented bench of dark-green brecciated serpentine extends round the building. The floor, also, is paved with marbles of various colours, and in the central part are two marble cenotaphs—the one supporting a recumbent figure—the late Prince Consort—attired as a warrior in plate and mail armour, sheathing a sword—"I have fought the good fight;" the other, of the late Duke of Albany. The interior of this chapel is the most magnificent piece of restoration—or perhaps one should almost say, of adaptation—which has been executed in England since the revival of the study of mediæval architecture.

The passage mentioned above brings us to the Dean's Cloister, a restored work of Edward III.'s age; thence, by a quaintly-cloistered passage to the "Hundred Steps," a steep descent leading into the town, and on the west by a fine portal—a good piece of Perpendicular work—to the space north of the chapel. The Deanery itself dates from the beginning of the sixteenth century, but has been much modernised. North of the chapel is the small Chapter-house, with other apartments; and overlooking the castle wall are a number of interesting buildings, among them the Library, St. George's School for the choristers, and houses of various dates. These form a series of groups which are often interesting and almost always picturesque.

T. G. BONNEY.

---

* The sarcophagus—as is well known—was afterwards used for the interment of Nelson, and is in the crypt of St. Paul's.

U U U

BEVERLEY MINSTER.

THE ancient town of Beverley is supposed to date from about A.D. 700, when the country hereabout, being low and marshy, owing to the frequent over-flowing of the river Hull, must have exhibited the alternate appearances of morass and lake; hence, it is said, arose the Saxon name of Beverlega, and subsequently Beverlac, or Lake of Beavers, which are alleged to have abounded in the contiguous waters. Professor Phillips, on the contrary, states that Beverley is simply Pedwer-llech, the ancient Petuaria. The town, without doubt, owes its importance as a great religious centre to the celebrated St. John of Beverley, the fifth Archbishop of York. This eminent prelate was born about 640, at the little village of Harpham-on-the-Wolds, twelve miles from Beverley. He was educated by Archbishop Theodore, and subsequently in St. Hilda's famous monastery at Whitby, and became a missionary-priest, travelling about to in-struct the rude and ignorant people in those turbulent times. For a period he lived in solitude as a hermit, but in 687 was called to the bishopric of Hexham, and was ultimately translated to the primacy of York in 705. He ordained the Venerable Bede, who speaks in affectionate terms of his master's piety and power of working miracles.

St. John founded a monastery on or near the site of the present minster, and endowed it with lands. When increasing years compelled him to resign his bishopric in 718, he retired to his monastery at Beverley, where he died three years later, and was buried in the porch called St. Peter's, within the church. In 1037 he was canonised by Pope Benedict IX., and his bones were deposited in a richly-decorated shrine, supposed to have been placed in the choir. This was lost when the church was destroyed by fire in 1188. In 1197 a search was made for his remains, which were found and then interred in the nave; and in 1644 his sepulchre was again uncovered, "wherein were several pieces of bone mixed with a little dust, yielding a sweet smell; also a pair of silver slippers, a knife, and some beads," with an inscription on lead recording the fire of 1188 and the interment of 1197. The saint's ashes were finally deposited in their former resting-place, in the centre aisle of the nave; and a subsequently-discovered mediæval inscription on the vaulting immediately above identifies the position.

THE PERCY SHRINE.

The sacred shrine of St. John of Beverley, like those of St. Thomas of Canterbury and St. Cuthbert of Durham, became the favourite resort of pilgrims from all parts. It is easy, therefore, to understand how the treasury was filled with the gifts of the pious, and the church gradually increased, until the superb edifice assumed its present stately and beautiful proportions.

Athelstane, King of the Saxons, in 937, being on a campaign to Scotland, visited Beverley on his way to York, and offered his prayers for success at the holy shrine. Then, drawing his dagger from its sheath, he deposited it on the high altar as a pledge, vowing that should he return victorious he would redeem it with costly offerings to the saint. Armed with a consecrated banner, the monarch set forth to meet the foe. He was victorious, the rebels flying before

v v v

his host on every side. On his return to Beverley the king amply redeemed his pledge by founding here a college of secular canons, endowing it with lands, and bestowing the privilege of sanctuary, which it enjoyed until the Reformation. The dagger was long preserved as a valued relic, and is believed to have been the knife which was found when the saint's ashes were discovered.

Beverley Minster, like many of our large English churches, has been the work of successive ages, and exhibits most perfect examples of the various styles of Pointed architecture, from the Early English period to the Perpendicular. The plan is that of a double cross, with the eastern transepts smaller than those at the chief intersection. The choir and transepts are of the Early English period, and the nave of the Decorated and Perpendicular. The exquisite proportions of the building, the harmonious grouping of the different styles of architecture, together with the variety and richness of ornament, charm and delight the observer.*

The west front is considered to be one of the finest examples of Perpendicular work in the country. The buttresses are decorated with niches. Of the multitude of statues which probably filled these, but one remains, on the north side of the north-west tower—a noble figure of a warrior in plate armour, bearing the arms of Percy on his breast. It doubtless represents the second earl, the son of Hotspur, who was slain at St. Albans, fighting for the Red Rose. The north tower contains a peal of eight bells which chime; in the south tower is a large funeral-bell. The nave has nine bays indicated externally by buttresses crowned with pinnacles; from these spring flying arches, which cross the parapet of the aisles and abut against the clerestory. The parapet of the aisles contains some curious bas-reliefs; those on the south side seem to refer to the history of Adam and Eve, their fall and expulsion from Paradise.

The north porch is Perpendicular, and of elaborate character; above it is a chamber or parvise, probably the residence of the watchman who admitted fugitives seeking sanctuary during the night. The great transept is Early English, with beautiful lancet windows. The eastern front of the church is also of the same period; but the east window is Perpendicular, having been inserted at a later date. At the intersection of the nave, transept, and choir rises a square basement, of modern work, upon a foundation intended to be continued as a great central tower, similar to that of York Minster.

The interior of the minster has a very imposing effect. There being comparatively little stained glass, it is light and cheerful; and it is maintained in perfect

* The dimensions of the minster are as follow:—Entire length, from east to west, 334 feet; breadth of nave, 64 feet; length of great transept, 169 feet; breadth of transept, 69 feet; height of nave, 66 feet; length of choir, 46 feet; breadth of choir, 26 feet; height of central tower, 107 feet; height of the two west towers, 200 feet.

order. The great east window is filled with ancient glass taken from various parts of the church, and although the design is, of course, irregular, the effect is wanting neither in richness nor in beauty. The nave has eleven lofty arches; the triforium consists of an arcade of plain Pointed arches, with quatrefoils in the spandrels, fronted by a second arcade of trefoil arches, on light columns of Purbeck marble. The clerestory has a gallery, where the adventurous can walk. Round the walls, beneath the windows of the aisles, is an arcade supported by Purbeck marble pillars, with figures of minstrels, angels, and monsters; some of these last are exceedingly quaint and full of humour, the old work being easily distinguishable from that of later date. The arcade is continued throughout the church, but without the figures. The groined vaulting of the entire building is simple and elegant. The great west window was filled with stained glass in 1859, and contains a variety of figures and groups referring to the history of Christianity in Yorkshire. The subjects of the windows under the north and south towers also refer to the early British Church.

The font, of Purbeck marble, is very large. It is probably older than any other feature of the building. Above is suspended a massive oak cover, richly carved and apparently of similar date to the carvings on the west door. These are of oak, with figures of the Evangelists, and below, their emblems, executed in very high relief; they are of the Renaissance period, and rather grotesque in character. On either side of the south door are two large leaden figures, painted; they formerly ornamented the old organ-screen, and were said to represent St. John and King Athelstane. It is probable, however, that they were purchased abroad, and were not originally designed as a pair, since they do not face each other.

Beneath one of the arches of the south arcade of the nave is a fine canopied tomb dating from about 1330. This is known as the Maiden Tomb. Tradition assigns it to two maiden sisters who are said to have given two of the common pastures to the town of Beverley. On one side of the south door of the great transept is a curious old painting on wood, representing Athelstane presenting a charter of privileges to St. John of Beverley. From the character of this rude picture it may be assigned to the year 1663, the date found upon a painting of the Royal Arms of Charles II., which hangs at the opposite side of the door.

The stained glass in the south window of the transept represents the Tree of Jesse or Genealogy of Christ, and was presented to the church in 1857. Near this is a curious bracket supported by minstrel figures, and projecting from one of the pillars. It is probable that this sustained a statue above an alms-chest; and we find that Roger Rolleston, brother of one of the Provosts of Beverley, by his will (1458), desires " to be buried in the church of St. John, before the image of the glorious Virgin, above the red chest." There are other references to this red chest in wills of the fourteenth and fifteenth centuries, and there was also a similar red chest under the great tower at York.

The new organ-screen (which supplanted a former classic one, erected in 1731) has been very finely carved by Messrs. Elwell, of Beverley. The wrought-iron gates are not yet completed. The organ, a magnificent instrument, was rebuilt some twelve years since, and placed on the north side of the choir, in order that the view of the entire church might be uninterrupted. Unfortunately, however, a group of small pipes has been placed upon the screen, presenting but an insignificant appearance.

The choir is fitted up in true cathedral style, with stalls having canopies of delicate tabernacle-work. The misereres, or carved movable seats, exhibit a variety of symbolic and humorous designs. There is the date 1520 upon one of the seats. Upon a shield in the choir appears the mediæval notion of a Beverley beaver, being an heraldic eagle displayed, with the substitution of a species of dog's head.

The altar-screen, an elaborate and beautiful work of the fourteenth century, had its western face entirely renewed in 1826; its top forms the ancient rood-loft, to which the visitor may ascend by a staircase, and whence a very fine view is attainable. The vaulting over the altar is decorated with fresco paintings of the Evangelists and other figure subjects, somewhat in the style of the early mediæval illuminators.

On the left of the altar is the renowned monument called the Percy Shrine, one of the finest examples of English mediæval sculpture. It is in a marvellous state of preservation, although the tomb itself and the brasses which were bedded in the upper slab have disappeared. The monument is now ascribed on the best authority to Eleanor Fitz-Alan, wife of Henry, first Lord Percy of Alnwick, who died in 1328; it is full of the most beautiful and interesting detail.

Near this is the Percy Chapel, above which hang some tattered military flags, with two ancient helmets. The only tomb remaining is that of Henry Percy, fourth Earl of Northumberland, who was killed near Thirsk in 1489. "Great dissatisfaction having been caused in the North by a subsidy levied for carrying on the war in Brittany, the earl, who was then Lord-Lieutenant, informed the King (Henry VII.) of the state of things, and prayed an abatement. The avaricious monarch replied that not a penny should be abated, which, repeated too frankly to the populace, cost the earl his life at the hands of the rabble, who broke into his house, and murdered him and several of his attendants. He had a magnificent funeral in Beverley Minster, 13,340 poor folks who were present receiving 2d. each, 500 priests 12d. each, and 1,000 clerks 4d. each." The altar-tomb is fairly perfect, but the effigy and canopy have disappeared. Round the tomb are

THE NAVE, LOOKING EAST.

shields of arms, and many niches in which silver statuettes ("weepers") were formerly placed.

At the entrance to the Percy Chapel stands the fridstool, which, with the font, is earlier than any other part of the building. It is a rude and perfectly plain stone chair, and is said by Spelman to have borne this inscription :—

" Hæc sedes lapidea Freedstol dicitur, i.e., Pacis Cathedra, ad quam reus fugiendo perveniens omnimodam habet securitatem." [" This stone seat is called Freed Stool, *i.e.*, the Chair of Peace, to which what criminal soever flies, hath full protection."] " The privilege of sanctuary doubtless gave considerable importance to this church, and was of greater extent than usual. From an account of the liberties of St. John of Beverley, it appears that the privilege extended from the church a mile every way; that the outer and second boundaries were marked by richly-carved crosses; that the third boundary commenced at the entrance to the church; and that the last included the high altar and the fridstool, which, placed near it, conferred the greatest security. Penalties were imposed on such as should violate the privilege of sanctuary, increasing in proportion to the degree of holiness ascribed to the successive distances. The seizure of a fugitive seated in the fridstool was inexpiable."

The minster, as a whole, appears to have suffered little from the lapse of time and the vicissitudes and needful restorations which have befallen it, though many beautiful and interesting works have no doubt been lost. Standing at the west end of the church, looking up the long vista, and marking the sunlight playing upon the rich carving and delicate work of the choir, listening to the powerful tones of the organ, the spectator feels that a more beautiful picture can scarcely be presented to his view. But could he have seen the building just before the Reformation, when it was thronged with a constant stream of worshippers, pilgrims and votaries, priests and monks, with other ecclesiastical dignitaries, and contemplated its glowing walls rich with colour, its decorated roofs, many altars, and all the gorgeous magnificence of the ancient faith, he would not have marvelled at the importance which the old poet attached to his pilgrimage when he wrote—

> " Come ye from the east, or come ye from the west,
>   Or bring relics from over the sea,
> Or come ye from the shrine of St. James the Divine,
>   Or St. John of Beverley."

M. C. PECK.

⁎ The writer is indebted to the several local histories, and particularly to a thoughtful and valuable paper by Mr. John Bilson, architect, of Hull.

THE CHAPELS IN "THE TOWER."

FOR KING AND CAPTIVE.

WILLIAM the Norman was not long in discovering that his seat on the throne of England was anything but secure. So, being a man of much practical ability for that time, he put more faith in physical coercion than in moral suasion, and built not a few strong castles to overawe his new subjects. London itself was not too conspicuous for loyalty, so just outside its wall, on the bank of the Thames, he founded a fortress, in a position which at once secured his communications with Normandy, and cut off the city from the sea. The construction was entrusted to Gundulf, Bishop of Rochester, some of whose work yet remains in his cathedral, and possibly—though this is doubtful—in the keep of the castle. Evidently he was a man in whose presence the modern jerry-builder would have found a short shrift and a long rope. He built here, as at Rochester, a work which time could scarce injure, and no fair usage of man destroy. The huge block of masonry now called the White Tower was the keep of his castle. It has been "uglified" by Wren, has been damaged or restored, at various times, in its details, especially externally; but both internally and in its main features it still remains as the tower of William the Norman and Gundulf the bishop.

The latter was careful that the garrison should not be deprived of spiritual comfort, so he constructed a chapel which occupies the south-eastern angle in an upper storey of the building. Its floor is on the same level as the great hall or dining-room of the keep, beneath which are the apartments designed more especially for the king's use. Mounting a narrow staircase—a staircase at the foot of which the two royal lads, Gloucester's victims, were hurriedly buried—we enter the chapel through a small door on the south side of the western wall. Its plan is simple, but effective. Its architecture, in keeping with the rest of the building, is of the plainest kind. On either side a narrow aisle is separated from the small central nave by massive circular columns, from the capitals of which spring strong semicircular arches supporting a triforium gallery. This has large, yet more simple, arched openings, one in each bay. The chapel terminates in the east in an apse, round which the aisle and triforium are carried. It would hardly be possible for the architecture to be plainer; the arches are relieved neither by moulding nor by order; the walls are of coarse masonry; the barrel vaulting of the roof, and the simple groining of the aisles, are rougher than the walls. An arch turned in the western wall, the circular columns, the rudely-carved capitals above, and the stilted arches in the apse—a necessary consequence of the nearer position of the columns in this part—are the only

approach, and it is but an approach, to ornament. Most of the windows have
been subsequently enlarged, but when all were in their original condition, the
building must indeed have been gloomy.

The apse mentioned above is visible from the exterior, projecting from top

THE INTERIOR OF ST. JOHN'S.

to bottom from the eastern front of the Tower, and encrusting, in a rather
unusual fashion, one face of the corner turret. The aisles enable us to appreciate
the massiveness of the construction. Beneath them, all is solid to the ground;
the columns are supported by one side, the outer wall by the other, of an
enormous mass of masonry, some sixteen feet in thickness. Thus for its two
lower storeys above the ground the White Tower was as if it stood on rock.
Against such a mass of masonry darts and missiles would be futile, fire and
battering-ram inoperative. It was in those days impregnable.

It was dedicated to St. John the Evangelist, and was used as the chapel
of the Court when the Tower was a royal residence, so that many of our kings
and queens, many of their subjects great in State or in Church, must have worshipped within its walls. The royal party, it is said, generally occupied the
triforium, entering it from the well-known "Council Chamber," which is on the

same level, and is over the dining-hall. As time went on, the royal visits became fewer and fewer—for the Tower must always have been too much of a fortress to be a commodious residence, and since Elizabeth no sovereign has sojourned within its walls. But no traditions of importance centre around this chapel, unless we so reckon this—that here Northumberland, in the days of Queen Mary, professed himself a member of the Church of Rome the day before his execution.

A CAPITAL IN ST. JOHN'S.

After the Civil Wars the chapel was desecrated. It was used as a receptacle for papers and rubbish; was whitewashed, plastered, and injured so far as such a solid structure could be; but a few years since, after the removal of the documents stored up there, it was thoroughly and carefully restored. A table of stone — perhaps of doubtful legality—has been erected in it. It is seated with chairs, and occasionally used for service, and is now even lighted by incandescent lamps.

The other chapel stands on Tower Green, near the north-west angle of the fortress. It is dedicated to "S. Petrus ad Vincula," a very unusual title for the saint.* The older part of the present building was erected by Edward I., but it replaced an earlier one, which probably was the work of Henry I., and certainly is mentioned in documents of the age of John. This chapel was adorned, as we learn from a royal warrant, by Henry III., who bestowed upon it, among other things, "two fair cherubim with cheerful and pleasant countenances," which were to be placed "on either side of the great crucifix." Fire and dilapidation had much injured the later chapel by the reign of Henry VIII., so it was then partially rebuilt. Of this date are the windows, except that over the west door, the arches of the nave, and the roof; so that at first sight the chapel appears

* Mr. Doyne Bell, whose valuable memoir has been followed in this article, states that he only knows of another instance, "S. Pietro in Vincoli," at Rome, where the reputed chains of the saint are exhibited.

to be a rather plain structure of Tudor age. In plan it is a two-aisled building, with a rather low-pitched roof, and a small belfry turret. The chancel is at the end of the southern aisle. Beneath the northern (at the east end of which is a small vestry) is a crypt, which probably belonged to the earlier chapel. This is not accessible to visitors, for it is nearly filled with coffins, but it is said to be a very plain structure.

Externally, St. Peter's Chapel offers little to attract. One or two tombs against the southern wall are indicative of the old burial-ground, which once extended for some distance towards the east, the site of which is now in part occupied by barracks. But on our way to the western door we turn aside for a moment to glance at a small enclosed area in the court, for it is the scene of more than one tragedy. Here was raised the scaffold for execution within the walls, and here perished Anne Boleyn, Katherine Howard, and Lady Jane Grey.

St. Peter's Chapel shared the usual fate of ecclesiastical buildings during the eighteenth and the early part of the present century. It was "beautified" with high pews, galleries, and plaster ceilings. Some changes for the better were made in 1862, but in the year 1876 a thorough and careful restoration was undertaken. The galleries and heavy wooden boxes were cleared away, the building was entirely refitted, the chancel was adorned with a reredos and a pavement, and many other improvements were effected. In Mr. Doyne Bell's work are pictures of the interior of the church before and after the restoration, which certainly do not tempt anyone to "bless the old and ban the new."

There is little to describe in the architecture of St. Peter's. It is a rather plain church, broad in proportion to its length, divided into two aisles of about equal width by a row of four-centred arches; the southernmost being prolonged into a chancel without any dividing arch; in the east wall of the nave are the remains of a piscina and hagioscope, and there are two monuments worth notice —one, the alabaster altar-tomb to Sir Richard Cholmondeley, Lieutenant of the Tower in the reign of Henry VII., and to his wife, now placed in the north-east angle of the chapel; the other, the great monument to the Blounts in the chancel. But its main interest—we might say, its whole interest—centres in those who lie beneath the shadow of its roof in nameless graves. *Væ victis!* might have been inscribed over its door, for the graves of those who had perished on the scaffold or died in the dungeons of the Tower were crowded beneath its floor. No apology need be made for quoting the words of Macaulay, for they express eloquently what all must feel, however imperfectly, while standing in this church:—"In truth, there is no sadder spot on earth. Death is here associated—not as at Westminster and St. Paul's, with genius and virtue, with public veneration and imperishable renown; not, as in our humblest churches and churchyards, with everything that is most endearing in social and domestic charities, but with whatever is darkest in human nature and in human destiny, with the savage triumph of implacable enemies, and the inconstancy, the ingratitude, the cowardice of friends; with all the miseries of fallen greatness and blighted fame. Thither have been carried—through successive ages, by the rude hands of gaolers, without one mourner following—the bleeding relics of men who had been the captains of armies, the leaders of parties, the oracles of senates, and the ornaments of Courts." Thither, too, have been carried, the historian might have added, the bodies of "tender and delicate women," nobly born and carefully nurtured, once the brightness of a home, and even idolised by a king; for the axe spared neither youth and beauty nor the grey hairs of venerable age; and even the steps of the throne sometimes proved the ascent to the scaffold.

The intra-mural interments had been so numerous, and, in some cases, so carelessly performed, that at the restoration of the chapel it was considered advisable, both for the security of the floor and for sanitary reasons, to dig up the earth within the walls of the nave. By Her Majesty's express command the greatest care was taken in this work; the coffins which were still perfect were removed to the crypt, the scattered bones were collected into cases and placed in the same receptacle. A brass plate was affixed to the western wall, giving a list of those who either died in prison or perished on the scaffold, and are known to have been buried within the chapel.

The chancel, however, is the spot of saddest memories; for beneath its floor lie the most illustrious among the victims of the axe. The first intention was not to disturb this resting-place, but to cover the old rough slabs in its eastern part with an ornamental pavement. But this part also of the floor was found, on examination, to be insecure, so that an investigation of the underlying ground became necessary. The earth was excavated in the eastern half of the chancel, between the great mural monument of the Blounts on the one side, and the brick vault on the other, which was constructed in 1871 to receive the body of Sir John Fox Burgoyne, once Constable of the Tower. A full and interesting account of this investigation will be found in Mr. Doyne Bell's work. Later interments, carelessly performed, had disturbed the older graves. The bodies evidently had been buried, as a rule, without coffins, and in some cases had even been covered with quicklime.* They had, indeed, been laid in consecrated ground, but "with the burial of a dog," as if they had been the lowest of malefactors. At most, only portions of the skeletons were found; but these, in some instances, were identified with fair certainty. The remains were placed separately in thick lead coffers, which were enclosed in strong wooden cases,

* The corpse of Anne Boleyn was "thrown into a common chest of elm-tree that was made to put arrows in, and buried in the chapel before twelve o'clock."

and then re-buried beneath the new pavement of parti-coloured marble, on which the names of the dead have been engraved.

As now arranged, a low step parts the floor of the chancel from that of the nave, and at about half its length a second similar step bounds the parti-

St Peter's Chapel.
on Tower Green
Herbert Railton

coloured marble pavement, on which the communion table is placed. The north chancel-wall is occupied by a grand monument of alabaster and marbles, erected to the memory of Sir Richard Blount and his son Sir Michael. This forms four arched compartments, beneath which are groups of kneeling figures. One half— that commemorating the father—was erected immediately after his death in 1564, the other just before the end of the same century; but the whole practically forms one monument. It is an exceptionally fine example of the sepulchral memorials

Y Y Y

of the Elizabethan age; but, unfortunately, it suffers by being much too large for the chapel.

By careful consideration of the incidental references in history, it has been found possible to indicate, with more or less certainty, the resting-places of the fifteen illustrious personages who were buried in this chancel; all but two of them after death by the axe. Immediately under the communion table—placed, like it, north and south—was laid the weak and ambitious Duke of Monmouth; the rest were arranged in two rows, the division between them being roughly indicated by the present change in level. Below the upper stage, to quote the chronicler's words, "there lyeth before the high altar in St. Peter's Church two Dukes between two Queens—to wit, the Duke of Somerset and the Duke of Northumberland, between Queen Anne and Queen Katherine—all four beheaded." To the north of Anne Boleyn's grave, it is believed, was that of her brother, Lord Rochford; to the south of Katherine Howard lay Lady Rochford, and beyond her the venerable Countess of Salisbury. In the lower row it is generally thought (though there is no direct evidence) that Lord Guildford Dudley was placed near the northern wall on the right hand of Lady Jane Grey, against whom was buried the Duke of Suffolk. By his side was the Duke of Norfolk, next to whom came his son, the Earl of Arundel, who died as a prisoner in the Tower; then the Earl of Essex; and, lastly, Sir Thomas Overbury, poisoned while in prison.

What a list of the blood-stained pages of English history! What a grim significance there is in the juxtaposition of some of these unfortunates! Somerset and Northumberland, rivals through life, made equal in their manner of death, united in their graves. Queen Anne Boleyn, whose guilt or innocence may be counted among the problems of history, but of whom it must at least be admitted that "Cæsar's wife was not above suspicion." Katherine Howard, in whose case it is to be feared that charity can do little even to extenuate; and Lady Rochford, her companion in guilt and in execution. The name of the Countess of Salisbury recalls one of the greatest crimes of the greatest English tyrant, and the unprecedented scene at her execution, for "she would not die, as a proud dame should, decorously." To what extent the blood-stained beginning of Queen Mary's blood-stained reign is recorded on this floor is not quite certain, but it is probable that the graves of Lady Jane Grey, her husband, and her father, were in the chancel; and if so, they could hardly have been in any other than the place indicated. Norfolk, Arundel, and Essex are memorials of the rare severity of Elizabeth, which, in the case of two at least, was forced upon her, while Overbury recalls the weakness of the foolish pedant, her successor.

But many another victim of the axe was laid within the walls of St. Peter's.

Bishop Fisher, for whom neither old age nor saintly life could plead; More, among the wisest and wittiest of men; Cromwell, their destroyer, more ruthless than his master, the man of "blood and iron," who at last went the way on which he had sent so many; Thomas Seymour, Lord High Admiral, who had married the widow of one king, and aspired to mate with the sister of another; Stafford, the last victim of the "Popish Plot," done to death by perjured knaves. Jeffreys also, judge of the "Bloody Assize," whom the Tower sheltered from popular vengeance, was for a time laid within these walls, and the list of "notable prisoners" is closed by Kilmarnock and Balmerino, and Lovat—all executed for their share in the rebellion of 1745.* With the last of these ends the catalogue of the victims of the axe in England. So strong even by that time had the feeling against political executions become, that it needed a second rebellion to bring so many high-born offenders to the scaffold, and it is now safe to prophesy that blood will never again be thus shed in England.

T. G. BONNEY.

---

* They were buried in coffins, but these, at the time of the restoration of the chapel, were found much damaged by later interments: the metal coffin plates were then removed, and are fixed against the neighbouring west wall.

SELBY.

A GREAT YORKSHIRE ABBEY.

TWENTY minutes south from York on the Great Northern Railway, the usual clatter of a railway station, a few minutes' walk along a quay and through a not very interesting town, and we find ourselves gazing at the church of Selby's famous abbey.

Besides the church (the only abbey church in Yorkshire left entire) nothing now remains of this once great establishment but the barn, which, by the way, is worth a visit, though now used half as a brewhouse and half as a stable. The fine gateway was pulled down in 1792. The church consists, as those belonging to monasteries usually do, of choir, transepts, and nave. A porch (covering a fine Norman arch) on the north of the nave, and a small side-chapel, used as a vestry, to the south of the choir, are the only additions to the simple cruciform structure. This last is often called the chapter-house, but it was not that of the monastery; over it is a chamber used as a schoolroom. It contains some graceful arches, and is adorned with pierced and crocketed pinnacles like those at the east end of the church.

The transepts are remarkably small, and the south one has lost much of its original character, having been partly destroyed by the fall of the upper part of the central tower in 1690. The lower part of the tower remains, with its Norman windows; but the top storey, which fell, was rebuilt according to the taste of the last century, and is the one thing in the outside of the church that fails to give pleasure. The open parapet which runs below the roof of the choir and choir aisles is much admired, as are also the pinnacles placed at each corner. There is a buttress on each side of the east window and two at right angles at each corner of the east end, and each is surmounted by a crocketed pinnacle. The effect is somewhat marred by a small window in the gable, the stiff little pattern of whose traceries is out of harmony with the bold lines of the larger one below.

The west front consists of a centre and two side divisions, separated by buttresses, and corresponding in breadth with the nave and aisles. The principal entrance is in the centre—a very beautiful Norman porch of five receding orders—above which is a graceful arcade of nine cusped arches, and over this a large Perpendicular window surrounded by Early English moulding. Each side division contains a pointed arch, which again encloses two smaller pointed arches. It was plainly the original intention for this façade to be flanked with

SELBY ABBEY, FROM THE SOUTH-EAST.

towers, but this was probably never carried out, and the buttresses are simply surmounted with pinnacles of a simpler design than those at the east end of the church.

To give any idea of the beauty of the interior, words utterly fail. Entering

THE WEST FRONT.

by the west door the visitor is at once sensible of the solemn grandeur of the nave. So perfect and harmonious is the effect that it takes some time for one to realise it is by no means all of one style. It is, in fact, a complete lesson in the gradual change from Norman, through Transitional, to perfect Early

English in the clerestory. Some clustered pillars in the north triforium are peculiar and much admired. The font, a very early Norman one, has a richly carved wooden canopy. The ceiling is of the time of Henry VII., and has some good carved bosses. It shows, among other designs, the three swans—the arms of the abbey. Passing eastward under the Norman arches of the tower, the glorious choir bursts into view. It is in the Middle Gothic or Decorated style; and, indeed, in its joyous bounding traceries, even verges into the Flamboyant. It is now in process of restoration. Lovely carved stones are being rescued from obscurity, and put together again; and in this way the screen, dividing the altar from the Lady Chapel, is now made nearly perfect. There are four good sedilia on the south side of the sanctuary, and some curious vestment-cupboards opposite to them. On boss and canopy and doorway there is an abundancy of beautiful and grotesque carving. Perhaps most striking of all are the brackets above the capitals, the figures on which at first sight appear to be those of spirits in pain. The position of the hands seems to indicate great internal agony, but the jocund faces belie this interpretation, and they are said to be comic portraits of the monks. With the " Purgatorio " in one's mind, two with their faces very close together suggest Paolo and Francesca; but, of course, if we are to accept the latter explanation, this theory would be quite inadmissible! In strong contrast to these active figures in the choir is the very beautiful and spiritual face of a nun, almost Egyptian in its calm, which adorns the capital of a pillar in the north transept.

That the town clustered round the monastery, rather than that the church was built for the town, is evident; and one wonders what could have induced the monks to select this site, this "home of seals;" for, excepting nearness to the river, there are no natural advantages. Tradition explains it in this way:— Benedict, a young monk in the monastery at Auxerre, saw in a vision the patron of that place, St. Germain, who commanded him, "like Abraham of old, to leave his own country and go to a land that he would show him (Gen. xii. 1); telling him, further, that there was a place in England called Selby, situated on the Ouse, near the city of York, that was ordained for his praise. The saint promised Benedict his protection, comfort, and counsel; and, in addition, the gift of the finger preserved on the altar. Benedict was ordered to open his arm between the shoulder-blade and elbow, and insert the finger for its safe custody, which he should be miraculously enabled to do without feeling any pain."

He took no notice of this vision, till it had been repeated three times; but he then made it known to his brethren, and asked leave of his Superior to depart. It was refused, and all tried to persuade him to remain, but without effect; so one night he took possession of the finger, and escaped to the coast. Having reached England in safety, he inquired his way to Salisbury, supposing that to be the place meant; but, finding it was not so, awaited further directions from the saint, which in due time were bestowed. The word Selby was distinctly pronounced, and the place shown in a vision. He resumed his journey, and arrived at Lynn, in Norfolk, and there embarked in a vessel bound for York, which had been waiting a fortnight for a favourable wind. Directly he and the finger were on board, the wind changed, and they were able to sail, and safely reached the Ouse. At the first sight of Selby he knew it to be the place shown in the vision, and he and his little band of followers landed, and set up their cross by the northern stream.

Those were dark days in the North. The greater part of Yorkshire had been ravaged by the Danes, the churches burnt, the monasteries destroyed, and the light of Christianity, which had burned so brightly under St. Aidan and the Culdees, was flickering very low. We read that "the country people never heard the name of a monk, and were frightened at their very habit." It is therefore not surprising that when Hugh, Norman Sheriff of Yorkshire, was passing down the Ouse in a boat, and saw so unusual a sight as the cross on the bank, he should land to interview the owner. He found him in prayer before his precious relic—the finger of St. Germain! The little band of "Pilgrim Fathers" then dwelt in a hut of wood and moss, sheltered by an "oak of vast size." But Hugh gave them his own tent as a shelter for the "gloriosus digitus," and sent carpenters to help in the building of a chapel.

We next find that "when, in accordance with the custom of the times, William determined to found monasteries, he selected two places, viz., Battle, in Sussex, in commemoration of the great victory of Hastings; and Selby, most probably in celebration of his conquests in the North. Both Simeon of Durham and Leland state that the abbey at Selby was founded in 1069; and on the visit of William in the following year, accompanied by his wife Matilda, his fourth and youngest son, Henry Beauclerk, afterwards Henry I., is said to have been born." A "Painted Chamber" in the abbot's house was long known as Matilda's room; though, unfortunately, a date on one of the beams proved it to have been only built in Abbot Deeping's time, viz., early in the sixteenth century.

Benedict was abbot for twenty-seven years. The church and monastic buildings were still of wood, and it was not till the reign of his successor, Abbot Hugh, that the present lordly church was begun on a site rather further from the river. The place of the humbler building is still called Church Hill, and the remains of many burials have been found there; but, of course, not a vestige of the church remains. Meanwhile the newly founded house grew and prospered. Dugdale gives a stupendous list of its possessions in Yorkshire, Lincolnshire, Leicestershire, and Northamptonshire, and of its privileges at home. Among the latter was that of "soc," or "soke"—the monopoly of flour-grinding in Selby—

which continued till quite recent years, when it was decided by law that the introduction of flour ground elsewhere could not be prevented. Part of the old "soke" mill is still standing.

William appears to have been wishful to make Selby equal with York, for it was a mitred abbey, and they were the only two north of the Trent. The possession of a mitre at that time bestowed a seat in Parliament; but, strange as it may seem to us now, this was then regarded more as a burden than an honour, and many instances are recorded in which exemption was claimed.

The list of the possessions of Selby Abbey was happily preserved when many other valuable papers were destroyed by the blowing up of the Round Tower at the corner of Marygate, York (1644). Roger Dodsworth, the York historian, had just made a copy of them. The earliest record of the Abbey of Selby is found in a chronicle, entitled "The History of the Monastery of Selby, which was founded in England, in honour of St. Germain, the Bishop of Auxerre, in the year 1069," written by a young monk of the abbey in the time of Abbot Gilbert, A.D. 1174. The monk writes "that of the many and great miracles wrought at this time, the memory of but few has been preserved;" but to our nineteenth-century eyes they seem *many*, and of a decidedly utilitarian type. For instance, when a large band of Saxon robbers attacked the church with a view to plunder, the hand of the leader, Syva, stuck to the wall as he was attempting to lift the door off its hinges; and there he had to stay till found by the monks in the morning; and on another and similar occasion, when a Norman robber put a lever under the door to prise it open, he suddenly fell back, "struck by St. Germain"! He then swelled in all his limbs, his skin being inflated till it almost burst; he became of hideous blackness, both his eyes were forced from their sockets, and after three days he died. But miracles of a more genial sort were also performed. The cure of a raging maniac is recorded by the application of the napkin of St. Germain and a relic of St. Agatha; and the son of Viscount Hugh was cured of fits by the touch of the finger, in token whereof Hugh gave two lights to the church to be burned after his death. In the time of the fourth abbot, Durannus (1127—1137), the church was miraculously preserved from a surrounding flood, and another time from fire, for the flames swept past it when the town around was burning.

The Abbot Benedict had in his youth hesitated between a military life and a monastic one, and the warlike spirit never entirely forsook him; for quite in his old age he challenged Stephen, the Abbot of York, to single combat, because he, by the king's orders, was going to take Benedict into custody in consequence of his too ferocious punishment of two monks who had robbed the monastery. He seized a shepherd's staff and cried, "Let us see who is the stronger." Stephen smiled, mounted his horse, and returned home. He is not the only instance of a very militant Selby churchman. Helias Paganellus, sixth abbot, was more than half a soldier; and held his own bravely in the stormy reign of Stephen. In 1320, again, the Scots had ravaged the greater part of Yorkshire, and made a raid on York itself. Archbishop Melton hastily collected an army of ten thousand men, mostly ecclesiastics, put himself and the Bishop of Ely at its head, and started in pursuit. They overtook the enemy at Myton-on-Swale on October 12th, 1320. The Scots had laid an ambuscade, and the " Church Party " were completely routed. About 4,000 of them fell, including 2,000 drowned in the Ouse, and 200 ecclesiastics. The latter lay on the field in full canonicals, and the battle has ever since been called the " Chapter of Myton." The Archbishop of York had a narrow escape, and the Lord Mayor (Nicholas Fleming) was killed; but the Abbot of Selby had provided himself with a " swifte horse," and escaped.

It is written of Abbot Benedict that " like as Jacob loved Leah and Rachel, he attended to both secular and spiritual affairs in the Church; " and the spirit appears to have clung to his establishment. For the monks of Selby were eminently practical as opposed to contemplative; and we find the second abbot, Hugh, working with his own hands at building the church, and receiving his wages at the end of the week along with the other workers. To this active spirit may no doubt be attributed the remarkable worldly success of so many who were here educated. The name of not one scholar is recorded, for even that of the young chronicler is lost. But we find Nicholas de Seleby, in the thirteenth century, three times Mayor of York and the first Member of Parliament elected for that city. Several others there were who were distinguished in civil affairs, but perhaps the most eminent of them was Ralph de Selby, a great favourite with both the Fourth and Fifth Henrys, who, in addition to holding a number of high ecclesiastical offices, became Baron of the Exchequer.

The last abbot was Robert Selby or Rodgers, who appears to have been a man of considerable tact, for though surrounded by the most active supporters of the insurrection called the " Pilgrimage of Grace," and no doubt sympathising with it, he contrived not to be embroiled in it. This was in 1536. The next year a Royal Commission was sent to investigate, but nothing much can have been discovered, for the abbot took his seat in Parliament two years later, secured good pensions for himself and twenty-three monks, and when, in the general dissolution, resistance was no longer possible, got comfortably across to France, taking with him " all the valuables and muniments which he could safely convey." The abbey was finally surrendered to the King on December 6th, 1539, and remained in his hands till August 26th, 1541, when the abbey itself and a large part of the surrounding property were granted " to Sir Ralph Sadler, Kt., in consideration of the sum of £736 paid down, and a yearly rent of

£3 10s. 8d., and subject, doubtless, to the payment of the pensions allowed to the abbot and monks." Sir Ralph, however, parted with his new possession the same year to Leonard Beckwith, and it passed, usually by purchase, to the

THE NAVE AND CHOIR, LOOKING EAST.

families of Shrewsbury, Walmsley, and Petre, and lastly to Lord Londesborough, the present owner.

The monks have passed away with their joys and their sorrows, and we profit by what their hands made. We may treat with contempt or ridicule their grinning caricatures of each other in the flesh, or representations of post-mortem discomfort. But may we not also think with shame how very few of the shoddy churches of the nineteenth century can possibly, after four hundred years, be in existence at all? And are we not bound to acknowledge that, in spite of the "High Art" twaddled about by "æsthetes," and the real progress made in what is undoubtedly good and beautiful, the "Dark Ages" before the Reformation were, architecturally speaking, "the good old times"?

CONSTANCE ANDERSON.

VIEW FROM THE SOUTH-EAST.

WIMBORNE MINSTER.

A SAXON FOUNDATION.

WIMBORNE MINSTER gives to Dorsetshire the distinction of possessing one of the oldest ecclesiastical establishments in England whose history can be traced back with any degree of certainty. From the Harleian MSS. and sundry monkish chronicles, including the *Annales de Derleye*, we learn that the nunnery from which the present foundation originated was built and endowed by Cuthberga, daughter of Kenred and sister of Ina, kings of the West Saxons in the earliest years of the eighth century, different authorities assigning to it various dates between 705 and 720. The earliest is probably the right one, for Regner in his Tracts alludes to an epistle thus dated from St. Aldhelm, Bishop of Sherborne, taken out of the register of Malmesbury, and including in his list of congregations possessing the liberty of election the monastery of "Winburnia," presided over by the sister of the King. Cuthberga herself married Egfred, or as he is quite as frequently called in early records, Osric King of Northumbria, from whom she obtained a divorce as soon as possible, and went to the Convent of Barking. Her sister Quinberga was a co-foundress with her of the institution at Wimborne, and the two princesses were both buried there. On their deaths both were canonised as saints, though Cuthberga seems to have been the more famous of the two, and the 31st of August was set apart to her memory. In the ancient "Use" of Sarum a special office was assigned to her as "a virgin, but not a martyr."

Of this ancient building, however, no traces are believed to exist, and it is not even thought that the present noble minster stands upon its site. Under Saxon rule it was probably the most important church foundation of the district,

THE NAVE, LOOKING WEST.

judging from the fact that the body of Ethelred I., brother of Alfred, was brought here for interment after his death in an encounter with the Danes, on some spot near, though local historians are divided as to its exact position. William of Malmesbury states that Alfred fortified Shaftesbury in 880, and Hutchins, the erudite historian of Dorset, infers that it is likely he would have enriched and beautified the establishment to his beloved brother's memory. However, there are very early chronicles which indicate that the foundation as a nunnery was either swept away by the invading Danes, or dissolved, for Edward the Confessor converted it into a Collegiate Church and Royal Free Chapel, with a house of secular canons attached, and then it is that we lose all records of the original institution, to meet fresh ones in the architecture of the standing walls.

Speaking generally and broadly, Wimborne Minster belongs to the long architectural period between Later Norman and Perpendicular. In shape it is cruciform, and consists of a central lantern tower, nave and choir, with aisles, transepts without aisles, western or bell tower, north and south porches, crypt, vestry, library, and a tiny priest's room over the north porch. The dates of these various portions can be accurately assigned from the early part of the twelfth to the middle of the fifteenth century, and the central tower is the oldest part, forming indeed the nucleus to which all else was subsequently added. This stands upon four semicircular arches, and all the other Norman piers which remain save these have pointed arches. Mr. C. H. Mayo, a local antiquary of great authority, speaks thus:—"The masonry is good, neither fine jointed nor very coarse. There is very little sculpture, the capitals being extremely plain except in the side arches of the choir, where they are rather rudely carved.

THE IVY TOWER.

These data, as we have no authentic record of the foundation of the church, would lead us to place it early in the twelfth century. The use of pointed arches abutting as these do on undoubtedly early solid piers, is not common; they must be as early specimens as are to be found anywhere of this form of arch." The original church when complete was probably about half the size of the present one, from the very careful estimates which Mr. Mayo was able to form during the restoration, commenced about 1855 and completed in 1857.

This tower is divided into four storeys, the piers of the arches having pairs of shafts, and on these rest first a dark triforium or gallery in the wall, then a clerestory with two windows, and a belfry storey shut away from the rest, and which can only be seen from outside. The triforium is the most interesting stage, having two broad and slightly pointed arches on each of the four sides, sparely adorned with carvings of grotesque heads and rude foliage. The gallery path is nowhere more than 4 feet 6 inches in breadth. This massive tower was originally surmounted by a tall spire of equal height, according to legend, with that of Salisbury, but this is only traditional. It fell in 1600, being finally blown down by a great gale, though the churchwarden's books for more than half-a-century previously contained entries regarding its patchwork repairs.

The next stage of Norman masonry occurs in the nave, the first three bays towards the western end being Later Norman. In all, there are six pier arches here, and on the first three, which are pointed, is chevron ornamentation. This marks the length of the original Norman edifice, and the end arches are presumably of the Decorated period, which commenced early in the fourteenth century; but they cannot lay claim to being considered architecturally the equals to those to which they are joined, and are but poor examples. Above them is a Perpendicular clerestory, which is thought from technical indications to have been built at the same time as the bell tower, or between 1448 and 1464. The aisles again belong to the Decorated order, and have no west windows. Those along the sides, five in number, have two graceful lights. The building material used here is Purbeck marble varied with red-brown sandstone; the two uniting to form a pleasing colour effect.

In the choir and its aisles we encounter Early English work. Wimborne Minster derives its strongly impressive aspect from its almost unique choir and presbytery, which are raised above the nave by some fifteen steps, seven of which lead up to the altar. This gives an imposing grandeur to the east end of the building, which rivals and even surpasses many of our cathedrals. The choir, therefore, is raised several feet above the aisles, which run the full length of the building, and are divided from it by a screen of masonry, solid save for a tall lancet window on either side, and a very richly moulded pier arch. The east window is a very fine specimen of Early English design, consisting of a tall triplet of lancets, the middle one being the highest. In the thin wall in which they are set separate openings are pierced, that above in the centre light being a quatrefoil, and those of the sides two sexfoil. Finely worked dog-tooth ornament appears on the middle light, and the rest of the mouldings are plain. The south choir aisle has a large five-light window at the east end, and its general character is Late Decorated. The north one resembles it, save in being a foot or so less in breadth, and that it has three windows of two lights each, besides its east one, instead of two with three lights. The crypt below the presbytery is vaulted, and supported on two pairs of columns. Early English and Decorated features are repeated here; and it is lighted by four windows, one of which remained for five centuries uncompleted, and was only finished in 1856. The north transept is longer than the south, and the additional length goes by the name of Brembre's Chantry. Its founder was one of the canons, who died in 1361, and, it is believed, was buried here. The south transept has an altar recess, and both incorporate a trace or two of Norman origin, though they are predominantly Early Decorated. The western or bell tower is the latest addition to the building, and appears to have been commenced about 1450, for the purpose of receiving the bells. It is connected with the nave by a lofty Perpendicular arch, and contains a peal of eight bells, of which the dates of the first six are 1629, 1686, 1686, 1600 (with the inscription "Sound out the Bells, in God Rejoice"), 1798, and 1528 (recast in 1629). Fixed to the south wall of this tower is a remarkable old orrery, on the Ptolemaic system. The earth is fixed in the centre, and the sun, moon, and stars revolve round it in their several places. A rod from the clock gives motion to its works, and it shows the relative positions of sun and moon, the daily age of the moon during the lunar month, and its daily distance from the sun. The invention is assigned to Peter Lightfoot, a monk of Glastonbury, and its date is approximately 1320, prior therefore to Copernicus' discovery of the true solar system in 1543. It still goes with perfect regularity. Wimborne too is proud of its clock upon this tower, which has a soldier sentinel to mark time's flight upon a pair of bells.

The history of the minster, subsequent to the hazy distances after its foundation and Norman re-building, does not take long to tell. Ecclesiastically it ranked as a deanery in the gift of the Crown, and we have a complete list of those who held this office between 1224 and 1547, when it was dissolved. Many of them were worthy men, but the most famous occupant of the deanery was Reginald Pole, the son of Margaret, Countess of Salisbury, who was born in 1500, and was only seventeen when he came to this post. He is not, however, buried in Wimborne, but at Canterbury, close to the site of Thomas A'Beckett's shrine. Another benefactress of the church was that great and good patroness of learning, Margaret, Countess of Richmond, the "Lady Margaret" of Cambridge Collegiate foundations, and mother of Henry VII. She endowed the original "Seminary," which, under Elizabeth, became a Grammar School, and she conferred other advantages upon the town, in memory of her parents, the Duke and Duchess of Somerset. She left some magnificent vestments to the church, and the 9th of July, until after the Reformation, was observed as an anniversary of her memory with a special Office and High Mass. On the abolition of the deanery the foundation became a Royal Peculiar and Exempt Jurisdiction, under the ministrations of three "Priest Vicars," elected by the Corporation. These served for a month in turn, and the Corporation had the power to appoint one of them — termed the "Official"—to hold courts and grant licences, and who, by virtue of this dignity, held his own visitations. Some of the oldest inhabitants still living can remember how the court used to be held in the north aisle, the official sitting at a desk, and having the other two priest vicars on either hand, while at a long table were the churchwardens and sidesmen, the vestry clerks and apparitors. But these anomalous livings were swept aside by an Act of Parliament some half a century ago, and though Wimborne was thus ministered to until 1876, it may now be regarded as a living held under the usual conditions, and under the jurisdiction of the Bishop of Salisbury.

The monuments in Wimborne Minster are of great interest, and first and foremost among them comes the brass let into the pavement of the presbytery to Ethelred I. It represents a crowned figure of three-quarter length, clad in kingly robes of ermine, holding a sceptre. The inscription runs thus:—

ORRERY IN BELL TOWER.

In hoc loco qviescit corpvs S[ti]
Ethelredi Regis West Saxonum martyris
Qva[no] D[on] 873–23 die Aprilis per manus
Dacorvm Paganorvm occvbvit—

and below it is a shield with a cross. Both Leland and Camden record the inscription, and the theory is that it is a copy of a much older one. The view is justified by the fact that a piece of a second brass plate was found between the leaves of one of the old books in the library, and it is inferred that the original was secreted for safety during the civil wars. Experts pronounce the effigy and shield to belong to the fourteenth century. In this connection a strange coincidence may be noticed, which seems to have escaped the attention of the numerous antiquarian writers who have discussed and described the building. The minster now shares with only two or three other churches in England—among them is one in or near Coventry, and another at Much Wenlock—the distinction of possessing no altar rails. These as a mere modern excrescence were removed in 1852, and now three fine old oak benches are placed before the table at which the communicants kneel. The late sexton, whose memory carried him back almost to Waterloo, and who was devoted to the old church and its traditions, could recall the time when there were ten of them, and they were placed upon the steps. The clerk, on the occasions of a celebration of the Sacrament, used to take his place at the lectern, and to say in a loud voice, "All who are prepared to receive the Holy Communion draw near." All who did so came to the chancel and remained kneeling at the benches or the choir-stalls, until the sacred elements were

THE LIBRARY.

brought to each one. This custom was discontinued with the abolition of the rails, and only three are now in use. But week-days and services alike these remain. The rails formerly were covered with "fair linen cloths," which, through all the days of strife and struggle, of conquests and crusades, in the Wars of the Roses, through the Reformation and martyrs' deaths, through the overthrow of the monarchy, the Commonwealth, the Restoration, and all the later pages of our history, have retained their old Saxon name of "The Houseling Linen." * And over the memorial to this gentle Saxon Prince the linen thus named in his own day is actually standing.

To come back, however, to the monuments. There is a very ancient one, unnamed, to a Knight Crusader, and under the pier arch, on the north side of

---

* The word "housel" for sacrament is pronounced obsolete in Johnson, though we recall Shakespeare's use of it in *Hamlet*, where the ghost says :—

> "Thus was I, sleeping, by a brother's hand,
>   Of life, of crown, of queen at once dispatched,
>   Cut off even in the blossoms of my sin,
>   Unhouseled, unanointed, unanneled."

R R R R

the presbytery, is one of Purbeck marble to Gertrude Courtenay, Countess of Devonshire. Her husband, the last Earl of Devonshire, was beheaded, with Margaret, Countess of Salisbury, and others, for conspiracy, in 1538, and she also was sentenced to death, but was pardoned. The tomb was foolishly opened at the close of the last century, and the body appeared so perfect that an idiotic effort was made to seat it upright, when it tumbled to fragments, while the brass shields and other interesting features of the tomb were lost or stolen. Under the opposite side is the large square monument to John Beaufort, Duke of Somerset, and his wife, the parents of Margaret, Countess of Richmond, upon which their effigies are finely carved in alabaster. As a work of art, however, the finest monument in the minster is the one in pure Italian Renaissance to Sir Edmund Uvedale, who died in 1606, and whose widow, as an inscription states, erected it "In dolefull dutie." It consists of a solid base, on which the worthy old knight is depicted as a soldier rising from sleep to obey the last trumpet call.

Close beside the organ, under an arch, is a massive coffin, or rather sarcophagus of slate, emblazoned with many coats of arms, and a date thus written, 1 6 9 3, or the years respectively 1691 and 1703; this contains the bones of a highly eccentric individual, named Anthony Ettricke, who directed in his will that he was to be interred in a consecrated spot, but neither in the church nor in the churchyard, a problem solved by the selection of a niche in the wall. The explanation of the two dates is thus given in Hutchins' veracious County History: "This Anthony Ettricke was bred to the law, and towards the latter end of his life grew very humoursome, phlegmatic, and credulous, of an impulse of spirit insomuch, that having once (as I have been credibly in- formed) a share in a ship and cargo, and receiving advice that the same was safely delivered in Portland Road, he was so far persuaded that the same ship would be lost before she could reach the port of London, to which she was consigned, that he sold his share therein, though at a very considerable discount. He had, however, the good fortune to be a great gainer in the end, for (agreeably to forebodings) the ship was lost in her passage. Whether these or other accidents in life gave him occasion, I cannot say, but he afterwards remained fully persuaded that he should die in the year 1691, and accordingly procured this tomb to be made, and had that date cut thereon as may be plainly seen, the same being altered to 1703, in which year he died and was buried. In the year 1692 he obtained a licence from the Rev. William Watkinson, official of Wimborne, for erecting this tomb, and for such liberty gave to the church for ever a rent of 20 shillings from a farm." When the Duke of Monmouth was captured after Sedgmoor on Horton Heath, about six miles from Wimborne, he was brought before this curious man as chief magistrate, and by him was sent to Ringwood for further examination, before being tried at Whitehall. Two of Defoe's daughters are buried in the north aisle. The oldest—Henrietta—married an officer of excise named John Boston, who was quartered in Wimborne; she died May 5, 1760. Her unmarried sister, Hannah, had evidently been staying with her, and just a year previously had been laid here to rest. There is a strong division of opinion as to whether or not Wimborne may claim Matthew Prior as a native. In the firm belief that it can do so, Mr. Weld Taylor and some other admirers of the poet have placed a brass to his memory in the western tower.

The library is situated over the vestry, and is approached through a small doorway under one of the Norman arches of the south aisle. It may claim to be a forerunner of our modern free libraries, for the collection of books which it contains was given by the Rev. William Stone in 1686, "for the free use of the townspeople of Wimborne." Its oldest possession is a manuscript of 1343, containing instructions for those having the care of souls, and entitled *Regimen Animarum*. It is neatly written on vellum with some pleasing initial letters, and has at the end a formula of absolution for the patient scribe. Nearly all the two hundred and fifty books in this library are fastened by about three feet of iron chain, on which is a stout ring running upon an iron rod. This enabled readers to consult the works at the desks provided, but not to carry them away. Among the most valuable works are a copy of the *Index Expurgatorius* of the Spanish Inquisition of 1601 and a sadly mutilated, but skilfully repaired, copy of the first edition of Raleigh's "History of the World" (1614). The organ contains some of the stops which were in the one built by Hayward of Bath in 1664 at a cost of £180, though it is often attributed to "Father Smith." Since then it has been much enlarged and improved; it now has three manuals, a "great," "choir," and "swell," with forty-two stops, and is one of the finest instruments in the south-west.

One word must be added in commendation of the admirable care with which the building is now kept. No one who visits it can fail to remark the decency and order of all its fittings and surroundings. Wimborne itself is a quiet country town, and but for this noble legacy from the dim past would enjoy little claim to notice. It is pleasant to record, therefore, that its inhabitants are worthily mindful of their valuable heritage, and guard with affectionate reverence the walls that are hallowed by so many prayers and historic associations.

MARY FRANCES BILLINGTON.

EVESHAM ABBEY.

A DESTRUCTIVE REFORMATION.

IN one of the loveliest spots in the West of England, known as the Vale of
Evesham, the River Avon with a curious bend encloses a little green peninsula in the south-east of Worcestershire, close to the borders of the counties of
Warwick and Gloucester.   In this little Avon-surrounded district is a tall and
singularly graceful tower of the purest Perpendicular work.   Like so many of
these peculiarly English Gothic towers, massiveness is combined with exquisite
grace and beauty.   The fabric is square, strengthened from base to parapet by
graduated buttresses with panelled fronts.   The fronts are entirely covered, save
where the gate and window arches occur, with panelled mullions under foliated
transoms, and the whole is surmounted by an embattled parapet delicately
pierced, and crowned with tapering pinnacles.   The tower to the summit of
the pinnacles is 110 feet, roughly speaking half the height of the graceful yet
massive tower of Gloucester, or to indulge in another comparison, half the
height of Wren's twin towers of Westminster Abbey.   This, with the exception
of a mutilated archway, is really all that remains of the once lordly abbey and
monastery of Evesham, one of the most notable abbeys of England.

The noble tower, the work of the last real abbot of Evesham, Clement
Lichfield, was completed just before the surrender of the monastery, A.D. 1539,
and was designed for a clock and bell tower.   It was built at the entrance of
the cemetery.

The story of Evesham Abbey goes back many, many centuries.   Eoves, the
swineherd of Ecgwin, third bishop of the Hwicci, while tending his animals was
startled with a vision of the Blessed Virgin.   He told his master, the bishop, what
he had seen.   The bishop accompanied his swineherd to the spot where the radiant
appearance had dazzled his servant.   The same vision was vouchsafed to Ecgwin,
who thence concluded that it was Mary's wish that a church should be erected
on that spot.   A very considerable tract of country was given by the Christian
King of Mercia, Ethelred, to Ecgwin, who, on the site of the vision, built the
first church and monastery.   The district became known as Eoves-holm, which
in time was contracted into Evesham.   Ecgwin subsequently resigned his
bishopric, and became the first abbot of the Evesham monastery.   The year of
our Lord 714 is usually given as the date of the founding of this great religious
house.   We possess few or no details of its history for the first two centuries.
But in the tenth century, like Gloucester and other "houses," it was one of the
battle grounds of the secular clergy and the monks, both claiming Evesham as

their own. As at Gloucester and so many other abbeys, the policy of Dunstan, which afterwards became the policy of Lanfranc and the school of Church reformers of the eleventh century, prevailed, and Evesham became the home of a great Benedictine colony.

After the Conquest the story of Evesham closely resembles that of Tewkesbury, Gloucester, and many other of the more important foundations. A monk, Walter of Cérisy, appointed abbot by William, determined to rebuild the abbey church on a grand and magnificent scale. He commenced with the massive crypt or undercroft, then proceeded with the choir above, and the great central tower as far as the first storey. By slow degrees the whole of the splendid abbey was completed about ninety years after Walter of Cérisy commenced it. Its outline was in form of a Latin cross, and it consisted of a nave, transepts, and choir, with a great central tower rising from the intersection of these divisions. From the bases of some of the nave columns which were discovered among the few fragments remaining, and, alas! removed as curiosities to a neighbouring park, it appears that Evesham Abbey possessed cylindrical piers of vast size, like those of the nave in Gloucester and Tewkesbury. Its length from east to west appears to have been about 300 feet; the length of Gloucester (without the lady chapel, which belongs to a later age) being 314 feet, Tewkesbury Abbey 286 feet long, and Hereford Cathedral 288 feet.

But when we look at Domesday Book and see what were the possessions of Evesham Abbey, we are not surprised that the great Norman abbot was determined to have a house of God in some way worthy of its great wealth. Even after the spoliation of Odo, Bishop of Bayeux, the Conqueror's half-brother, and Urse d'Abitot, the rapacious sheriff of the county, who confiscated some 12,000 acres of the abbey land, it was registered as owning 21,862 acres, mostly in the neighbourhood of Evesham.

As years passed on, the abbey increased in power. It claimed exemption from all episcopal control, and as early as A.D. 1163 its abbot received the mitre. Its interior decorations were of unusual magnificence. It was fitted with shrines of elaborate workmanship, enclosing relics of ancient Mercian kings and bishops. We have a record of one of them which will help us to form some conception of its pre-Reformation grandeur. The shrine of St. Ecgwin, the founder of this famous house, was partly the work of Abbot Mannie, a contemporary of Edward the Confessor. Mannie was reckoned the best goldsmith of his day. This exquisite shrine was made of gold, studded with sparkling gems, and when the lights were lit in the church, the dusky gleaming of the gold and gems is said to have positively lit up this Holy House of God. The numberless services were rendered with great pomp and ceremony, and at vast cost. The vestments of the lord abbot and of the officiating priests were gorgeous and

ALL SAINTS' CHURCH.   THE BELL TOWER, EVESHAM ABBEY.   ST. LAURENCE'S CHURCH.

U U U U

costly, and an enormous number of sacred and other vessels belonging to the abbey were of solid silver, not a few of them enriched with gems.

With a fierce recklessness, with a strange disregard for what was beautiful and venerable, the Commissioners of King Henry VIII. swept away many of our inimitable abbeys and the exquisite buildings which so often surrounded them. Nowhere, though, was their savage thirst for destruction perhaps so wantonly gratified as in the stately monastery of Evesham. The estates were confiscated and parcelled out, and the abbey was dismantled and given away to Sir Philip Hoby, a gentleman of Worcestershire, who shortly afterwards seems to have leased out the magnificent buildings of abbey and monastery as *a quarry for stone*. These were of so vast an extent that in 1657, considerably more than a hundred years after the suppression, the quarry was not yet worked out, for we find in the book of the Corporation of Evesham this curious entry: "That the churchwardens of the several parishes in the borough no longer sell limestone indiscriminately, of or belonging to the churches, but preserve the same for public use." The noble conventual library was scattered, according to some, in part devoted to the flames.*

I know of none of the greater monastic foundations which has suffered like Evesham. Scarcely can it, with its mouldering chapter-house arch and solitary tower, be called even a ruin; and yet against the mighty monastery which lay beneath the shadow of the glorious abbey church so utterly destroyed, no charge of wrong-doing or evil living is extant. Its historian,† after weighing the evidence with care, arrives at the deliberate judgment that Evesham comes within that catalogue of religious houses strangely enough referred to in the Act of King Henry VIII.,‡ where thanks are given to God that "within divers and great solemn Monasteries of this Realm, religion is right well kept and observed."

Our great abbey was not connected with many of the stirring scenes of English history. It was too near the ancient cities of Gloucester and Worcester to become an important national centre. But in the reign of Henry III., Evesham stands out prominently in the story of England. It was a time of sore peril for the country. Were the immortal provisions of the great Charter wrested from King John to be trampled under foot? There were men who encouraged the Sovereign to enter upon this course. Had it succeeded there had been no splendid story of England to tell. That it failed was owing in great measure to the noble and heroic devotion of one man —Simon de Montford—whose gallant resistance, though he, as so many of earth's great ones, died apparently in defeat and dishonour, successfully taught

* May's "History of Evesham," pp. 144, 145.
† May, p. 146.   ‡ 27 Henry VIII., c. 28.

his countrymen what was the deadly peril and how they should ward it off. De Montford was in the Abbey of Evesham when the news of the appearance of Prince Edward — afterwards Edward I.—and a numerous well-appointed force was brought him. There was no escape for the English hero save by a doubtful flight. So with sadly unequal forces he gave battle, and he and his devoted band of followers were cut to pieces. The scene of the bloody encounter—known in history as the Battle of Evesham—was on a woody hill washed by the Avon, over against the green peninsula on which the fair abbey and the monastery of Ecgwin of Evesham were built. The body of the English patriot was shamefully mutilated, but eventually laid to rest in the choir of the abbey church. For long years the tomb of De Montford became a shrine to which vast numbers of pilgrims to Evesham, especially the sick and ailing, resorted. Many legends are extant of wonderful cures worked at the grave of the dead hero. The tomb of De Montford was destroyed when the abbey was surrendered to the Commissioners of Henry VIII. in the sixteenth century.

The pilgrim to the site of the lost abbey of Evesham, standing near the poor remains of the monastery wall, is surprised to see in close proximity to the tall and graceful solitary bell-tower of Abbot Lichfield, two fair-sized churches, each with its own tower and spire, only a few yards separating the twin churches and the Lichfield bell-tower. These two churches were chapels founded by the monks of the great abbey for the use of the dwellers in the town, the splendid abbey church being generally reserved—except probably on the occasion of the more important festivals—for the constant services of the monastery. These chapels, dedicated respectively to St. Laurence and to All Saints, were served exclusively by the abbey monks, who arranged and provided everything for the services.

The twin churches are now united under the charge of the Vicar of Evesham. One is tempted, however, sadly to regret this thirteenth century arrangement of the monks, which provided parish churches for the dwellers in the little town clustering round their great house; for had they not existed at the time of the Reformation it is probable that the inhabitants of Evesham, like the people of the neighbouring Pershore and Tewkesbury, would have made interest with the ruthless Commissioners of Henry VIII. and purchased, for their own use as a parish church, the whole, or at least a part, of the noble abbey whose complete disappearance we so bitterly mourn.

Each of the twin churches dates back to the thirteenth century, St. Laurence being the older of the two. The tower and the spire of the original church still remains, but with this exception, successive additions and restorations have destroyed most of the old work. But the glory of St. Laurence is a small chantry erected by Clement Lichfield, the builder of the bell-tower.

This exquisite little chapel was built in order that daily mass might be performed for the repose of the founder's soul. It is square, and four richly ornamented fans round a carved pendant form a most perfect ceiling, which is still in admirable preservation. The once rich altar is gone, and all the elaborate ornamentation has disappeared; but even in its scarred beauty it is very lovely.

RUINED ARCH LEADING TO VESTIBULE OF THE CHAPTER-HOUSE.

The other church, All Saints, which has been sadly damaged and disfigured, also possesses a beautiful fan-roofed chantry; built, too, by Abbot Clement Lichfield, who prepared this little chapel as his last earthly resting-place.

Both these interesting churches or chapels are used at the present day. All Saints has been elaborately restored, and presents the appearance of a beautiful and thoroughly devotional parish church. St. Laurence, too, has been partially rebuilt, and is now in process of a more complete and thorough restoration under the watchful care of the present vicar, who is justly proud of these precious remains of the handiwork of the monks.

H. DONALD M. SPENCE.

PERSHORE.

THE FRAGMENT WHICH REMAINS.

FROM a very early period no district in England was so rich in monastic foundations as the old Hwiccian Land—roughly including the present counties of Gloucestershire and Worcestershire. At the close of the eighth century there were no less than twenty-four of these monasteries in the district in question. On some of these old sites have been erected stately abbeys which are still with us—such as Tewkesbury, and the lordly pile of Gloucester. On some of them only a ruin or a hallowed memory remains, such as Evesham; here and there a glorious fragment, more or less carefully preserved, tells its story of Christian worship for more than a thousand years.

In this latter class of time-honoured sacred buildings in the Hwiccian Land the abbey of Pershore is a notable example—a noble monument of Norman devotion and skill of the eleventh and twelfth centuries, curiously and quaintly varied by the more decorative work of the Early English school of builders of the thirteenth and fourteenth centuries. It was condemned to utter destruction by Henry VIII. and his rough lieutenant, Cromwell, and only partially rescued from these ruthless and careless spoilers by the self-denying far-sightedness of the poor inhabitants of Pershore, who—for what was to them a great sum— bought back from the rapacious Minister of King Henry VIII. a fragment of the glorious abbey which they loved so well, and of which they were so justly proud.

The Norman nave of Pershore Abbey was at this sad period of its history pulled down, as also were the lady chapel with other parts of the grand abbey, such as the beautiful chapel of St. Eadberg, and the far-reaching buildings of the great monastery. Two centuries ago—weakened no doubt by the wholesale destruction of so large a portion of the pile in the days of Henry VIII.—the great north transept fell. Our own times have witnessed a complete and thorough restoration and careful repair of the beautiful fragment of the old abbey which remained.

This fragment includes the south transept of the original Norman church, the piers and arches of the tower, and very slight remains of the north transept and the Norman nave; to these older parts of the great church we happily can add the choir, built in the first half of the thirteenth century, almost in its entirety—a most noble specimen of the earlier Pointed style, usually known as " Early English "—the two upper storeys of the tower, the lower storey of which formed an exquisite lantern, the lantern pronounced by the late Sir Gilbert

Scott " to be, with the single exception of Lincoln Cathedral, probably the most beautiful feature of its class to be found in any English church."

The great church of which we possess this lovely fragment has a story reaching back twelve hundred eventful years. Two brothers, Oswald and Osric,

PERSHORE, FROM THE NORTH-EAST.

nephews of King Ethelred of Mercia, the son of the famous Penda, received grants of land—the one at Gloucester, the other at Pershore—probably as outposts against the dreaded incursions of the British from South Wales. One of these princes, Osric, was the founder of the cathedral of Gloucester. The other, Oswald, was the traditional builder of Pershore Abbey. The year of our Lord 689 was probably the date of the erection of the first church by Oswald, who died fighting with his brother Osric (subsequently King of Northumbria) A.D. 729.

From incidental notices in monastic cartularies and in other early documents, we gather that the Pershore Church and Monastery continued to be a centre of mission and other work for God during the eighth and ninth centuries. Like many religious foundations it suffered grievously at the hands of bands of Danish invaders, and in common with other monastic foundations its possession was disputed by the secular clergy, usually probably represented by a small college of canons, and by the regulars, the monks. In the year of our Lord 972 it became remodelled on the Benedictine rule, and from that date monks of this order occupied it until the Reformation, when the monastery was suppressed.

The great prosperity of our abbey in Saxon times seems to have been brought about in this wise. Some eighty years before the Norman Conquest a rich Saxon noble became, from some reason not known to us, deeply interested in Pershore and its ancient church. His name was Egel-wada, and he held the high office of Earl of Dorset. This munificent noble splendidly restored the abbey and the buildings clustered round it, and then purchased for an enormous sum from his aunt, the Abbess of St. Mary, Winchester, the precious relics of Eadberg, a nun held in great reverence by the Saxon Church. Eadberg, who was subsequently canonised, was a granddaughter of King Alfred, and a nun of extraordinary piety. After her death her bones were reputed to work wondrous miracles of healing. The possession of these wonder-working relics, which brought a great influx of pilgrims and strangers to worship in the restored and beautiful abbey, and the rich gifts and endowment of land of Earl Egel-wada, raised the monastery of Pershore to a high position among the Saxon religious houses of the tenth and eleventh centuries.

These prosperous days came to an end in the later years of King Edward the Confessor, who seems to have had no scruple in confiscating not a little of the broad lands of Pershore, and bestowing them on his favourite Abbey of West-Minster, then rapidly rising in Thorny Island by the Thames water. Some twenty-eight manors were taken away from the monastic possessions, and nineteen of these were given to the foundation of the new abbey.

In common with all other Saxon foundations Pershore was more or less impoverished as a result of the Norman Conquest. For a long period the value of land was much depreciated, and rapacious Normans—like Urse d'Abitôt, the sheriff of Worcester, who possessed vast powers in this part of England—heavily oppressed with exactions the Saxon proprietors who escaped confiscation. But the abbey suffered less than most Saxon foundations, for it had the good fortune of being ruled over at this juncture by Eadmund, a man widely respected for his high and stainless character. The next abbot but one was Guido, who was probably an Italian, and certainly a great builder. The grand Norman abbey church of Pershore was his work. The responds of the nave—those half-columns we see still outside the west-end of the church—closely resemble the lofty round massive pillars peculiar to Gloucester and Tewkesbury. Indeed the Norman abbey at Pershore of Abbot Guido must have closely resembled the glorious Gloucester Minster and the slightly smaller sister church of Tewkesbury, and the three must have been the fruit of one inspiration, the architect of Serlo of Gloucester most probably designing them all. The Norman south transept of Pershore Abbey is still standing much as Guido's workmen left it, and is, in its quaint irregularity and strange, stern beauty, intensely interesting to the archæologist and the architect. We have in the church two "memories" of the Crusades. In the transept there is a rude carving of three elephants' heads on a small capital, a remembrance of what the artist had seen in the East. The other "memory" is a more interesting one. It is the beautifully wrought effigy of a crusader of mark, Sir William de Harley. It has unfortunately been fixed on the top of a stone coffin with which it has nothing to do. This crusader was Lord of Harley in Shropshire, who fought in the first crusade, and was knighted at Jerusalem, tradition says, by the hand of Godfrey de Bouillon.

In the year 1204 Gervase became abbot. Dissatisfied, as were so many of the monk-architects of the thirteenth century, with the grave, fortress-like Norman work, he determined to rebuild the choir with graceful pointed arches and rich tracery. During his long reign of thirty years his beautiful work was almost completed. It is with us still, but little harmed by time and neglect, save for the disappearance of the gold and colour which once relieved much of the sombre greyness of the walls, and is a very noble example of Early English architecture.

Pershore, after the confiscation in the time of Edward the Confessor, and the subsequent impoverishment consequent on the Norman Conquest, was evidently never a wealthy house. Yet the Pershore monks, in spite of their poverty, were lavish and splendid in their magnificent buildings. The thirteenth century witnessed the designing and erecting of the noble Early English choir, which took the monks some thirty years to complete. A disastrous fire, which happened near the end of that century (the thirteenth), seriously injured the Norman nave, and especially damaged the tower. So terrible was this conflagration that forty years later we read of the ruinous state of the nave and tower. The monks, after restoring their nave, set themselves, somewhere about the year 1330, to rebuild their tower — a truly magnificent piece of work, which still remains to us almost in its fresh beauty. We have no record of the details of this superb work. The very name of the great architect is lost. But Sir Gilbert Scott, who in 1865, with vast skill, conducted the restoration works, is convinced that the same master mind that guided the builders of the gorgeous central tower of the magnificent cathedral of Salisbury, planned the smaller but still exquisitely beautiful tower of Pershore Abbey. "Every

feature," says our learned nineteenth century architect, "in Salisbury and Pershore is alike; the lower stage is merely a plainer version of the corresponding
stage at Salisbury, the great distinction being that it is but one, whereas. there
are two in the prototype, and a spire in addition."

THE NAVE, LOOKING EAST.

In the thirty-first year of Henry VIII.'s reign the confiscation of the abbey
lands was completed. The abbot and the monks were pensioned. The nave,
the north transept, and the lady chapel were pulled down, as well as the
monastic buildings. The beautiful chapel of St. Eadberg, the granddaughter of
the beloved King Alfred, which was on the south of the choir, was probably

destroyed at the same time.   Then it was that the people of Pershore—" poor folks they must have been, .came forward with their little offerings, and bought the remnant of the church, that they might make it their parish church for ever."

From the time of the Reformation, the poverty of the people, and the small interest generally felt in these splendid memorials of a little understood past, allowed the noble fragment of the glorious abbey gradually to decay. The great north transept, as we have said, fell; two large buttresses were erected to support the massive tower; vast galleries were put up, reaching well-nigh half down the choir. The matchless lantern was shut out from view by a floor unskilfully built beneath it. The south transept, which still defied the wear and tear of time and neglect, was shut off from the choir and converted into a parish schoolroom. In 1861 the tower showed signs of giving way. Then the people of Pershore awoke from their long torpor, and, guided by their devoted and energetic vicar, the late Dr. Williamson, set themselves to repair and to restore their noble choir, transept, and tower. The result of the work* has been to give us back, exquisitely restored, one of the noblest fragments of Norman and Early English work our country possesses—a grand example of the learning and piety of our age, which, while incapable of erecting a Pershore Abbey, has sense and discrimination to appreciate and love these mighty efforts of a power and genius which exist no longer.

H. Donald M. Spence.

* The parishioners are said to have expended some £10,000 on their abbey, while the late Sir Gilbert Scott directed the restoration. The still incomplete task has been taken in hand with great success by the present Vicar of Pershore, Archdeacon Walters. I may here mention that many of the details in this study have been taken from two admirable unpublished lectures on the abbey by the late Prebendary Wickenden, of Lincoln.

INDEX.

—◆◇◆—

Y